CW01261354

A HISTORY OF NIHILISM IN THE NINETEENTH CENTURY

Nihilism – the belief that life is meaningless – is frequently associated with twentieth-century movements such as existentialism, postmodernism and Dadaism, and thought to result from the shocking experiences of the two World Wars and the Holocaust. In his rich and expansive new book, Jon Stewart shows that nihilism's beginnings in fact go back much further to the first half of the nineteenth century. He argues that the true origin of modern nihilism was the rapid development of Enlightenment science, which established a secular worldview. This radically diminished the importance of human beings so that, in the vastness of space and time, individuals now seemed completely insignificant within the universe. The author's panoramic exploration of how nihilism developed – not only in philosophy, but also in religion, poetry and literature – shows what an urgent topic it was for thinkers of all kinds, and how it has continued powerfully to shape intellectual debates ever since.

JON STEWART is Research Fellow in the Institute of Philosophy at the Slovak Academy of Sciences. He is the author of many books, most recently *An Introduction to Hegel's Lectures on the Philosophy of Religion: The Issue of Religious Content in the Enlightenment and Romanticism* (2022) and *Hegel's Century: Alienation and Recognition in a Time of Revolution* (Cambridge University Press, 2021), which was the Philosophy category prizewinner in the 2021 PROSE Awards.

A HISTORY OF NIHILISM IN THE NINETEENTH CENTURY

Confrontations with Nothingness

JON STEWART
Slovak Academy of Sciences

CAMBRIDGE
UNIVERSITY PRESS

CAMBRIDGE
UNIVERSITY PRESS

Shaftesbury Road, Cambridge CB2 8EA, United Kingdom

One Liberty Plaza, 20th Floor, New York, NY 10006, USA

477 Williamstown Road, Port Melbourne, VIC 3207, Australia

314–321, 3rd Floor, Plot 3, Splendor Forum, Jasola District Centre, New Delhi – 110025, India

103 Penang Road, #05–06/07, Visioncrest Commercial, Singapore 238467

Cambridge University Press is part of Cambridge University Press & Assessment, a department of the University of Cambridge.

We share the University's mission to contribute to society through the pursuit of education, learning and research at the highest international levels of excellence.

www.cambridge.org
Information on this title: www.cambridge.org/9781009266703
DOI: 10.1017/9781009266734

© Jon Stewart 2023

This publication is in copyright. Subject to statutory exception and to the provisions of relevant collective licensing agreements, no reproduction of any part may take place without the written permission of Cambridge University Press & Assessment.

First published 2023

Printed in the United Kingdom by TJ Books Limited, Padstow, Cornwall

A catalogue record for this publication is available from the British Library.

A Cataloging-in-Publication data record for this book is available from the Library of Congress.

ISBN 978-1-009-26670-3 Hardback

Cambridge University Press & Assessment has no responsibility for the persistence or accuracy of URLs for external or third-party internet websites referred to in this publication and does not guarantee that any content on such websites is, or will remain, accurate or appropriate.

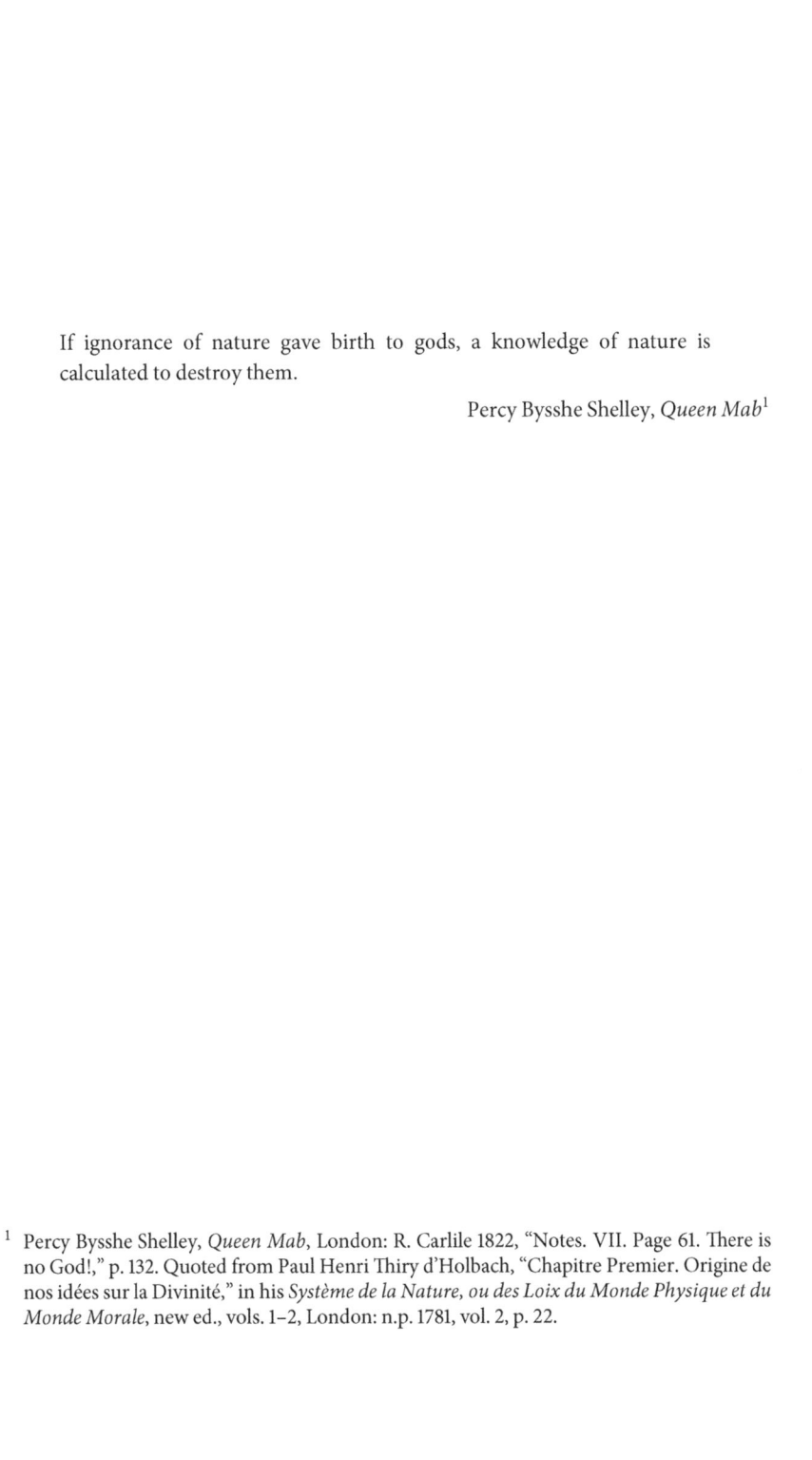

If ignorance of nature gave birth to gods, a knowledge of nature is calculated to destroy them.

Percy Bysshe Shelley, *Queen Mab*[1]

---

[1] Percy Bysshe Shelley, *Queen Mab*, London: R. Carlile 1822, "Notes. VII. Page 61. There is no God!," p. 132. Quoted from Paul Henri Thiry d'Holbach, "Chapitre Premier. Origine de nos idées sur la Divinité," in his *Système de la Nature, ou des Loix du Monde Physique et du Monde Morale*, new ed., vols. 1–2, London: n.p. 1781, vol. 2, p. 22.

CONTENTS

List of Figures   *page* viii
Preface   ix
Acknowledgments   xi

    Introduction   1

1 Jean Paul's Vision of Nihilism and Plea for the Doctrine of Immortality   35

2 Klingemann and the Absurdity of Nothingness in *The Nightwatches*   64

3 Nihilism in English Romanticism: Byron and Shelley   99

4 Schopenhauer's Theory of Human Suffering and Lack of Meaning   126

5 Büchner's Account of the Reign of Terror as a Mirror of Human Existence   149

6 Poul Martin Møller's Criticism of Hegelianism and the Danish Discussion of Nihilism   173

7 Kierkegaard and the Indefinability and Inexplicability of Death   201

8 Turgenev's Portrait of a Nihilist   237

9 Nietzsche's Vision of the Past and the Future of Nihilism   259

10 The Importance of Nihilism in the Nineteenth Century   280

Selected Bibliography on Nihilism   308
Name Index   311
Subject Index   316

FIGURES

0.1 The cover of Johann Andreas Segner's *Einleitung in die Natur-Lehre*, 3rd edition. Göttingen: Abram Vandenhoecks seel. Wittwe (1770) *page* 29
1.1 Joshua Reynolds, *David Garrick between Tragedy and Comedy* (1761) 46
2.1 Detail from Michelangelo, *The Last Judgment* (1541) 69
2.2 William Hogarth's etching, *The Tailpiece, or the Bathos* (1764) 88
3.1 Colossal bust of Rameses II, the "Younger Memnon" (1250 BC) 122
7.1 [Niels Prahl], *Det menneskelige Livs Flugt, eller Døde-Dands, hvorudi ved tydelige Forestillinger og Underviisnings-Vers viises, hvorledes at Døden uden Persons Anseelse, dandser af med Enhver, endog ofte uformodentlig, fra Verden til Evigheden; Afbildet ved lærerige Stykker, og Samtaler imellem Døden og Personerne, Forlagt og besørgt til sine Landsmænds Nytte og Fornøyelse af Thomas Larsen Borup* (1762) 229

PREFACE

This book is the culmination of a lifelong reflection on the problem of nihilism. I became interested in this issue at an early stage in my academic education and continued to return to it frequently over the subsequent years. In a sense this is a book that I have long wanted to write, and so it is with a great sense of gratification that I see it now appear. When I began work on it, I proudly imagined that I knew a fair bit about nihilism. But in the course of the work, I learned a great deal that was new to me. This project afforded me the opportunity to discover some new authors and revisit some old ones with whom I was already familiar. The research on this book has vastly expanded my knowledge of and appreciation for the problem.

Some authors such as Dostoevsky and Nietzsche have long been associated with nihilism, and their portrayals and analyses of the issue have been repeated so often that they have almost become a cliché. Since these connections have already been treated so thoroughly, I have tried to direct my focus to lesser-known figures who also played an important role in the development of the concept of nihilism. I have dutifully given some attention to the well-known figures associated with nihilism, but I have not made them my primary focus or treated them in a systematic, let alone exhaustive, manner.

I believe that the work adds something original to the research literature, providing a new explanation of the origin of nihilism in the modern context. It should therefore be of interest to scholars in philosophy, religious studies, German literature, Scandinavian Studies, and English Romanticism. Moreover, the book has been written so that it is accessible to students and generally interested readers. The reason for this is that I believe that everyone has feelings of anxiety, despair, hopelessness, and dark thoughts about death. There are times when all of us struggle to find meaning in life. Thus, nihilism is a topic that concerns everyone and is part of the human condition. It should therefore not be regarded as a purely academic issue. Because of this I have tried to frame this study not solely as an academic work designed for research specialists. I have refrained from engaging in lengthy polemics with other authors who have written on this theme. In the note apparatus, I have directed interested readers to the relevant works in the secondary literature for further reading. But I have avoided making these works explicit dialogue partners for my study.

All biblical quotations used in the present work are taken from the well-known translation, the New Revised Standard Version. The quotations from Shakespeare refer to the new scholarly edition *The New Oxford Shakespeare*.[1] Since the present investigation is a study in the history of ideas and concepts, it is important to understand the individual works under examination in their historical context. For this reason, I have tried to use the original editions of these works and not later reprints. However, in a few cases I have availed myself of later editions, but only when there was some compelling philological reason to do so. In line with my desire to make this study as accessible as possible to a broad readership, I have also provided references to standard English translations for the works treated here.

---

[1] *The New Oxford Shakespeare. The Complete Works*, modern critical ed., general eds., Gary Taylor, John Jowett, Terri Bourus, and Gabriel Egan, Oxford: Oxford University Press 2016.

ACKNOWLEDGMENTS

This work has been significantly improved by the useful suggestions and criticisms of Roe Fremstedal, Stephen Dowden, Katalin Nun Stewart, Robert Wicks, and Daniel Conway. I am very grateful to them for their generous help. I am forever thankful to Hilary Gaskin of Cambridge University Press for her kind support of my work.

I would also like to thank Samuel Abraham and František Novosád for affording me the opportunity to teach a class on some of this material, entitled "The Origins of Existentialism: The Problem of Nihilism" at the Bratislava International School of Liberal Arts (Slovakia) in the spring of 2021. I would also like to express my gratitude to Zoltán Gyenge for the chance to teach a variant of this class for graduate students at the University of Szeged in Hungary in the Fall Semester of 2021. The manuscript profited enormously from the in-class discussions, and I am grateful to my students for their enthusiastic engagement and insights. I am thankful to Katalin Nun Stewart for her attractive cover design for this book.

My work on this project builds on a lecture that I gave entitled "The Problem of Nihilism in the Danish Golden Age," which was presented at the annual conference of the Society for the Advancement of Scandinavian Studies in Minneapolis, Minnesota, on May 12, 2017. The lecture at the conference took place in the context of a stream, "The Crisis of the Danish Golden Age and Its Modern Resonance," that I organized together with my friend Nate Kramer, to whom I remain eternally grateful.

I would also like to acknowledge the great help and support of my friends and colleagues at the Institute of Philosophy at the Slovak Academy of Sciences: Peter Šajda, Róbert Karul, Jaroslava Vydrová, František Novosád, Alžbeta Kuchtová, Ivana Kováčiková, and Lucia Jankovičová. I am deeply grateful to the director of the institute, Richard Sťahel, for providing me with an academic context that gives me the freedom to pursue this and other projects.

This work was produced at the Institute of Philosophy of the Slovak Academy of Sciences. It was supported by the Agency APVV under the project "Philosophical Anthropology in the Context of Current Crises of Symbolic Structures," APVV-20-0137.

Introduction

"All is vanity."[1] The words of Ecclesiastes echo disturbingly through the ages. We all want to think that what we do in life is meaningful. It is this belief in the importance of our projects that gives us the motivation to carry them out, even though they might be very difficult and demand many sacrifices. We have all had the experience of being assigned some task that we took to be completely meaningless, and as a result we struggled to complete it, and even if we managed to do so, we did it poorly with only the minimum effort and engagement. The belief in the value of our lives and actions seems to be among the most fundamental of human needs. If we were firmly convinced that our existence was utterly meaningless, it would be hard to muster the interest and motivation to do anything. Indeed, in extreme cases this can lead to depression and even suicide. But generally, most people, in their busy modern lives, never give much thought to these matters. We simply follow our regular routine and lose ourselves in the many daily tasks at hand. Our mundane activities seem to provide us with a sufficient sense of purpose to keep us going or at least to distract us sufficiently so that we do not constantly raise the question of the meaning of our lives. But in times of crisis the words of Ecclesiastes haunt us and force us out of our complacency. We begin to wonder if, in the big picture, what we have worked for or achieved ultimately amounts to anything at all. This calls into question the meaning of our very existence. In philosophy this is known as the problem of nihilism.

The present work is a study of nihilism. Its goal is to determine the origin of the modern concept of nihilism and trace its development in Western culture in the nineteenth century. This is potentially a very broad topic, and so I have limited myself to an investigation of what I take to be some of the key texts in which the concept of nihilism is present. I have tried to identify the nihilistic elements in these works and determine precisely how each of the authors understands the problem. Here at the outset, it will be necessary to define what we mean by nihilism so that it can be readily identified in the works under examination.

---

[1] Ecclesiastes 1:2. All biblical translations are from the New Revised Standard Version.

0.1 The Concept of Nihilism

It would be a mistake to think of nihilism as a single concept or problem. Rather, it is a complex constellation of related concepts and problems. For this reason, there have been many attempts to define and categorize various kinds of nihilism.[2] Literally the belief in nothing (in Latin *nihil*), nihilism can be understood as the troubling idea that nothing is ultimately valuable or meaningful, including our own existence. The world itself is meaningless. While this might be regarded as its basic meaning, the term "nihilism" has, however, been used in various ways, branching off from this. One of the purposes of the present study is to identify these different meanings and to understand their relations to one another by exploring the origin and development of the basic set of issues that gave rise to the concept in the modern context.

This question is complicated by the fact that the idea of the lack of value or meaning in human life existed long before the word "nihilism" was coined and gained currency. Thus, if we wish to understand the full scope of the question, it is necessary to broaden the investigation to include works where the relevant issues are present, although the term that we usually use to designate it is absent. In what follows I will briefly sketch what are commonly taken to be key elements related to the concept of nihilism. These can be defined by the different causes that lead to the idea of the meaninglessness of the universe.

0.1.1 Death

Humans have always feared death, and the idea of nihilism is closely connected with human mortality. The thought of the vanity of our mundane existence arises in part from the awareness of the brevity of our lives and the sobering and inescapable reality of death. Ecclesiastes notes, "For the fate of humans and the fate of animals is the same; as one dies, so dies the other. They all have the same breath, and humans have no advantage over the animals; for all is vanity. All go to one place; all are from the dust, and all turn to dust again."[3] In this sense humans, for all their accomplishments, differ in no way from the rest of nature. So a sense the meaninglessness of life can easily seem to follow from an awareness of death, which is thus commonly associated with nihilism.

In the ancient Sumerian epic, the king Gilgamesh experienced a crisis of meaning when his beloved friend Enkidu died. For the first time he feels anxiety in the face of death. He sees the bodies of the dead floating in the river and knows that this too will be his fate.[4] These events cause him to realize the

---

[2] See, for example, Donald A. Crosby, "Types of Nihilism," in his *The Spectre of the Absurd: Sources and Criticisms of Modern Nihilism*, Albany: State University of New York Press 1988, pp. 8–36.
[3] Ecclesiastes 3:20.
[4] *The Epic of Gilgamesh*, trans. by N. K. Sanders, Harmondsworth: Penguin 1960, p. 72.

finitude of his own existence and reflect on his own death. The threat of death evokes great terror in him, and he becomes obsessed with finding a means to avoid it. Ultimately, he undertakes a long and perilous journey to discover the key to immortality. This is thus the story of a rich and powerful king who has everything that he wants yet is deeply vexed since he knows that one day he will die. The anticipation of death deprives him of all joy in life.

In the vastness of space and time, we live for but a moment and then disappear again. In his *Pythian Odes* Pindar laments, "Man's life is a day. What is he? / What is he not? A shadow in a dream / Is man."[5] Human existence is an ephemeral reality. Entire peoples come and go quickly. In the *Iliad* the Lycian warrior Glaucus says, "As is the generation of leaves, so is that of humanity. / The wind scatters the leaves on the ground, but the live timber / Burgeons with leaves again in the season of spring returning. / So one generation of men will grow while another / dies."[6] Our entire life seems just to be a part of the natural cycle of nature that cannot be stopped or avoided.

The fear of death is not only limited to oneself but also to those whom one loves and cares about. When someone close to us dies, in addition to the natural sadness and grief, people often feel a sense of disorientation. We struggle to understand the meaning of the death of our loved ones. There seems to be something wrong with the universe that would allow such a thing to happen. This is particularly troubling in the case of the death of young people. There is great pathos in Virgil's portrayal of the souls of dead children in Elysium in the *Aeneid*: "Here voices and loud lamentations echo: / the souls of infants weeping at the very / first threshold – torn away by the black day, / deprived of their sweet life, ripped from the breast, / plunged into bitter death."[7] What meaning could there possibly be in innocent children dying? What purpose could this possibly serve? Why did they not have the chance to grow up and happily live out their lives? It seems impossible to give satisfying answers to these kinds of questions.

This problem illustrates the deep-seated need to believe that death is not what it immediately seems to be – complete annihilation – since this frightening idea is difficult for people to accept and leads to a struggle for meaning. Many religions have a conception of an afterlife that offers a degree of solace in the face of the inevitability of death. The fact that this idea is so widespread demonstrates the importance of this issue for human beings. However, the modern scientific view seems to rule out the possibility of surviving death in any form. According to this view, we simply die, decompose, and turn to dust.

---

[5] Pindar, *The Odes*, trans. by Maurice Bowra, Harmondsworth: Penguin 1969, "Pythian VIII," p. 237, lines 95–97.
[6] *The Iliad of Homer*, trans. by Richmond Lattimore, Chicago, and London: University of Chicago Press 1951, Book VI, lines 146–150, p. 157.
[7] *The Aeneid of Virgil*, trans. by Allen Mandelbaum, New York: Bantam 1981, Book VI, p. 147.

What we understand as our personality, our individuality, or, if one will, our soul originates in our brain. When we die, our brain stops working, and then our personality dies as well. It is difficult to conceive of a life after death without a physical body or a brain, both of which make it possible for us to be who we are. For most people, this is a depressing and anxiety-evoking thought. Like Gilgamesh, many people would be happy to find some way to escape death. If we are born just to die after a short life, our existence seems meaningless in the immensity of the universe. However, if we continue forever after death, then we are clearly something special, and our lives and afterlives have a significance beyond that of the rest of nature.

Modern science and medical advances have made it possible to overcome diseases that have plagued humanity through the ages. Today's medicine can be regarded as nothing short of miraculous in comparison with the medical practices of only a century ago. Despite this, death stubbornly resists all our scientific efforts. While life expectancy has gradually risen, and recent research into slowing the process of aging has been promising, the fundamental fact of death remains. This is a part of nature that human ingenuity seems helpless to change. The ancient problem of mortality is thus still with us today and constitutes a part of the modern conception of nihilism.

0.1.2 The Fear of Being Forgotten

Connected with the issue of nihilism and death is the inevitability that we will all in time be completely forgotten. While for most people dying is a terrifying thought in itself, being forgotten seems in some ways almost even worse. This is also a point about which Ecclesiastes reminds us: "The people of long ago are not remembered, / nor will there be any remembrance / of people yet to come / by those who come after them."[8] Even if one managed to accomplish something important and meaningful in life, all memory of it will fade into oblivion over time. Ultimately, it will be as if one never even existed. This thought undermines the idea that anything is meaningful with respect to one's life as an individual. Whatever meaning one can find is only fleeting and relative. The fear of being forgotten is thus also associated with the concept of nihilism.

In the ancient world, kings and nobles with great wealth were usually generally free from worrying about obtaining the basic necessities of life. As a result, they had the luxury of reflecting on the broader philosophical issues concerning the meaning of their existence. Even though these were powerful people who enjoyed great respect and recognition in their societies, some of them were still troubled by the question of meaning. For the ancients more so than today, death was very much present and highly visible. Child mortality was commonplace. There was an awareness of human vulnerability, finitude,

---

[8] Ecclesiastes 1:11.

and the brevity of life. Even the rich and powerful could not avoid thinking about the grim prospect of their demise. The anxiety of the leaders of antiquity is reflected in the various ways in which they tried to overcome death by ensuring that their memory would live on.

Throughout history people from different times and cultures have continually struggled with this issue. They endeavored to do something spectacular by which they would be remembered. For example, the Egyptian pharaohs mobilized enormous resources in order to create massive pyramids as funeral monuments to themselves. Obsessed with their own death, they wanted to leave behind a visible mark of the glory of their reign. Their immediate message to one who beholds the pyramids for the first time seems to be that someone very important created these colossal structures and is worthy of respect because of it. The story of the Tower of Babel in Genesis can be seen as an expression of the same desire. The people say, "Come, let us build ourselves a city, and a tower with its top in the heavens, and let us make a name for ourselves; otherwise, we shall be scattered abroad upon the face of the whole earth."[9] They fear that, as a people, they will be forgotten by the world if they do not mark their existence with some magnificent achievement that everyone would recognize.

The Greek heroes in Homer were motivated by the warrior ethic, according to which they would be remembered long after their deaths for their illustrious deeds. Their victories in battle were of interest even to the gods themselves, and this provided the lives of the warriors with a sense of meaning and purpose. Homer describes their exploits as if they were fighting on a stage for all to see. He is careful to note who fought bravely and who did not. It was important for the Greeks to know that later generations would recall with praise their brave combats and victorious battles. On his travels home to Ithaka, Odysseus proudly states his name to those people he meets along the way so that his adventures will be remembered. In later times the Greeks celebrated their Olympian victors lavishly, and this general recognition gave the sense that their fame would be enduring even long after their deaths.

Greek and Roman literature is full of explicit examples of the value placed on attaining a lasting name for oneself. The Greek historian Polybius observes with fascination the Roman customs for honoring their dead relatives. He explains that the elaborate funerary processions, effigies, and eulogies for the ancestors all serve the purpose of inspiring "young men to endure the extremes of suffering for the common good in the hope of winning the glory that waits upon the brave."[10] To his mind it is completely obvious that the attainment of fame in battle is the *raison d'être* of men.

---

[9] Genesis 11:4.
[10] Polybius, *The Rise of the Roman Empire*, trans. by Ian Scott-Kilvert, Harmondsworth: Penguin 1979, p. 347.

Both the Greeks and the Romans sought to win an enduring reputation not just in the military context but also in other spheres such as the sciences and the arts. Ovid ends his *Metamorphoses* with a recognition that he will one day die, but he is consoled by the fact that his work will bring him immorality of reputation: "That day which has power over nothing but my body may, when it pleases, put an end to my uncertain span of years. Yet with my better part I shall soar, undying, far above the stars, and my name will be imperishable .... I shall live to all eternity, immortalized by fame."[11] According to Pliny the Younger, this knowledge of one's enduring fame plays an important role in the pursuit of the good life: "my idea of the truly happy man is of one who enjoys the anticipation of a good and lasting reputation, and, confident in the verdict of posterity, lives in the knowledge of the fame that is to come."[12] He regards the "love and longing for a lasting name" to be "man's worthiest aspiration."[13]

The Roman historian Sallust makes an argument similar to that of Ovid, that it is noble to seek the immortality of fame by means of higher cultural achievements in the arts and letters:

> All human beings who want to be superior to the other animals ought to struggle with every resource not to be like cattle passing silently through life. It is natural for the cattle to hang their heads and obey their stomachs, but all our strength is situated in our mind as well as our body: we use the mind more for control, the body for servitude; the one we have in common with the gods, the other with the beasts. And so I think it more upright to seek glory with our inner resources than with our physical strength and, since life is itself brief, to make the memory of our lives as long as possible.[14]

Sallust is indirectly in a polemic here with the traditional heroic ethic, which concerns exclusively martial prowess and bodily strength. He suggests an alternative to this by arguing that fame can also be achieved by means of the use of the mind. This is what separates the human from the animal. For Sallust, history writing was thus the means to overcome the oblivion of death.

Likewise, the Roman emperors tried to win great victories, expand Roman territories, and embark on ambitious building projects in order to leave their mark after their death. The deification of Egyptian pharaohs, Roman emperors, and Incan rulers can also be seen as a way to achieve the immortality of

---

[11] Ovid, *Metamorphoses*, trans. by Mary Innes, Harmondsworth: Penguin 1955, Book XV.870–879, p. 357.

[12] Pliny, *The Letters of the Younger Pliny*, trans. by Betty Radice, Harmondsworth: Penguin 1963, Book IX.3, p. 235.

[13] Pliny, *The Letters of the Younger Pliny*, Book V.8, p. 145.

[14] Sallust, *Cataline's Conspiracy*, in *Cataline's Conspiracy, The Jugurthine War, Histories*, trans. by William W. Batstone, Oxford: Oxford University Press 2010, p. 10. See also *The Jugurthine War*, ibid., p. 52: "the extraordinary deeds of intellectual talent are, just like the soul, immortal."

reputation and fame. The medieval knight followed a Christian code of chivalry and embarked on ambitious undertakings in the service of faith in order to ensure a special place for himself both at court and in heaven. All of this can be seen as motivated by the fear of disappearing forever and leaving behind no trace of one's existence.

A moving modern image of the fear of being forgotten can be found in the life and work of John Keats. There was a history of tuberculosis in the family, and the poet took care of his younger brother Tom who died of the disease in 1818. In that same year he wrote the poem "When I Have Fears That I May Cease to Be" in which he reflects on his own mortality and expresses concerns that he might not have the chance to live long enough to develop his poetic art fully.[15] When he himself showed symptoms, he was advised to go to Italy in the hope that the warmer climate would help to improve his condition. When he arrived in Rome in November of 1820, he only had a few months left to live. With his medical training, Keats knew that he was dying and that there was nothing that could be done to save him. Melancholy at leaving life at the age of 25, he believed that his works would be forgotten. When he was on his deathbed, he formulated an inscription that he requested be put on his tomb: "Here lies One Whose Name was writ in Water."[16] This is made more poignant by the fact that, also at his request, his name does not appear on the tomb but only the words "a young English poet." The inscription reflects a bitterness at what Keats believed to be his fate.

The desire to be remembered after death is reflected indirectly in the many efforts that have been made to erase the memories and records of certain people. Often referred to the *damnatio memoriae* or the "condemnation of memory," this can involve the destruction of tombs and monuments or the deletion of inscriptions or records. During his reign in the thirteenth century BC, the Egyptian pharaoh Akhenaten introduced monotheism with the cult of Aten (or Aton). However, after his death the angered priests took their revenge by destroying images of him and chiseling away or deleting his name wherever it appeared in writing. The practice of the desecration of graves is still known to this day. This shows the value that is placed on establishing a legacy or at least a name that will be long remembered.

In all these cases, it is evident that there is a deeply rooted need to give one's life some meaning by ensuring that one will be remembered posthumously. If death is inevitable, then being remembered after death is the best that can be hoped for. As the examples above illustrate, historically, some people have gone to extravagant lengths to create a memory of themselves if they had the social position, the time, the ability, and the resources to do so. The goal is often

---

[15] John Keats, "When I Have Fears That I May Cease to Be," in *The Complete Poems*, ed. by John Barnard, 3rd ed., London: Penguin 1988, p. 221.
[16] See Walter Jackson Bate, *John Keats*, New York: Oxford University Press 1966, p. 694.

to see one's life as a part of something greater, that is, something in relation to the state, the gods, or the universe as such. It has been quite plausibly argued that in this way a large part of human culture is created by the anxiety about death, finitude, and the terrifying specter of being forgotten.[17]

A case might be made that today, with the increased numbers of people enjoying financial well-being and security, this problem has increased in the sense that more people now find themselves with the leisure to reflect on what appears to be the emptiness and meaninglessness of life. The need to be remembered has thus become even more widespread. In recent times, this need accounts for the tremendous growth in the publication of genres such as memoirs, autobiographies, and letters. It can also help to explain the staggering rise of social media sites, which people zealously use to spread the word about not only what they regard as their great accomplishments but also the trivialities of their daily lives. The issue of the meaning of our lives is thus a very old problem but also a very current one that is expressed in an ever-increasing variety of new forms.

0.1.3 Suffering

High on the list of things that humans fear most is pain and suffering. From our earliest childhood, we know that we will periodically experience pain. This is a necessary feature of the fact that, in order to live, we must inhabit bodies. Our bodies are equipped with nerves and pain detectors that alert us when we are in danger. If our hand were burning and we were unaware of it, we could easily be mortally harmed before we took action. While this sensitivity to pain serves an important function in our survival, it is difficult to cope with and can lead to great anxiety. In some ways this can be even worse when our loved ones are in great pain, and we are helpless to do anything about it. When we or those close to us suffer, we ask how such a thing could happen or what the point of it could be. Why do we suffer and have pain? This common reaction demonstrates that suffering is related to the question of meaning. The value of everything is called into question if we feel that we are suffering, and there is no reason for or meaning to it. For this reason, people desperately try to find some meaning in their suffering – for example, God is testing them, or it is a part of a larger divine plan that will later lead to something good. But if suffering people feel that these kinds of explanations are implausible, they can easily end in nihilism and meaninglessness.

In a sense it seems like we have been created to suffer. Our bodies require constant attention. We cannot go for very long without food, water, or sleep. We must be constantly attentive to fulfilling our basic needs. No sooner do we satisfy one natural drive than the call of another arises and must be attended to. We spend most of our lives catering to these. Indeed, making money can be

---

[17] See Jan Assmann, *Death and Salvation in Ancient Egypt*, trans. by David Lorton, Ithaca and London: Cornell University Press 2001.

seen in this context as a means of securing what we require to satisfy our needs for food, shelter, and security.

Early human beings must have been acutely aware of the central role of suffering in life. Living in small groups, they must have regularly experienced women in childbirth, broken bones, painful diseases, and death. In the absence of anesthesiology or any knowledge of modern medicine, these must have been terrifying, traumatizing, and puzzling experiences. Moreover, prehistorical people were regularly exposed to the elements and had to struggle daily to find food. They could rarely relax and feel comfortable. This raises the question of meaning since if human existence is merely a struggle to survive, then what could the point of this be? Is our whole life simply an evolutionary sacrifice required to perpetuate the species? The things that usually give our lives meaning, such as our projects, accomplishments, family, and so on, all seem to presuppose that we have attained a minimum level of well-being whereby we are not constantly in pain or suffering, since this would undermine our ability to do anything or even enjoy the company of our loved ones.

As the story goes, the young Buddha, known as Siddhartha, was raised in a sheltered way in the confines of the palace of his father. Sequestered from the real world, he was prevented from seeing old age, death, and other miseries. When he finally left the palace for the first time, he was shocked to see the suffering that the outside world contained. Deeply troubled to see the large role that pain plays in human existence, he set off on the road to reflection and developed a doctrine for how to avoid the suffering that is such a fundamental part of the basic human condition. Inspired by Buddhism, Schopenhauer followed much the same trajectory in his philosophy. According to his view, when we are prevented from satisfying our basic needs, we suffer. For this reason, he claimed that life itself is constant suffering.

The fact that pain and suffering are an inevitable part of life raises the question of meaning. Traditionally, this has been an argument against the existence of God, for if God is omnipotent and all-loving, then why does he allow people to suffer? If he is omnipotent, then he can always step in and stop it at any time. If he is all-loving, then he would surely be inclined to do so (in contrast to a malevolent deity). Given this, it is difficult to reconcile the enormous amount of suffering in the world with the usual conception of God. This well-known problem is illustrated in the Book of Job. Why do kind and innocent people suffer, while rogues flourish and go unpunished? The fact of suffering seems to undermine the belief in God and meaning. We suffer, and there is no meaning or point to it.

0.1.4 Atheism

According to many thinkers, one of the basic ideas behind modern nihilism is the feeling of meaninglessness that follows from the realization that God does not exist. Without God, there is a deep sense of abandonment and loneliness in a hostile world. It is frightening to be subject to the many trials and tribulations that we are confronted with in life without any higher power to comfort or help us. The absence of God is, however, not just about this feeling of abandonment, but it also concerns our fundamental sense of meaning. If God exists, then all truth, meaning, and value come from him. But if not, then the very idea of truth and meaning no longer seems possible. For this reason, atheism is often closely associated with nihilism. Nietzsche's idea of the death of God in Western society is thus often regarded as a key diagnosis of the rise of nihilism and loss of meaning.

The scientific view of the world, according to which the universe was created by natural forces, can seem depressing. In the great void of space there are countless atoms rushing at enormous speeds, which by chance come into interaction with one another to produce an infinite variety of results over seemingly infinite time. What is particularly disturbing is the thought that there is no conscious plan or goal to any of it. The universe was not created by anyone for any purpose. There are merely natural forces and accidents at work that have no consciousness or meaning.

By contrast, the idea that human beings were created by an all-powerful and loving God is comforting. It gives us a great sense of satisfaction to think that God made us for a special purpose as a part of his divine plan for the universe. On this view, we are separate from the rest of nature and have an absolute meaning. However, the scientific view tells us that we evolved from earlier species over a very long period of time in accordance with basic principles of nature and chance variations. There is nothing special about us since the same forces that created a mouse or a fly also produced human beings. We have no absolute meaning but are merely one among an enormous number of species, most of which have already gone extinct. This picture offers little comfort or meaning.

It should be noted that nihilism does not necessarily need to imply atheism, although the two are often associated. A nihilistic perspective can still be consistent with a belief in God, as, for example, in the case of Ecclesiastes. Nihilistic elements can also be found among the ancient Mesopotamians and Greeks, who were polytheists. Likewise, a deist or a pantheist might have a belief in the divine and at the same time be vexed by nihilism. One can thus still despair of the lack of meaning in life and human finitude, while at the same time believing in the divine. It all depends on one's conception of God or the gods and what other religious or philosophical doctrines one subscribes to.

0.1.5 Ethical and Value Relativism

The idea that God does not exist leads to the problem of relativism, which is often associated with nihilism.[18] If there is not a single ruling force in the universe

---

[18] There is a vast literature on relativism, only some of which connects the problem with nihilism. See E. M. Adams, *Philosophy and the Modern Mind: A Philosophical Critique*

that defines meaning, then it might be argued that it follows that all meaning is relative, with everyone having their own idea about it. Without any absolutes, whether religious or secular, it seems that there is no final truth about such matters and no value in the deeper sense. Human beings are obliged to create their own truth and meaning, but this seems hopelessly impoverished and arbitrary in comparison to the former divine standard. If there is no absolute meaning, then, it is claimed, there is no meaning at all that anyone can really convince themselves to believe in. Nothing can be taken seriously anymore.

Forms of relativism have existed since antiquity. Some of the surviving fragments of the pre-Socratic thinkers, such as Heraclitus and Xenophanes, evidence relativistic ideas.[19] The Greek historian Herodotus observes the relativity of custom and tradition and concludes, "Such, then, is how custom operates; and how right Pindar is, it seems to me, when he declares in his poetry that 'Custom is the King of all.'"[20] Since each person has his or her own values and customs, it is impossible to speak of any one thing as being universally right or wrong. Even the things that we might find the most offensive and abhorrent are common practice somewhere. Similarly, the question of relativism or nihilism is often a central issue in Plato's portrayal of Socrates' struggle with the Sophists. For example, in the *Gorgias* Callicles argues that laws and traditions are simply the artificial constructs of the weak, intended to restrain those who are stronger by nature.[21] In Book I of the *Republic*, Socrates tries to answer a similar argument from Thrasymachus, who violently asserts that justice is simply a convention imposed by the stronger.[22] The implication is that there is no real truth or justice, but these are just arbitrary words that we use to seek our own advantage.

of Modern Western Civilization, Chapel Hill: University of North Carolina Press 1975, especially pp. 34–35, pp. 77–105; Michael Krausz and Jack W. Meiland (eds.), *Relativism: Cognitive and Moral*, Notre Dame and London: University of Notre Dame Press 1982; James Dreier, "Moral Relativism and Moral Nihilism," in *Oxford Handbook of Ethical Theory*, ed. by David Copp, Oxford: Oxford University Press 2006, pp. 240–264.

[19] *A PreSocratics Reader*, ed. by Patricia Curd, trans. by Richard D. McKirahan Jr., Indianapolis and Cambridge: Hackett 1995. Heraclitus: "The sea is the purest and most polluted water: to fishes drinkable and bringing safety, to humans undrinkable and destructive" (p. 33). "Pigs rejoice in mud more than pure water" (p. 35). "Pigs wash themselves in mud, birds in dust or ash" (p. 35). Xenophanes: "Ethiopians say that their gods are flat-nosed and dark, Thracians that theirs are blue-eyed and red-haired" (p. 26). "If oxen and horses and lions had hands and were able to draw … horses would draw the shapes of gods to look like horses and oxen to look like oxen, and each would make the gods' bodies have the same shape as they themselves had" (p. 26).

[20] Herodotus, *The Histories*, trans. by Tom Holland, with notes by Paul Cartledge, London: Penguin 2013, Book III, chapter 38, p. 207.

[21] Plato, *Gorgias*, trans. by Walter Hamilton and Chris Emlyn-Jones, London: Penguin 2004, p. 67, 483b–c.

[22] *The Republic of Plato*, trans. by Allan Bloom, New York: Basic Books 1968, Book I, pp. 13–34, 336b–354c.

The Roman thinker Cicero perceived the looming danger of relativism if a general skepticism comes to undermine traditional religious beliefs. In his main work on religion, *The Nature of the Gods*, he explains this as follows:

> Piety like any other virtue cannot long endure in the guise of a mere convention and pretense. When piety goes, religion and sanctity go with it. And when these are gone, there is anarchy and complete confusion in our way of life. Indeed, I do not know whether, if our reverence of the gods were lost, we should not also see the end of good faith, of human brotherhood, and even of justice itself, which is the keystone of all the virtues.[23]

Cicero thus anticipates a central motif in the modern discussion by connecting ethics and values with religious belief. On this view, a genuine belief in the existence of a solid foundation of justice is essential for societies to exist at all. Basic ideas of ethics cannot be regarded simply as "mere convention," since this amounts to relativism. Rather, they must be seen to have a firm, objective grounding.

In the seventeenth century Descartes was aware of the importance of God for promoting moral behavior. In his famous *Meditations on First Philosophy*, when describing one of his motivations for writing the work, he comments, "since in this life the rewards offered to vice are often greater than the rewards of virtue, few people would prefer what is right to what is expedient if they did not fear God or have the expectation of an after-life."[24] The idea of divine justice is thus seen as the motivation for people to act ethically. Without the lure of divine rewards and punishments, people would simply do as they please with no concern for right or wrong.

The issue also exercised the authors of the Enlightenment. In the same spirit as Cicero, Lessing, in his drama *Nathan the Wise*, portrays the concern of moral decay in the absence of belief in God. The Patriarch of Jerusalem is vexed by the threat of atheism, to which he believes the Sultan who reigns over the city is indifferent. The Patriarch exclaims, "I'll show him how dangerous it is for a state when one doesn't believe anything! All civic bonds are undone, ripped to pieces, when a human being is allowed to believe nothing. Away! Away with such wickedness!"[25] The Patriarch thus sees belief in God as the assurance of a common value system, without which a destructive relativism would result.

Similarly, in 1769 Voltaire argued, in *God and Human Beings*, that morality comes from the idea of God. Evildoers tend to commit their criminal activity

---

[23] Cicero, *The Nature of the Gods*, trans. by Horace C. P. McGregor, with an Introduction by J. M. Ross, Harmondsworth: Penguin 1972, p. 70.

[24] René Descartes, *Meditations on First Philosophy*, trans. by John Cottingham with an introduction by Bernard Williams, Cambridge: Cambridge University Press 1986, p. 3.

[25] Gotthold Ephraim Lessing, *Nathan the Wise with Related Documents*, trans. and ed. by Ronald Schlecter, Boston and New York: Bedford/St. Martin's 2004, p. 81, Act 4, Scene 2.

in the dark or in places where they cannot be seen. In this way they hope to escape detection and subsequent punishment. Voltaire argues that belief in God plays a beneficial role in such cases by preventing people from committing crimes when no one is around to see them.[26] The ever vigilant, all-seeing eye of God inhibits potential offenders from acting on their worse impulses since they know that even if they manage to escape human justice, they will never be able to hide from divine punishment. Once again, God is the guarantor of justice, and without this belief people would decide about what to do based on what they thought they could get away with instead of what they thought was right.

A similar thought is expressed by Kant in his *Lectures on the Philosophical Doctrine of Religion*. He describes the dangers of atheism by claiming,

> the dogmatic atheist ... directly denies the existence of a God and ... declares it impossible that there is a God at all. Either there never have been such dogmatic atheists, or they have been the most evil of human beings. In them all the incentives of morality have broken down; and it is to these atheists that moral theism stands opposed.[27]

This explains why Kant regularly refers to atheists as moral scoundrels.[28] Without any God to guide their actions, atheists can only be evil people since they act in a completely unprincipled manner, following their immediate drives, desires, and wishes, with no concern for others. For Kant, this kind of disrespect for ethics is unworthy of human beings who possess the faculty of reason.

In the nineteenth century Feuerbach makes the same observation as Kant about the suspicion of atheists in his own day: "Atheism was supposed, and is even now supposed to be the negation of all moral principle, of all moral foundations and bonds: if God is not, all distinction between good and bad, virtue and vice, is abolished."[29] All these views express the sentiment that humans are not sufficiently endowed with benevolence that they are able to pursue the good on their own. On the contrary, they need God as a control to ensure that they follow the path of morality. Thus, since the atheist does not believe in God, he must be an unprincipled person who regards all ethical values as illusions.

---

[26] Voltaire, *God and Human Beings*, trans. by Michael Shreve, Amherst, New York: Prometheus Books 2010, pp. 17–21. See also ibid., p. 157: "If the state's law punishes known crimes, let us proclaim a God who punishes the unknown crimes."

[27] Immanuel Kant, *Lectures on the Philosophical Doctrine of Religion* in *Religion and Rational Theology*, ed. and trans. by Allen W. Wood and George di Giovanni, Cambridge and New York: Cambridge University Press 1996, p. 355.

[28] Kant, *Lectures on the Philosophical Doctrine of Religion*, p. 407: "Hence without God I would have to be either a visionary or a scoundrel [sc. with regard to ethics]." Ibid., p. 415: "anyone who denies [the postulate of God] would have to be a scoundrel."

[29] Ludwig Feuerbach, *The Essence of Christianity*, trans. by George Eliot, New York: Harper & Row 1957, p. 202. See also p. 274.

The concern is that this loss of the divine grounding of ethics will lead to chaos and mayhem. Some people might take this realization of the absence of God opportunistically to justify all kinds of wicked actions that they believe will further their own ends. If everything is relative, then evil actions can be argued for just as well as good ones. This is summed up in Ivan Karamazov's oft-quoted statement that if God does not exist, then "everything is allowed."[30] In short, if there is no God, then there is no meaning or ethics. There is nothing intrinsically good or evil. This leaves it up to individuals to judge their own actions any way that they like since there is no external standard of measure. From these examples, it should be clear that the question of relativism was an important issue from the earliest times of ancient philosophy and that this issue is closely connected to nihilism.

Advocates of atheism often claim that there is a great sense of liberation in abandoning the idea of God. One can act as one wishes without the feeling of being under divine surveillance all the time. Despite this apparent advantage, the atheistic view opens the door for wicked people to do whatever they want with no fear of punishment or even scruple of conscience. Once the belief in God becomes dubious, any kind of ethics or system of morality based on religion seems to be built on a very unstable foundation. Given this, people of the modern age sometimes feel that they are in a crisis since they are apparently deprived of meaningful or persuasive reasons for acting morally. The problem of establishing an ethics in the absence of a divine grounding can in many ways be seen as one of the main problems of modern philosophy, perhaps most notably in existentialism.

If values are relative, then those who follow traditional customs, institutions, and beliefs as if they were absolute seem to be unreflective conformists, who live under childish delusions. This gives rise to different forms of social criticism grounded in nihilism. This reaction can be regarded as a destructive form of revolt against the views of the past, which, it is thought, rest on irrational beliefs in religion or repressive institutions inherited from history. Once one has seen through the thin veneer of legitimacy covering these, all of society appears to be absurd.

But by calling into question the basic customs and beliefs that the mainstream subscribes to, one makes oneself an outsider in society. A great sense of alienation arises since it is impossible to identify with the values that are generally held. Modern literature is full of characters like this. For example, Diderot's protagonist in *Rameau's Nephew* leads an unusual life with no clear goals or ambitions apart from simple hedonism. He rejects the values that govern social life in France at the time. He repeats Ecclesiastes' word "vanity" in reference to the traditional duties of defending one's homeland, having

---

[30] Fyodor Dostoevsky, *The Brothers Karamazov*, vols. 1–2, trans. by David Magarshack, Harmondsworth: Penguin 1958, vol. 2, p. 691.

friends, enjoying a position in society, and raising children.[31] By contrast, he amusingly explains what he thinks is important by claiming that the ultimate and "final outcome of life" is to defecate "easily, freely, pleasantly, and copiously every evening."[32] Friedrich von Schlegel's *Lucinde*, published in 1799, shocked the contemporary reader with its criticism of bourgeois sexual mores. It criticized the repression of the natural desires and passions by the accepted morality of the day. The protagonist Julius rejects values such as decency and bourgeois respectability.

This form of nihilism can well overlap with politics, and, for this reason, it is sometimes referred to as "political nihilism" in order to distinguish it from moral or ethical nihilism.[33] The standard example of this is Turgenev's Bazarov in *Fathers and Sons*. This famous character rejects not just old-fashioned customs and beliefs but also the repressive social and political institutions of Czarist Russia, which he dedicates himself to tearing down. In this sense nihilism can seem close to anarchism. The past rests on hypocrisy and oppression, where no real meaning can be found. Therefore, everything must be destroyed before a new start can be made to rebuild society based on rational, scientific principles.

Given this diversity of accents or emphases, it is no wonder that there has been confusion about the precise meaning of the term "nihilism." All these aspects are related to one another in different ways, and thus they can be taken together in different combinations. Different authors focus on different parts of the problem, while ignoring others. But I submit that all of these represent a thematic or semantic cluster that renders the term "nihilism" meaningful. What connects all of these is the fundamental sense of the lack of meaning in human existence, which was mentioned at the outset. The sense of meaninglessness can come from the different causes mentioned here: the prospect of death and annihilation, the fear of being forgotten, suffering, the loss of the faith in God, and the lapse in the belief in any absolutes concerning truth and meaning. There are thus many roads that lead to nihilism.

0.2 The Question of the Origin of Modern Nihilism

From the brief examples mentioned above, it is clear that the problem of nihilism is nothing new and can probably be found in one form or another in any period of history insofar as death and suffering are fundamental to the human condition. However, the twentieth century is the period best known for thematizing this issue. Most histories of this topic start with Nietzsche as a late

---

[31] Diderot, *Rameau's Nephew and D'Alembert's Dream*, trans. by Leonard Tancock, Harmondsworth: Penguin 1966, p. 65.
[32] Diderot, *Rameau's Nephew*, p. 52.
[33] See Crosby, "Types of Nihilism," pp. 9–11.

nineteenth-century precursor to the problem of nihilism and then move on from there.[34] For example, one author writes,

> Nietzsche set the stage for the epic drama of metaphysical despair that was acted out in the twentieth-century mind ... His struggles to cure himself of this sickness of soul prefigure the metaphysical conflicts ... in the twentieth century. He sounded the cry of spiritual alienation that is the leitmotif of nihilism .... Practically the entire history of twentieth-century thought ... is foreshadowed in Nietzsche's work.[35]

While this is perhaps a bit overstated, it is true that nihilism appears as an important topic in several philosophical, literary, and artistic schools of the twentieth century, and for this reason it is understandable that the concept is usually associated with this period.

Most recently, the relativistic element of nihilism has often been associated with *postmodernism* in the thought of Derrida, Lyotard, and Baudrillard.[36] In this context, the very idea of an objective truth is called into question. The postmodernist arguments about the impossibility of determining any fixed meaning in things or of communicating unambiguously have done much to undermine many traditional assumptions about epistemology. They seem to leave us wallowing in skepticism and nihilism, uncertain of anything at all.

The key issues related to nihilism are probably associated most frequently with the famous philosophical and literary movement of *existentialism*,[37] and

---

[34] One important exception to this is Michael Allen Gillespie's excellent *Nihilism before Nietzsche*, Chicago: University of Chicago Press 1996.

[35] Charles I. Glicksberg, *The Literature of Nihilism*, Lewisburg: Bucknell University Press 1975, pp. 20.

[36] See Anthony King, "Baudrillard's Nihilism and the End of Theory," *Telos*, vol. 112, 1998, pp. 89–106; David Will Slocombe, *Nihilism and the Sublime Postmodern: The (Hi)Story of a Difficult Relationship*, New York: Routledge 2006; Shane Weller, "Postmodernism and Nihilism," in his *Modernism and Nihilism*, Houndmills: Palgrave Macmillan 2011, pp. 137–165; Peter van Zilfhout, "Traces of Nihilism," in *Enduring Resistance: Cultural Theory after Derrida*, ed. by Sjef Houppermans, Rico Sneller, and Peter van Zilfhout, Leiden: Brill 2010, pp. 99–117; Ashley Woodward, "Nihilism and the Sublime in Lyotard," *Angelaki: Journal of the Theoretical Humanities*, vol. 16, no. 2, 2011, pp. 51–71; Ashley Woodward, *Nihilism in Postmodernity: Lyotard, Baudrillard, Vattimo*, Aurora, CO: The Davies Group 2009; Ashley Woodward, "Nihilism and the Postmodern in Vattimo's Nietzsche," *Minerva: An Internet Journal of Philosophy*, vol. 6, no. 1, 2002, pp. 51–67; Gianni Vattimo, *The End of Modernity: Nihilism and Hermeneutics in Post-modern Culture*, trans. by Jon R. Snyder, Cambridge: Polity Press 1994; David Michael Levin, *The Opening of Vision: Nihilism and the Postmodern Situation*, New York and London: Routledge 1988.

[37] See Walter Veit, "Existential Nihilism: The Only Really Serious Philosophical Problem," *Journal of Camus Studies*, 2018, pp. 211–236; Julian Young, "Nihilism and the Meaning of Life," in *The Oxford Handbook of Continental Philosophy*, ed. by Brian Leiter and Michael Rosen, Oxford: Oxford University Press 2007, pp. 463–493.

existential nihilism has been designated as a specific type.[38] This can be seen, for example, in Heidegger's concept of being-towards-death, according to which our consciousness of our own mortality and finitude plays a constitutive role in what it is to be human. Similarly, Camus treats nihilism explicitly in *The Myth of Sisyphus*, where he raises the question of what prevents us from committing suicide in a world without meaning. He uses the Greek mythological figure of Sisyphus as a symbol of a person trying to rebel against the meaninglessness of his existence. Sartre gives an account of the ontological priority of nothingness, according to which we are confronted with the world as something negative, and it is up to us as individuals to give things meaning. The existentialist topics of despair, anxiety, alienation, rebellion, and freedom are all closely related to the nihilistic experience, which many existentialist novels depict.

Related to existentialism, the *theater of the absurd movement* in drama has also been closely tied to the concept of nihilism.[39] Its leading figures, such as Beckett, Ionesco, and Genet, tried to create dramatic pieces that expressed the meaninglessness and absurdity of the human condition. Their works defy the traditional rules for drama, usually lacking a clear storyline, a conflict, character development, or a conclusion. The dialogues of their characters are often discontinuous and fragmented. The absurd plays are designed to puzzle the audience instead of offering answers to anything.

Through these different schools, nihilism has been seen as a concept characteristic and representative of the twentieth century as a whole. This seems to fit with the historical context of the rise of fascism, the Second World War, and the Holocaust.[40] The existentialists, for example, explicitly linked their movement to the experience of the war and its atrocities, which implicitly called into question the very meaning of civilization. In the wake of the war,

---

[38] Crosby, "Types of Nihilism," pp. 30–36.
[39] See the work by Martin Esslin credited with introducing the term, *The Theater of the Absurd*, New York: Anchor 1961; Maurice Marc LaBelle, *Alfred Jarry: Nihilism and the Theater of the Absurd*, Albany: New York University Press 1980; Glicksberg, "Ionesco and the Comedy of the Absurd," in his *The Literature of Nihilism*, pp. 222–233, and ibid., "Samuel Beckett: The Cosmic Nihilist," pp. 234–245; Shane Weller, *A Taste for the Negative: Beckett and Nihilism*, New York: Routledge 2004; Steven Miskinis, "Enduring Recurrence: Samuel Beckett's Nihilistic Poetics," *ELH*, vol. 63, no. 4, 1996, pp. 1047–1067; Harry E. Stewart, *Jean Genet: From Fascism to Nihilism*, New York: Peter Lang 1993.
[40] In this context fascism has often been taken to be synonymous with nihilism. See Karl Löwith, *Martin Heidegger and European Nihilism*, trans. by Gary Steiner, ed. by Richard Wolin, New York: Columbia University Press 1995; Stefan Elbe, "European Nihilism and Annihilation in the Twentieth Century," *Totalitarian Movements and Political Religions*, vol. 1, no. 3, 2000, pp. 43–72; Heinrich Fries, *Nihilismus. Die Gefahr unserer Zeit*, Stuttgart: Schwabenverlag 1949; Hermann Rauschning, *The Revolution of Nihilism: Warning to the West*, trans. by E. W. Dickes, New York: Alliance Book Corporation 1939; Hermann Rauschning, *Masken und Metamorphosen des Nihilismus: Der Nihilismus des XX. Jahrhunderts*, Frankfurt am Main: Humboldt-Verlag 1954.

intellectuals were left asking how it could have happened. They were forced to acknowledge the darker side of the human psyche. Further, they explored the question of meaning in extreme situations of hopelessness and despair.

But the issue of nihilism can be traced back even further. The artistic movement known as Dadaism, which arose in the context of the First World War, has often been associated with nihilism by calling into question the meaning of conventional values of society and celebrating irrationality, chaos, and nonsense.[41] Shaken by the events of the war, the Dadaists were critical of nationalism, capitalism, colonialism, and violence. They regarded modern culture to be in a state of crisis and moral bankruptcy, which they tried to work against. Dadaism was a sweeping international movement with centers in major cities such as Paris, Berlin, Zürich, and New York. The socially critical nihilism and nonconformism of its followers garnered a wide following.

Most philosophical accounts of the history of nihilism begin, as noted, with Turgenev or Nietzsche in the second half of the nineteenth century.[42] The reason for this is presumably that these writers used the term explicitly and were instrumental in making it well known in Europe. According to the canned textbook versions of the story, nihilism begins with these thinkers and was later picked up on by the existentialists. Turgenev's portrayal is primarily concerned with sociopolitical criticism, whereas Nietzsche's more comprehensive view of nihilism includes religion, ethics, politics, metaphysics, and epistemology. While it is true that they both use the term "nihilism," their understanding of the issue is rather different, despite some points of overlap.

It has also been claimed that modern nihilism can be traced back even earlier to the works of the Romantic movement.[43] This view follows the account given by Hegel, who sees the rise of relativism and nihilism as resulting from the German Romantics' misapplication of Fichte's philosophy of subjectivity.[44] Hegel examined the issue of relativism in the *Phenomenology of Spirit* (1807), the *Philosophy of Right* (1821), and the posthumously published *Lectures on the History of Philosophy* (1833–36). While the first two works explore the conceptual structure of different

---

[41] See Shane Weller, "From Flaubert to Dada," in his *Modernism and Nihilism*, pp. 77–101; Anne-Marie Amiot, "Georges Ribemont-Dessaignes: du nihilisme Dada au dithyrambe dionysiaque," *Noesis*, vol. 7, 2004 (online journal); Laurent Margantin, "Dada ou la boussole folle de l'anarchisme," *Lignes*, vol. 16, no. 1, 2005, pp. 148–159.

[42] See, for example, Julian Young, "Nihilism and the Meaning of Life," in *The Oxford Handbook of Continental Philosophy*, ed. by Leiter and Rosen, pp. 463–493.

[43] See Mădălina Diaconu, *Pe marginea abisului. Søren Kierkegaard și nihilismul secolului al XIX-lea*, Bucharest: Editura Științifică 1996; Alexey Ponomarev, *Das Problem des Nihilismus in der deutschen und russischen Romantik aus kultur-komparatistischer Perspektive*, Marburg: Tectum Verlag 2010.

[44] See Otto Pöggeler, "Hegel und die Anfänge der Nihilismus-Diskussion," in *Der Nihilismus als Phänomen der Geistesgeschichte in der wissenschaftlichen Diskussion unseres Jahrhunderts*, ed. by Dieter Arendt, Darmstadt: Wissenschaftliche Buchgesellschaft 1974, pp. 307–349.

0.2 THE QUESTION OF THE ORIGIN OF MODERN NIHILISM

forms of relativism,[45] his *Lectures* examine this as a historical phenomenon. It is here that Hegel sketches his view about how the Romantics mistakenly applied Fichte's theory to real life and ended up with a nihilistic criticism of everything.[46] In this context his favorite target is the relativism of Friedrich von Schlegel and his followers. While the ancients denied the validity of the individual subject and saw the truth as dwelling in the objective world that was divinely ordained, in the modern world, by contrast, the pendulum has swung to the other extreme. Modernity tends to regard the individual as the sole source of truth, independent of the external sphere. According to Hegel, relativism and nihilism are thus characteristic of the excesses of the modern worldview. Hegel's plea is to restore the proper balance between subjective and objective. The truth rests not in the one or the other exclusively, but in the dialectical relation between them. In *The Concept of Irony*, Kierkegaard explicitly follows Hegel's account about the development of relativism and nihilism from Fichte to the German Romantics.[47] Instead of using the term "nihilism," he refers to the phenomenon as "irony."[48] The Romantics criticize all traditional values and customs in an ironic manner in order to undermine them. The guiding idea is that individuals, on their own, have the right to pass judgment on society since there is no outward, objective truth.

There have thus been many conflicting views about the origin of nihilism. As we have seen, this issue is particularly difficult given the fact that the term is used in different ways, and in many instances the issue is present without the term being used at all. In this work I will try to trace what I take to be the true origins of modern nihilism that can be regarded as the precondition for the later movements that have been briefly mentioned here. I would like to argue that previous accounts of this issue, by focusing on one or the other later school, fail to recognize the historical and cultural background of nihilism that became a particularly widespread problem in the nineteenth century.

---

[45] See *Hegel's Phenomenology of Spirit*, trans. by A. V. Miller, Oxford: Clarendon Press 1977, "The Law of the Heart," pp. 221–228, "Virtue and the Way of the World," pp. 228–235, "The Spiritual Animal Kingdom," pp. 236–252, "Dissemblance or Duplicity," pp. 374–383, and "The Beautiful Soul," pp. 384–409; Hegel, *Sämtliche Werke. Jubiläumsausgabe*, vols. 1–20, ed. by Hermann Glockner, Stuttgart: Friedrich Frommann Verlag 1928–41, vol. 2, pp. 283–292, 292–301, 303–322, 471–484, 484–516; Hegel, *Elements of the Philosophy of Right*, trans. by H.B. Nisbet, ed. by Allen Wood, Cambridge and New York: Cambridge University Press 1991, "The Forms of Subjectivism," § 140, pp. 170–184; Hegel, *Sämtliche Werke. Jubiläumsausgabe*, vol. 7, pp. 204–223.

[46] See Hegel, *Lectures on the History of Philosophy*, vols. 1–3, trans. by E. S. Haldane, London: K. Paul, Trench, Trübner 1892–96; Lincoln and London: University of Nebraska Press 1995, vol. 3, pp. 479–512; Hegel, *Sämtliche Werke. Jubiläumsausgabe*, vol. 19, pp. 611–646.

[47] See Jon Stewart, *Faust, Romantic Irony, and System: German Culture in the Thought of Søren Kierkegaard*, Copenhagen: Museum Tusculanum Press 2019 (*Danish Golden Age Studies*, vol. 11), pp. 66–100.

[48] See K. Brian Söderquist, *The Isolated Self: Irony as Truth and Untruth in Søren Kierkegaard's On the Concept of Irony*, Copenhagen: C. A. Reitzel 2007 (*Danish Golden Age Studies*, vol. 1), pp. 23–26.

0.3 Nihilism and the Rise of Science in the Seventeenth and Eighteenth Centuries

Although we tend today to associate nihilism and related views with the twentieth century, in fact this basic idea goes back to some of the earliest philosophical, literary, and religious texts, and it reappears throughout history. Given the enormity of the material, it would be impossible to give a responsible overview of the history of nihilism in general within the framework of a single book. Instead, this study focuses on one specific period, namely, the nineteenth century. But this choice of focus is by no means arbitrary, as will be seen in the following. This study aims to show, among other things, that the background for the tradition of twentieth-century nihilism and existentialism was already well established in the nineteenth century. The root cause of the problem of modern nihilism was not so much the trauma of the World Wars but rather goes back to a considerably earlier period.

My thesis is that the true origin of modern nihilism can be found in the rapid development of the sciences in the Enlightenment that established a secular worldview that gradually displaced the traditional religious conception of the universe. The scientific perspective revealed the tiny, seemingly insignificant role of humans in the universe. This was a radical, new idea with far-reaching consequences. This modern scientific view led to a struggle with nihilism, which then became an important topic for thinkers in the first half of the nineteenth century, long before Turgenev and Nietzsche made the term fashionable.[49] It is no accident that the term "nihilism" was coined at around the beginning and not at the end of the nineteenth century.[50]

The scientific revolution that took place during the Enlightenment witnessed the confirmation and general acceptance of the Copernican picture of the heliocentric universe. This was the origin of many conceptual shifts that followed. At the beginning of the eighteenth century, Edmund Halley (1656–1742) determined that the stars were not fixed, as had long been thought, but rather moved. By comparing the modern star catalogue from 1712 with that of Hipparchus in the second century BC, he noticed that there was a great variation in the positions of some of the stars. This was evidence that the stars had moved since the time of Hipparchus. This idea contradicted the accepted view that the stars were tiny points of light on the crystal sphere that enclosed the universe and that was located just past the orbit of Saturn. The evidence suggested that the stars were much farther away and were moving on their own. They were at different distances out in space.[51] With this discovery the

---

[49] Glicksberg acknowledges the role of the sciences in a very general way, but he confines himself to the twentieth century and fails to trace the roots of this development in the nineteenth century. See Glicksberg, *The Literature of Nihilism*, pp. 43–52.

[50] On the historical use of the term "nihilism," see the helpful discussion in Johan Goudsblom, *Nihilism and Culture*, Totowa, NJ: Rowman and Littlefield 1980, pp. 3–7.

[51] See John Gribben, *Science: A History 1543–2001*, London: Penguin 2002, pp. 201f.

estimation of the size of the universe increased. This had the effect of making the earth and its inhabitants look considerably smaller. Moreover, from the idea that the stars were moving on their own arose the suspicion that the stars might in fact be other suns seen at a great distance. If the sun was just one among a great many others, then there seemed to be nothing special or unique about it. Moreover, with the development of optics new telescopes allowed astronomers to probe deeper into space. In 1781, William Herschel discovered Uranus, a planet beyond where the crystal sphere was thought to be. These new discoveries radically changed the view of the importance of human beings in the universe. While previously humans were thought to have played a central role in the big picture, now they started to look much less significant.

Halley pushed back the limits not only of space but also of time. It was generally accepted that the earth was created in 4004 BC. This calculation, made by the Irish Archbishop James Ussher (1581–1656), was based on counting the generations listed in the Bible back to the beginning. Halley approached the question more scientifically by trying to determine the date of the biblical flood by observing the subsequent effects of erosion that were visible. His new calculation determined that the Creation must have taken place much earlier than Ussher imagined.[52] By increasing the length of time since the creation, Halley began to put into perspective the shortness of human lifespans compared to the geological timeframe. It is true that the ancients were aware of the brevity of life and the smallness of the human sphere, but the discoveries of modern sciences reduced the scale of this even further by several degrees of magnitude.

There were also great advances made in the fields of botany, zoology, and biology. John Ray (1627–1705) and his friend and assistant Francis Willughby (1635–72) collected an enormous amount of empirical data on plants, animals, fish, and insects. This allowed them to make the first catalogue of the different species and their relations to one another. Ray published several different works on the classification of plants, which included increasing numbers of specimens. He first made a study of the local plants around Cambridge. Then he expanded this to include the other plants of England. Then he made a tour of Europe, which culminated with his classification of plants in his *Historia Plantarum*.[53] He also wrote an overview of classifications of animals and reptiles.[54] A similar work on birds and fish appeared posthumously.[55] His research represented the beginning of modern taxonomy.

---

[52] See Gribben, *Science*, pp. 194f.
[53] John Ray, *Historia plantarum species hactenus editas aliasque insuper multas noviter inventas & descriptas complectens*, vols. 1–3, London: Clark 1686–1704.
[54] John Ray, *Synopsis Methodica Animalium Quadrupedum et Serpentini Generis*, London: S. Smith & B. Walford 1693.
[55] John Ray, *Synopsis Methodica Avium et Piscium; Opus Posthumum*, vols. 1–2, London: William Innys 1713.

This work was carried on by the Swedish botanist and zoologist, Carl Linnaeus (1707–78), who first published his *Systema Naturae* in 1735.[56] This book was revised and reprinted in several subsequent editions. What is regarded as the definitive edition, entitled *Systema naturæ per regna tria naturæ, secundum classes, ordines, genera, species, cum characteribus, differentiis, synonymis, locis*, followed in 1758. Yet a further expanded edition appeared between 1766 and 1768.[57] The work contains some 10,000 species of plants and animals, a sign of the author's obsession with collecting specimens. Linnaeus created a hierarchical classification of the world of nature based on a binomial system (i.e., a two-word Latin name). His system gave names to all the different species that he meticulously catalogued. The radicality of Linnaeus's view of nature was found in the fact that he was the first to include human beings, which he designated *homo sapiens*, in a system of the natural world. His overview of nature thus regarded humans as a continuous part of the rest of nature. Humans could no longer be separated as something special and important in God's creation. They were creatures belonging to the animal kingdom just like pigs and goats.[58] This suggested that human immortality was a myth since, as a part of nature, humans also die and decompose like other animals.

Linnaeus's theories were important for establishing a point of departure for the modern theory of evolution. Erasmus Darwin (1731–1802), the grandfather of Charles Darwin (1809–82), originally popularized Linnaeus's ideas with a poetic work, entitled *The Loves of Plants*, which enjoyed a wide readership.[59] Later he presented his early notions about evolution in his *Zoonomia*.[60] Here the elder Darwin explains that species have changed over time and provides examples of how plants and animals have been modified under human domestication.[61] By artificial selection humans have, for example, been able

---

[56] See Gribben, *Science*, pp. 213–219.
[57] Carl Linnaeus, *Systema naturæ, sive regna tria naturæ systematice proposita per classes, ordines, genera, & species*, Leiden: Theodorum Haak 1735; *Systema naturæ per regna tria naturæ, secundum classes, ordines, genera, species, cum characteribus, differentiis, synonymis, locis*, vols. 1–2, 10th ed., Stockholm: Laurentii Salvii 1758–59; *Systema naturæ per regna tria naturæ, secundum classes, ordines, genera, species, cum characteribus, differentiis, synonymis, locis*, vols. 1–3 [vol. 1 in two parts], 12th ed., Stockholm: Laurentii Salvii 1766–68. The title translates, *The System of Nature through the Three Kingdoms of Nature, according to Classes, Orders, Genera and Species, with Characters, Differences, Synonyms, and Places*.
[58] Linnaeus was convinced that humans belonged to the same genus as the apes. However, for fear of the response from the religious establishment, he decided to place *homo sapiens* as the sole member of its own genus. For the sake of appearances, he thus tried to maintain the special place of humans in the universe. See Gribben, *Science*, p. 219.
[59] Erasmus Darwin, *The Botanic Garden*, Part II: *Containing the Loves of the Plants, a Poem: with Philosophical Notes*, London: Joseph Johnson 1789.
[60] Erasmus Darwin, *Zoonomia; or, the Laws of Organic Life*, vols. 1–2, London: Joseph Johnson 1794–96.
[61] See Gribben, *Science*, p. 333.

to breed faster horses. He further notes how animals have adapted to their environments and developed certain characteristics that help them survive in their local surroundings. Darwin posits the idea that all living creatures might have evolved from a single simple life form. This largely diminished the role of God since, while the divine can be regarded as the creator of the first living thing, there is no need for God to create each species one at a time or to interfere in the process of development once it has begun. Erasmus Darwin thus anticipated the work of Jean-Baptiste Lamarck (1744-1829) and Charles Darwin. Although he never came up with the idea of evolution by natural selection, his basic intuition was correct. Like Linnaeus, he presented the picture of human beings as a part of nature. They had been produced by the same natural processes as all other living things. This was a new idea that seemed shocking to most people at the time. Since people then did not tend to think of the lives of animals as particularly meaningful, this raised the question about what was fundamentally different about humans that gave them meaning, when after all they were also mortal like the animals.

Linnaeus also took up the issue of the age of the earth. The Dane Niels Steensen (Nicolaus Steno) (1638-86) discovered sediment patterns that indicated the presence of large bodies of water far inland. This was confirmed by the discovery in the sediment of an ancient shark tooth that Steensen compared with a modern one. This was evidence that the seas had shifted over long periods. As the waters receded, they left behind deposits in the sediment that over time became fossilized. Thus, the different strata of rock that Steensen found were at some point in the distant past underwater. Linnaeus seized upon this idea and argued that the entire earth was once covered with water that gradually receded over a long period. But this process would take far longer than the ca. 6,000 years that were thought to have elapsed since the creation. Thus, although no precise date for the creation could be fixed, Linnaeus concluded that the earth must be much older than previously imagined.

The French naturalist, Georges-Louis Leclerc, Comte de Buffon (1707-88), also presented a new argument that pushed back the date of the creation of the earth even further and seemed to be able to determine it with greater precision.[62] He claimed that the earth was created when a comet collided with the sun and material was thrown out on impact. Gradually, this material came together to form the planet and began to cool. Buffon's estimate of the earth's age is based on the time needed for the cooling to take place. He experimented with iron balls of different sizes. These were heated until they were red hot, and then he measured how long it took them to cool. He used this as his basis for measurement by inserting into the calculation the size of the earth in the place of the size of the balls of iron. According to his calculations, it would have taken the earth some 75,000 years to cool off. This was a radical new concept that

---

[62] See Gribben, *Science*, pp. 225f.

made a human lifetime seem even shorter than ever before. Once again, human existence seemed to be less and less significant in the universe.

One could continue to enumerate several more important discoveries of the age, but the pattern here should be clear. Each new step in science had, in one way or another an influence on the way in which humans understood themselves and the world around them. With each new discovery, the significance of human existence seemed to be diminished.

All these discoveries, however important they were, would never have had any widespread influence if it were not for the fact that a key part of the Enlightenment program concerned popularizing scientific knowledge. The goal was *to enlighten* the common people and get them to abandon their superstitious beliefs. As the general population became more literate, more journals and publications began to appear that explained the new scientific discoveries to a lay audience. For example, in 1738 Voltaire and his companion, the scientist Émilie du Châtelet (1706–49), popularized Newton's discoveries with their book *Éléments de la philosophie de Newton*.[63] The massive *Encyclopédie, ou dictionnaire raisonné des sciences, des arts et des métiers* (1751–72 and with supplements 1776–80), created by Denis Diderot and Jean Le Rond d'Alembert, was widely read and helped to increase the general level of knowledge about the sciences. With seventeen volumes of articles and another eleven volumes of illustrations, this work attempted a systematic and up-to-date overview of all accumulated knowledge in the different fields. Buffon's massive *Histoire Naturelle* (1749–1804) also played a great role in expanding the interest in science among less-educated readers.[64] As the general title indicates, the work covered a tremendous amount of material in several scientific fields.

Likewise, this period saw the birth of the modern academies of science, many of which had their own publications to present the work of their members.[65] There was an increase in the number of popular lectures on science for the general public, which took place outside the academies. Science was no longer a matter for a small cadre of experts but instead was something that far more people had access to than ever before in history. This meant that the implications and meaning of the scientific discoveries of the day were more broadly discussed. This played an important role in the rapid spread of the scientific worldview during the eighteenth century.

The role and importance of science in society was thus completely different in 1600 than it was in 1800. At the beginning, science was the purview of an elite

---

[63] Voltaire [and Émilie du Châtelet], *Éléments de la philosophie de Newton, donnés par M. de Voltaire*, Paris: Prault 1738.
[64] [Buffon], *Histoire Naturelle, générale et particulière, avec la description du Cabinet du Roi*, vols. 1–36, Paris: L'Imprimerie Royale 1749–1804.
[65] These later became the origin of the numerous specialized academic journals that we know today.

group of scholars, but by the end it was an important part of the mainstream discourse. The rapid growth that simultaneously took place in many different fields gradually shaped a new scientific view that became ever more dominant. Each new scientific breakthrough seemed to call into question different traditional religious beliefs about the nature of the universe and the role of human beings in it. This shift was the beginning of the crisis of modern nihilism.

0.4 The Enthusiastic Views Accompanying the Rise of Science

The thinkers of the Enlightenment in the eighteenth century appealed to reason as the sole standard of truth and used this to criticize politics, religion, and society. For many, this new scientific worldview was an exhilarating and liberating conception. The Enlightenment ideals enjoined people to remove the shackles of superstition and political oppression that they had submitted to for centuries. They should embrace their own freedom and autonomy by thinking for themselves and using their own faculty of critical reason. Thinkers such as Voltaire, Rousseau, Condorcet, Lessing, and Kant offered powerful messages of social, political, and personal emancipation. The advances in the sciences made the case for the new worldview very persuasive. Nobody wanted to be left behind to wallow in ignorance and superstition. Those who did not fully embrace this new worldview were regarded as reactionary.

The scientific worldview thus represented a point of pride among the freethinkers of the Enlightenment. Through human reason, nature was finally giving up her secrets. People were no longer stifled by absurd and irrational beliefs. With science there seemed to be no limits to human progress. There was no problem that could not be solved. All of this led to an optimistic view of the future. In some circles it was believed that it was possible to restructure society on purely rational and scientific grounds, and this would lead to the elimination of long-standing social ills such as poverty and inequality.[66]

This was the picture at the turn of the century in the wake of the French Revolution. Thinkers thus began to come to terms with what a secular, scientifically based worldview would look like and what its implications would be for the different spheres of life. It is here that the problem of nihilism in its modern form began to emerge. The challenge of nihilism presented a problem for the optimistic worldview of the Enlightenment. It seemed to expose the dark side of science that risked outweighing whatever concrete benefits scientific advancement had to offer. Thus, authors who focused on nihilism saw the need to qualify the unbridled praise of science that was part and parcel of the Enlightenment project.

---

[66] From this arose various conceptions of utopianism in the eighteenth and nineteenth centuries, e.g. in thinkers such as Henri de Saint-Simon, Charles Fourier, Étienne Cabet, Robert Owen, and others.

The new scientific worldview presented a conception of human beings that collided with the picture presented by Renaissance Humanism. The thinkers and artists of the Renaissance tended to glorify the human as something special and dignified in contrast to the rest of creation. We need only think of the artistic works of Leonardo da Vinci, Michelangelo, and Raphael, or Pico della Mirandola's much-celebrated argument for the dignity of humanity and human achievement. By contrast, the seventeenth- and eighteenth-century view tended to reduce the human to the physical sphere. Science taught that humans were ultimately no different from the animals and other created beings. Finite and mortal, human beings were bound by nature and had come about by means of natural processes. This challenged the widespread belief in immortality that was supported by the church.

Moreover, the earth no longer occupied a special place in the universe but rather was only one of a number of planets, circling only one of a vast number of stars. Doubts about the idea of a personal God meant that it was impossible to justify the meaning of one's existence by appeal to a special relation to the divine or a special role in some grand scheme. Gradually, the place of humans in the universe seemed to grow smaller and smaller. The scientific worldview that people were so keen to embrace offered very little by way of consolation. It presented a sober picture of a cold, godless universe that was utterly indifferent to human interests. This was a chilling realization. Nihilism can thus be regarded as a stumbling block to the cocksure attitude of the deists and freethinkers of the Enlightenment, who failed to see the full implications of their views. While they were busy congratulating themselves, they did not realize that their unqualified celebration of science would in fact carry with it a negative side.

0.5 Science as Forbidden Knowledge

Instead of science offering a program for human liberation, it suddenly seemed rather to lead to misery. As in Genesis, the tree of knowledge of good and evil is the source not of human development and wisdom but rather of despair. This is also a motif that can be found in Ecclesiastes: "And I applied my mind to know wisdom and to know madness and folly. I perceived that this also is but a chasing after wind. For in much wisdom is much vexation, and those who increase knowledge, increase sorrow."[67] According to this view, there are certain things that it is better not to know and that science should not interfere with. The blind pursuit of science does not lead to the good life but ends in sadness and anxiety.

The potential danger of scientific knowledge was perceived by thinkers and writers at the end of the nineteenth century. We find this motif in Schiller's

---

[67] Ecclesiastes 1:17–18.

poem "The Veiled Statue at Sais," which was published in 1795 in his journal *Die Horen*.[68] The poem describes how a youth, zealous for knowledge, goes to Sais in ancient Egypt to learn from the wise men in the temple. He enquires about a veiled statue of the goddess Isis and is told that the goddess has proclaimed that it is forbidden to raise her veil since beneath it lies the truth. Driven by insatiable curiosity, the youth sneaks into the temple at night and, despite the prohibition, removes the veil so that he can look upon the goddess directly and see the pure, unfiltered truth. The priests find him the next day languishing on the floor of the temple, hardly able to speak. The youth represents the spirit of modern science with its unquenchable thirst to know everything. Like the encyclopedists, he wants to collect knowledge in a systematic fashion and gain a complete overview of all the fields. The poem serves as a warning that there are some things that are best left alone, for if people were to know about them, they would be unable to live with the truth.

This can be regarded *in nuce* as a metaphor for the problem of nihilism. The young man wants to know everything and drives scientific enquiry to its furthest extreme. The statue represents scientific knowledge. When the youth sees it, he learns something that he cannot live with, and this spells doom for him. He experiences deep anxiety and dies an early death. Nihilism is the result of a sober, consistent scientific way of thinking. Science gives us information about the universe that we are curious to learn about. But when we transfer the scientific worldview to ourselves, it becomes disturbing since it seems to deprive human existence of all meaning. Like the misguided youth in the poem, we struggle to know how to continue our lives with the knowledge that the universe is meaningless and that we are utterly insignificant in it.

This motif can also be found in what has been regarded as the quintessential modern legend of Faust, especially in the version by Goethe. In this story the scholar Faust is tired of conventional science and yearns for greater wisdom. This is promised him by Mephistopheles, to whom Faust agrees to give his soul in exchange. Here again the main issue is hidden knowledge that is best left unknown. In order to get it, Faust, like Schiller's zealous youth, must sacrifice

---

[68] Friedrich Schiller, "Das verschleierte Bild zu Sais," *Die Horen*, vol. 1, no. 9, Tübingen: J. G. Cotta 1795, pp. 94–98 (English translation: "The Veiled Statue at Sais," in *The Poems and Ballads of Schiller*, trans. by Sir Edward Bulwer Lytton, Bart., New York: Thomas Y. Cromwell & Co. n.d., pp. 88–91). See Herbert Hager, "Friedrich Schiller. Das verschleierte Bild zu Sais," in *Wege zum Gedicht. II Interpretationen von Balladen*, ed. by Rupert Hirschenauer and Albrecht Weber, Munich: Schnell und Steiner 1963, pp. 190–202; Norbert Klatt, "'…des Wissens heisser Durst.' Ein literarischer Beitrag zu Schillers Gedicht *Das verschleierte Bild zu Sais*," *Jahrbuch der deutschen Schillergesellschaft*, vol. 29, 1985, pp. 98–112; Jon Stewart, "The Movement from East to West: Hegel's Interpretation of the Egyptian Goddess Neith," in *Etica, Politica, Storia Universale, Atti del Congresso Internazionale (Urbino, 24–27 Ottobre 2018)*, ed. by Giacomo Rinaldi and Giacomo Cerretani, Rome: Arcne Editrice 2020, pp. 105–134.

his life. In both cases, the desired knowledge can be understood as the nihilism that comes with a purely scientific view. Both protagonists perish in the end, due to having breached this forbidden knowledge.

The inspiration for Schiller's poem comes from Plutarch's work *Isis and Osiris*, which constitutes a part of his *Moralia*. Following the Greek practice of associating gods and goddesses of foreign religions with those of the Greek pantheon, Plutarch writes, "In Sais the statue of Athena, whom they believe to be Isis, bore the inscription: 'I am all that has been, and is, and shall be, and my robe no mortal has yet uncovered.'"[69] Schiller slightly revises this in the poem as follows: "'Til I' – thus saith the goddess – 'lift this vail, / may it be raised by none of mortal-born.'"[70] Schiller's poem points out that there really is such a thing as forbidden knowledge, which must be respected.

Of particular interest is that fact that Schiller's poem can be seen as a reaction to the use of the motif from Plutarch by the Hungarian natural scientist János András Segner (1704–77), known best by his German name Johann Andreas von Segner. In 1746 Segner published his introductory textbook to the natural sciences entitled *Einleitung in die Natur-Lehre*.[71] The image, taken from Plutarch's account, is depicted on the cover (Figure 0.1). The veiled goddess, representing nature, is represented with a thick robe that covers her entire body. Prevented from seeing her directly, the followers of science hasten after her. One of them employs a pair of compasses to measure the length of her stride, while another is on the verge of lifting her robe. What is interesting here is that Segner, a son of the Enlightenment, ignores the context of the image as one concerning forbidden knowledge. Instead, by placing it on the cover of his textbook, he distorts it to being a celebration of the ingenuity of the natural sciences to penetrate the secrets of nature. Segner belongs to the zealots of modern science, who can see no problematic or dangerous sides to it.

Schiller's poem and Goethe's drama raised a critical question about the enthusiastic praises of modern science in the eighteenth century such as that of Segner. Is the search for scientific knowledge really the highest and most important human task? Will modern science really solve all human problems? Will human reason find a solution to everything? Today these kinds of questions take on a sense of greater urgency. After the two World Wars, the Holocaust, the use of atomic bombs, and the rapid destruction of the environment, the

---

[69] See *Isis and Osiris* in *Plutarch's Moralia*, vols. 1–16, trans. by Frank Cole Babbitt, London: William Heinemann Ltd., Cambridge, MA: Harvard University Press 1936 (*Loeb Classical Library*, vol. 306), vol. 5, chapter 9, p. 25.

[70] Schiller, "Das verschleierte Bild zu Sais," *Die Horen*, vol. 1, no. 9, Tübingen: J. G. Cotta 1795, pp. 94–98 ("The Veiled Statue at Sais," in *The Poems of Schiller*, p. 95.).

[71] Johann Andreas Segner, *Einleitung in die Natur-Lehre*, Göttingen (n.p.) 1746. Note that the same cover image is used for the third edition, which is shown here: Johann Andreas Segner, *Einleitung in die Natur-Lehre*, 3rd ed., Göttingen: Abram Vandenhoecks seel. Wittwe 1770.

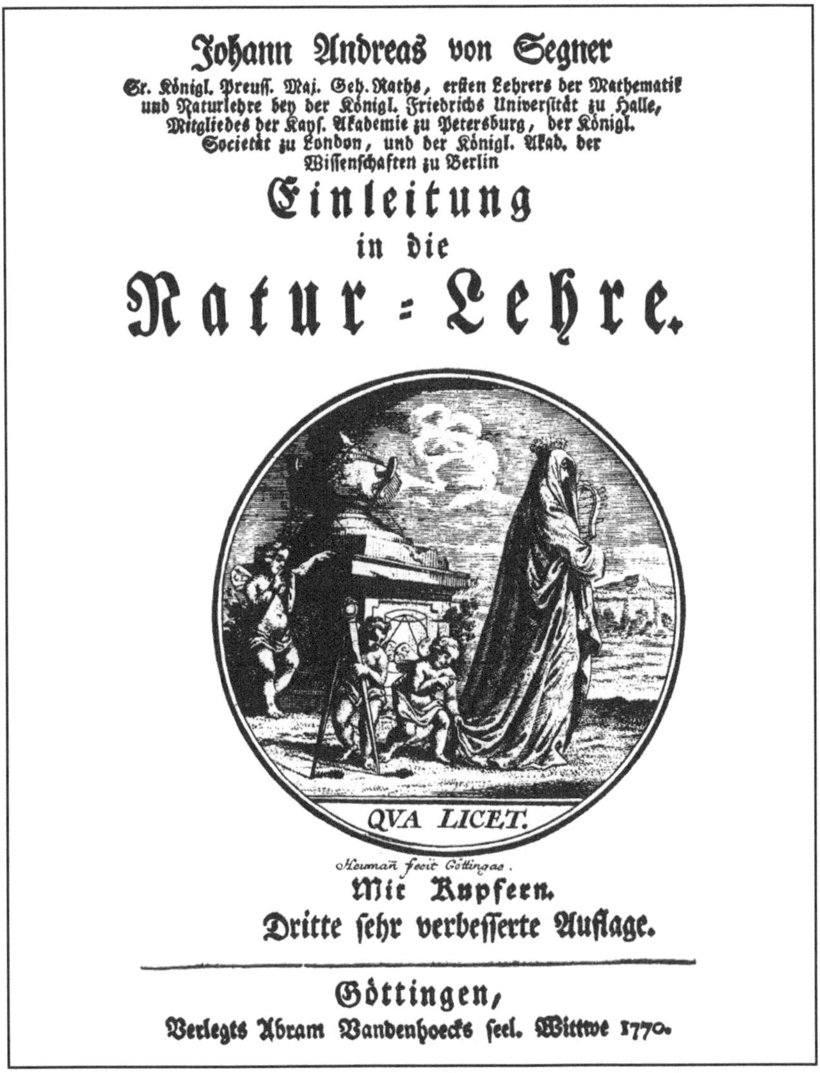
Johann Andreas von Segner

Sr. Königl. Preuss. Maj. Geh. Raths, ersten Lehrers der Mathematik und Naturlehre bey der Königl. Friedrichs Universität zu Halle, Mitgliedes der Kays. Akademie zu Petersburg, der Königl. Societät zu London, und der Königl. Akad. der Wissenschaften zu Berlin

Einleitung in die Natur-Lehre.

QVA LICET.

Heuman fecit Gottingae.

Mit Kupfern.

Dritte sehr verbesserte Auflage.

Göttingen,
Verlegts Abram Vandenhoecks seel. Wittwe 1770.

Figure 0.1 The cover of Johann Andreas Segner's *Einleitung in die Natur-Lehre*, 3rd edition. Göttingen: Abram Vandenhoecks seel. Wittwe (1770)

promise of science seemed hopelessly naïve in the twentieth century. However, this concern about the dangers of unfettered scientific inquiry and a purely scientific worldview were already clear to thinkers and writers in the nineteenth century.

One important offshoot of the Enlightenment demand for reason and the development of the sciences can be found in the sphere of politics. The idea of the divine right of kings seemed to be grounded in superstition and not rationality. Scholars such as Hobbes, Locke, and Rousseau tried to ground political legitimacy on the consent of the governed. They wanted to establish this view on rational argumentation and not tradition. This new approach to politics planted the seeds for the American Revolution in 1776 and the French Revolution in 1789. The eighteenth and nineteenth centuries thus represent a dynamic period in Western history where social and political changes were taking place very quickly. These revolutions cast a great shadow of doubt on both the politics and the religion of previous periods. The thinkers of the Enlightenment advocated new ideals such as individual freedom and democracy, and the revolutionaries were keen to tear down older political institutions and create new ones based on reason. These political changes also contributed to the rise of nihilism. The replacement of monarchy with a democracy of limited suffrage strengthened the idea that there was no truth in politics. Everyone has their own ideas about what would be beneficial for the state. But in contrast to the unlimited authority of the king, the democratic principle acknowledges a kind of relativism. In the end, no one really knows what is best. Democracy is simply a forum for competing arguments about it, but no one expects any absolutes to arise from this. This marked a major shift in thinking that contributed to nihilism. When the French Revolution descended into the Reign of Terror, it seemed to many to be a confirmation of the dangers of democracy and too much freedom. This nihilistic period was seen as a terrible warning about what can happen when traditional beliefs are abandoned.

Another obvious offshoot of the rise of Enlightenment reason was that the central authority of the church in all elements of life began to be eroded, and faith in traditional religious institutions and beliefs gradually became a matter of doubt. The erosion already began with the rise of Protestantism, with the diminution of the ecclesiastical hierarchy and the new doctrine that it was up to the conscience of each individual to believe what they saw fit based on their own personal inspiration. This pointed in the direction of relativism since it gave the power to each individual believer instead of to a single central authority. As a result, many different forms of Protestantism quickly sprung up.

The Enlightenment took up an even more radical attack on the church. It criticized all religion as superstitious nonsense. Thus, religious believers and representatives of the religious establishment were derided and caricatured. During the French Revolution members of the clergy along with their churches were attacked. Rationalism and naturalism had rendered traditional belief no longer plausible, and there seemed to be nothing else to replace it with. The only plausible religious view seemed to be that of deism.

This situation led to a sense of disorientation, which raised the specter of nihilism, relativism, and a dismissal of religion altogether. With the loss of God and monarchy, people were left confused and uncertain. The fundamental pillars of their worldview had fallen away, and they felt abandoned and alone.

There was a sense that many of the institutions that had previously been held in such deep reverence had now been exposed for their shortcomings. What had once been greatly valued no longer possessed any value at all. While many scholars have focused exclusively on the collapse of traditional religious belief or political revolution as the cause of nihilism, I wish to argue that neither of these was the original cause, but rather the consequences of the quick development of the sciences. To be sure, the radical changes in the religious and political landscape were important, but these are best seen as a part of a broader social context.

0.6 Theses and Methodology

In this work I wish to try to gain an overview of the various treatments of nihilism in the nineteenth century. The problem was addressed by a large number of very different kinds of thinkers, writers, dramatists, and artists from different traditions. These texts come from a variety of fields – philosophy, theology, literature – and represent several literary genres: academic treatises, edifying literature, poetic works, dramas, and novels. I wish to see how the authors articulate the problem of nihilism and how they propose to address it.

The methodology used here will be that which is commonly associated with the history of ideas. I will examine the original writings of the key figures who provided some kind of account of or response to nihilism. I wish to understand these accounts in the specific contexts in which they originally appeared. I will proceed in a chronological fashion so that it will be possible to trace the influences of the earlier works on the later ones. I wish to bring out the different elements of this broad constellation of problems that are usually associated with nihilism: meaninglessness, anxiety, despair, atheism, and immortality. The goal will be to explore and critically evaluate the different notions and their relations to one another. In this study I will not confine myself to cases when the word "nihilism" itself is used. Instead, I will examine several other works as well where the constellation of issues that we know as nihilism is discussed, even though it might be described with other words. The main question is how the authors understand the problem, its origin, and its possible solutions.

It might be argued that my selection of authors is somewhat odd or idiosyncratic, differing significantly from what one would expect from a book on the history of nihilism in the nineteenth century. Notably, one would expect a chapter on Dostoevsky since he is such a major figure whose relation to nihilism is generally recognized. By contrast, writers, to whom entire chapters have been dedicated, such as Klingemann and Møller, are not well known, and others, such as Jean Paul and Büchner, are almost never read by philosophers. In an overview work of this kind, it is of course impossible to give an exhaustive account, and difficult choices had to be made about what to include and what to omit. The main criterion for my selection was that I wanted to present a new reading of the role of nihilism in the nineteenth century instead of simply rehearsing old analyses of figures with whom the reader is already familiar. The themes concerning nihilism in Dostoevsky and Nietzsche are so well known that they have virtually become a cliché. I thus did not want to make these thinkers the main focus of the work, although I did include a chapter on Nietzsche. I am convinced that the history of nihilism in the nineteenth century is far richer and broader than has been recognized by previous readings. In order to demonstrate this, I have needed to introduce some lesser-known figures who were important for their treatment of nihilism, although their contributions are little recognized.

I will try to argue for five distinct theses. My first and primary thesis is, as just sketched, that the problem of modern nihilism arose in the wake of the scientific development during the Enlightenment and the concomitant criticism of politics and religion. I wish to argue that modern nihilism came about as an unwelcome result of the growing power of the sciences, which created the modern worldview. It arose as an attempt to reconcile the emerging scientific worldview with the human needs for meaning, purpose, direction, and hope. It should be noted that this is not to say that all the figures examined here were enthusiastic followers of the Enlightenment program. In fact, many of them were critical of it. The point is rather that the scientific developments during the Enlightenment were so compelling that they could not be ignored even by those critical of the movement in general. The fact that nihilism originates in the new worldview that came with the sciences shows the strong connection between the sciences and culture of the period. The scientific advances sketched above might seem at first glance to be completely irrelevant for the authors that I wish to examine in the following. However, a closer look reveals how strongly their depictions of nihilism were influenced by the sciences in their day. Little work has been done to establish these connections.

My second thesis is that the problem of nihilism was not a local issue confined only to a specific place or country. Instead, when seen as a development that arose after the French Revolution, it was something central to the general zeitgeist of the entire nineteenth century in Europe and the West. In histories of philosophy in the nineteenth century, it is common to divide the different schools of thought and traditions along nationalist lines. There is German idealism, British utilitarianism, and French positivism, and so on. Each country is thus portrayed as pursuing its own philosophical agenda more or less independent of the other. However, I wish to show that the problem of nihilism is one that transcends national borders and philosophical traditions. It appears in a number of different countries in a more or less prominent manner. This suggests that the problem had something to do with the specific cultural conditions of the time.

My third thesis is that the problem of nihilism was not limited to philosophy. In fact, it received detailed treatment in works of poetry, drama, and other forms of literature. The problem of nihilism is in some ways less of an academic issue than a practical one. Even the most unreflective person has moments when they question the value of their lives. This explains why the literary and dramatic portrayals of nihilism are in some ways more effective and powerful than the purely philosophical ones.[72] They are able to depict aspects of life that general readers can readily identify with.

Historians of philosophy have often missed this point largely because the treatments of nihilism in the nineteenth century have often come from literary works that stand outside the philosophical canon and are thus often little known to philosophers. Moreover, as noted, these literary texts often do not use the term "nihilism" itself, but nonetheless the set of issues that they treat is clearly very similar to that of their twentieth-century successors, who use the term freely. Historians of philosophy who want to treat the issue of nihilism in the nineteenth century usually go straight to the philosophers Schopenhauer and Nietzsche, who have long been associated with the issue. However, their works need to be understood in a broader context of thinking about this topic in the literature of the nineteenth century.

My fourth thesis is that the problem of nihilism is more widespread than has been acknowledged in the past. While there have been many studies on the topic of nihilism in relation to some of the individual thinkers and authors discussed, almost all of these are specialized works that are confined to a single thinker. However, my claim is that in order to appreciate the importance of nihilism in the nineteenth century, it is necessary to step back and gain a broader perspective, which will allow us to see these thinkers as part of a much larger discussion. Sadly, modern specialization too often leads us to miss the forest for the trees, and I submit that the issue of nihilism in the nineteenth century is a case in point of this kind of distortion. My goal is to try to connect the dots to allow the big picture to appear. What surprisingly emerges from this is that nihilism is a central problem for many of the thinkers of the period and not just for Schopenhauer and Nietzsche. The first half of the nineteenth century has especially been neglected in this regard. The issues associated with nihilism in the nineteenth century are therefore far more widespread than has been generally appreciated before.

My fifth thesis is that discussions of nihilism in the nineteenth century anticipate almost all the key topics of the existentialist movement. Of course, nineteenth-century thinkers, such as Nietzsche and Kierkegaard, have long been regarded as forerunners of existentialism, and so this might come as little surprise. But the critical thrust of this thesis is that the discussions of nihilism go far beyond the work of these purported proto-existentialists. Indeed, their work on the issue can only be properly appreciated when it is seen in its

---

[72] See Jon Stewart, *The Unity of Content and Form in Philosophical Writing: The Perils of Conformity*, London, New Delhi, New York, and Sydney: Bloomsbury 2013.

immediate historical context and in dialogue with other thinkers of their own period. It might be claimed that some of their uniqueness and originality is slightly dented when it becomes clear how many other thinkers were involved in the discussion. However, I believe that establishing connections among all these thinkers makes them more interesting and gives us a greater understanding and appreciation for what is original in their thought.

This study thus intends to present a broader overview and a more accurate picture of the rise and development of modern nihilism than previous accounts. Moreover, since our own times stand in the tradition of the twentieth-century schools of thought influenced by nihilism, the hope is also that we can find some insight into this issue that will be relevant for our own age, which is also very much under the spell of modern science.

1

Jean Paul's Vision of Nihilism and Plea for the Doctrine of Immortality

The German writer Johann Paul Friedrich Richter (1763-1825), known best by his pseudonym Jean Paul, was concerned with the problem of nihilism and specifically human mortality throughout his life.[1] His concern with this issue was presumably motivated at least in part by the fact that he experienced the deaths of his close friends Adam Lorenz von Oerthel (1763-86), Johann Bernhard Hermann (1761-90), Christian von Oerthel (1775-92), and Karl Philipp Moritz (1756-93). Moreover, Jean Paul's younger brother Heinrich (1770-89) committed suicide in 1789 at the tender age of 19. On November 15, 1790, Jean Paul had a mystical vision of himself on his own deathbed, and this experience had a profound effect on him. Death thus must have seemed ever-present, and he had a lifelong obsession with it.[2] His works are filled with motifs related to this topic. It has been claimed that Jean Paul's "work provides some of the most striking documents of nihilism in European Literature."[3] While Jean Paul consistently wants to reject nihilism, it always remains for him a terrifying possibility.

Before embarking on a career as a writer, Jean Paul studied theology. Although he abandoned this and was critical of the church and certain forms of organized religion, Jean Paul clearly nourished some religious intuitions. Yet his constant return to the issue of nihilism seems to suggest that his soul was somehow divided. The power and clarity with which he paints the picture of a

---

[1] For Jean Paul's life, see Kurt Wölfel, "Johann Paul Friedrich Richter. Leben, Werk, Wirkung," in *Jean Paul-Studien*, ed. by Bernhard Buschendorf, Frankfurt am Main: Suhrkamp 1989, pp. 7-50; Günter de Bruyn, *Das Leben des Jean Paul Friedrich Richter. Eine Biographie*, Frankfurt am Main: Fischer Taschenbuch Verlag 1998 [1975]; Max Kommerell, *Jean Paul*, Frankfurt am Main: Vittorio Klostermann 1933; Walter Harich, *Jean Paul*, Leipzig: H. Haessel 1925; Paul Nerrlich, *Jean Paul. Sein Leben und seine Werke*, Berlin: Weidmann 1899.
[2] See Käte Hamburger, "Das Todesproblem bei Jean Paul," in *Jean Paul*, ed. by Uwe Schweikert, Darmstadt: Wissenschaftliche Buchgesellschaft 1974, pp. 74-105; Jacob Günter, "Das Nichts und die Welt. Die metaphysische Frage bei Jean Paul," *Logos*, vol. 21, 1932, pp. 65-89.
[3] Timothy J. Casey, editorial introduction to *Flower, Fruit, and Thorn Pieces in Jean Paul: A Reader*, ed. by Timothy J. Casey, trans. by Erika Caset, Baltimore and London: The Johns Hopkins University Press 1992, p. 161. See also Walther Rehm, *Jean Paul, Dostojewski: Zur dichterischen Gestaltung des Unglaubens*, Göttingen: Vandenhoeck & Ruprecht 1962.

nihilistic or atheistic worldview is evidence that he has a deep understanding of and appreciation for these perspectives.

Jean Paul is often cast in the role of a literary writer par excellence, but he was also profoundly well versed in the rapid developments of the sciences of his day. His works are replete with examples and images from nature that have been drawn from his knowledge of the sciences. A part of his genius can be seen in his attempt to bring together the results of the modern scientific revolution with a more traditional humanistic perspective. It is from this combination that the issue of nihilism arises.

While the term "nihilism" does not appear in the two works by Jean Paul that we will be exploring here, it should be noted that he does in fact employ the term elsewhere.[4] He regards the German Romantics with great alarm since he believes that they have taken to heart Fichte's concept of the self-positing ego and have turned this into a justification for a radical rejection of traditional values. For this reason, Jean Paul designates the Romantics "poetic nihilists" in his *Preschool of Aesthetics*.[5] According to his view, the Romantics reject the validity of the entire external objective world. Instead, they regard themselves as the sole origin of truth, like an atomistic self-positing ego. On this account, the Romantic nihilists are simply relativists. Jean Paul's use of "nihilism" in this context is thus somewhat different from that of the focus of the present study, namely, nihilism in the sense of despair at the meaninglessness of human existence. For our purposes two other texts by Jean Paul are far more important than *Preschool of Aesthetics*, namely, "The Dead Christ Proclaims that There Is No God" and *The Valley of Campan*.

1.1 The Message of the Dead Christ

One of Jean Paul's most important works is the novel *Flower, Fruit, and Thorn Pieces; Or, The Wedded Life, Death, and Marriage of Firmian Stanislaus Siebenkæs*, which appeared in three volumes from 1796 to 1797.[6] The story tells of the life of a lawyer, named in the title, and his ill-fated marriage. Jean Paul borrows the terms "flower piece" and "fruit piece" from art, where they refer to

---

[4] See *Jean Paul: A Reader*, ed. by Casey, pp. 242f.; Michael Allen Gillespie, *Nihilism before Nietzsche*, Chicago: University of Chicago Press 1996, p. 106.

[5] Jean Paul, *Vorschule der Aesthetik nebenst einigen Vorlesungen in Leipzig über die Parteien der Zeit*, vols. 1–3, 2nd augmented edition, Stuttgart and Tübingen: J. G. Cotta 1813, vol. 1, § 2, "Poetische Nihilisten," pp. 3–12.

[6] Jean Paul, *Blumen-, Frucht- und Dornenstücke oder Ehestand, Tod und Hochzeit des Armenadvokaten F. St. Siebenkäs im Reichsmarktflecken Kuhschnappel*, vols. 1–3, Berlin: In Carl Matzdorff's Buchhandlung 1796–97 (English translation: *Flower, Fruit, and Thorn Pieces; Or, The Wedded Life, Death, and Marriage of Firmian Stanislaus Siebenkæs*, trans. by Alexander Ewing [London: George Bell and Sons 1897]; note that this English translation, which is based on a later German edition, moves "The Dead Christ" to a different place in the text).

still-life paintings depicting a group of flowers or fruits. The initial idea was to write a text that contained a number of short, unrelated works that would each individually represent a fruit or flower piece. However, Jean Paul abandoned this idea in favor of a continuous story. But despite this, remnants of a discontinuous work remain with various stories. After the preface, he inserts into the text two "flower pieces" and one "thorn piece," which are set apart from the running narrative. By calling these parts of his work a "flower piece" or a "fruit piece," Jean Paul seems to suggest that he presents to the reader a pleasing picture of diverse human relations for contemplation. But then by expanding this also with "thorn pieces," the implication seems to be that the picture is not just pleasing but also in some aspects painful to behold.

The most famous part of the work is the short chapter entitled "The Dead Christ Proclaims That There Is No God."[7] This work appears as the first flower piece, which follows immediately after the preface. Although this is only a short text, Jean Paul worked on it over an extended period of time. It was translated several times and caused a great stir in the literary world of the day. The piece consists of a short introduction and then a dream sequence, which is followed by an awakening and a return to reality, which represent the conclusion of the chapter.

The piece concerns the value of the belief in God, which the modern sciences call into question. Jean Paul tries to follow the scientifically based denial of God to its logical conclusion in order to show that this leads to a horrifying view that no one can accept. The author notes that most people casually believe in God but fail to appreciate fully how important this belief is for them. Especially academics, whether theists or atheists, discuss this issue in a sober yet almost indifferent manner, apparently without realizing that they too as individuals are implicated in the results. This anticipates Kierkegaard's complaint about how scholars tend to be so absorbed in their analyses that they forget to ask themselves what their relation is to the issue. The twentieth-century existentialists were also critical of what they regarded as overly abstract philosophy or what Merleau-Ponty called "high-altitude thinking."[8] They tried to promote a form of philosophy that was related to real life and concrete human situations. Jean Paul clearly shares this sentiment and, in this respect, can be said to anticipate this aspect of existentialist thinking. A part of Jean Paul's strategy is to present his argument by means of images and not just sterile arguments. The images that he depicts in "The Dead Christ" are so powerful and provocative that they are potentially more effective than traditional forms of philosophical reasoning and persuasion. Here again he anticipates a part of the argumentative strategy

---

[7] For useful accounts of this text, see J. P. Vijn, *Carlyle and Jean Paul: Their Spiritual Optics*, Amsterdam and Philadelphia: John Benjamins Publishing Company 1982.

[8] See, for example, Maurice Merleau-Ponty, *The Visible and the Invisible*, trans. by Alphonso Lingis, Evanston, IL: Northwestern University Press 1968, p. 73.

of the existentialists, many of whom also wrote novels and plays alongside their more strictly philosophical treatises.

This is the point of departure since the unnamed narrator in "The Dead Christ" concedes that he too has been complacent in regard to his beliefs in God: "I myself was suddenly horror-struck at the perception of the poison-power of that vapor which strikes with such suffocating fumes to the heart of him who enters the school of Atheistic doctrine."[9] Jean Paul depicts what he regards as the nefarious nature of the rejection of the belief in God. The idea that this took place suddenly (and not over a long period of time) implies that his crisis of faith was the result of some new information from the sciences that called his belief into question. When one denies the existence of God, the result is the following:

> The whole spiritual universe is shattered and shivered, by the hand of Atheism, into innumerable glittering quicksilver globules of individual personalities, running hither and thither at random, coalescing, and parting asunder without unity, coherence, or consistency. In all this wide universe there is none so utterly solitary and alone as a denier of God.[10]

The idea seems to be that without belief in God, one is left with an empty mechanistic world where things happen by chance with no greater *logos* or purpose. This is the vision of the universe as consisting of atoms in the void with nothing more. The stated goal of the chapter is then to bring home to the reader the gravity of this way of seeing the world, which is rarely fully appreciated.

Without God, nature itself loses its meaning and becomes an "immeasurable corpse."[11] For the atheist there is nothing left to do but mourn this loss "until he himself crumbles and falls away from it into nothingness .... [T]he immeasurable universe has become for him but the cold iron-mask upon an eternity which is without form and void."[12] The atheist must live with this disconsolate picture of the universe in the absence of God and, by implication, the absence of meaning. The implicit question is whether anyone, even the most devoted scientific mind and critic of religion, can fully embrace this view in all its details. Is it really possible to live believing that one's life has no meaning and that one will revert to dust after death?

The narrator reflects on the fears of children, which often come out in the form of dreams. He argues that we should try to preserve these dreams since

---

[9] Jean Paul, *Blumen-, Frucht- und Dornenstücke*, vol. 1, p. 2 (*Flower, Fruit, and Thorn Pieces*, p. 260).
[10] Jean Paul, *Blumen-, Frucht- und Dornenstücke*, vol. 1, p. 2 (*Flower, Fruit, and Thorn Pieces*, p. 260).
[11] Jean Paul, *Blumen-, Frucht- und Dornenstücke*, vol. 1, p. 2 (*Flower, Fruit, and Thorn Pieces*, p. 260).
[12] Jean Paul, *Blumen-, Frucht- und Dornenstücke*, vol. 1, pp. 2f. (*Flower, Fruit, and Thorn Pieces*, p. 260).

1.1 THE MESSAGE OF THE DEAD CHRIST   39

they serve to highlight certain things about life. Frightening dreams can serve to inform our disposition and life decisions. In this way he introduces his own dream, which he had when he fell asleep on a hillside one summer evening. This is the centerpiece of "The Dead Christ." In his dream he sees himself in a graveyard with the spirits of the dead, who were coming out of their coffins. According to the Gospel of Matthew, this is what happened after Jesus' death on the cross: "The tombs also were opened, and many bodies of the saints who had fallen asleep were raised."[13] Jean Paul's narrator portrays the nature around him in apocalyptic terms: the sky darkens, avalanches rumble in the distance, and an earthquake strikes below his feet. This also corresponds to the signs that accompany the crucifixion in Matthew, where it is said that "darkness came over the whole land"[14] and the "earth shook, and the rocks were split."[15] The message is that the world without God is an inhospitable place. But Jean Paul evokes these images also in order to emphasize the seriousness of the situation, which concerns not just individuals but the entire universe. The narrator enters the church where the dead are assembling. Jean Paul alludes to the ancient Greek designation σκιαί by referring to them as "shadows" or "shades."

With no explanation or motivation given, it is described how Christ descends to them and is immediately recognized since he is expected. The dead ask, "Christ! Is there no God?" to which he answers, "There is none."[16] Christ goes on to explain,

> I have traversed the worlds, I have risen to the suns, with the milky ways I have passed athwart the great waste spaces of the sky; there is no God. And I descended to where the very shadow cast by Being dies out and ends, and I gazed out into the gulf beyond, and cried, "Father, where art Thou?" But answer came there none, save the eternal storm which rages on, controlled by none; and towards the west, above the chasm, a gleaming rainbow hung, but there was no sun to give it birth, and so it sank and fell by drops into the gulf. And when I looked up to the boundless universe for the Divine eye, behold, it glared at me from out a socket, empty and bottomless. Over the face of chaos brooded Eternity, chewing it forever, again and yet again. Shriek on, then, discords, shatter the shadows with your shrieking din, for He is not![17]

Since Christ was responsible for so many people believing in God, it seems fitting that he be the one to announce that in fact God does not exist. In some ways it is difficult to imagine anyone else making such an announcement and

---

[13] Matthew 27:52.
[14] Matthew 27:45.
[15] Matthew 27:51.
[16] Jean Paul, *Blumen-, Frucht- und Dornenstücke*, vol. 1, p. 6 (*Flower, Fruit, and Thorn Pieces*, p. 262).
[17] Jean Paul, *Blumen-, Frucht- und Dornenstücke*, vol. 1, p. 7 (*Flower, Fruit, and Thorn Pieces*, p. 263).

having any credibility. There are many atheists who make the same claim, but when it comes from Christ, it is a much more powerful statement. There is, however, something odd in the fact that Christ seems to go to work like a natural scientist who looks for God in some physical space in the universe in the way that one might look for a star or galaxy. According to this depiction, Christ possesses the ability to travel quickly to any place in the universe, and due to this he has been able to make a complete survey. Apart from the role of Christ, Jean Paul's description of the universe is the one presented by the sciences. The universe contains numerous suns and galaxies in the vastness of space. Further, it endures seemingly for eternity. The idea of the absence of God is clearly motivated by the breakthroughs in science, which have left no place for the divine. The passage speaks of the great movements of the universe as an "eternal storm which rages on, controlled by none." These are natural forces at work without any need of a conscious guiding deity.

The scenario that Jean Paul seems to want to invoke is an alternative version of the Second Coming, the Last Judgment, and the Resurrection of the Dead. The end of time has come, and Christ returns. The dead arise in bodily form in order to meet him and be judged. But to their great surprise and disappointment, he declares that there is no God, thus dashing their hopes for eternal life. Instead of taking up residence in heaven, they immediately dissolve into the dust of nothingness. They do not have the opportunity to be judged, and their good deeds go unrecognized and unrewarded. All the people are subject to the same fate: complete destruction. No exceptions are made. Jean Paul invites his readers to imagine what the end of the world would look like according to a purely scientific view and without the aforementioned Christian dogmas. What results is a terrifying, comfortless vision.

The dead children then awaken and ask Christ, "'Jesus, have we no Father?' He made answer, with streaming tears, 'We are orphans all, both I and ye. We have no Father.'"[18] This is a play on the passage in John, where Christ promises exactly the opposite: "I will not leave you orphaned; I am coming to you."[19] Jean Paul's inversion of this contains great pathos since the dead children were cheated out of a full life on earth, and now they too are denied an afterlife in heaven. The children asking for a father can be regarded as a metaphor for human existence: humans are all orphans in a strange and hostile world with no one to protect or look after them. Everyone is utterly alone in the vast universe governed only by mechanical forces. There is no deity to help us in times of need or to comfort us in our moment of distress.

Everyone has a yearning for peace, comfort, and reconciliation. Much of the success of religion can be ascribed to this deep inner need of people, who

---

[18] Jean Paul, *Blumen-, Frucht- und Dornenstücke*, vol. 1, pp. 7f. (*Flower, Fruit, and Thorn Pieces*, p. 263).

[19] John 14:18.

live their lives with restlessness, anxiety, and sorrow. One wants to believe that there is a caring, loving God looking over one's life as an individual. But now, in Jean Paul's frightening dream scenario, Christ declares that, despite our deep-seated need, our "wounds will not be healed.... [T]here is no healing hand, no everlasting Father."[20] According to this view, there is no solution to the anguish in the human soul. This is a permanent fixture of the human condition. We cannot expect any liberation from this when we die. Instead, all that awaits us after death is annihilation.

In the dream the end of time has come but without God to redeem anyone. The final destruction of the universe is then a purely natural event that takes place according to the laws of physics. Christ is portrayed as witnessing this end of the universe on a grand scale. He observes all the galaxies, planets, and stars being destroyed (presumably in an event such as the Big Crunch – the opposite of the Big Bang – when the gravity of the universe causes all matter to contract):

> And as he gazed upon the grinding mass of worlds, the wild torch dance of starry will-o'-the-wisps, and all the coral banks of throbbing hearts – and saw how world by world shook forth its glimmering souls on to the ocean of death – then He, sublime, loftiest of finite beings, raised his eyes towards the nothingness and boundless void, saying, "Oh dead, dumb, nothingness! necessity endless and chill! Oh! mad unreasoning chance – when will ye dash this fabric into atoms, and me too?"[21]

The image that Jean Paul tries to evoke is that Christ can observe the universe as a whole in all of its workings. He can see everything, for example, how stars and galaxies develop and die. Now, he can see the apocalyptic end of all things. In all the vastness and the majesty of the universe, he can find ultimately only nothingness. However many tiny dots of light there might be, they are all overwhelmed by darkness. Being is vastly outweighed and destroyed by nothingness. There seems something mad about the idea that the vast universe with all its components will in the end disappear into nothingness. Star after star will be extinguished and reduced to atoms. The universe is an "ocean of death," one "great corpse trench."[22] In the passage the role of chance is also emphasized. In contrast to the old view of a wise entity ruling the universe, now chance simply goes its way, destroying star after star, life after life, without having any conscious agency. All human existence is simply a matter of a fortuitous combination of events that arose by chance. There was no grand design, plan, or meaning. It was simply atoms interacting in the void of space according to fixed laws.

---

[20] Jean Paul, *Blumen-, Frucht- und Dornenstücke*, vol. 1, p. 10 (*Flower, Fruit, and Thorn Pieces*, pp. 264f.).
[21] Jean Paul, *Blumen-, Frucht- und Dornenstücke*, vol. 1, pp. 8f. (*Flower, Fruit, and Thorn Pieces*, pp. 263f.).
[22] Jean Paul, *Blumen-, Frucht- und Dornenstücke*, vol. 1, p. 9 (*Flower, Fruit, and Thorn Pieces*, p. 264).

In the vast universe, the tiny and insignificant role of human life is emphasized. Christ continues, "Wretched being! That petty life of thine is but the sigh of nature, or the echo of that sigh. Your wavering cloudy forms are but reflections of rays cast by a concave mirror upon the clouds of dust which shroud your world – dust which is dead men's ashes."[23] As Ecclesiastes claimed, after death we all turn to dust.[24] Human life itself is just one small outcome of many natural processes. The lives of individuals, or even the entire species, are miniscule in this picture, given the vast number of other planets and species, and given the enormous time scale of the universe in comparison to human life.

This frightening dream ends with an apocalyptic vision: "And then a great immeasurable bell began to swing ... to toll the last hour of time and shatter the fabric of the universe to countless atoms – when my sleep broke up, and I awoke."[25] At the end of the universe everything, large and small, is destroyed. When the narrator awakens, he is greatly relieved that it was all only a bad dream. He rejoices that he can return to his belief in God and meaning in the universe. This happy end is presumably the reason why Jean Paul dubs this a "flower piece" instead of a "thorn piece." Now instead of hearing the bells announcing the end of the world, it is as if he hears the joyous bells of nature ringing in "a rich, soft, gentle harmony."[26] Since his vision was just a nightmare, it is safe to return to the happy world that he always knew. This seems a strange way to end the text since after such a dramatic and disturbing description, the narrator seems to tell the reader that none of it really matters. The described events have made no impact on his belief system.

This is an intense and powerful story that seems intended to shock and provoke the reader. It is designed to show what a terrible picture the secular, scientific worldview leads to if it is carried through to the end. Jean Paul's intent seems to be to say that this picture is so frightening that no one can live with it. If one were to regard this as a philosophical argument, then it can be seen in the form of a *reductio ad absurdum*. As its first premise it assumes the truth of the scientific worldview. Then it sets about to develop the consequences of this. Finally, it demonstrates that these consequences, if not contradictory (or absurd), are in any case impossible to accept. In this sense the text can be interpreted as a refutation of a purely scientific conception of the universe. It will be noted that no attempt is made to demonstrate that the scientific worldview is wrong on any given point. But rather

---

[23] Jean Paul, *Blumen-, Frucht- und Dornenstücke*, vol. 1, p. 9 (*Flower, Fruit, and Thorn Pieces*, p. 264).
[24] Ecclesiastes 3:20.
[25] Jean Paul, *Blumen-, Frucht- und Dornenstücke*, vol. 1, p. 11 (*Flower, Fruit, and Thorn Pieces*, p. 265).
[26] Jean Paul, *Blumen-, Frucht- und Dornenstücke*, vol. 1, p. 11 (*Flower, Fruit, and Thorn Pieces*, p. 265).

the argument is simply that humans cannot lead their lives with this belief. The implication is that some space must still exist for some form of religious belief that offers us peace of mind.

There is a point to the fact that this episode is portrayed as a bad dream. The idea of a world without God is a terrifying prospect. Visions like the one that Jean Paul depicts haunt the consciousness of even the most pious Christian. Even if one is quick to reject the scientific worldview, there always remains a degree of doubt. One can never be completely certain. This doubt returns to us periodically when we have a crisis of faith. But it is always there in the recesses of the mind. The followers of psychoanalysis would say that the idea of a universe without God and meaning is so frightening that we repress it from our consciousness, and as a result it comes out in our dreams.

The text emphasizes the natural processes of the universe, mentioning key ideas from physics and astronomy: atoms, the void, movement, eternity, necessity, and so on. The developments of eighteenth-century science are clearly foremost in Jean Paul's mind. The point of departure for his analysis of nihilism and the related issues is thus the result of modern science, which, to his mind, represents a menacing specter.

1.2 The Beginning of *The Valley of Campan*

Jean Paul returns to the issue of nihilism in his novel *The Valley of Campan* from 1797.[27] While "The Dead Christ" was concerned with refuting the denial of God, this work is concerned with refuting the denial of the doctrine of immortality. This novel, which has as its subtitle *Discourses on the Immortality of the Soul*, contains elements of a dialogue in the spirit of Berkeley's *Three Dialogues between Hylas and Philonous* (1713) and Hume's *Dialogues concerning Natural Religion* (1779). Although primarily known as a *littérateur*, Jean Paul was also very familiar with philosophy. With his *Clavis Fichtiana* (from 1800),[28] he raised a polemic against Fichte, and, in many works, he often mentions thinkers such as Kant and Leibniz. Despite the subtitle of *The Valley of Campan*, the importance of this text has not been appreciated by mainstream philosophy. In the Preface or "Vorbericht" Jean Paul explains that Kant's critical philosophy has offered an argument for the belief in God and immortality, but not everyone is able to understand or appreciate this given that it appears in the

---

[27] Jean Paul, *Das Kampaner Thal oder über die Unsterblichkeit der Seele; nebst einer Erklärung der Holzschnitte unter den 10 Geboten des Katechismus*, Erfurt: bei Wilhelm Hennings 1797 (English translation: *The Campaner Thal and Other Writings*, Boston: Ticknor and Fields 1864).

[28] Jean Paul, *Clavis Fichtiana seu Leibgeberiana*, Erfurt: in der Henningsschen Buchhandlung 1800. See Wolfgang Harich, *Jean Pauls Kritik des philosophischen Egoismus: Belegt durch Texte und Briefstellen Jean Pauls im Anhang*, Frankfurt am Main: Suhrkamp 1968.

context of a complex philosophical system.[29] The idea is that Jean Paul's novel can offer a kind of proof that will be considerably more accessible to the reader than Kant's account. So once again, as with "The Dead Christ," Jean Paul is proposing an alternative kind of philosophical argumentation and persuasion in the form of a narrative.

At the end of the work Jean Paul adds a series of woodcuts that are the occasion for reflections on the Ten Commandments in the Catechism. This appendix, which proved controversial, uses as its model a work entitled *Ausführliche Erklärung der Hogarthischen Kupferstiche* by Georg Christoph Lichtenberg (1742–99).[30] In this text Lichtenberg gives detailed descriptions and analyses of the then quite popular satirical pictures by the English painter and engraver William Hogarth (1697–1764).

The storyline of Jean Paul's novel is fairly straightforward: a small group takes an excursion in the Valley of Campan in the Pyrenees, and they discuss the issue of immortality as they go. The unnamed first-person narrator, who, the reader later learns, is Jean Paul himself, writes regular updates about the journey to his friend Victor. The novel purports to be a collection of these. The events are said to take place in 1796, that is, a year before the publication of the work. The text is divided into chapters called "stations" that the author uses to give an account of each segment of the journey.

The handful of characters each have an opinion about the issue of immortality. The narrator's friend Karlson has training in chemistry and is presumably a natural scientist. He represents the position of naturalism and does not believe in the immortality of the soul. This is the position that all the others try to refute in one way or another. There is also a chaplain, who is a Kantian and thus believes in both God and immortality. This is significant since at the time Kant represented perhaps the important scholarly attempt to rescue the doctrine of immortality. Given this, one might think that Jean Paul would be sympathetic to the Kantian approach, but this is not the case. The chaplain cuts an arrogant and unsympathetic figure who is pedantic and blind to the beauties of nature. His aloof disposition to such issues is the object of criticism. The narrator jokingly calls the disagreeable and humorless man "Phylax."[31] Also in the group are Baron Wilhelmi with his fiancée Gione and her sister Nadine. These three

---

[29] Jean Paul, *Das Kampaner Thal*, p. ii (n.b. the "Vorbericht" is not translated in the English translation).

[30] G. C. Lichtenberg, *Ausführliche Erklärung der Hogarthischen Kupferstiche, mit verkleinerten aber vollständigen Copien derselben von E. [rnst Ludwig] Riepenhausen*, vols. 1–13, Göttingen: Heinrich Dieterich 1794–1833 (in English, see *The World of Hogarth. Lichtenberg's Commentaries on Hogarth's Engravings*, trans. by Innes and Gustav Herdan, Boston: Houghton Mifflin Company 1966; *Hogarth on High Life. The Marriage à la Mode Series, from Georg Christoph Lichtenberg's Commentaries*, trans. and ed. by Arthur S. Wensinger and W. B. Coley, Middletown, CT: Wesleyan University Press 1970).

[31] Jean Paul, *Das Kampaner Thal*, p. 42 (*The Campaner Thal*, p. 22).

1.2 THE BEGINNING OF *THE VALLEY OF CAMPAN* 45

are less educated philosophically. They represent the voice of common sense. They believe in immortality but do not have developed philosophical positions to ground their views. They tend not to lead the discussion but instead mostly to chime in on occasion to support the one argument or the other in favor of immortality. Finally, there is the narrator, Jean Paul.[32] He provokes the chaplain and offers a number of arguments in refutation of Karlson's naturalism.

The setting of the story in the Valley of Campan is significant. It is portrayed as a kind of earthly paradise, and Jean Paul dwells in some detail on the beauty of nature found there. This picture of a happy and harmonious nature, which is pleasant to human beings, stands in stark juxtaposition to the hostile picture of nature found in "The Dead Christ." In *The Valley of Campan*, this positive view in a sense anticipates Jean Paul's case for human immortality. Death and finitude would be antithetical to such a natural world. The idea is that the beautiful and harmonious world of nature would in itself seem to imply human immorality.

The story begins *in medias res* with the 501st Station, with the narrator and his friend Karlson at an inn where a wedding and a funeral are taking place at the same time. The funeral is for the youngest daughter of the owner of the inn, and the juxtaposition between the two events – the death of the daughter and the beginning of married life for the bride – create a tension that underscores the fragility of human existence. Here Jean Paul seizes the occasion to make a comparison between happiness and sadness, tragedy and comedy, in human life:

> When fate harnesses to Psyche's car, the merry and the mourning steed together, the mourning one ever takes the lead; i.e. if the muses of Mirth and Sorrow play on the same stage in the same hour, man does not, like Garrick, follow the former; he does not even remain neutral, but takes the side of the mourning one. Thus we always paint, like Milton, our lost Paradise more glowingly than the regained one, – like Dante, hell better than purgatory.[33]

Without any real argument, Jean Paul claims that tragedy is more primary or higher than comedy. It has often been noted that Milton's *Paradise Lost* is more compelling than his *Paradise Regained* and Dante's *Inferno* is the most vivid part of the *Divine Comedy*. Jean Paul alludes to a painting by the English artist Joshua Reynolds (1723–92) entitled *David Garrick between Tragedy and Comedy* (Figure 1.1). This painting depicts Thalia, the muse of comedy, and Melpomene, the muse of tragedy, trying to induce the English playwright and theater manager David Garrick (1717–79) to write and perform something in their genre. As Jean Paul indicates, Reynolds portrays Garrick as somewhat apologetically going with Thalia, despite the angry protest of Melpomene.

---

[32] Jean Paul, *Das Kampaner Thal*, p. 75, p. 101 (*The Campaner Thal*, p. 37, p. 49).
[33] Jean Paul, *Das Kampaner Thal*, p. 20 (*The Campaner Thal*, pp. 7f.). Translation slightly modified.

Figure 1.1 Joshua Reynolds, *David Garrick between Tragedy and Comedy* (1761)

Jean Paul's preference for tragedy over comedy (and his implicit critique of Reynolds) is relevant for his treatment of nihilism. As we have seen in "The Dead Christ," the scientific worldview that Jean Paul presents leads to an unbearable nihilism. This is portrayed with a high degree of pathos with crying dead children and the apocalyptic vision of the end of the universe. This is a tragic picture, and there is nothing to laugh at. *The Valley of Campan*, while more subtle, follows in this same spirit of pathos. However, as we will see in Chapter 2, humor is also a possible response to nihilism.

Karlson is disproportionately moved by the death of the daughter of the innkeeper and especially the grief of her young lover. When the narrator asks him why he is so disturbed, Karlson reveals his story. When he was in Lausanne with the others, Karlson had secretly fallen in love with the already engaged Gione, who suddenly fell seriously ill. After a deep swoon, it was believed that she had died, and her apparent death was immediately reported to him. Overwhelmed with grief over the death of his secret love, Karlson precipitously left the group and returned to the Rhein Falls near Schaffhausen in Switzerland. Karlson explains that he was particularly grieved since he does not believe in immortality: "For he believed, as most world-men among whom he had grown

1.2 THE BEGINNING OF *THE VALLEY OF CAMPAN* 47

up do – perhaps, also, too much accustomed to analyzed ideas and opinions by his favorite study, chemistry – that our last sleep is annihilation."[34] Here the narrator seems to imply that Karlson was educated by men of the Enlightenment, who disdainfully rejected any religious view of the world. The narrator explains that the experience threw Karlson into a nihilistic state: "he was long imprisoned in the dark, cold, serpent's nest of envenomed pains; they entwined and crawled over him, even to his heart."[35] This description recalls some of the images from "The Dead Christ." The point is clear that the rejection of the idea of human immortality leaves one in complete despair.

Sad and alone, Karlson writes a short text called "Grief without Hope" that he sends as a condolence to his friend Wilhelmi for the loss of his fiancée. Here at the beginning the text is only mentioned, but towards the end of the work a full paraphrase of it appears. When Wilhelmi receives Karlson's letter, he writes back immediately and explains that the whole thing was a mistake and that thankfully Gione had just fallen unconscious for a time but was revived and is now alive and well. Wilhelmi then invites Karlson to rejoin them for their tour of the Pyrenees. Thus ends Karlson's story.

Upon hearing this, the narrator is happy to accompany Karlson back to meet his friends in the Valley of Campan, where the group is waiting to celebrate the nuptials of Wilhelmi and Gione. This gracious gesture cannot hide the somewhat awkward element that Karlson, in his letter, more or less revealed his love for Wilhelmi's fiancée. Despite this, Wilhelmi is not angry with his friend, and Gione is likewise not upset.

Karlson and the narrator depart for the valley. They arrive in the evening and rejoin the others in a large cave that is referred to as a paradise and Elysium, suggesting that they have died and this was their reward, a place where everyone was happy and friends find each other again: "it seemed as if the world had ceased, Elysium had opened, and the separated, covered, sub-terrestrial regions cradled only tranquil, but happy souls."[36] This makes sense in that Gione appeared to have died. The meeting in the cave is full of gracious gestures on all sides with everyone glad to see each other again, despite the fact that it is now known to all that Karlson was or is in love with his friend's fiancée. But as in heaven, in this cave of paradise there are no conflicts or bouts of envy or jealousy. Everyone is happy, and the mood is harmonious. This image can be said to prefigure Jean Paul's case for immortality. By enjoining his readers to envision a scene from Elysium where old friends are reunited in joy, the idea of life in heaven seems less far-fetched. It is after all in some respects similar to happy experiences with which we are already familiar from our mundane existence. The suggestion is that this might count for some kind of empirical evidence for

---

[34] Jean Paul, *Das Kampaner Thal*, p. 15 (*The Campaner Thal*, p. 10).
[35] Jean Paul, *Das Kampaner Thal*, p. 15 (*The Campaner Thal*, p. 10).
[36] Jean Paul, *Das Kampaner Thal*, p. 24 (*The Campaner Thal*, p. 14).

immortality that the scientists could accept. As was the case with "The Dead Christ," visualization is an important tool that Jean Paul uses to make his literary *argument* for immortality. In his view, this is more effective than barren proofs about abstract concepts.

The narrator describes the great feeling of happiness that everyone felt at the moment. The power of joy is prior to that of grief: "And therefore fatherly fate, thou spreadest the flowers of joy, as nurses do lilies in the nursery of life, that the awakening children may sleep the sounder! O, let philosophy, which grudges our *pleasures*, and blots them out from the plans of Providence, say by what right did torturing *pain* enter into our frail life?"[37] Joy is what God and the prospect of immortality offer. However, philosophy looks at this with a critical eye and cannot accept it, thereby taking away from us the comfort that this view gives. But the idea is that humans deserve this joy and even have a right to it. This seems to be a criticism of the Stoics or Kant for their negative view of pleasure. Enjoying life is human, and so why should we try to deny or repress it in the name of abstract ethical principles?

Karlson learns that Gione and Wilhelmi are to be married the next day, and here the chapter closes as it began, with the juxtaposition of a wedding and death. The young Gione, once mistakenly taken for dead, now prepares for her wedding ceremony and a new life with Wilhelmi. But in contrast to the depressing mood at the beginning of the chapter with the death of the young daughter of the owner of the inn and the image of her grieving lover, now the mood is one of joy, harmony, and hope.

1.3 The Refutation of the Kantian View of Immortality

The 503rd Station sees the group set out on their excursion through the valley. It features a discussion primarily between the narrator and the Kantian chaplain. Given that Kant was the leading philosopher at the time and that his theory of immortality enjoyed a following, Jean Paul feels the need to address it. The narrator begins with some critical reflections about Kant for neglecting poetry and human emotion. He then turns to refute Kant's theory of immortality. This might seem odd given that Jean Paul also ultimately wants to argue for the same conclusion. Although he agrees with Kant that humans are immortal, he finds Kant's reasoning dubious. Indeed, Jean Paul believes Kant's general approach to the issue to be mistaken. Instead of addressing the individual with issues of real concern, Kant's philosophy is an arid exercise in logic and abstraction. On this point Jean Paul anticipates the existentialists' criticism of abstract reasoning and their call for philosophy to address the lived experience of the individual.

---

[37] Jean Paul, *Das Kampaner Thal*, p. 28 (*The Campaner Thal*, p. 15).

1.3 THE REFUTATION OF THE KANTIAN VIEW OF IMMORTALITY 49

The discussion is prompted by Nadine, who playfully considers the idea that flowers have souls. The materialist Karlson soberly rejects the notion. At this point the ever-serious chaplain, who has no sense for persiflage, gives a brief account of Kant's notion of immortality with the following argument:

> No immortality but that of moral beings can be discussed, and with them it is a postulate or apprenticeship of practical sense. For as a full conformity of the human will to the moral law, with which the just Creator never can dispense, is quite unattainable by a finite being, an eternally continuing progress, i.e., an unceasing duration, must contain and prove this conformity in God's eyes, who overlooks the everlasting course. Therefore, our immortality is necessary.[38]

Immortality only makes sense for rational beings created by God and not for flowers. According to Kant in the *Critique of Practical Reason*,[39] God created humans and endowed them with the faculty of reason so that they could act morally. The *telos* or ultimate goal is then to achieve moral perfection. Since our life in this world is too short for us to attain this, it follows that we must have another life after death, where we continue on the way to the moral perfection that God demands of us. The eternity of immortality must exist since we must continue forever to try to approach moral perfection, which is an unreachable goal. While Jean Paul clearly addresses himself to this argument from Kant's *Critique of Practical Reason*, it should be noted that Kant's view changes in his later work *Religion within the Boundaries of Mere Reason*, published in 1793, where the highest good is in fact attainable but only by means of divine grace.[40]

Karlson issues a series of penetrating criticisms of this Kantian view. He asks for details about exactly what the development towards the goal of moral perfection will look like:

> How can a righteousness, scattered and dispersed over an interminable period of time, satisfy Divine Justice, which must require this righteousness in each portion of the period? And has the constant approximation of man towards this state of purity been proved? And will not the number, if not the grossness of faults, in this infinite space, increase with the number of virtues? And what comparison will the list of faults bear to that of the virtues at the examination?[41]

---

[38] Jean Paul, *Das Kampaner Thal*, pp. 58f. (*The Campaner Thal*, pp. 29f.).
[39] Immanuel Kant, *Critik der practischen Vernunft*, Riga: Johann Friedrich Hartknoch 1788, pp. 219–223 (English translation: *Critique of Practical Reason*, trans. by Lewis White Beck, Indianapolis: Bobbs-Merrill 1956, pp. 126–128).
[40] Immanuel Kant, *Die Religion innerhalb der Grenzen der bloßen Vernunft, zweyter vermehrte Auflage*, Königsberg: Friedrich Nicolovius 1794, pp. 84–105 (English translation: *Religion within the Boundaries of Mere Reason* in *Religion and Rational Theology*, ed. and trans. by Allen W. Wood and George di Giovanni, Cambridge and New York: Cambridge University Press 1996, pp. 108–117).
[41] Jean Paul, *Das Kampaner Thal*, pp. 59f. (*The Campaner Thal*, p. 30).

With these questions, suddenly Kant's theory appears complicated to the point of being implausible. There is no evidence that people improve morally and get closer to moral perfection over time. Indeed, many get worse. In an infinity of time, one's immoral acts would also increase as would one's moral acts. But even if one managed to make some progress, this would not remove the guilt of past infractions (or the continued accumulation of them). The change in the temporal framework would not alter the mental disposition of the individual, which, for Kant, is the locus of morality, specifically in the good will. What is required is a change in the individual's way of thinking. But an infinity of time is neither required for this nor a guarantee of it. Karlson also critically asks about how moral comparisons of people might look according to this view:

> Will, in the sight of the Divine eye, the moral purity of two different beings – for instance, a seraph and a man, or of two different men, as Robespierre and Socrates – be equally contained in two equally long, i.e., eternal, courses of time? If on comparing the two, a difference appears, then one of them cannot have attained the so-called perfection and must still be mortal.[42]

Kant's view seems to make moral comparisons of people impossible. The *Critique of Practical Reason* seems to confuse moral imperfection with being mortal, while associating immortality with moral perfection. But Kant then has problems with accounting for the moral differences between different people. He simply suggests that everyone makes essentially the same progress towards the good. This view levels all human beings since everyone is striving towards perfection for eternity, which implies that everyone will at some point pass through the same stages of increasing perfection, even if they might have started from a fairly low or fairly high position. But this is counterintuitive since we want to make moral distinctions between such different characters as Robespierre and Socrates.

The chaplain hastens to remind Karlson that Kant does not mean this as an argument that demonstrates the truth of immortality. Instead, Kant believes that it cannot be proven, but rather that it must be presupposed as a postulate of practical reason, which is demanded for ethics to make sense. Karlson also objects to this idea: "It is a strange axiom to presuppose the truth of an opinion from its indemonstrability."[43] Thus the chapter ends with Karlson's materialism clearly having refuted the Kantian conception of immortality based on ethics.

The argument between the chaplain and Karlson continues in the next chapter, the 505th Station. The chaplain asks for permission to present some arguments for immortality, and Wilhelmi agrees. He supports the idea of

---

[42] Jean Paul, *Das Kampaner Thal*, p. 60 (*The Campaner Thal*, p. 30).
[43] Jean Paul, *Das Kampaner Thal*, p. 61 (*The Campaner Thal*, p. 31).

1.3 THE REFUTATION OF THE KANTIAN VIEW OF IMMORTALITY 51

giving scholarly proofs for such things, adding, "The Owl of Minerva, as all other owls, is said to forebode destruction to a household, by settling on its roof. But I hope it is not so."[44] The Owl of Minerva of course represents scientific knowledge. Wilhelmi recalls that some believe that this kind of knowledge is destructive (as it was to the initiate at the Temple at Sais in Schiller's poem, "The Veiled Statue at Sais").[45] So Wilhelmi is in favor of allowing science to try to prove the existence of immortality, hoping that it will not backfire and leave everyone in despair. The narrator emphasizes that the fate of everyone is tied to the issue of immortality, and so everyone has a deep personal interest in such a proof being successful.

The skeptic Karlson catches a day-fly that changes forms throughout its development, only to die after a single day. Karlson seems to want to draw an analogy to the human wishes for immortality. He argues from the perspective of the day-fly:

> In my opinion, a philosophical ephemera would argue thus. What! I should have uselessly accomplished all my various changes, and the Creator had no other intention in calling me from the egg to the grub, then to a chrysalis, and at last to a flying being, whose wings must burst another covering before death, with this long range of spiritual and corporeal developments, he should have had no other aim than a six hours' existence, and the grave must be the only goal of so long ... a course?[46]

From the perspective of the fly, all of this effort would seem absurd if the whole thing only ends in death after a short life anyway. The implication seems to be that this is also the human perspective, only on a smaller scale. Although humans live longer lives than day-flies, they find it difficult to believe that all their efforts and strivings serve no purpose and end only in destruction.

The example of the day-fly raises the question of scale. Of course, from the human perspective a day-fly seems completely small and insignificant. But this is not the case for the day-fly itself since its life is all that it knows. In *The Essence of Christianity* Feuerbach makes the same point about how the worldview of each creature is limited to its own horizon of experience. He claims that for the day-fly its short lifetime seems normal since this is all that it knows.[47] Thus, everything has its own specific relative place in the grand scheme of things.

---

[44] Jean Paul, *Das Kampaner Thal*, p. 69 (*The Campaner Thal*, p. 35).
[45] Friedrich Schiller, "Das verschleierte Bild zu Sais," *Die Horen*, vol. 1, no. 9, Tübingen: J. G. Cotta 1795, pp. 94–98 (English translation: "The Veiled Statue at Sais," in *The Poems of Schiller*, trans. by Edgar A. Bowring, New York: Hurst & Co. Publishers 1884, pp. 182–184). This poem was discussed in the Introduction above, pp. 27–28.
[46] Jean Paul, *Das Kampaner Thal*, pp. 70f. (*The Campaner Thal*, pp. 35f.).
[47] Ludwig Feuerbach, *Das Wesen des Christenthums*, Zweite vermehrte Auflage, Leipzig: Otto Wigand 1843, p. 11 (English translation: *The Essence of Christianity*, trans. by Marian Evans, New York: Calvin Blanchard 1855, p. 27).

There is a great ladder or chain of being where the individual members are separated only by degrees. When we talk about meaning, it is always something relative that is determined by the entity's place in the big picture. From the human perspective, it would appear that the human world is invested with great importance vis-à-vis the day-fly. But this forgets that there is a much higher and grander perspective that transcends the human, namely, the macrolevel perspective of planets, solar systems, and galaxies. From this point of view, the human world looks as tiny and insignificant as the world of the day-fly from the human perspective. The argument is that everything appears relative, yet each has its own significance and relevance from the position of a divine observer who can see everything: "every relative conclusion must be based on something positive, which only eternal eyes, which can measure the whole range of innumerable degrees, can truly weigh."[48] Paradoxically, the relative standard presupposes an absolute one. Therefore, even the day-fly has its significance, although it might seem negligible from the human perspective. While this might seem very small, it is not nothing. Note that the examples here are drawn from the natural sciences. It is specifically from the side of scientific observation that the idea of immortality and meaning seems impossible. These ideas make no sense when it is a question of day-flies and planets. Why then would it make sense for human beings who find themselves in some intermediary stage in the chain of being? The narrator, Jean Paul, concludes that the universe must represent a continually developing system and not something that is created once and for all. This system is harmonious, and everything has its proper place and role in the grand scheme.[49]

1.4 Karlson's Two Arguments against Immortality

The arguments concerning immortality continue in the next chapter, the 506th Station. Now the focus turns to Karlson's objections to immortality, which are grounded in his scientific worldview. The narrator asks the skeptic and scientifically educated Karlson to explain his objections. To initiate the discussion, he provides Karlson with prompts to two oft-heard arguments against immortality that he asks Karlson to elaborate on. The first argument the narrator suggests is "the simultaneous decay and destruction of the body and the soul."[50] Karlson takes up the challenge and gives materialist arguments that are intended to show how everything that is taken to be mental or spiritual is actually tied necessarily to the physical body. Memory, imagination, and all other mental faculties are made possible by the brain and would not exist without it. The motif of the chapter is the inner and the outer sides of the human being.

---

[48] Jean Paul, *Das Kampaner Thal*, p. 72 (*The Campaner Thal*, p. 36).
[49] Jean Paul, *Das Kampaner Thal*, p. 75 (*The Campaner Thal*, p. 37).
[50] Jean Paul, *Das Kampaner Thal*, p. 84 (*The Campaner Thal*, p. 41).

1.4 KARLSON'S TWO ARGUMENTS AGAINST IMMORTALITY 53

There is an outward side, namely, the body, but there is also an inward side, our personalities, with all our mental and ethical faculties, that seem to be something spiritual or nonphysical. This represents something invisible within us. Karlson's argument is that the two sides are necessarily connected, and it is an illusion to think of the inward side as something free and independent from the physical body. Both sides die together. All human experience shows that when the body dies, all the spiritual or inner qualities also die. There is thus no verifiable evidence that any part of a human being survives death.

The second argument suggested by the narrator is "the absolute impossibility of ascertaining the mode of life of a future existence, or as the Chaplain would say, to see into the spiritual world from the sensuous one."[51] At the prompting of the narrator, Karlson then turns his attention to an elaboration of this refutation of immortality. Karlson argues that there is no evidence of any second sphere beyond the physical one. People tend to imagine such things based on their own experience with this world, but these are only vague analogies, which have no confirmation in empirical reality.[52] There is no scientific grounding for human immortality, which is a sheer product of the imagination. The idea of spiritual beings living without bodies eternally after death flies in the face of every principle of science. It is impossible to explain how such a thing could even be vaguely consistent with a scientific worldview.

The narrator issues a counterargument to Karlson's positions. He first takes up the reductionist argument that the soul is just the physical brain and thus dies with it. He reasons that there is a second world, that is, the sphere of immortality, which "is already contained in this physical first one."[53] The world of immortality is not some transcendent sphere but exists here and now in "*Virtue, Truth, and Beauty*," which cannot be explained by the "dark, dirty clump of the sensuous world."[54] The triad of virtue, truth, and beauty is repeated like a mantra throughout the rest of the text. These are things that even the scientist believes in, yet they are not physical entities. The narrator argues that the mental and the physical or the inner and the outer are not identical, or rather the inner cannot be simply reduced to the outer as the materialists try to do. He gives the following examples: "Grief has no resemblance to a tear, – shame, none to the cheek-imprisoned blood, – wit, none to champagne, – the idea of this valley, none to its portrait on the retina."[55] The materialists constantly attempt to make reductions of this kind in order to show that the inner or mental sphere is nothing more than the physical. But the objection is that these things are not the same. Our inner feeling of sadness and grief might be expressed by a tear, but

---

[51] Jean Paul, *Das Kampaner Thal*, p. 84 (*The Campaner Thal*, p. 41).
[52] Jean Paul, *Das Kampaner Thal*, p. 88 (*The Campaner Thal*, p. 43).
[53] Jean Paul, *Das Kampaner Thal*, p. 88 (*The Campaner Thal*, p. 43).
[54] Jean Paul, *Das Kampaner Thal*, pp. 88f. (*The Campaner Thal*, p. 43).
[55] Jean Paul, *Das Kampaner Thal*, p. 90 (*The Campaner Thal*, p. 44).

the experience of it is very different from the physical shedding of the tear. The tear does not explain sadness and is not identical to it. Likewise, we know how images are formed by means of their imprint on our retina, but this in no way explains the full idea of the thing that we have in our minds and that seems to have nothing to do with the physiology of our eyes. The inner experience of being in love cannot be understood as the hormones that are released by the glands in our endocrine system. There thus seems to be something separate that transcends the physical being of our bodies.

The suggestion is also made that the inward, nonphysical element is the will. This is what makes it possible to move the physical body, although the will itself is not something physical.[56] As an additional argument, Wilhelmi uses the example of Socrates as a moral character. If something were to cause damage to Socrates' brain, this would not mitigate the fact that he was a moral character, even though his behavior might change. So, the character of being moral is independent of the physical body. This is further demonstrated by the fact that our mental exertions are quite different from our physical exertions and seem generally to be separate from them. Even if we are physically very tired, we can still move our bodies by means of our will. Thus, the narrator, Wilhelmi, and to a lesser degree the chaplain, are all keen to refute Karlson's view that immortality is impossible. With this ends the 506th station.

The final station is number 507. This is the longest chapter, and it represents the narrator's, that is, Jean Paul's view on immortality. Specifically, he offers several arguments to contradict Karlson's naturalistic position. Having refuted the reductionist, materialist view, he continues by taking up the second objection presented by Karlson, namely, the lack of evidence for any other world beyond the empirical one that we know. It is conceded that the more we learn about the natural sciences, the more impossible it seems that there is any reason to believe in the continuation of some life or existence after death in some other place. According to the modern scientific view, that is, "the increasing proofs and apparatus of chemistry and physiology," death is complete annihilation, and there is no escaping this.[57]

Jean Paul addresses the second argument of Karlson with a kind of agnosticism. It is true that we have no knowledge or experience of another world where the dead souls dwell, but this does not rule out the possibility that such as world does in fact still exist.[58] We cannot clearly imagine or portray such a world, but there is nothing wrong with this. There are many cases where we believe in things that we do not immediately see. When we see a mountain descending into the sea, we assume that it continues under the water, even though we do not see this part directly. It might be argued on Jean Paul's behalf that even

---

[56] Jean Paul, *Das Kampaner Thal*, p. 92 (*The Campaner Thal*, p. 44).
[57] Jean Paul, *Das Kampaner Thal*, p. 102 (*The Campaner Thal*, p. 49).
[58] Jean Paul, *Das Kampaner Thal*, pp. 105f. (*The Campaner Thal*, p. 51).

1.4 KARLSON'S TWO ARGUMENTS AGAINST IMMORTALITY

science makes assumptions about things that it cannot empirically observe, for example, the inside of black holes or dark matter. However, the objection here is obvious: such entities can be observed *indirectly* by their effects on things that can be observed. Moreover, they are completely in harmony with the laws of physics in contrast to the idea of immortal souls.

Wilhelmi and Nadine propose a view that was well known at the time, namely, that other planets were inhabited with the souls of the dead. This seemed in some ways logical given that science had postulated that there were presumably other habitable planets in orbit around other stars. Given that we do not see any dead souls here on earth, might it not be the case that they have simply migrated to one of these other planets? Wilhelmi and Nadine draw analogies with well-known natural phenomena in the world in order to give their views a scientific grounding: "Nadine said: 'One day I so pictured the inhabitants of a lemon-tree to myself. The worm on the leaf may think it is on the green earth, the second worm on the white bud is on the moon, and the one on the lemon believes itself to be upon the sun.'"[59] The worms on the one part of the tree cannot imagine that there is life on the other parts since these are so far away and their environments appear so different. So also, by analogy, there might well be inhabited planets with other human beings that we are unaware of simply because of their great distance from us.

There is nothing in itself to object to this, but it will be noted that this is not, strictly speaking, an argument for immortality. An additional argument is needed to explain how the inhabitants of the second world are in fact the deceased souls from the first. How, after death, could the souls miraculously fly to another planet where they would live a new existence? Karlson points out that if one were dead, one would need a new body to be transported to another planet. How would the dead be able to receive a new body for their journey and new life? To this the narrator Jean Paul can only respond that this must be a miracle, just as one's first body can be regarded as a miracle.[60] The new body would need to be one suited to the chemical and atmospheric conditions of the host planet, and thus there would be a variation among human beings such as is the case on earth between peoples who live in, for example, very hot or very cold climates.

Karlson points out that if it is true that the other planets are inhabited, they will have their own inhabitants and will not be the home of migrant dead souls from earth. Jean Paul is forced to concede that this cannot be a satisfying argument for immortality. While it might well be that the universe is teeming with life on different planets, this has nothing to do with the idea of a continued life after death for humans.

---

[59] Jean Paul, *Das Kampaner Thal*, p. 107 (*The Campaner Thal*, p. 52).
[60] Jean Paul, *Das Kampaner Thal*, p. 106 (*The Campaner Thal*, p. 51).

1.5 The Argument for Immortality and Karlson's Conversion

Jean Paul then makes his strongest case for immortality. He believes that it is a mistake to conceive of immortality as being in some other physical place such as heaven or on another planet. Instead, we have the seeds of immortality already within us as living beings. He earlier distinguished between the inner and the outer world. While the outer world is simply our physical bodies, we also have an inner life that cannot be reduced to our bodies. Continuing from the earlier discussion, he returns to the three key elements of our inner world: virtue, truth, and beauty.[61] These three elements are completely separate from our physical being and cannot be explained by it. It is commonly thought that we develop these ideas in our character as we grow and are educated. But this is mistaken. Instead of creating them ourselves, they exist in us already, and "we merely recognize them."[62] This sounds similar to Socrates' doctrine that learning is merely recollection of what we know from past lives. For Jean Paul, these are proofs that we possess something that is higher than the physical body and that endures when the body perishes. Thus, the second world of immortality is not another physical place outside us, but rather it is within us the whole time. It always already exists in every human being and is the part of us that lives on when our physical bodies die. The misunderstanding lies in how philosophers have understood this inner world as something that we create or that arises by socialization. Instead, it is something that is implanted within us at birth and that ensures our continued existence. Virtue, truth, and beauty extend far beyond the physical body and point to a higher, nobler sphere of human existence, where humans rise above nature.

Wilhelmi raises the objection that these things might well have been implanted in us "for the enjoyment and preservation of the present life."[63] Jean Paul quickly dismisses this objection by pointing out that this would mean that these noble qualities would be subordinated to our base, physical inclinations and desires and would serve as a means for them. Only when our physical desires are met do humans long for something higher, for example, virtue, truth, and beauty. So there is a qualitative difference between the physical needs of our body and our intellectual or spiritual side. Due to the fact that we recognize these things within ourselves, we realize that we have an immortal nature that is different from our physical body. Since we are immortal or have immortal elements, we are not entirely at home in the world where we are born. We belong to a higher place and thus feel a sense of alienation with the world we see around us. Jean Paul concludes the argument as follows: "we are immortal, and ... the second world in us demands, and proves a second world beyond us."[64] The world of

---

[61] Jean Paul, *Das Kampaner Thal*, p. 110 (*The Campaner Thal*, p. 53).
[62] Jean Paul, *Das Kampaner Thal*, p. 111 (*The Campaner Thal*, p. 53).
[63] Jean Paul, *Das Kampaner Thal*, p. 114 (*The Campaner Thal*, p. 55).
[64] Jean Paul, *Das Kampaner Thal*, p. 119 (*The Campaner Thal*, p. 57).

1.5 ARGUMENT FOR IMMORTALITY & KARLSON'S CONVERSION

virtue, beauty, and truth that we find within ourselves implies that there must be an immortal sphere outside us where these things exist, unburdened by the physical sphere.

Both Nadine and Gione are moved by the argument for immortality that Jean Paul gives. In this mood, Nadine presents to Jean Paul the letter of condolence that Karlson wrote to Wilhelmi at the beginning of the work when he believed that Gione had died. The introduction of the letter marks an important shift in the conversation. Until now the discussion covered well-known arguments for and against immortality. It had the character of a scholarly debate. But now by presenting the letter, Nadine moves the discussion from a detached academic issue to one of deep personal interest that involves a large emotional element. Nadine presumably sees that the arguments back and forth are not leading anywhere. But she knows of Karlson's love for Gione, and she uses his letter to remind him of his grief for her. This puts Karlson in a completely different frame of mind. Now it is no longer a dry academic debate, but instead it concerns him intimately. This proves to be the key to convince Karlson of the importance of believing in immortality.

In the short note, "Grief without Hope," Karlson expresses his *grief* for Gione, but he cannot entertain any *hope* of ever seeing her again since he does not believe in immortality and is convinced that in death humans meet with complete and final destruction. Karlson contrasts his view with that of Nadine, who shares his grief but, by contrast, maintains hope in immortality. He writes,

> Human blood paints the fluid figure called man on the monument, as oil on marble forms forests. Death wipes away the man and leaves the stone. O Gione! I would have some consolation, if thou wert but far away from us all, on a clouded forest, in a cave of the Earth, or on the most distant world in space. But thou art gone, thy soul is dead, not only thy life and thy body.[65]

Karlson has difficulties reconciling his scientific knowledge that there is no life after death with his deep wish that there would be an afterlife at least for his beloved Gione, whose apparent sudden death he was struggling to accept. By contrast, Gione's sister Nadine, while also sad, can at least take comfort in the consolation of believing that Gione continues in some postmortem existence. The point is that Karlson's worldview offers him no form of consolation whatsoever: "But I, Gione, stand beside your ruins with unalleviated pain, with undestroyed soul; and grieving, think of you until I also dissolve. And my grief is noble and deep for I have no hope!"[66]

Karlson's letter underscores the split between the intellectual and the emotional side of human beings. The scientist Karlson has no problem denying the

---

[65] Jean Paul, *Das Kampaner Thal*, p. 125 (*The Campaner Thal*, pp. 59f.).
[66] Jean Paul, *Das Kampaner Thal*, p. 126 (*The Campaner Thal*, p. 60).

idea of immortality from an intellectual point of view. But when his own secret love, Gione, appears to die, his emotional side is left completely vulnerable and without any resources to deal with the situation. A life without hope seems unbearable. By introducing the letter, Nadine confronts Karlson directly with the nihilistic consequences of his view in order to show that no one can in good faith live without the belief in immortality. The narrator, Jean Paul, is terrified to witness Karlson's condition: "how horrible and fearful the eternal snow of annihilating death seemed to me, placed beside the noble form it should have covered; how frightful the thought."[67] The very idea of the wonderful Gione being annihilated forever is too much even to imagine. He asks if anyone can really truly believe in this as Karlson claims. He conjures up a number of powerful images suggesting the meaninglessness of human existence if everything is destined for destruction:

> But let the disbeliever of immortality imagine a life of sixty minutes instead of sixty years, and let him try if he can bear to see loved, noble, or wise men only aimless, hour-long air-phantoms, hollow thin shadows which fly towards the light and are consumed by it, and who, without path, trace, or aim, after a short flight, dissolve into their former night. No; even over him steals a supposition of immortality.[68]

Not even the most ardent atheist scientist can maintain this view consistently. Jean Paul notes that the sober, scientific, rationalistic view ignores the important emotional side of human beings, which must also be acknowledged: "all arguments were poeticized into feelings."[69] This proves to be key to Jean Paul's case for immortality that causes Karlson's conversion. Abstract thinkers such as followers of Kant are focused on vapid "word arguments,"[70] and they thus completely neglect their own feelings, which in cases such as death and suffering are far more profound than abstract logical argumentation.

Jean Paul invokes another powerful image about the end of the earth as it is consumed by the sun – an imagine akin to the picture presented in "The Dead Christ":

> And when at last, after a thousand, thousand years, our earth is dried up by the sun's heat, and every living sound on its surface silenced, will an immortal spirit look down on the silent globe, and gazing on the empty hearse moving slowly on, say: "There the churchyard of humanity flies into the crater of the sun; on that burning heap many shadows, and dreamers, and wax-figures, have wept and bled, but now they are all melted and consumed: Fly into the sun, which will also dissolve thee, thou silent desert with thy swallowed tears, with thy dried up-blood." No, the crushed worm dares raise himself to his Creator, and say: "Thou canst not have made me only to suffer."[71]

---

[67] Jean Paul, *Das Kampaner Thal*, p. 127 (*The Campaner Thal*, p. 60).
[68] Jean Paul, *Das Kampaner Thal*, pp. 127f. (*The Campaner Thal*, pp. 60f.).
[69] Jean Paul, *Das Kampaner Thal*, p. 228 (*The Campaner Thal*, p. 61).
[70] Jean Paul, *Das Kampaner Thal*, p. 127 (*The Campaner Thal*, p. 60).
[71] Jean Paul, *Das Kampaner Thal*, pp. 129f. (*The Campaner Thal*, p. 61).

1.5 ARGUMENT FOR IMMORTALITY & KARLSON'S CONVERSION

Karlson objects to this by asking by what right the worm, that is, human beings, can raise such a question. The answer that Gione gives is that God himself gives us the right to do so since he created us for a purpose. But this response is obviously question-begging since it presupposes a Christian or theistic worldview that includes a conception of immortality and meaning, which is precisely what is at issue.

Jean Paul makes a final impassioned plea to Karlson by returning to the two difficulties that were discussed above: (1) the lack of evidence to explain our continued existence apart from the body, and (2) the lack of evidence for a second world or sphere of existence where the dead souls dwell. With this he seems to grant that the previous responses to these difficulties were inadequate. He asks,

> Are two difficulties, based too on the *necessary ignorance* of man, sufficient to overthrow a belief, which explains a thousand greater difficulties, without which our existence is without aim, our sufferings without explanation, and the holy Trinity in our breast three furies, and three terrible contradictions?[72]

The idea seems to be that the notion of immortality solves so many other problems for one's worldview in general that it would be absurd to abandon it out of concern for the much smaller problems raised by the two objections against it. The "holy Trinity" alludes to virtue, truth, and beauty, which science cannot explain by means of physical objects. So it is best, for the sake of consistency, just to assume immortality, so that the other elements of one's worldview will fall into place. This is legitimate since it is impossible for humans to know everything, and some assumptions must be made anyway. This sounds very similar to Kant's argument with the postulates of practical reason, despite the fact that his approach was dismissed earlier. Jean Paul's claim is that it is absurd to believe that "there can be no aim and no object in the whole spiritual universe."[73] This is, however, the nihilistic view of Karlson, according to which the world is not in harmony but rather represents an "eternally jarring discord."[74]

By this point in the narrative most all of the interlocutors are emotionally moved to tears. The beautiful Gione, harboring her secret love for Karlson, goes to him and takes him by the hand, saying, "You are the only one among us who is tormented by this melancholy belief, – and you deserve to have one so beautiful!"[75] This is too much for Karlson to bear, and finally he capitulates, abandoning his scientific view of human mortality:

> This word of concealed love overpowered his long-filled heart, and two burning drops fell from the blinded eyes, and the sun gilded the holy tears,

---

[72] Jean Paul, *Das Kampaner Thal*, pp. 133f. (*The Campaner Thal*, p. 63).
[73] Jean Paul, *Das Kampaner Thal*, p. 136 (*The Campaner Thal*, p. 64).
[74] Jean Paul, *Das Kampaner Thal*, p. 137 (*The Campaner Thal*, p. 65).
[75] Jean Paul, *Das Kampaner Thal*, p. 138 (*The Campaner Thal*, p. 65).

and he said, looking towards the mountains: "I can bear no annihilation but my own, – my whole heart is of your opinion, and my head must slowly follow."[76]

He allows his reason ("my head") to yield to his deep emotion ("my whole heart"). Karlson, who formerly had "blinded eyes," can now finally see the truth. With this, the debate finally ends with victory for the advocates of immortality, although its specific details remain sketchy. The key is Karlson's love for Gione, which is more powerful than his rational scientific disposition. Under normal circumstances, he would presumably have stuck firmly to the scientific view. But his recent, highly emotional experience of being mistakenly informed of the death of Gione produced a great inner turmoil in his heart. Despite his scientific reason, he cannot bring himself to believe that his beloved Gione, now happy and healthy, will truly die one day, and nothing will survive of her. There is a real point to his appeal to the emotions in contrast to sterile reason. Jean Paul clearly believes that reason alone can be misleading. His point was to make immortality persuasive to people in a way that philosophy, for example, in the form of Kantian reasoning, could not. The appeal to human emotion, he believes, can do this. The emotions can be understood as a kind of argument, although science does its best to exclude them from all discussion in order to keep up the pretense of objectivity.

Jean Paul seems not to note the inconsistency in the argument between the transcendent value of truth and the willingness to change it due to emotional need. Along with virtue and beauty, truth was one of the transcendent characteristics listed as evidence of an immortal side of human beings. But this would suggest that the truth has an unshakable and sacred position in human life. Yet, with the argument that is ultimately given, Karlson is prevailed upon to give up what he knows to be true for the sake of what is in effect an emotional need. But, of course, for the scientist something is true regardless of what we might feel about it. We cannot change the truth simply due to our personal wishes. The truths of mathematics and geometry are what they are independent of whether we think that they are good or bad, interesting or boring, vexing or emotionally fulfilling. Thus, if Karlson is certain that the doctrine of annihilation is supported by the best scientific evidence, it would seem contradictory for him to give this up merely because he does not like the idea, and it does not suit his emotional commitments. In science the two views must be kept strictly separate: what is the case, based on scientific evidence, and what we personally think about this. The moment that these two perspectives are mixed, science is compromised. There can, of course, be no doubt that we have a strong interest in such things as our mortality, but this merely means that we should be doubly cautious not to let this interfere with our scientific evaluation of the matter.

---

[76] Jean Paul, *Das Kampaner Thal*, pp. 138f. (*The Campaner Thal*, p. 65).

There is a long description of the beauty of nature, with the implication that it is a wonderful, harmonious system in which humans are at home. God has created these wonders for us, and human immortality is a natural part of it. Having been profoundly moved by the foregoing discussion, the narrator and the others experience a kind of ecstasy upon viewing the wonders of nature. This gives them a glimmer of the immortal life. The narrator reports to his friend Victor, "in this moment it was with each of our enraptured souls as if from its oppressed heart earth's load had dropped away; as if from her mother's arms, the earth were giving us, matured into the fatherly arms of the infinite spirit; as if our little life were over! To ourselves, we seemed the immortal, the exalted."[77]

This ecstasy is also represented by their taking a trip in two hot air balloons floating in the valley. The trip in the air is a kind of preview of death and immortality as the soul ascends effortlessly, taking leave of its mundane existence. First, Gione ascends alone, and then the narrator, Jean Paul, makes the trip in the air with Nadine. By leaving the earth and the material sphere, they get a sense for the immortal life without a body. They float over the houses and the mountains and seem to touch the moon and the stars. This feeling of elation and rapture seems to serve as a kind of confirmation for the truth of the conclusion to their discussion. Immortality does truly exist, and it is possible for human souls to depart from their bodies and the mundane sphere. As the narrator and Nadine return to the ground, they are both so moved that they can hardly speak.

This account of rising in the hot air balloons as an anticipation of the afterlife represents the counterpart or bookend corresponding to the scene of the friends being happily reunited in the Elysium-like cave at the beginning of the work. Both accounts are presented as a kind of ecstatic experience. This plays a role in Jean Paul's argument. The idea is that God shows us immortality in the beauties of this world. It will be recalled that in Jean Paul's introduction, the Campan Valley is described as a wondrous, magical place, a piece of the divine on earth.[78] It is unnecessary to seek abstract scholarly arguments for proofs of immortality since evidence for it is all around us if we are able to see it for what it is. We can feel the truth of immortality in ourselves when we have such experiences as the ones described here.

1.6 Jean Paul's Final Work and Death

After the publication of *The Valley of Campan*, Jean Paul was still not finished with the issue of immortality. In 1821, with the death of his son Max (1803–21), Jean Paul was plunged into a profound grief. This caused him to throw himself into a new project, *Selina or on Immortality*, which was to be the sequel

---

[77] Jean Paul, *Das Kampaner Thal*, p. 141 (*The Campaner Thal*, p. 66). Translation slightly modified.
[78] Jean Paul, *Das Kampaner Thal*, pp. 4f. (*The Campaner Thal*, pp. 3f.).

to *The Valley of Campan*. He worked on this book during the last years of his life, and at his death it remained unfinished and was only published posthumously in 1827 by Jean Paul's friend Christian Georg Otto.[79] The work contains a similar set of characters who represent the next generation of those found in *The Valley of Campan*. The lead character Selina is the daughter of Gione, and Alexander is the son of Karlson. The new cast take up a discussion of the question of human immortality. There is a degree of pathos in the work in that Jean Paul presumably knew that he was dying as he was writing it. As early as 1824 he began experiencing health problems that only increased. His eyesight gradually became worse until he went completely blind. He died on November 14, 1825.

It is fair to say that Jean Paul struggled with the issue of immortality and meaning in the universe his entire life. His knowledge of the most recent developments in the natural sciences made it impossible for him to ignore the sober naturalistic worldview that was becoming increasingly popular at the time. But he was terrified by this picture and was desperate to find some way if not to demonstrate human immortality, then at least to make it plausible. In the end his argument rests not so much on a scientific foundation as a psychological one. For human beings the thought of our infinitesimal place in the universe and our complete annihilation with death is simply too much to bear. This idea is so vexing that it is better to have recourse to some more comforting view that gives us hope. Without this, our lives become impossible. While from a scientific point of view, it might appear that we are finite and meaningless beings in a vast universe, this surely cannot be the final word.

While Jean Paul clearly wants to argue for human immortality, he has great insight into the scientific worldview that denies this. For this reason he is able to portray such a view so colorfully in "The Dead Christ." In *The Valley of Campan* he writes insightfully,

> On the whole, I find fewer men than one would imagine who decidedly believe in, or deny, the existence of a future world. Few dare to deny it, as for them this life would then lose all unity, form, peace, and hope; few dare to believe it, for they are startled at their own purification and at the destruction of the lessened earth. The majority, according to the promptness of alternating feelings, waver poetically between both beliefs.[80]

This nicely captures the problem of nihilism at the time. Many people wanted to embrace the new scientific worldview, yet they also still wanted to maintain certain elements of the traditional religious worldview that offered them comfort. The struggle between these two views was an inner struggle in many individuals.

---

[79] Jean Paul, *Selina, oder über die Unsterblichkeit*, vols. 1–2, Stuttgart and Tübingen: J.G. Cotta 1827.
[80] Jean Paul, *Das Kampaner Thal*, p. 103 (*The Campaner Thal*, p. 50).

Jean Paul frames the issue as an either/or proposition. Either one believes in immortality and can thus live a happy and flourishing life, or one rejects the idea and leads a miserable life filled with the fear of death and the absence of meaning. It might have appeared this way at the end of the eighteenth century, but today one could argue that the consequences of rejecting immortality are not nearly as grave as Jean Paul seems to think. Today there are many people who reject the idea of immortality but have not lapsed into a desperate nihilism. They are perfectly able to find other sources of meaning and purpose in their lives. In this sense it might be argued that Jean Paul exaggerates the problem of nihilism that comes with the development of Enlightenment science. There seems to be a lot of middle ground between the acceptance of either immortality or nihilism that Jean Paul fails to see.

For Jean Paul, the threat of the meaninglessness of the universe is closely connected to the question of human immortality. He believes that if humans are not immortal but simply perish forever with death, then the universe has no meaning or purpose. He does not make any attempt to sketch in a positive manner what this meaning might be, but for whatever it is, it has something to do with human existence continuing forever. Thus, he retains this part of the traditional Christian picture of the cosmos, where humans occupy a central role and are in a sense the very reason for the existence and course of the universe. Without human beings, the universe would be a dead, empty shell. Here the triad of concepts of God, meaning, and immortality are intimately connected.

Jean Paul's writings on this subject are couched in truly moving and powerful prose. His attempt to give an overview of the universe and at the same time touch the human heart is nothing short of breathtaking. He has a great gift for creating stirring images that hauntingly stick in the minds of readers. But the question is whether his argumentation is as good as his literary bluster.

2

Klingemann and the Absurdity of Nothingness in *The Nightwatches*

The mysterious work *The Nightwatches*, ostensibly by the pseudonym Bonaventura, was published at the end of 1804 with the year 1805 appearing on the title page.[1] It is an odd text that took a long time to find its way into the canon of German literature. There was an extended controversy about the author of the work, and many leading figures of German letters were suggested as possible candidates, such as Clemens Brentano and Friedrich von Schlegel. Only in 1987 was more definitive evidence found that the true author was the

---

[1] The work was originally published as *Journal von neuen deutschen Original Romanen in 8 Lieferungen jährlich*, Dritter Jahrgang 1804. Siebenten Lieferung, *Nachtwachen*, Penig: bey F. Dienemann und Comp. 1804. It contains a second title page that reads as follows: *Nachtwachen. Von Bonaventura*, Penig: bey F. Dienemann und Comp. 1805. All references are to this original edition. There are a number of modern German editions. See *Nachtwachen. Von Bonaventura*, ed. by Steffen Dietzsch, Leipzig: Reclam 1991. The earlier facsimile edition is also useful: *Nachtwachen. Von Bonaventura*, ed. by Raimund Steinert, Weimar: Gustav Kiepenheuer Verlag 1916. See also the bilingual edition, *Die Nachtwachen des Bonaventura*, ed. by Gerald Gillespie, Edinburgh: Edinburgh University Press 1973 (English translation: *The Nightwatches of Bonaventura*, trans. by Gerald Gillespie, Chicago and London: University of Chicago Press 2014). For secondary literature, see Thomas Böning, *Widersprüche: Zu den "Nachtwachen. Von Bonaventura" und zur Theoriedebatte*, Freiburg im Breisgau: Rombach Verlag 1996; Ina Brauer-Ewers, *Züge des Grotesken in den Nachtwachen von Bonaventura*, Paderborn: Schönigh 1995; Richard Brinkmann, *"Nachtwachen von Bonaventura": Kehrseite der Frühromantik*, Pfullingen: Niske 1966; Kathy Brzović, *Bonaventura's "Nachtwachen": A Satirical Novel*, New York: Lang 1990; Horst Fleig, *Literarischer Vampirismus. Klingemanns Nachtwachen von Bonaventura*, Tübingen: Niemeyer 1985 (*Studien zur deutschen Literatur*, vol. 83); Linde Katritzky, *A Guide to Bonaventura's "Nightwatches,"* New York: Lang 1999; Peter Kohl, *Der freie Spielraum im Nichts: Eine kritische Betrachtung der "Nachtwachen von Bonaventura,"* Frankfurt am Main: Lang 1986; Walter Pfannkuche, *Idealismus und Nihilismus in den "Nachtwachen von Bonaventura,"* Frankfurt am Main: Lang 1983; Rado Pribic, *Bonaventuras "Nachtwachen" and Dostoevsky's "Notes from the Underground": A Comparison of Nihilism*, Munich: Otto Sagner 1974 (*Slavistische Beiträge*, vol. 79); Jeffrey Sammons, *The "Nachtwachen von Bonaventura": A Structural Interpretation*, The Hague: Mouton 1965; Dorothee Sölle-Nipperdey, *Untersuchungen zur Struktur der Nachtwachen von Bonaventura*, Gottingen: Vandenhoeck & Ruprecht 1959; Thomas F. Barry, "Madness and the Disoriented Self in Bonaventura's *Nightwatches*," *The Journal of the Midwest Modern Language Association*, vol. 19 no. 1, 1986, pp. 50–58.

dramatist August Klingemann (1777–1831).[2] Originally, Klingemann studied philosophy in Jena with some of the greatest philosophers of the age, such as Fichte and Schelling. However, his true love was drama, and he became director of the theater in his native town of Braunschweig. There he produced the first performance of Goethe's *Faust* in 1829. Klingemann's background in the theater is clearly in evidence in *The Nightwatches*, which contains constant references to playwrights, dramatic works, and histrionics. Klingemann authored a handful of novels and a large number of plays. Despite this, he has remained a lesser-known figure in German literature.

The Nightwatches represents an intriguing text in which nihilism and the meaninglessness of human existence play important roles. The novel is written in the first person by a night watchman named Kreuzgang, whose name is a play on the fact that he was found at a crossroads as a baby. The name is also an echo of the motif of the cross (*Kreuz*) that appears in the work. As the novel progresses, Kreuzgang's story emerges bit by bit. He was a poet, an actor, a puppeteer, and was committed for a time to an insane asylum. Only later does he become a night watchman. Throughout his life Kreuzgang seems to become more and more disillusioned with the lies and folly of human life and more and more convinced of its meaninglessness. In a sense *The Nightwatches* can be regarded as a *Bildungsroman* in reverse. Instead of a young man going out into the world to discover himself and develop into manhood in a positive way, Kreuzgang begins with some semblance of normalcy but then becomes increasingly disenchanted with the world until he finally at the end hits bottom and fully embraces nihilism. In contrast to Jean Paul's *The Valley of Campan* with its tender moments of love and moving scenes of sublime rapture, and "The Dead Christ" with its the dark, gloomy, and pessimistic mood, *The Nightwatches* has tones of humor and satire. For Klingemann's protagonist there is apparently nothing sad or tragic about the nihilism of the world. One finds little of the pathos that was in abundance in Jean Paul.

The Nightwatches does not follow the linear narrative structure of traditional storytelling. Instead, it consists of a series of fragmented tableaus or individual scenes, which fluidly pass from the one into the other. While there is a sort of continuity and harmony in Jean Paul's storyline, Klingemann presents a mishmash of carefully framed scenes of horror, cruelty, and despair. It can be understood as a gallery of personalities or as a mosaic of strange images and stories. The brilliant detail of the individual scenes is testimony to Klingemann's skill as a director for the stage. The only discernible red thread is the gradual unfolding of Kreuzgang's life, which emerges only in a scattershot and nonchronological fashion.

---

[2] See Ruth Haag, "Noch einmal: Der Verfasser der 'Nachtwachen von Bonaventura,'" *Euphorion*, vol. 81, no. 3, 1987, pp. 286–297. See the overview of the discussions about the authorship of *The Nightwatches* in Gerald Gillespie, "Afterword: Authorship and Reception," in his edition of *The Nightwatches of Bonaventura*, trans. by Gerald Gillespie, pp. 127–135.

Kreuzgang goes out at night and observes different people in their ordinary lives. He sees their cruelty, suffering, and folly. Much of the work takes place at night, in darkness, with no shortage of scenes in cemeteries. The suggestion is that during the day people are free to engage in the illusions of social life and to play whatever role they wish. But in the end, it is all a lie. The truth of the hollowness of human existence comes out clearly only at night, and therefore the night watchman is the perfect observer. The realm of night brings out frightening truths that people try not to think about during the day, but these haunt our dreams and nocturnal thoughts. People feel much more comfortable in the warmth of the sun, where they can thrive in their natural folly.

2.1 Kreuzgang's Social Critique

In the first of the sixteen nightwatches, Kreuzgang observes at a distance first a poet and then a dying freethinker surrounded by his family. The sick man is under no illusions about what awaits him: "He gazes palely and calmly into empty nothingness, into which he intends to penetrate after an hour, in order to sleep forever the dreamless sleep."[3] This stands in contrast to the poet who nourishes "dreams of immortality" by means of his poetic works,[4] despite the fact that at the moment he labors in obscurity.

The dying man is surrounded by his wife and children, who make for a tender scene. However, he is also attended by a priest who threatens him with the fires of hell if he does not immediately convert to Christianity. This is the first of many images critical of religion that can be found in *The Nightwatches*. The priest is portrayed as cruel and unfeeling, tormenting the dying man in his final moments. The priest is directly associated with the devil himself and becomes increasing angry and impatient when the man calmly accepts death without repentance. Kreuzgang praises the dying man for not giving in to the priest for fear of death. He suggests that only petty minds are vexed by the thought of death, whereas the more noble soul is not concerned with it. Unable to bear the idea of annihilation, the limited mind must create the fictions of heaven and an afterlife.

Kreuzgang displays a sense of sympathy for the family of the deceased, who believe that the dead man will still wake up and be revived. He even tries to comfort the dead man by singing a dirge so that the last thing that the deceased hears will not be the railing of the priest. This is a disturbing picture. Here initially Kreuzgang is portrayed as a feeling person with some sensitivity to the suffering of others. Later in the text, he describes human suffering with a tone of indifference.

A very different side of his personality emerges in the "Sixth Nightwatch," where Klingemann's social criticism comes out perhaps most clearly. Here

---

[3] [Klingemann], *Nachtwachen*, p. 5 (*The Nightwatches of Bonaventura*, p. 2).
[4] [Klingemann], *Nachtwachen*, p. 3 (*The Nightwatches of Bonaventura*, p. 2).

Kreuzgang suggests that the world is not an orderly cosmos but rather a chaos.[5] This picture radically contradicts the conception of a harmonious mechanistic universe governed unwaveringly by natural laws. Without a sense of order in the universe, humans would be constantly confused and disoriented. There is a deep psychological need for stability and predictability, which allows for the possibility of finding meaning in life. Kreuzgang further recalls that as a youth he believed that "as soon as possible the Creator will have to set about deleting and nullifying the world as a miscarried system."[6] This suggests an absurd world where humans are never at home – a key motif in twentieth-century existentialism. These ideas seem to defy the value of Enlightenment science, which presupposes a sense of regularity and harmony in the universe, something that Kreuzgang wants to call into question.

At the end of the eighteenth century, millenarian groups appeared and prepared for the end of days that they believed would take place at the end of 1799. Kreuzgang explains how on the final day of that year, at 11 p.m., he decided, as a part of his official duties as night watchman, not to shout out the time but rather to proclaim that the Last Judgment had arrived. He then watches with amusement how people react to this news: "many ecclesiastical and worldly gentlemen leaped in fright from their feathers and into perplexity, since they were not prepared for anything so unexpected."[7] Usually people complacently live their lives without much thought to their death or divine judgment. But now that this appears imminent, the thin veneer of reason and respectability that surrounded people disappears immediately. The nobles are suddenly terrified since they know that their esteemed social status will not help them. They rush to make amends for all the injustices that they have committed during their lives. The idea of equality before God that dissolves all mundane social distinction is a frightening prospect:

> Offices were resigned, ribbons and decorations were taken off by unworthy possessors with their own hands; pastors solemnly promised to give their flocks in the future, in addition to good words, a good example into the bargain, if only the Lord God would this one time rest satisfied with their return to reason.[8]

The atheist or freethinker in the "First Nightwatch" appeared to be a noble figure, who went to his death at peace. By contrast, almost everyone else in society is terrified at the prospect and scrambles to repent and make amends as soon as possible in order to avoid God's negative judgment.

---

[5] [Klingemann], *Nachtwachen*, p. 94 (*The Nightwatches of Bonaventura*, p. 41).
[6] [Klingemann], *Nachtwachen*, p. 94 (*The Nightwatches of Bonaventura*, p. 41).
[7] [Klingemann], *Nachtwachen*, p. 95 (*The Nightwatches of Bonaventura*, p. 42).
[8] [Klingemann], *Nachtwachen*, pp. 96f. (*The Nightwatches of Bonaventura*, p. 42).

Klingemann thus describes human society as a web of lies and hypocrisy. The ploy of the announcement of the Last Judgment serves to expose this with perfect clarity. The clothes and trappings that people use to establish their social status now fall away, and people are in a sense equal, at least for a brief moment. Klingemann's background in the theater is evident here since he portrays humans as simply acting different roles but with no real substance or truth behind them. As the famous line from Shakespeare's *As You Like It* goes,[9] the world is a stage where everyone has a part to play, but, for Kreuzgang, fools take this seriously and regard their roles with great gravity:

> Oh, how can I describe how before me on the stage the people ran into one another and in confusion and fear prayed and cursed and moaned and howled; and how the disguise fell from the countenance of every mask on this great ball, collapsed by the trumpet's summons; and how people discovered kings in beggars' clothes and the reverse, weaklings in knights' armor, and so almost always a contrast between dress and man.[10]

As a theater director, Klingemann was attentive to how people act not just on the stage but also in the world. Realizing that the line between theater and real social life is a thin one, he has an attentive eye towards how people constantly pretend and lie in their social roles. The reversals between kings and beggars, weaklings and knights, serve as illustrations of the distorted reality of social life.

Kreuzgang himself plays the role of a director by setting up the scene and watching how the actors, that is, the townspeople, play it out. He frequently employs language from the theater to describe the situation: "The scene unfolded drolly enough at this false Last Judgment alarm, during which I played the sole calm onlooker, whereas all others had to serve me as passionate actors."[11] His role as spectator emphasizes his social position as an outsider. In this regard he notes that the only other person to retain his calm was his acquaintance, the city poet, "who scornfully looked down from his garret window into the Michelangelo painting."[12] Here the allusion is of course to Michelangelo's famous work, *The Last Judgment* (Figure 2.1), which portrays the Second Coming of Christ, who is shown issuing the individual judgments. The painting, like the scene presented by Klingemann, displayed a great sense of movement and agitation. Like the

---

[9] Shakespeare, *As You Like it*, Act 2, Scene 7, lines 138–139, p. 1718. Klingemann's extensive use of Shakespeare has been explored in some detail. See Katritzky, *A Guide to Bonaventura's "Nightwatches,"* pp. 16–26; Klaus Bartenschlager, "Bonaventuras Shakespeare. Zur Bedeutung Shakespeares für die *Nachtwachen*," in *Großbritannien und Deutschland. Europäische Aspekte der politisch-kulturellen Beziehungen beider Länder in Geschichte und Gegenwart. Festschrift für John W.P. Bourke*, ed. by Ortwin Kuhn, Munich: Goldmann 1974, pp. 347–371.

[10] [Klingemann], *Nachtwachen*, p. 97 (*The Nightwatches of Bonaventura*, pp. 42f.). Translation slightly modified.

[11] [Klingemann], *Nachtwachen*, p. 95 (*The Nightwatches of Bonaventura*, p. 42).

[12] [Klingemann], *Nachtwachen*, p. 98 (*The Nightwatches of Bonaventura*, p. 43).

Figure 2.1 Detail from Michelangelo, *The Last Judgment* (1541)

townspeople in Kreuzgang's story, the people in Michelangelo's painting are full of despair and regret for the way they have lived their lives. Most of the figures are portrayed as naked or scantily clad so that they cannot hide their sins. Likewise, in Kreuzgang's account people's masks and costumes fall as they show their true selves for the short time of the crisis.

The power of the image of lawyers and politicians scrambling before the Last Judgment can be appreciated when we contrast it to the theories of social and political life at the time. In the tradition of German idealism, thinkers such as Kant (who is mentioned directly in the chapter),[13] Fichte, and later Hegel tried to present the state and the social order as a rational entity. Even though this might not always be immediately evident, there is a hidden reason or *logos* that develops in human institutions and practices. But, for Klingemann, rationality is a blind dogma of the Enlightenment that has no reality. His point seems to be that all of this is sheer self-deception. There is nothing but absurdity and hypocrisy in human society, where the rich and the powerful exploit the poor and the weak. While Kreuzgang rejects certain elements of the Enlightenment, such as this, he remains a believer in the new scientific worldview in the sense that it teaches the inevitability and finality of death.

Kreuzgang addresses the crowd in order to heighten their fear and prolong their anxiety about the Last Judgment. Given that this is the final day of the world, he enjoins his auditors to look back on all human history and reflect on what has been achieved. Kreuzgang asks, "what, however, have we accomplished in it [sc. history]? – I maintain: nothing at all!"[14] Thus, all the struggles and sacrifices made in human history through so many years have been in vain.

---

[13] [Klingemann], *Nachtwachen*, pp. 105f. (*The Nightwatches of Bonaventura*, p. 46).
[14] [Klingemann], *Nachtwachen*, p. 100 (*The Nightwatches of Bonaventura*, p. 44).

In all their time on earth, humans have not managed to achieve anything meaningful at all. History is a sheer chaos of conflicting struggles with no deeper truth or significance. Here again we can recall the ideas of Kant and Hegel about how reason works in history and develops human culture to ever greater heights. Indeed, for these thinkers, there is a teleological development in history that aims toward a divinely ordained end. For Klingemann, this is sheer illusion that anyone who has seriously studied the dynamics of history can recognize.

Kreuzgang then goes through the different respectable professions and argues that they have been meaningless and have achieved nothing. Philosophers, scholars, theologians, jurists, statesmen, and even princes and rulers are all exposed as fakes and hypocrites. While they command social respect, their work is useless and even nefarious. The philosophers have not managed to establish any enduring truths. The theologians have created factions that have led to religious wars and persecutions. The statesmen and princes rule only to enrich themselves with no thought of the people they are governing. They thus have no scruples about exploiting people for their personal benefit.

Given all of this, when we look back at all of human history and society, there is nothing to be proud of. Continuing his speech, Kreuzgang imagines God's assessment of human accomplishment:

> Behind you lies the whole of world history like a silly novel, in which there are some few tolerable characters and a legion of wretched ones. Ah, your Lord God made a mistake only in this one regard, that he did not himself elaborate it but left it up to you to write in it. Tell me, will he indeed consider it now worth the effort to translate the botched thing into a higher language, or must he not rather, when he sees it lying before him in its whole shallowness, tear it to shreds in wrath and deliver you with all your plans over to oblivion? I can't see it any other way![15]

Given this, it is impossible to imagine that we have reason to expect any kind of divine reward for our efforts. Human life and society are meaningless, and it is of our own making. The human race fully deserves God's condemnation.

Like Jean Paul's Karlson, Kreuzgang issues a criticism of Kant directly.[16] According to the *Critique of Pure Reason*, space and time are not properties of the external world itself but instead are part of the human cognitive apparatus. In Kant's language, they are forms of sensible intuition that make it possible for us to perceive discrete objects. They are thus subjective and not objective. But if this is true, then how can Kant make a case for immortality, which seems to imply a continued existence in space and time? How can this be possible if space and time are subjective and are not real features of the external world?

---

[15] [Klingemann], *Nachtwachen*, p. 104 (*The Nightwatches of Bonaventura*, p. 45).
[16] [Klingemann], *Nachtwachen*, pp. 105f. (*The Nightwatches of Bonaventura*, p. 46).

At length, the townspeople begin to pick up on the fact that Kreuzgang is playing a joke on them and that his announcement of the Last Judgment was only a false alarm. They are quick to resume their social roles and forms of hypocrisy. Although the authorities are understandably upset with Kreuzgang, he escapes legal action and is mercifully regarded simply as a fool. Here we find an interesting inversion where the fool is in fact the wise one who has insight into the hypocrisy of the world, whereas the real fools are those who play their meaningless social roles every day and thus live in hypocrisy. The work is known for its use of irony and is full of inversions of this kind, which are intended to satirize commonly accepted beliefs and practices. In any case, the citizens return to their life of lies and complacency once the threat of the impending Last Judgment is gone. The experience and fear of imminent divine condemnation do not serve as a wake-up call for them to mend their ways. Instead, they embrace once again their lives of hypocrisy without a second thought. There is a criticism here of how seriously people take themselves, even though the facts speak for the nihilistic truth that nothing matters.

2.2 The Tragedy of Man

The "Eighth Nightwatch" returns to the poet in the garret apartment who was introduced in the "First Nightwatch." He had produced an epic work, a tragedy entitled *Man*, and was anxiously awaiting the verdict of the publishing house about whether it would be accepted for publication. Curious about the result, Kreuzgang goes up to the poet's apartment to ask about the publisher's response. He finds that the poet has hung himself in despair upon learning that his manuscript was rejected. The account of the poet's suicide is rather matter of fact and even perversely humorous. The description of the situation portrays it as a dramatic scene in a theater. Kreuzgang's aloof response to the horrific sight underscores his unusual emotional life and his misanthropy.

It was seen that although Kreuzgang was deemed an idiot for proclaiming the false alarm of the end of the world and the Last Judgment, there was an inversion in the roles in that his proclamation exposed the hypocrisy of his fellow citizens. Previously, he was the only one who could see things as they truly are, while everyone else continued to play their role in the charade of social life. This motif of inversion appears again in connection with the suicide of the poet: "in a land wholly peopled by the lame, a single exception is ridiculed as a queer, perverse *lusus naturae*; likewise, in a state full of no one but thieves, honesty alone would have to be punished with the rope."[17] The implication is that the poet is the sane one for his honest portrayal of humanity, and the rest of society are insane since they cannot bear to face the truth. Thus, the

---

[17] [Klingemann], *Nachtwachen*, p. 135 (*The Nightwatches of Bonaventura*, p. 59).

rejected magnum opus of the poet contains some valuable insights about the human condition despite the appearance of the contrary.

Kreuzgang finds the poet's suicide letter, which is entitled "Letter of Refusal to Life." It begins with the statement "Man is good for nothing."[18] This contains a double entendre since it could in the first instance refer to the poet's tragedy, which, since it was rejected by the publisher, is good for nothing. Or it can be taken in the broader sense that humanity itself has no redeeming features and is good for nothing. Here the poet expresses his disappointment with life and the fate of his work.

Kreuzgang rescues the manuscript of the poet's tragedy from the hungry mice and then reads the prologue to *Man*, which is fittingly told by a clown (*Hanswurst*). This is an echo of Shakespeare's famous line from *Macbeth*: Life "is a tale / Told by an idiot, full of sound and fury, / Signifying nothing."[19] Klingemann has replaced "an idiot" with "a clown." While one would expect a tragedy about the human condition or history to be told by a person keen to praise human achievements, instead it is a story more suitably narrated by a fool. The poet explains his use of the clown by saying that people have become complacent and lazy, and thus what is needed is someone who will provoke them and irritate them so that they will become reflective.[20] The poet's goal thus resembles Socrates' mission as the gadfly of Athens who tries to disabuse his fellow citizens of their mistaken views.

The clown begins by referring to the incipient theory of evolution of Erasmus Darwin,[21] who was mentioned above.[22] According to his theory, humans are descended from apes. This is another example of how science leads us to conclusions that run contrary to our wishes and hopes. According to the Judeo-Christian tradition, humans have a divine element in themselves that separates them from the rest of nature. This is how we like to think of ourselves. We would prefer not to regard ourselves as advanced apes, but this is the sad fact of the matter. The clown's view stands in sharp contrast to Jean Paul's more positive assessment of human nature, according to which a human being is "a beautiful demi-god."[23] For Jean Paul, humans have a dignity and value that is special and unique in nature. For Kreuzgang, this is a laughable delusion.

The natural origin of humans as descended from apes confirms the clown's view of human beings as foolish and worthless. There is nothing dignified or

---

[18] [Klingemann], *Nachtwachen*, p. 140 (*The Nightwatches of Bonaventura*, p. 61).
[19] Shakespeare, *Macbeth*, Act 5, Scene 5, lines 26–27, p. 2561.
[20] [Klingemann], *Nachtwachen*, pp. 143f. (*The Nightwatches of Bonaventura*, p. 62).
[21] [Klingemann], *Nachtwachen*, pp. 144f. (*The Nightwatches of Bonaventura*, p. 62).
[22] See the Introduction, Section 0.3, pp. 22–23.
[23] Jean Paul, *Das Kampaner Thal oder über die Unsterblichkeit der Seele; nebst einer Erklärung der Holzschnitte unter den 10 Geboten des Katechismus*, Erfurt: bei Wilhelm Hennings 1797, p. 134 (English translation: *The Campaner Thal and Other Writings*, Boston: Ticknor and Fields 1864, p. 63).

grand about human existence. Life is not something serious as people like Jean Paul think – instead it is humorous. It must thus be portrayed with humor and irony. The clown argues that

> Man is a facetious animal by birth, and he merely acts on a larger stage than do the actors on the small one inserted into this big one as in *Hamlet*; however importantly he may want to take things, in the wings he must still put off crown, scepter, and theatrical dagger and creep into his little dark chamber as an exited comedian, until it pleases the director to announce a new comedy.[24]

Humans are always playing roles and wearing masks in social life in general, which is the "larger stage," in contrast to the "small one," which is the theater, strictly speaking. Klingemann makes reference here to the play within a play, entitled *The Murder of Gonzago*, that appears in *Hamlet*.[25] When a troupe of actors come to Elsinore Castle, Hamlet enjoins them to perform this work, which he has modified with some extra lines. Since the plot resembles the murder of his father, Hamlet hopes that he will be able to expose his uncle Claudius as the murderer by the latter's reaction to the performance. In that context Hamlet blurs the distinction between the fiction of the play and the reality of the murder of his father. The large stage (of society and reality) and the small one (of the theater) are mixed into one.

The theater gives the illusion that it is the only place where people dress up and play roles. Here again we see the metaphor of human life resembling a play, which is also found in Macbeth's soliloquy: "Life's but a walking shadow, a poor player, / That struts and frets his hour upon the stage, / And then is heard no more."[26] Humans act on a stage with an audience, but in the end they are still only animals like monkeys, and when they are not on stage they realize inwardly that they are only playing a role and are nothing in themselves. Much of life is spent trying to keep up the facade and not show other people the impoverished beings we really are:

> If he tried to show his ego *in puris naturalibus* or even only in a nightshirt and with sleeping cap, by the devil, everyone would flee from its shallowness and worthlessness; but hence he bedecks it with garish theatrical patches and holds the masks of joy and love before his face in order to appear interesting and to elevate his voice through the speaking tube attached inside; then the ego finally looks down onto these tatters and imagines to consist of them.[27]

---

[24] [Klingemann], *Nachtwachen*, p. 148 (*The Nightwatches of Bonaventura*, p. 64).
[25] Shakespeare, *Hamlet*, Scene 9, pp. 2043–2053 (in editions that divide the play into acts, this appears in Act 3, Scene 2).
[26] Shakespeare, *Macbeth*, Act 5, Scene 5, lines 23–25, p. 2561.
[27] [Klingemann], *Nachtwachen*, p. 149 (*The Nightwatches of Bonaventura*, p. 64).

Human life is governed not by the truth but by masks of respectability. Masks play a key role in the work. While we all wear masks, which are necessary for social life to exist, they also make possible lies, hypocrisy, and deception. The recognition that we receive from others based on our masks allows us to deceive ourselves as well. We cannot bring ourselves to accept the "shallowness and worthlessness" of the human condition.

Behind the masks with the lies, the charades, and the hypocrisy there is only death. This too is something that humans take great care to conceal from themselves and others:

> The death's-head is never missing behind the ogling mask, and life is only the cap and bells which the Nothing has draped around to tinkle with and finally to tear up fiercely and hurl from itself. Everything is Nothing and vomits itself up and gulps itself greedily down, and even this self-devouring is an insidious sham, as if there were something, whereas if the choking were once to cease, precisely the Nothing would quite plainly make its appearance and would be terror-struck before it; by this cessation fools understand "eternity"; but it is the real Nothing and absolute death, since life, on the contrary, arises only through a continual dying.[28]

The motif of nothingness runs throughout the work. The masks that we wear in society cover over what most people would regard as their true self. But Klingemann makes the more radical claim that there is no true self, and instead the mask merely hides our finitude and mortality. Behind the masks is the dust of death. He captures this brilliantly with the oxymoron "Everything is nothing." Everything that we take to be substantial will ultimately disappear. Here Klingemann leaves no doubt about the question of immortality. Only fools allow themselves to believe that there is some enduring soul behind the masks that will survive death. Life ends not in eternity but in nothingness and annihilation.

This part of Klingemann's descriptions of the human condition anticipates Sartre's analysis of how people live in bad faith. Like Sartre's famous example of the waiter described in *Being and Nothingness*, people want to believe that there is some fixed, eternal substance in their social roles. The reactions of others to us in our roles seems to confirm this. But ultimately this is something contingent and mutable. The waiter wears the mask of a waiter in order to demonstrate to others and to himself his ontological substance as a waiter, but this is self-deception. Like Sartre, Klingemann gives ontological priority to the nothingness. It seems that Klingemann would agree with Sartre that there is ultimately no stable ontological self that stands behind all the masks.

---

[28] [Klingemann], *Nachtwachen*, p. 150 (*The Nightwatches of Bonaventura*, pp. 64f.).

But there is a recognition that the clown's nihilistic view is a difficult truth to live with. Most people are abhorred by such thoughts, and people with such views are unwelcome in polite society:

> If one were ready to take [this] consideration seriously, it could easily lead to the madhouse; but I take it merely as Clown and thereby conduct the prologue up to the tragedy, in which the poet, of course, has taken it to a higher plane and even invented a God and an immortality in it, in order to make his characters more significant.[29]

Humans cannot live with the nothingness, and so they create fictions to make things easier for themselves. This also applies to the German idealists who believe in the illusion of meaning in human life and history. As was the case with Kreuzgang's announcement of the immanent end of the world and the Last Judgment, so also here with the poet's tragedy, *Man*, Klingemann has created a new context in which to expose the folly about the meaning of life and the dignity of humanity.

2.3 The Creator of the World

In the "Ninth Nightwatch" Kreuzgang has been committed to a mental institution. Here once again an inversion of roles is at work with the categories of madness and sanity. At the beginning he speaks about "the general insane asylum,"[30] by which he means society at large, in contrast to the smaller one, which is the insane asylum properly speaking. This mirrors his parallel, seen in the previous nightwatch, between the larger stage (sc. society) and the smaller one (sc. theater in the strict sense), where people are always acting and playing roles.[31] While, as noted above, Shakespeare says all the world is a stage,[32] Klingemann seems to suggest all the world is an insane asylum. Kreuzgang introduces his fellow inmates to the visiting Doctor Oehlmann, and his descriptions make it clear that people are judged to be psychologically disturbed because they do not conform to the mores of accepted social life. It is thus an inverted world. In fact, when the specific reasons are given for their insanity, these should rather be regarded as praiseworthy traits. Kreuzgang explains that one of the inmates "sits here simply because he has advanced too far culturally by half a century; a number of this type are still wandering around free, whom, however, as is fitting, people consider to be all mad."[33] To be ahead of one's time is not something laudable but rather is regarded as insanity. Another inmate "held talks

---

[29] [Klingemann], *Nachtwachen*, pp. 150f. (*The Nightwatches of Bonaventura*, p. 65).
[30] [Klingemann], *Nachtwachen*, p. 154 (*The Nightwatches of Bonaventura*, p. 67).
[31] [Klingemann], *Nachtwachen*, p. 148 (*The Nightwatches of Bonaventura*, p. 64).
[32] Shakespeare, *As You Like it*, Act 2, Scene 7, lines 138–139, p. 1718.
[33] [Klingemann], *Nachtwachen*, p. 159 (*The Nightwatches of Bonaventura*, p. 69).

that were too reasonable and understandable."[34] The implication is of course that being unreasonable and incomprehensible is what counts for sanity.

This is presumably in part a criticism of the convoluted academic language that dominated university philosophy at the time. This meant that when one spoke or wrote in a way that was more comprehensible, one risked not being taken seriously in philosophical circles. It will be recalled that Jean Paul was also critical of the tendency of university philosophers to write in a way that only they and their colleagues could understand. There is also a criticism of conformity in society, which ostracizes people who stand out as somewhat different from the crowd. Someone who is culturally advanced beyond the rest makes people feel uncomfortable.

One of the most intriguing of Kreuzgang's fellow inmates is one who believes he is God and has created the world. Doctor Oehlmann and Kreuzgang stop to listen to his long monologue. While the world creator is satisfied with much of what he has created, he has some misgivings about having created human beings:

> But this tiny speck, into which I blew a living breath and called it man, does now and then annoy me with his little spark of godhead which I implanted in him in overhaste and over which he became deranged. I should have recognized at once that so little divinity could lead only to evil, for the poor creature no longer knows in what direction to turn.[35]

Humans have become confused and arrogant. They want to be immortal like God but would only be bored with it. Mortality is thus necessary. The world creator explains, "I also feel bad about utterly destroying it [sc. humanity]; for the mote does often dream so very pleasantly of immortality and thinks, just because it dreams such a thing, it must come true."[36] The idea of immortality is simply a self-delusion on the part of small and utterly insignificant beings who have no understanding of their real place in the universe. Yet this self-delusion is what counts as sanity. Here the reader senses that this is not intended to be understood as the ramblings of a madman but in fact is an accurate portrayal of the human condition that only the one dubbed mad dares to state explicitly. Such a person who speaks the truth is ostracized from society since his claims that there is neither immortality nor meaning in existence make most people nervous.

The creator of the world issues a criticism of the pride that people take in the advancement of the sciences during the Enlightenment. Now that humans believe that they have begun to understand the laws of physics, they arrogantly imagine that they know the thoughts of God himself. They are quick to organize the natural world into systems of thought and then praise themselves that

---

[34] [Klingemann], *Nachtwachen*, p. 159 (*The Nightwatches of Bonaventura*, p. 69).
[35] [Klingemann], *Nachtwachen*, p. 162 (*The Nightwatches of Bonaventura*, p. 70). The "living breath" is of course an allusion to Genesis 2:7.
[36] [Klingemann], *Nachtwachen*, p. 163 (*The Nightwatches of Bonaventura*, p. 71).

they have matched God's intelligence. The creator of the world explains how "from pulpits and lecterns serious speeches are buzzing about the wise arrangement of nature."[37] This shows human presumption and pride, as if humans were in any position to comprehend the work of the creator of the universe and pass judgment on it. Klingemann's depiction of this madman creates a situation where the reader is forced to imagine the universe and the role of human beings from the perspective of God. He then draws out the implications of this perspective, which strike most people as disturbing, indeed, disturbing enough to be regarded as mad.

The creator of the universe says, "the speck fancied itself to be god and constructed systems in which it admired itself."[38] In the previous nightwatch, the clown who narrates the poet's tragedy *Man* complains that people "absolutely don't see through themselves, and Man shall finally consider himself as God or at least, like the idealists and world history, form himself on such a mask."[39] The "Thirteenth Nightwatch" criticizes the Enlightenment for arrogantly elevating the human to the status of semi-divine: "our enlightened century stands upright and we ourselves endeavor to pass for middling gods."[40] Clearly this is a part of Klingemann's satire of human vanity and arrogance. Despite the tiny role humans play in the universe, they ascribe to themselves a role like the divine.

Klingemann's depiction of the creator of the world can be contrasted with the exchange between Karlson and Gione in Jean Paul's *The Valley of Campan*.[41] It will be recalled that Jean Paul imagines the end of the earth plunging into the sun and being incinerated, thus wiping out every trace of human existence. He then appeals to Karlson by asking if this can really be God's purpose. He imagines humans thus protesting against this. Karlson then asks what right humans have to make this protest, to which Gione responds that God himself has given us this right by creating us. This picture implies a positive philosophical anthropology that believes that humans are part divine and have a special value and dignity that goes beyond nature. But according to the view of Klingemann's world creator, this is exactly what is denied. He has a very negative picture of human nature, and this would seem to undermine the force of Gione's response. If there is nothing special about humans, and we are simply continuous with the rest of nature and, moreover, are even unrepentant moral failures, then what right would we have to expect or even demand immortality? Gione's more traditional religious view assumes that people are redeemable, which the world creator denies.

Kreuzgang also criticizes once again the folly of academics by ridiculing their doctor's hats and pretentious robes. Academics feel the need to distinguish

---

[37] [Klingemann], *Nachtwachen*, p. 166 (*The Nightwatches of Bonaventura*, p. 72).
[38] [Klingemann], *Nachtwachen*, p. 163 (*The Nightwatches of Bonaventura*, p. 71).
[39] [Klingemann], *Nachtwachen*, p. 151 (*The Nightwatches of Bonaventura*, p. 65).
[40] [Klingemann], *Nachtwachen*, p. 224 (*The Nightwatches of Bonaventura*, p. 96).
[41] Jean Paul, *Das Kampaner Thal*, pp. 129f. (*The Campaner Thal*, p. 61).

themselves for their important social status by means of their attire and most importantly their academic caps. These are a part of their social masks. They come to associate this with knowledge and even seem to believe that just by changing hats they can reach great insights in the different fields:

> Traffic in dissertations on the quickest method for curing sicknesses, and release the patient himself from his illness by the shortest way! Embrace the dying man, after a swift switch of hats, as a legal friend and set his house in order, and finally, merely by donning a robe, show him the right way to heaven as a divine friend? In this way, as in a factory through different machines, highest and ultimate things could be attained through different hats.[42]

People thus run through the course of life with the assistance of learned specialists, who are there to meet our every need. Medical doctors, lawyers and theologians all strive to attain the hat of the doctor in their field since this is a symbol of knowledge and prestige that commands respect. It is as if they possess something infinitely important and valuable merely with a doctor's hat. This is a critique of what is regarded as human wisdom in general. Academic knowledge is simply vanity and arrogance. It is suggested that the German philosophers are pretentious in their attempts to create complete systems of knowing, thus imitating God. Here mention is made explicitly of Fichte and Friedrich von Schlegel.[43]

In describing his own mental ailment, Kreuzgang formulates the ironic inversion clearly: "I find everything rational absurd, just as vice versa."[44] This can be regarded as a nihilistic rejection of all conventional human thought, which is merely a patchwork of misunderstandings, lies, and self-delusions. What counts as respectable beliefs and commonly accepted ideas are shams and ideologies, which fall apart under closer examination. Here again we find a similarity to Socrates' critique of traditional knowledge and the misplaced pride that specialists take in it. Kreuzgang concludes his self-assessment: "But on closer examination I found everything vain … It is my *idée fixe* that I consider myself more rational than the reason deduced in systems and wiser than professional wisdom."[45] Since Kreuzgang has reached this conclusion by observing and reflecting on human life and activity, the doctor prescribes as a cure that he desist from thinking. This can be regarded as the beginning of a long tradition of thought, which includes Kierkegaard, Dostoevsky, and Camus, who all use sickness as a metaphor for reflection. To be healthy in the eyes of society, it is best to follow traditional views without calling anything into question. With this recipe, the problem of nihilism will never arise. One need only blindly follow the crowd.

---

[42] [Klingemann], *Nachtwachen*, pp. 170f. (*The Nightwatches of Bonaventura*, pp. 73f.).
[43] [Klingemann], *Nachtwachen*, p. 167 (*The Nightwatches of Bonaventura*, p. 72).
[44] [Klingemann], *Nachtwachen*, p. 170 (*The Nightwatches of Bonaventura*, p. 73).
[45] [Klingemann], *Nachtwachen*, p. 171 (*The Nightwatches of Bonaventura*, p. 74).

The text raises some important and quite modern questions about the nature of mental health, which can be seen as anticipating the work of twentieth-century thinkers such as Foucault. Who is really to say what constitutes what is normal in this sphere? Kreuzgang claims that what others regard as sickness he himself considers "higher health" and vice versa.[46] He compares the insane with the professors at the universities and asks who decides which people belong to the one category or the other. He again ironically suggests that the present state of things represents an inversion of the truth. Since the world finds the truth of nihilism and meaninglessness unbearable, it creates illusions to make life more palatable, and it persecutes and ostracizes those who see through these and remind others of the sad but true state of things.

2.4 Death and the Image of Nature

The theme of death plays a central role in the "Tenth Nightwatch." The first image that the reader is presented with is a sleepwalker carrying a baby at a perilous height.[47] In sleep he is oblivious to the danger and is observed by his wife who dares not wake him, lest he be startled and fall to his death with the child. This can in some ways be regarded as a metaphor for human life in general. Humans are constantly in danger, and death can happen at any time. Yet they are unaware of it and go on blindly with their daily lives, as if there were no threat. Unknowingly, we are always dangling just above the precipice, and the real danger can only be seen by an outsider observing the situation from a distance.

Nature is the other key motif in this chapter. It is portrayed as indifferent to human desires and needs, sometimes nourishing and sometimes destroying. Kreuzgang describes the winter scene:

> Everything is cold and stiff and raw, and the limbs have dropped from the torso of nature, and it still stretches only its petrified stumps toward the sky without their garlands of blossoms and leaves. The night is quiet and almost terrible, and cold death is present in her as an invisible spirit that grips subdued life.[48]

Kreuzgang sees a beggar trying to stay awake in the cold and in danger of freezing to death. He asks himself if he should try to help and repeats the famous lines of Hamlet: "Shall I cheat death of a beggarly life? By the devil, I really do not know what is better – to be or not to be!"[49] The obvious implication is that death is perhaps preferable to the life of suffering that the beggar must endure.

---

[46] [Klingemann], *Nachtwachen*, p. 172 (*The Nightwatches of Bonaventura*, p. 74).
[47] [Klingemann], *Nachtwachen*, p. 174 (*The Nightwatches of Bonaventura*, p. 75).
[48] [Klingemann], *Nachtwachen*, p. 175 (*The Nightwatches of Bonaventura*, p. 75).
[49] [Klingemann], *Nachtwachen*, p. 176 (*The Nightwatches of Bonaventura*, p. 76). See Shakespeare, *Hamlet*, Scene 8, lines 57–91, pp. 2040f. (in editions that divide the play into acts, this appears in Act 3, Scene 1).

Kreuzgang reflects on the images that the bourgeois paint on the walls of the interiors of their houses. Nature is among their favorite motifs. It is always presented as warm and bountiful, providing a nourishing home for human beings. But this is only an imagined, artistic conception of nature. The truth is quite different. Nature can also be violent and destructive to human plans and designs: nature, "capricious and peevish as any old woman, now warms her children and now crushes them."[50] The idea of nature as a loving mother is a one-sided picture that people recount to one another in order to feel better about the world. But nature can also be a terrible and hostile force. Klingemann returns to this motif in the "Thirteenth Nightwatch," where the beauties of nature are celebrated, but when it comes to the question of the human being, nature is mute. It provides us with no answers to the deepest issues about human existence. When we ask, we receive only an empty echo of our own voice as a response.[51]

The beggar dies of the cold, and it is recounted how he lost his young wife, which presumably led him to despair. Under the heading "The Dream of Love," Kreuzgang distinguishes between the illusion of love and the sobering fact that lovers also die. He notes that we hold close the dream of love, but we ignore the reality of its outcome in death. The imagined dead wife in an afterlife is much more palatable than that of a decaying corpse and the annihilation of the person. This imagined picture we can cultivate and keep close to our heart at all times:

> The white rose of death is more beautiful than her sister, for she reminds one of life and makes it desirable and precious. Over the mound of the beloved's grave her figure hovers eternally youthful and garlanded, and reality never deforms her features and does not touch her that she grow cold and her embrace terminate.[52]

Monuments representing the dead remain and serve as a help for our memories. Such an image remains happily unchanged in our minds. But this does not mitigate the fact of death.

This passage might well be contrasted with Jean Paul's account of the power of love and the human spirit, which seems to make it impossible to believe in human mortality and meaninglessness. Klingemann would presumably regard this view as an absurdity or a dream. It has no basis in reality, which is governed by cruel nature. The comparison is made even more explicit with the description that Klingemann gives of a simultaneous wedding celebration and funeral, the image with which Jean Paul begins *The Valley of Campan*. Like Jean Paul, Klingemann compares the "dance music and the death chant."[53] Likewise the two brides, one alive and one dead, are disturbingly compared.

---

[50] [Klingemann], *Nachtwachen*, p. 176 (*The Nightwatches of Bonaventura*, p. 76).
[51] [Klingemann], *Nachtwachen*, p. 219 (*The Nightwatches of Bonaventura*, p. 94).
[52] [Klingemann], *Nachtwachen*, p. 178 (*The Nightwatches of Bonaventura*, p. 76).
[53] [Klingemann], *Nachtwachen*, p. 178 (*The Nightwatches of Bonaventura*, p. 77).

2.4 DEATH AND THE IMAGE OF NATURE

The funeral procession for the deceased bride goes out and walks through the frozen streets with the casket. Kreuzgang poignantly notes the reaction of indifference of the world: "But nearby, youths are still singing and carousing and squander life and love and poetry in a brief swift intoxication that by morning is dispelled – when their deeds, their dreams, their hopes, their wishes, and everything around them has become sober and grown cold."[54] This too can be regarded as an image of human life in general. People frivolously pursue silly activities and fail to recognize that with every hour their lives are ticking away. They live for quick gratification and never think of their own death. They thus fail to appreciate the brevity of their existence and waste the precious time that they have.

Kreuzgang goes to visit an embittered porter who stands guard outside the wall of the cloister of nuns. The porter converses with a black bird. The allusion is to the legend of Oedipus and the Sphinx found, for example, in Sophocles. The Sphinx stood guard at the entrance to the city of Thebes and prevented anyone from entering until they could answer its riddle correctly. According to the story, the Sphinx asked what kind of creature goes on four legs in the morning, on two at midday, and on three in the evening. The answer is a human being. Children crawl on all fours before they learn to walk on two legs, and then in old age humans are assisted by a cane, and thus walk, as it were, on three legs. Klingemann plays on this, and the porter asked the black bird about a similar mysterious creature:

> "Do you know that creature"—the porter spoke—"whose countenance laughs insidiously when its interposed mask gushes tears; which names God when it is thinking about the devil; which inside, like an apple on the dead sea, contains poisonous dust, while its peel, blossoming red, invites to pleasure; which utters melodic tones through its ingeniously twisted speaking trumpet, while screaming revolt into it; which like the sphinx smiles kindly only in order to mangle, and like the snake merely embraces so intimately for the purpose of pressing its deadly sting into your breast? —Who is this creature, Blackie?" "Man!" croaked the animal in an unpleasant fashion.[55]

Like the ancient riddle, the question here tries to bring together contradictory characteristics of human nature. More importantly, this hints at Kreuzgang's frequent criticism of people for hypocrisy and dissimulation. They are able to think one thing but express something entirely different with whatever mask they happen to be using.

The porter explains the activity taking place in the nunnery. One of the nuns has become pregnant and given birth. Now on that very evening she is to be

---

[54] [Klingemann], *Nachtwachen*, p. 181 (*The Nightwatches of Bonaventura*, p. 78).
[55] [Klingemann], *Nachtwachen*, p. 183 (*The Nightwatches of Bonaventura*, p. 78).

punished by death, being immured alive. From behind the wall of the cemetery, Kreuzgang observes how the nuns come in a procession with the offender, bringing her to her living tomb. But he admits that, despite the cruelty of the punishment, he does not feel moved by the situation. He describes his emotions as running through a scale. Returning to images from drama, Kreuzgang again imagines how humans put on different masks in different situations in life. But they all come and go, and nothing endures: "Life runs past man, but so fleetingly that he calls to it in vain to stand still for him a moment so he can discuss with it what it wants and why it is looking at him. Then the masks whisk by, the sentiments, one more distorted than the other."[56] It is as if humans are not in control of their true character, which is always hidden beneath the masks that pass from one to the other so quickly. Indeed, Kreuzgang raises the question of whether there really is any such thing as a true self behind the masks: "Does no I stand in the mirror, when I step before it – am I only the thought of a thought, the dream of a dream?"[57] Perhaps all of the different roles that we are forced to play deprive us of the opportunity of ever discovering if we are anything else beyond these roles. Are we as humans really an insubstantial nothingness, mere thoughts that correspond to nothing in reality? Here again we find an important contrastive point with Jean Paul, which celebrates the individuality of each person. This is what allows us to form firm relations of friendship and love. But, for Klingemann, people are merely a meaningless dance of masks.

2.5 Kreuzgang's Criticism of Romantic Love

The juxtaposition between real life and the pretended life on the stage of dramaturgy is again an important motif in the "Fourteenth Nightwatch." Kreuzgang explains how he played the role of Hamlet, and the actress portraying Ophelia went insane, just like her character. The role of Hamlet is appropriate for Kreuzgang since it is Hamlet who questions the meaning of life with the famous "To be or not to be" soliloquy,[58] which is referred to explicitly.[59] Kreuzgang is reunited with the actress of Ophelia in the insane asylum, where they are incarcerated in adjoining cells.

Here we gain insight into Kreuzgang's character. At first, he is cynical, and, in harmony with what the reader has seen previously, he sees no deeper truth or meaning in the world or human existence. He appears as a kind of misanthrope who has nothing but disdain for human conventions and beliefs. He explains,

[56] [Klingemann], *Nachtwachen*, pp. 186f. (*The Nightwatches of Bonaventura*, p. 80).
[57] [Klingemann], *Nachtwachen*, p. 188 (*The Nightwatches of Bonaventura*, p. 80). The issue of whether there is a real person behind the masks is taken up again in the "Fourteenth Nightwatch."
[58] Shakespeare, *Hamlet*, Scene 8, lines 57–91, pp. 2040f. (In editions that divide the play into acts, this appears in Act 3, Scene 1).
[59] [Klingemann], *Nachtwachen*, p. 246 (*The Nightwatches of Bonaventura*, p. 105).

2.5 KREUZGANG'S CRITICISM OF ROMANTIC LOVE

"A fellow like me, who is composed of hate and anger and, unlike other human children, seems to have been born not from his mother's body but rather from a pregnant volcano, has little sense for love and the like."[60] But he confesses that now a feeling of love has come over him for the actress. As his love develops, his view of the world comes to resemble more and more the conventional bourgeois belief system with all its absurdities and illusions. He characterizes this as a disease:

> indeed, the symptoms grew more and more critical, and I began to wander about engrossed in myself and felt myself almost human and meekly disposed toward the world. Once I even thought it might be the best possible one, and man himself something more than the first animal on it, indeed, that he had his own worth and could perhaps even be immortal.[61]

Hypnotized by love, he relents in his sober, nihilistic view of the world. Like Jean Paul's Karlson, he is induced by love to see the value of human beings and to believe in their immortality. The satirical allusion to Leibniz's theory of the best of all possible worlds suggests the depth of his folly. A part of him struggles to resist falling in love, but his emotions are overpowering, and he is unable to withstand them.

This split in Kreuzgang's character is evident in his love letter to Ophelia, where he describes love as a kind of cruel joke that is played on humanity. We fall in love and then are parted from our beloved by death, which results in great grief and suffering. It is as if there were an "evil fiend" tormenting people with love in order to make their lives more miserable.[62] Nature has instilled the sentiment of love in us in order that we mate and reproduce. But this is but a trick that nature plays on us. Love itself is simply an illusion that only leads to sadness. It is far better to hate the world and other people since only in this way can one be truly independent and self-sufficient. Kreuzgang tries to discourage Ophelia with Hamlet's line: "Get thee to a nunnery."[63] But in the same letter he cannot hold back declaring his love for her.

In her response, Ophelia raises the question of the difference between theater and reality, between the dramatic role being played and the actress herself. In her epistemological reflections, she calls into question whether there is any final truth at all:

> Does anything in itself exist, or is all only word and breath and much fantasy? —See, now I will never be able to find out whether I am a

---

[60] [Klingemann], *Nachtwachen*, p. 233 (*The Nightwatches of Bonaventura*, p. 100).
[61] [Klingemann], *Nachtwachen*, pp. 238f. (*The Nightwatches of Bonaventura*, p. 102).
[62] [Klingemann], *Nachtwachen*, p. 242 (*The Nightwatches of Bonaventura*, p. 103).
[63] [Klingemann], *Nachtwachen*, p. 241 (*The Nightwatches of Bonaventura*, p. 103). Shakespeare, *Hamlet*, Scene 8, line 120, p. 2042 (in editions that divide the play into acts, this appears in Act 3, Scene 1).

dream—whether it is merely play or truth, and whether the truth in turn is more than play—one shell covers the next, and I am often on the verge of losing my mind over this.[64]

This can be read, in a sense, as a commentary on Kant's epistemology, which claims that we can only know representations and not things as they are in themselves. Kant's critics pointed out that since everything is a representation as an object of consciousness, the very idea of a thing-in-itself, apart from consciousness, is an absurdity. Everything must be seen from a certain perspective or via certain modes of knowing, and there is no divine view from nowhere that has immediate access to things.

It will be noted that Kreuzgang indirectly alludes to Kant's theory of space and time as faculties of human perception in his letter of Ophelia. He speaks of the "metaphysical sophistries that [he] brought back from the university."[65] Then he explains to Ophelia, "according to the newest school we do not know whether we are in fact standing on our feet or on our heads, except that we have assumed the first by ourselves on trust and in faith."[66] According to the Kantian view, we can only know what appears to us as a representation or an object of perception, and we must assume that there are things-in-themselves behind these, but this cannot be demonstrated metaphysically and is thus a point of faith. We cannot know if we are "standing on our feet or on our heads" since space is not a fact about the world but only a part of our perceptual apparatus. Therefore, we cannot know if there is really space outside us, and if there is, what our attitude in it might be.

Ophelia then takes up the issue of the real self (raised earlier in the "Tenth Nightwatch") behind all the roles that we play in life. Does such a thing exist? She toys with the question of nominalism. Is love something that really exists or is it too just a word or a name?[67] She desperately searches for her true self, independent of her dramatic roles. In response, Kreuzgang, under the guise of his former role of Hamlet, argues that everything is mere acting, or in Kantian language, everything is representation with nothing real or substantial. Ophelia's dualistic conception of a real person in contrast to a role is misconceived. There are only roles and no true persons. There is nothing lasting since representations are always fleeting and changing:

> It is all role, the role itself and the play-actor who is behind it, and in him in turn his thoughts and plans and enthusiasms and buffooneries—all belongs to the moment and swiftly flees, like the word on the comedian's lips. —All is even but theater, whether the comedian may be playing on

---

[64] [Klingemann], *Nachtwachen*, pp. 243f. (*The Nightwatches of Bonaventura*, p. 104).
[65] [Klingemann], *Nachtwachen*, p. 240 (*The Nightwatches of Bonaventura*, p. 103).
[66] [Klingemann], *Nachtwachen*, p. 240 (*The Nightwatches of Bonaventura*, p. 103).
[67] [Klingemann], *Nachtwachen*, p. 243 (*The Nightwatches of Bonaventura*, p. 104).

2.5 KREUZGANG'S CRITICISM OF ROMANTIC LOVE

earth itself or two steps higher on the boards, or two steps lower in the ground, where the worms pick up the cue of the exiting king.[68]

In the "Eighth Nightwatch," the distinction was made between the society's large stage and the smaller theatrical stage.[69] Here the same idea is found with the actor "playing on earth itself or two steps higher on the boards." It is all the same in theater and in real life since we are always playing a role. But here a new dimension is added to the dualism when Klingemann mentions playing one's role "two steps lower in the ground," that is, when one is dead. Even death itself is a role. There is nothing enduring about us or the situation:

> everything vanishes again, though, and extinguishes and transmutes itself—including the spring in the human heart; and when the props are wholly removed, only an odd naked skeleton stands behind, without color and life, and the skeleton grins at the other comedians still dashing about.[70]

All human activity looks absurd from this perspective, which sees everything as vain. In a sense the skeleton is a metaphor for the Kantian thing-in-itself. Death is the only thing that is stable and enduring, in contrast to the representations. Yet, death itself is also nothing: "See, there the skeleton stands and casts a handful of dust into the air and now collapses itself; but afterward sardonic laughter resounds. That is the world spirit, or the devil – or the Nothing echoing!"[71] Death thus seems to mock all our activities and dreams, even the sentiment of love. Ophelia nonetheless continues in the belief that she has a true self that she just needs to discover if she can only cast aside the role she is playing.

Kreuzgang, qua Hamlet, quotes the first lines of the soliloquy: "To be or not to be."[72] The argument that Shakespeare's Hamlet gives is that, despite all the difficulties and trials of life, most people do not immediately commit suicide because they fear that something worse might await them after death. This fear motivates us to endure the many hardships and sufferings involved in human existence. Kreuzgang is critical of this view. In his role of Hamlet, he claims that he was naïve to have thought such things previously. Now, however, he is fully disabused of any conception of immortality and thus the prospect of any form of suffering after death. Death is simply nothingness.

After Kreuzgang and Ophelia consummate their love, as he predicted, it ends sadly. Although he enjoyed moments of happiness, Kreuzgang has a premonition of the end with a vision of the nothingness: "The storm raged wildly

---

[68] [Klingemann], *Nachtwachen*, pp. 245f. (*The Nightwatches of Bonaventura*, p. 105).
[69] [Klingemann], *Nachtwachen*, p. 148 (*The Nightwatches of Bonaventura*, p. 64).
[70] [Klingemann], *Nachtwachen*, p. 246 (*The Nightwatches of Bonaventura*, p. 105).
[71] [Klingemann], *Nachtwachen*, p. 246 (*The Nightwatches of Bonaventura*, p. 105).
[72] [Klingemann], *Nachtwachen*, p. 246 (*The Nightwatches of Bonaventura*, p. 105). Shakespeare, *Hamlet*, Scene 8, lines 57–91, pp. 2040f. (in editions that divide the play into acts, this appears in Act 3, Scene 1).

about the madhouse. – I lay against the bars and looked into the night, beyond which there was nothing further to be seen in heaven and on earth. It was for me as if I were standing close to the Nothing and cried into it, but there was no more sound."[73] He thus anticipates the death of Ophelia in the neighboring cell. He continues,

> I imagined I was passing away. Then I saw myself with me alone in the Nothing; only the late earth was still flickering far out in the distance, as an extinguishing spark—but it was only a thought of mine that was just ending. A single tone quavered gravely and earnestly through the void—it was time chiming out, and eternity now set in.[74]

This frightening and sobering picture of death can be contrasted with Jean Paul's ecstatic vision (in *The Valley of Campan*) of rising into the night sky with a hot-air balloon, where he is deeply moved by what he takes to be a proof of his immortality and the profound meaning that humans have in the universe. While Kreuzgang has his vision, his beloved Ophelia dies with their stillborn child at her breast. By contrast, the image for Jean Paul is one of everlasting love and life. Given such depths of human suffering, Kreuzgang even has a laudatory word for death: "Praise God there is a death, and afterward no eternity!"[75] In her own way, Ophelia also praises death, which she conceives as the only way to escape her role in the play.

We are left with a powerful melancholy image of Ophelia who endures great suffering, dies, and departs from an indifferent world. Klingemann continues with the theatrical images: "There the curtain fell, and Ophelia exited – no one applauded, and it was as if no viewer were present."[76] The silence evokes a sense of nihilism, the despair that human life is finite, and there is no greater meaning or eternal life that can be expected. This can be seen as an image of human existence in general. Humans live and die on their own small planet with no God looking over them to see their plight. The entire human race will one day be extinguished, and there will be no one to witness that it was ever even there. Each of us pursues our goals and projects with a general indifference to the many others who die every day.

The difference between the power of love in *The Nightwatches* and in Jean Paul's *The Valley of Campan* is striking. Klingemann portrays love as a sad and tragic matter that yields only fleeting moments of happiness but always ends in separation and death. At the beginning and at the end, with only a brief space of time in between, Kreuzgang is a cynic with regard to love. It is something that should be avoided at all costs since it always ends in grief. Being in

---

[73] [Klingemann], *Nachtwachen*, pp. 249f. (*The Nightwatches of Bonaventura*, p. 106).
[74] [Klingemann], *Nachtwachen*, p. 250 (*The Nightwatches of Bonaventura*, p. 107).
[75] [Klingemann], *Nachtwachen*, p. 252 (*The Nightwatches of Bonaventura*, p. 107).
[76] [Klingemann], *Nachtwachen*, p. 253 (*The Nightwatches of Bonaventura*, p. 108).

2.6 The Nothingness of Human Existence

love is idiocy that only blind fools succumb to. By contrast, in Jean Paul the love we feel for another person is a key argument for immortality since it is, to his mind, inconceivable that God would create us and allow us to love one another, only then to destroy us. Despite his scientific mindset, Karlson cannot bring himself to believe that his beloved Gione will one day die and be destroyed forever. It is his love for her that caused him to capitulate and to give up his purely naturalistic position.

2.6 The Nothingness of Human Existence

At the start of the "Sixteenth Nightwatch" Klingemann refers to William Hogarth's etching *The Tail Piece of the Bathos* from 1764 (Figure 2.2).[77] It was noted in the previous chapter that Hogarth was also an inspiration for Jean Paul and Lichtenberg.[78] Hogarth was known for his satirical paintings, and it is easy to imagine that he would have been a favorite of Klingemann. *The Tail Piece* was Hogarth's last work, which he made knowing that he only had a short time left to live. The motif of the end of the world is thus to be understood also as referring to the end of Hogarth's life and work. The idea of the work as a "tail piece" refers to the fact that it was intended to be the final illustration in a volume of his collected sketches.

The Tail Piece portrays the end of the world with the grim reaper or Father Time as the central motif. He is portrayed with the wings of an angel and the horns of the devil, and he holds a scythe. After the destruction of all humanity, the reaper says his last word, "Finis," and is on the point of death. He holds in his hand his last will and testament, which states that he leaves behind all the atoms in the universe to chaos. Hogarth's image contains many symbols of the passage of time: an hourglass, a sun dial, a candle burning, a newspaper called *The Times*. There are also many indications of the vanity of human accomplishment: a broken gun, a broken broom, a broken pipe, a broken crown, a broken palate, a dilapidated house, a tombstone, a broken church tower. Each of these can be seen as symbols of the different spheres of life: the military, domestic life, royalty, politics, the church, and art. There is a theatrical allusion, which Klingemann also uses, with a book containing a dramatic work opened to the last page, where it reads, "*exeunt omnes*."[79] The sun is depicted in the background riding a broken chariot that is plunging downward. The satirical element in Hogarth's work can be found in its sober atmosphere that offers no hint

---

[77] [Klingemann], *Nachtwachen*, p. 272 (*The Nightwatches of Bonaventura*, p. 117). See also *Nachtwachen*, p. 59 (*The Nightwatches of Bonaventura*, p. 26); *Nachtwachen*, p. 123 (*The Nightwatches of Bonaventura*, p. 54). See Gerald Gillespie, "Night-Piece and *Tail-Piece*: Bonaventura's Relation to Hogarth," *Arcadia*, vol. 8, 1973, pp. 284–295.

[78] Chapter 1, Section 1.2, p. 44.

[79] See [Klingemann], *Nachtwachen*, p. 248 (*The Nightwatches of Bonaventura*, p. 106).

Figure 2.2 William Hogarth's etching, *The Tailpiece, or the Bathos* (1764)

of immortality or redemption. In this way it can be seen as a criticism of earlier artists who portray death as leading to a glorious afterlife of bliss in heaven. Here, by contrast, the end of the world and of all human life is accompanied by no higher purpose. This is a disturbing image that Kreuzgang invokes.[80]

This final chapter of *The Nightwatches* takes place in a cemetery, as usual, at night. Kreuzgang wanders through the graves and contemplates the dead lying under them. The role of nature is important here. Instead of a beautiful, vibrant, living nature, as we would expect in Romantic poetry, here Kreuzgang presents us with a picture of dead nature. He refers to an "expired rotting tree" that "crumbles wholly into dust."[81] Even nature itself cannot escape the fate of death. It comes into being, decays, and passes out of existence.

---

[80] For the connection between Klingemann and Hogarth, see Gillespie, "Night-Piece and Tail-Piece."

[81] [Klingemann], *Nachtwachen*, p. 274 (*The Nightwatches of Bonaventura*, p. 118).

2.6 THE NOTHINGNESS OF HUMAN EXISTENCE

There is a poet among the graves, struggling in vain to compose a piece about nature. Kreuzgang observes him and then falls asleep among the graves. A dream about the poet comes to him, which is described as follows:

> Then in my sleep I heard the storm come up, and the poet wanted to set the thunder to music and compose words for it, but the tones eluded arrangement and the words seemed to explode and scatter in disarray as single incomprehensible syllables. Sweat stood on the poet's brow because he could inject no sense into his nature poem—the fool had hitherto tried poetizing solely on paper.[82]

The poet works with regularities of rhyme and meter. Since he wants to write about nature, he tries to formulate his descriptions of it in this way, but nature defies him. The point is that there is no reason or *logos* in nature. It is absurd to ask nature for an explanation of death or the destruction of the earth. There is no answer to this. There is no other "why" than the basic laws of physics and biology. This conception of an irrational nature with no interest in human needs is antithetical to the view of nature in German idealism. The idealists known for their philosophy of nature, such as Schelling and Steffens, conceived of nature as the external rationality of the human mind. It has its own principle that develops on its own in a way that is comprehensible to reason.

The poet next tries his hand at a poem about immortality. But he also fails in this. He uses a skull as a support for the paper he is writing on, and the skull seems to mock his undertaking. Like Jean Paul, the poet wants to depict immortality in a positive and hopeful manner, "like the radiant sunrise after the deepest darkest night."[83] But Kreuzgang recognizes these as mere "fantasies."[84] The poet, engrossed in his work, fails to notice that the graves have opened and the dead are staring at him, as if to demonstrate the absurdity of his idea of immortality. The grim image of the smiling corpses and skeletons is proof enough of the finality of death. In his poem, he depicts the Last Judgment, which will awaken the dead, but "none wished to awake."[85] The dead seem to reject his conception of immortality:

> below they all merely shook indignantly and turned from him onto their sides as so to sleep more tranquilly and show him the naked backs of their heads. —"What, is there then no God!" he exclaimed wildly, and the echo gave him back the word "God" loudly and perceptibly. He stood there, now quite naïve, and chewed on his pen.[86]

This, of course, recalls Jean Paul's image of Christ returning from the heavens to announce that there is no God, and the dead listening to his message

---

[82] [Klingemann], *Nachtwachen*, pp. 274f. (*The Nightwatches of Bonaventura*, p. 118).
[83] [Klingemann], *Nachtwachen*, p. 276 (*The Nightwatches of Bonaventura*, p. 118).
[84] [Klingemann], *Nachtwachen*, p. 276 (*The Nightwatches of Bonaventura*, p. 118).
[85] [Klingemann], *Nachtwachen*, p. 276 (*The Nightwatches of Bonaventura*, p. 119).
[86] [Klingemann], *Nachtwachen*, pp. 276f. (*The Nightwatches of Bonaventura*, p. 119).

incredulously. Here in *The Nightwatches*, there is something significant about the fact that the word "God" is echoed back to the poet. This seems to suggest that the idea of God is a human convention. We can hear the echo of the word when it is spoken in the world, but again, as with Jean Paul's "The Dead Christ," we look for God in vain in the universe itself.[87] This seems to anticipate Feuerbach's idea that God is a projection or objectification of ideas of the human mind. According to this view, God is simply an echo or reflection of human properties but not an independently existing external being. Although the poet tries to describe immortality, his pen does not write. It is as if the pen knows that there is nothing to write about and prevents the poet from producing absurd fabrications. Again, as with "The Dead Christ," all of this is but a dream.

When Kreuzgang awakens, he sees a Bohemian gypsy woman who turns out to be his mother. She recounts to him the beginning of his life's story. She reveals that his father was an alchemist, whose nearby grave Kreuzgang had already noted. He learns that he was conceived at the moment when his father succeeded in conjuring the devil. Kreuzgang and nihilism are thus associated with the demonic. His mother directly observes that he bears a striking resemblance to the devil.[88] This raises the question of Klingemann's intentions with the piece. Does he thereby mean to suggest that we should not take seriously Kreuzgang's nihilistic worldview since it is a product of the devil or that Kreuzgang himself represents the devil? Or does it mean that we all have in us a part of the devil, which appears when we have certain moods that lead to nihilistic thoughts? The story is nothing short of a personal revelation for Kreuzgang, who at least gains insight into his life and character, however depressing that might be. His mother wishes to see his father again, and so she begins the macabre work of exhuming him.

While she is digging, Kreuzgang walks around the cemetery with a visionary who claims to be able to see the dead in their graves, provided that their bodies have not completely turned to dust. The more they have decomposed, the less of them he can see. This emphasizes the inevitable destruction or disappearance of the living after their dead bodies decay. But it also reflects symbolically the way in which the memory of the dead gradually disappears in the minds of the surviving relatives and friends as time passes. After a few generations and the passage of enough time, there is no one remaining to think of a specific dead person, who then disappears from living memory altogether. The man tells Kreuzgang that he is there to find his deceased beloved, despite the

---

[87] See Jean Paul, *Blumen-, Frucht- und Dornenstücke oder Ehestand, Tod und Hochzeit des Armenadvokaten F. St. Siebenkäs im Reichsmarktflecken Kuhschnappel*, vols. 1–3, Berlin: In Carl Matzdorff's Buchhandlung 1796–97, vol. 1, p. 7 (English translation: *Flower, Fruit, and Thorn Pieces; Or, The Wedded Life, Death, and Marriage of Firmian Stanislaus Siebenkæs*, trans. by Alexander Ewing, London: George Bell and Sons 1897, p. 263).

[88] [Klingemann], *Nachtwachen*, p. 280 (*The Nightwatches of Bonaventura*, p. 120).

2.6 THE NOTHINGNESS OF HUMAN EXISTENCE 91

fact that seeing the ghosts of the other dead is so frightening for him. As they walk along together, the man tells Kreuzgang about the lives of the dead whose graves they pass. They see the grave of Kreuzgang's Ophelia, and the man can in fact see her with her child. Finally, the man finds his dead beloved and tries in vain to embrace her.

In the interim Kreuzgang's mother ultimately manages to dig up his father, but instead of being emotionally moved by this, Kreuzgang reflects on a worm that is eating the decomposing body. He addresses the worm as follows:

> On how many kings' and princes' brains have you gorged yourself, you plump parasite, to attain this degree of corpulence? How many philosophers' idealisms have you reduced to this your realism? You are an irrefutable proof for the real utility of ideas, as you have crammed yourself valiantly with the wisdom of so many heads.[89]

The point seems to be that the ideas of philosophy are all ultimately empty productions of the human mind with no reality. In the end all ideas are reduced to nothing, and material being always trumps the ephemeral thought. Yet even physical being itself decays. A part of Klingemann's criticism seems to be directed specifically at the German idealists, Kant, Fichte, and the young Schelling. The implicit critique is that notions of God, immortality, and even meaning in life belong to the realm of ideas, which have no reality in the real world. This applies to the entire sphere of religion, which consists of ideas, or, if one will, illusions. On Kreuzgang's nihilistic view, "in the inner Pantheon all gods crash down from their pedestals,"[90] having been exposed as fraudulent. This can be regarded as an anticipation of Nietzsche's criticism of religion.

Kreuzgang contrasts the heights reached by kings and princes in their prime with their inevitable death, where even a tiny worm has power over them:

> Where now is the eye that smiled so enchantingly or commanded so threateningly? —You, satirist, sit alone in the empty socket of bone and peer insolently and maliciously about and make the head into your dwelling (and something even worse), in which formerly the schemes of a Caesar and an Alexander were born.[91]

This recalls the famous graveyard scene in Shakespeare's *Hamlet*.[92] Contemplating the skull of the deceased Yorick, the former court jester whom he knew in his youth, Hamlet notes that this is the sad fate of all human beings. Even the greatest names in human history, such as Alexander the Great or Julius Caesar, end up as bare skulls and then dust. The greatest accomplishments of

---

[89] [Klingemann], *Nachtwachen*, p. 289 (*The Nightwatches of Bonaventura*, p. 123).
[90] [Klingemann], *Nachtwachen*, p. 290 (*The Nightwatches of Bonaventura*, p. 124).
[91] [Klingemann], *Nachtwachen*, pp. 289f. (*The Nightwatches of Bonaventura*, p. 124).
[92] Shakespeare, *Hamlet* Scene 18, pp. 2081–2088 (in editions that divide the play into acts, this appears in *Hamlet*, Act 5, Scene 1).

humanity ultimately are only trivialities of the human mind that in the end amount to nothing. The sober truth is that everything dies and decomposes, and no human achievement, regardless of how great, ever endures. Death is always the victor:

> What now is this palace that can enclose a whole world and a heaven; this fairy castle in which love's wonders enchantingly delude; this microcosm in which all that is great and splendid and everything terrible and fearsome reside together in embryo, which brought forth temples and gods, inquisitions and devils; this tailpiece of the creation—the human head!—shelter for a worm! —Oh, what is the world if that which it thought is nothing, and everything in it only transitory fantasy![93]

The argument is that human accomplishment is merely a thought, and thought has no reality. Therefore, no human accomplishment can ever have any enduring reality or truth. With an allusion to Kant, Kreuzgang mocks the idea of "the autonomy of spirit,"[94] which, since it is just an idea, can never conquer death and the destruction of the world.

In the end Kreuzgang fully embraces the nothingness of human existence, which he has been arguing for all along: "I will look fiercely into Nothingness and pledge fraternity with It, that I may perceive no further human traces when, at last, It seizes me, too!"[95] This is the train of thought that Kreuzgang has as he exhumes his father's body and opens the lid of the casket. He seems in no way moved by any kind of natural filial feeling.

Kreuzgang reflects on the place of the earth in the universe and argues that the existence of other planets and life on them in no way changes the fact of human mortality. The facts of the cosmos hold little consolation to him:

> ... no doubt countless stars are sparkling and swimming there above us in heaven's ocean, but if they have worlds, as many clever heads assert, then there are also skulls on them and worms, as here below; and that holds throughout the whole immensity, and the Basel dance of death merely grows all the merrier and wilder thereby and the ballroom grander.[96]

His view can be juxtaposed to the more optimistic one presented by Jean Paul, who cannot believe that in the end all the life on earth and in the entire universe will be extinguished. It is simply unthinkable that God would create the world in this way. But for Klingemann, while humans yearn for some kind of God who can offer consolation, there is nothing but the cold force of nature. The universe itself has no "heart."[97]

---

[93] [Klingemann], *Nachtwachen*, p. 290 (*The Nightwatches of Bonaventura*, p. 124).
[94] [Klingemann], *Nachtwachen*, p. 290 (*The Nightwatches of Bonaventura*, p. 124).
[95] [Klingemann], *Nachtwachen*, p. 291 (*The Nightwatches of Bonaventura*, p. 124).
[96] [Klingemann], *Nachtwachen*, p. 292 (*The Nightwatches of Bonaventura*, p. 125).
[97] [Klingemann], *Nachtwachen*, p. 293 (*The Nightwatches of Bonaventura*, p. 125).

2.6 THE NOTHINGNESS OF HUMAN EXISTENCE 93

Kreuzgang seems to suggest that the correct disposition to this is first to reject all the illusory forms of consolation that constitute human culture in general. This includes the idea of love, which is a deception that always ends in death and grief. These views, of course, separate him from most everyone else in society, who all doggedly cling to their illusory beliefs for fear of the gloomy alternative. But once one realizes that the only true principle of the universe is nothingness, the only authentic response is laughter, even in the face of death: "I refuse to love and will remain quite cold and frozen so as to be able, if possible, to laugh away when the giant's hand crushes me, too!"[98] He criticizes the religious idea of prayer, which he regards as in a sense begging the gods for entry into heaven. It is absurd to think that one will be granted immortality for "a little morality" and "comparative virtue."[99] These belong to the cherished but absurd illusions of religion. Kreuzgang instead proposes a disposition of defiance in the face of the nothingness. In this way at least a modicum of human dignity is preserved. This anticipates the motif of rebellion that is so prominent in the work of the existentialists, such as Camus.

Kreuzgang observes that his father's body has completely decomposed into dust and become nothing. He repeatedly echoes the word "nothing" in the final lines of the work:

> "At my touch all crumbles into ashes, and there is only a handful of dust lying yet on the ground, and a few satisfied worms creep secretly away like moral funeral orators who have outdone themselves at the banquet of sorrow. I strew this handful of paternal dust into the air and it remains —Nothing!" On the grave beyond, the visionary is still standing and embracing Nothing! And the echo in the charnel house cries for the last time *nothing*![100]

The universe is on an inevitable course hurling towards destruction, and this involves the annihilation of everything: galaxies, solar systems, and all living creatures. It is absurd to seek a theodicy in nature or progress in the human or natural sphere. That all human existence ends in nothing seems clearly to be the message. Even though it is difficult for people to accept this, it is the hard truth of the matter. Most people prefer to live in an unreflective state by throwing themselves into traditional belief systems, which are simply a patchwork of fantasy. Although they might enjoy their delusions, they cannot completely escape slipping into nihilistic notions. The nagging thought of nihilism comes out involuntarily in moments of anxiety or despair. As was illustrated in "The Dead Christ," this is often the subject of our nightmares. It belongs to the realm of the night, which we try to repress and forget during the day when we escape into our unreflective routines and habits.

---

[98] [Klingemann], *Nachtwachen*, p. 293 (*The Nightwatches of Bonaventura*, p. 125).
[99] [Klingemann], *Nachtwachen*, p. 295 (*The Nightwatches of Bonaventura*, p. 126).
[100] [Klingemann], *Nachtwachen*, p. 296 (*The Nightwatches of Bonaventura*, p. 126).

We have seen the strong influence of the existential side of Shakespeare on Klingemann. In this same context, we can think of Prospero's famous lines from *The Tempest*:

> Our revels now are ended. These our actors,
> As I foretold you, were all spirits, and
> Are melted into air, into thin air;
> And, like the baseless fabric of this vision,
> The cloud-capped towers, the gorgeous palaces,
> The solemn temples, the great globe itself,
> Yea, all which it inherit, shall dissolve;
> And, like this insubstantial pageant faded,
> Leave not a rack behind. We are such stuff
> As dreams are made on, and our little life
> Is rounded with a sleep.[101]

While the immediate reference of these remarks is to the play, which, once performed, disappears, there is an unsettling suspicion that this is also intended to refer to life and the world in general. Kreuzgang's echo of "nothing" and his images of skulls, skeletons, and dust seem to be consistent with this view of all human existence melting away and dissolving into nothing.

2.7 Klingemann and Jean Paul

The Nightwatches can be fruitfully compared with the works by Jean Paul that were discussed in the previous chapter.[102] Both address the problem of nihilism, but their conclusions are quite different. For Jean Paul it is primarily love that prevents people from slipping into nihilism. Despite their knowledge of the modern natural sciences, most people still cannot bring themselves to believe that there is really no deeper meaning in the universe and that human beings face complete annihilation with death. For Jean Paul, this is simply not in harmony with the dignity of human beings. We recall Jean Paul's encomium for virtue, beauty, and truth that reside in the human heart alone and that raise us above nature. By contrast, Klingemann has a much more cynical picture of human nature. Humans are liars, hypocrites, and fools. On this view, Jean Paul's triad of virtue, beauty, and truth is an illusion sprung from human arrogance and vanity. There is no reason to think that there is anything redeeming about human beings whatsoever. Even if God existed, what reason would he possibly have to grant such creatures immortality or to attach the meaning of the universe to them? In the final scene of *The Nightwatches* the lover tries in

---

[101] Shakespeare, *The Tempest*, Act 4, Scene 1, lines 148–158, p. 3118.
[102] For the comparison of Jean Paul with *The Nightwatches*, see Andreas Mielke, *Zeitgenosse Bonaventura*, Stuttgart: Hans-Dieter Heinz Akademischer Verlag 1984; Katritzky, *A Guide to Bonaventura's "Nightwatches,"* pp. 13–16.

vain to embrace his dead beloved. There is no hope or consolation here. This marks a strong contrastive point to the all-conquering power of love in Jean Paul, embodied in Karlson's deep affection for Gione. For Klingemann, the inability to regain the dead lover who disappears into nothingness inevitably leaves us with a sense of nihilism. Moreover, Kreuzgang's sad affair with Ophelia illustrates the futility of love. By contrast, the power of love for the dead is, for Jean Paul, a proof for immortality. In a word, while Jean Paul is drunk with optimism and hope, Klingemann leaves the reader with disconsolate pessimism.

A comparison of the end of *The Valley of Campan* with that of *The Nightwatches* makes it clear that while Jean Paul wants to offer a solution to the problem of meaninglessness in the universe, Klingemann seems to have no such program. While the latter suggests that laughter is an appropriate response, there is little in *The Nightwatches* that can be conceived as offering any consolation or hope. The universe is what it is, and there is no point in trying to dress it up as if it were conducive to our desires. All such attempts only end in illusions and forms of self-deception.

The endings of "The Dead Christ" and *The Nightwatches* also represent another important point of contrast. In Jean Paul's work the narrator awakens from a bad dream and is again immediately reconciled with the world and religious belief. There is a great sense of relief that God still exists and that there is still meaning in the universe. It is as if the whole idea of Christ coming down and declaring that there is no God is just a thought experiment that leaves no lasting mark. By contrast, the final images of *The Nightwatches* offer no form of peace or reconciliation. There is just the repeated empty echo of "nothing." The human condition is a bad dream from which we never awake.

Yet another key point of contrast between Klingemann's and Jean Paul's respective responses to nihilism can be found in Klingemann's humor and Jean Paul's pathos. While there are a few light moments of playfulness in the texts by Jean Paul that we explored, with regard to the key issue of immortality or nihilism there is no humor whatsoever. For him, this is an issue of the greatest possible gravity. By contrast, Klingemann emphasizes the absurdity of existence in the face of nihilism. For him, the lack of meaning is something that is used towards humorous and satirical ends. He exposes the absurdity of how seriously people take themselves and their lives. His motto is "Just leave me laughter my whole life long, and I will hold out here below!"[103] The story of humanity is appropriately introduced by a clown. Klingemann's work can probably be best described as a tragicomedy, a term that he uses himself to describe world history.[104] If all human society and history are just a farce, then the rational

---

[103] [Klingemann], *Nachtwachen*, p. 260 (*The Nightwatches of Bonaventura*, p. 111).
[104] [Klingemann], *Nachtwachen*, p. 60 (*The Nightwatches of Bonaventura*, p. 27).

person is the one who regards it as such and not those who meticulously construct fantasies around it and put on a serious face.[105]

The distinction between the approaches of Jean Paul and Klingemann can be captured by Joshua Reynolds' painting, *David Garrick between Tragedy and Comedy* (Figure 1.1) that was referred to by Jean Paul in *The Valley of Campan*. As was discussed in the previous chapter,[106] in this painting Reynolds shows the dramatist David Garrick caught in a dilemma between the muses of comedy and tragedy. To Jean Paul's disapprobation, Reynolds portrays Garrick as choosing comedy. For Jean Paul, the seriousness of human existence dictates that tragedy be given the primary position. The issue of nihilism is thus a serious and sober affair. By contrast, Klingemann chooses the muse of comedy for his response. Laughter is the correct disposition to the meaninglessness and finitude of human existence. The two sides represented in the views of Jean Paul and Klingemann are reflected in Virginia Woolf's *A Room of Her Own*, where she writes, "the beauty of the world, which is so soon to perish, has two edges, one of laughter, one of anguish, cutting the heart asunder."[107]

Another key point of contrast can be illustrated by the characters of Karlson and Kreuzgang. In effect they both seem to represent in general the same sober scientific view of the world. But despite this similarity, they are very different. Karlson is a well-adjusted member of society with a group of friends for whom he has great affection. He even harbors a love for Gione and thus has a fairly normal emotional life. By contrast, Kreuzgang is a loner and an outsider who is completely alienated from mainstream society. With the exception of Ophelia, he keeps people at a distance and is unable to have any feelings for others. Even in the case of Ophelia, he tries to resist falling in love as best he can and regards amorous relations as pure folly. He is unmoved at the sight of the poet who hanged himself,[108] or the young boy who committed suicide to escape the Last Judgment and the boredom that comes with immortality.[109] He is even unmoved at the sight of the decomposing corpse of his own father. All these horrific images leave him cold. Kreuzgang clearly has a more cynical edge than Karlson. A part of Klingemann's portrayal of Kreuzgang in this way seems to suggest that anyone who wants to hold the nihilistic view consistently will end up in an emotional vacuum, in a state of alienation from the rest of humanity. Kreuzgang is a radical nonconformist and social deviant, and for this reason he is committed to an insane asylum. Anyone wishing to tread this path will be condemned to the life of a lonely outcast. For Jean Paul's Karlson, this price is too high to pay, and he finally capitulates on the key point

---

[105] [Klingemann], *Nachtwachen*, p. 73 (*The Nightwatches of Bonaventura*, p. 32).
[106] Chapter 1, Section 1.2, pp. 45–46.
[107] Virginia Woolf, *A Room of One's Own*, London: Hogarth Press 1935 [1929], p. 25.
[108] [Klingemann], *Nachtwachen*, pp. 134f. (*The Nightwatches of Bonaventura*, pp. 58f.).
[109] [Klingemann], *Nachtwachen*, p. 98 (*The Nightwatches of Bonaventura*, p. 43).

of immortality and thereby rejoins respectable society. But there is no such repentance for Kreuzgang, who insists on the nihilistic view to the end.

Despite their differences, Jean Paul and Klingemann are in agreement in their rejection of German idealism, which they believe is so hypnotized by the victory parade of modern science that it does not even fully appreciate the issue of nihilism. Its feeble attempts to address the problem are regarded as overly naïve and optimistic with regard to human nature and the power of reason. The German idealists fail to grasp the full depths of human despair in the face of a barren universe, antithetical to human wishes. Instead, they still attempt to resolve the problem by embracing some form of religious solution. Human nature is not an embodiment of pure reason, and nature itself is not the externalization of it. Instead, nature is a horrible, inhospitable place that can only lead to despair. In the end, nature crushes all forms of life in the entire universe. The German idealists fail to see that their praise of reason is just one more unfounded fantasy of the human mind.

2.8 Klingemann's Message

With Klingemann's rejection of the German idealists' abstract philosophical reflection on metaphysical issues that are irrelevant for the individual, we can see an anticipation of twentieth-century existentialism.[110] Klingemann believes that thinkers such as Kant and Fichte end in absurdities. Their approach to philosophy has nothing to do with the real life of people, which is an important point of emphasis in existentialism. So wrapped up in their meaningless abstractions, the philosophers of the age fail to see the problem of meaning that is right in front of them. Like Jean Paul, Klingemann thus rejects the university philosophy of the day as irrelevant. Even when it does ostensibly address serious issues such as nihilism, it renders them ridiculous by taking them up into the world of abstractions. For Kreuzgang, philosophers and scholars in general are simply highly educated fools. Like the existentialists, Klingemann can be seen as making a plea for rendering philosophy relevant by dropping the hopeless abstractions of conceptual analysis and focusing instead on real-life experiences.

Another point of contact with existentialism is the motif of the echo that recurs in *The Nightwatches*. While humans seek meaning in the universe, there is none to be found. The only kind of meaning that exists is what we put there. Human experience thus does not come from our interaction with the world or God but rather is only an echo of our own voice. This rings empty for one expecting a deeper transcendent meaning. The echo tells us that we are alone in the universe with no God to help us. The existentialists also put emphasis on the primacy of

---

[110] For the connection between Klingemann and existentialism, see Gerald Gillespie, "Bonaventura's Romantic Agony: Prevision of an Art of Existential Despair," *Modern Language Notes*, vol. 85, 1970, pp. 697–672; Kenneth M. Ralston, *The Captured Horizon: Heidegger and the "Nachtwachen von Bonaventura,"* Tübingen: Max Niemeyer Verlag 1994.

bare existence itself with nothing more. This bare existence is something that disturbs us, as is illustrated by Sartre's famous analysis of the tree in *Nausea*.[111]

Likewise, Klingemann's motif of rebellion in the form of Prometheus and the Titans also anticipates existentialism,[112] such as, for example in the work of Albert Camus. Klingemann seems to regard the idea of revolting against a meaningless universe as a hopeless gesture. It is absurd to think that rebellion can ever be successful. However, he seems to agree with Camus that in rebellion we have at least a means of salvaging the dignity and integrity of human existence.

What exactly is Klingemann's message with this strange work? Is he really recommending the nihilistic position of the strange Kreuzgang? This would presumably be saying too much. However, it seems clear that there is something about Kreuzgang's social criticism and sober view of human existence that must be taken seriously, as is the case with Hogarth's paintings and engravings, which many people regard as cynical. Klingemann seems to be enjoining people to abandon their illusions and accept the harsh truths about the nature of the universe, which includes human existence. Perhaps using Juvenal and Hogarth as his models, Klingemann can be read as a satirist intent on exposing the many aspects of human folly.[113] As we have seen, a part of this is social criticism aimed at the common traditions and beliefs by which people live their lives. Kreuzgang thinks that people are "waking sleepers"[114] who need to be awakened to the sad facts of the world.

The main objection issued in *The Nightwatches* seems to be the scientific one: we all just turn to dust in death. Our minds or ideas are necessarily connected to our bodies, and so when our bodies turn to dust, our minds are also destroyed forever. Human existence is meaningless in the universe. As was the case with Jean Paul, the issue of nihilism arises as a result of the new scientific worldview. Kreuzgang is critical of the pride of the Enlightenment thinkers and their naïve zeal to carry out their project. He has recognized that the conclusion that they should have already drawn, based on their scientific intuitions, is nihilism. The scientists are fools like everyone else for pretending not to see this and continuing to live with many of the traditional beliefs that they are ostensibly trying to tear down. In this regard Kreuzgang can be seen as a forerunner of Nietzsche, who, while accepting the basics of the scientific worldview of the day, ultimately extends the nihilistic critique to include this sphere as well.

---

[111] Jean-Paul Sartre, *La nausée*, Paris: Gallimard 1938, pp. 179–191 (English translation: *Nausea*, trans. by Lloyd Alexander, New York: New Directions 1964, pp. 126–135).

[112] See, for example, *Nachtwachen*, p. 60 (*The Nightwatches of Bonaventura*, p. 27); *Nachtwachen*, p. 202 (*The Nightwatches of Bonaventura*, p. 87); *Nachtwachen*, p. 228 (*The Nightwatches of Bonaventura*, p. 97); *Nachtwachen*, p. 295 (*The Nightwatches of Bonaventura*, p. 126).

[113] The thesis of Katritzky's work is that *The Nightwatches* is a form of Menippean satire. See Katritzky, *A Guide to Bonaventura's "Nightwatches."*

[114] [Klingemann], *Nachtwachen*, p. 78 (*The Nightwatches of Bonaventura*, p. 35).

3

Nihilism in English Romanticism

Byron and Shelley

Nihilism is an important theme in the anglophone tradition. It is probably best known from the so-called graveyard poets from the beginning of the eighteenth century: Thomas Gray (1716–71), Thomas Parnell (1679–1718), Robert Blair (1699–1746), and Edward Young (1683–1765). This tradition was particularly influential for the later well-known English Romantics Lord Byron (1788–1824) and Percy Bysshe Shelley (1792–1822). There are many texts from these poets that could be treated in this context. However, I will limit myself to a few brief examples, namely, Bryon's dramatic work *Manfred* and Shelley's short poem "Ozymandias."

Some interpreters have pointed out nihilistic elements in the work of Lord Byron.[1] He regularly treats themes such as despair and death, often employing motifs such as darkness and desolation. He is also a merciless social critic, calling into question the reigning value system of bourgeois culture. It is difficult to pin down exactly what Byron's final position is on nihilism, but there can be no doubt that this is a central issue in his writings. It has been noted that Byron can be read as anticipating the existentialist movement,[2] but more work needs to be done on this connection.

Bryon published his short tragedy *Manfred* in 1817.[3] The circumstances of the composition of this work oblige one to read it as a very personal piece, despite the many fantastical aspects it contains. The background to this

---

[1] See, for example, John Watkins, "Byron and the Phenomenology of Negation," *Studies in Romanticism*, vol. 29, no. 3, 1990, pp. 395–411; Robert Gleckner, *Byron and the Ruins of Paradise*, Baltimore: Johns Hopkins University Press 1967; Charles LaChance, "Naïve and Knowledgeable Nihilism in Byron's Gothic Verse," *Papers on Language and Literature*, vol. 32, no. 4, 1996, pp. 339–368; Charles LaChance, "Nihilism, Love, and Genre in *Don Juan*," *Keats-Shelley Review*, vol. 11, 1997, pp. 141–166; Jerome McGann, *Byron and Romanticism*, Cambridge: Cambridge University Press 2002, see pp. 136, 168, 185; Brian Wilkie, "Byron and the Epic of Negation," in *Twentieth Century Interpretations of Don Juan*, ed. by Edward E. Bostetter, Englewood Cliffs, NJ: Prentice-Hall 1969, pp. 73–84.

[2] See Jason Pauly, *Designing Byron's Dasein: The Anticipation of Existentialist Despair in Lord Byron's Poetry*, dissertation, McGill University, 2008.

[3] Lord Byron, *Manfred, A Dramatic Poem*, London: John Murray 1817. See also the useful edition by Peter Cochran, *Manfred: An Edition of Byron's Manuscripts and a Collection of Essays*, Newcastle upon Tyne: Cambridge Scholars Publishing 2015.

involves the events that led Byron to leave England for good in 1816. He married Anne Isabella Milbanke (Annabella) (1792–1860) at the beginning of 1815, but their marriage was unhappy.[4] Depressed and angry, he began to drink. When Annabella gave birth to their daughter Ada (1815–52) at the end of the year, things only got worse. She began to suspect that her husband had gone insane. By March of 1816 they had reached an agreement for a legal separation. Annabella alleged, among other things, that Byron had homosexual lovers. She was also convinced that he had had incestuous relations with his half-sister, Augusta Leigh (1783–1851). When the ugly details of the separation became known, a scandal ensued that compelled Byron to leave London. He subsequently went to Switzerland, where he rented the Villa Diodati at Lake Geneva for the summer. It was there in June of 1816 that the famous group – which included Shelley, Mary Godwin (later Mary Shelley (1797–1851)), her stepsister (another of Byron's former lovers) Claire Clairmont (1798–1879), and John Polidori (1795–1821) – entertained each other with ghost stories. In September Byron made an excursion through the Alps near Bern and wrote the first draft of *Manfred*. The work was completed by February 1817.[5]

In the drama the protagonist Manfred is tormented by the fact that he committed incest with his beloved sister Astarte, and that this ultimately led to her death.[6] This key element of the story closely resembles Byron's forbidden relations with Augusta Leigh and indeed seems to confirm the veracity of the affair. Given this, it is difficult to read the story of Manfred without thinking of him as somehow representing Byron himself. It was presumably emotionally troubling for Byron to have to abandon his life in London so suddenly and to have to endure the gossip about him there. His *Manfred* can be seen as a personal rumination on his fate and self-imposed exile. It can be argued that Byron thus uses the work indirectly to confess his misdeed. More importantly for our purposes, the poem contains a number of nihilistic motifs.[7]

---

[4] For Byron's colorful biography see Leslie A. Marchand, *Byron: A Biography*, vols. 1–3, New York: Alfred A. Knopf 1957; Peter W. Graham, *Lord Byron*, New York: Twayne 1998; Karl Friedrich Elze, *Lord Byron: A Biography*, London: John Murray 1872; John Galt, *The Life of Lord Byron*, London: Henry Colburn and Richard Bentley 1830; Richard Lansdown, *The Cambridge Introduction to Byron*, Cambridge: Cambridge University Press 2012; Fiona MacCarthy, *Byron: Life and Legend*, London: John Murray 2002. See also *Byron's Letters and Journals*, vols. 1–12, ed. by Leslie A. Marchand, Cambridge, MA: Harvard University Press 1973–82.

[5] Lord Byron, *Manfred, A Dramatic Poem*, London: John Murray 1817. All references in the following refer to this first edition. This edition, however, does not provide line numbers, and so I have added these in brackets.

[6] See Atara Stein, "I Loved Her and Destroyed Her: Love and Narcissism in Byron's *Manfred*," *Philological Quarterly*, vol. 69, 1990, pp. 189–215; D.L. MacDonald, "Incest, Narcissism and Demonality in Byron's *Manfred*," *Mosaic*, vol. 25, no. 2, 1992, pp. 25–38.

[7] See Michael Allen Gillespie, *Nihilism before Nietzsche*, Chicago: University of Chicago Press 1996, pp. 121–125.

3.1 The Warning about the Pursuit of Knowledge in Byron's *Manfred*

Like Schiller's poem "The Veiled Statue at Sais," Byron's *Manfred* tells the story of a man who is tormented by knowledge and in a sense dies as a result of it. The tragedy can thus be read as a critique of the modern value attached to scientific knowing.[8] Manfred is a kind of Faustian figure zealous for learning.[9] He pursues his occult studies alone in a tower in the Alps. Over time he attains powers of magic that allow him to evoke supernatural spirits.

Manfred is influenced in part by what can be regarded as the existentialist moments in Shakespeare, to whom Byron pays homage by using the lines from Hamlet as the motto that appears on the title page: "There are more things in heaven and earth, Horatio, / Than are dreamt of in your philosophy."[10] This hints at Byron's use of *Hamlet* in some of the themes and motifs in the work.[11] Specifically, it suggests a limitation of human knowledge. In the original context of Shakespeare, "philosophy" refers to what was at the time called the philosophy of nature or natural philosophy, that is, what we today call the natural sciences. Thus, it does not refer, as is often thought, to what is now understood as the discipline of philosophy. It will be recalled that Hamlet's statement comes after he has spoken with the ghost of his father. The encounter with the supernatural realm is of course something that cannot be understood or explained by the sciences. Similarly, in *Manfred*, the protagonist has just seen the ghost of his sister, and this prompts him to acknowledge his awareness of the limitations of science when he says that he knows "philosophy / To be of all vanities the motliest, / the merest word that ever fool'd the ear / From out the schoolman's jargon."[12] Like Hamlet, he criticizes the pride of human knowledge. This also recalls the claim of Ecclesiastes that science and knowing are ultimately useless when it comes to the question of the meaning of life.

At the outset of the work Manfred complains that he is unable to sleep since he is haunted by a fixed thought that he cannot put out of his mind. He declares, "But grief should be the instructor of the wise; / Sorrow is knowledge: they who know the most / Must mourn the deepest o'er the fatal truth, / The Tree of

---

[8] See Mark D. Merritt, "Natural History, Manfred, and the Critique of Knowledge," *European Romantic Review*, vol. 9, no. 3, 1998, pp. 351–360.

[9] See Cochran, "*Manfred* and Dr. Faustus," and "*Manfred* and Faust," in his *Manfred: An Edition of Byron's Manuscripts and a Collection of Essays*, pp. 167–172, pp. 173–180, respectively. Jean Malaplate, "Goethe et Byron, Faust et Manfred, une conversation interrompue," in *Lord Byron: A Multidisciplinary Open Forum*, ed. by Thérèse Tessier, Paris: n.p. 1999 pp. 147–167.

[10] Shakespeare, *Hamlet*, Scene 6, lines 165–166, p. 2021 (in editions that divide the play into acts, this appears in Act I, Scene 5).

[11] See Cochran, "*Manfred* and Shakespeare," in his *Manfred: An Edition of Byron's Manuscripts and a Collection of Essays*, pp. 195–200; G. Wilson Knight, "Byron and Hamlet," *Bulletin of the John Rylands Library*, vol. 45, no. 1, 1962, pp. 115–147.

[12] Byron, *Manfred, A Dramatic Poem*, p. 55, Act III, Scene I [lines 9–12].

Knowledge is not that of Life."[13] Since here grief and sorrow are associated with knowing, Manfred refers to the trees of knowledge and life that are found in the Garden of Eden as recounted in Genesis.[14] It is a sin to eat from the tree of knowledge as Adam and Eve did. Their punishment was expulsion from Eden and mortality. Thus, knowledge is an antipode to life since it results in suffering and death. This can clearly be seen as a motif for the nihilism that follows from a barren scientific worldview. Byron's account recalls Jean Paul's argument that it is impossible to live with the nihilistic and atheistic view that comes with science. Such knowledge leads only to despair and anguish. Schiller's image of the overzealous youth in "The Veiled Statue at Sais" is also relevant in this context. After gaining the forbidden knowledge, he is found completely incapacitated, languishing on the floor of the temple: "Ever from his heart / Was fled the sweet serenity of life / And the deep anguish dug the early grave."[15]

Manfred explains in more detail how his knowledge has not been able to help him in any way to escape his grief. Instead, he has become numb to the world, and nothing seems to matter anymore:

> Philosophy and science, and the springs
> Of wonder, and the wisdom of the world,
> I have essayed, and in my mind there is
> A power to make these subject to itself—
> But they avail not: I have done men good,
> And I have met with good even among men—
> But this avail'd not: I have had my foes,
> And none have baffled, many fallen before me—
> But this avail'd not: —Good, or evil, life,
> Powers, passions, all I see in other beings,
> Have been to me as rain unto the sands,
> Since that all-nameless hour.[16]

With the repetition of "avail not" Manfred emphasizes the worthlessness of knowing with respect to the existential questions. While science and knowledge might be assets in certain practical matters, when it comes to deeper questions such as life, they are useless. Manfred's great knowledge has been no help to him. On the contrary, it was his desire to know that led him to sin. The scientist's knowledge of the universe is of no help when trying to understand the meaning of one's existence. Instead, it only seems to make the problem worse by drawing attention to the brevity and fragility of human life.

---

[13] Byron, *Manfred, A Dramatic Poem*, p. 7, Act I, Scene I [lines 9–12].
[14] Genesis 2:9, 16–17.
[15] Friedrich Schiller, "Das verschleierte Bild zu Sais," *Die Horen*, vol. 1, no. 9, Tübingen: J.G. Cotta 1795, p. 98 (English translation: "The Veiled Statue at Sais," in *The Poems and Ballads of Schiller*, trans. by Sir Edward Bulwer Lytton, Bart., New York: Thomas Y. Cromwell & Co. n.d., p. 91).
[16] Byron, *Manfred, A Dramatic Poem*, p. 8, Act I, Scene I [lines 13–24].

Only later do we learn the reason for Manfred's grief, namely, his incest with his sister Astarte. This represents forbidden knowledge as in the story of the Fall, which also has a sexual element with the symbol of the apple. After eating of it, Adam and Eve are transformed and realize for the first time that they are naked. Byron's choice of the name makes sense in this context since in antiquity Astarte was a goddess of sexuality worshipped throughout the Near East. Manfred's sexual relation to his sister torments his mind to the point that he only wishes for death. Using his magical knowledge, he summons the spirits of nature in order to ask them to put him out of his misery by erasing his memory forever. Only this will give him peace from the pangs of guilt from which he suffers. He tries to call forth the spirits, but they do not come. They arise only with the third try when he calls them in the name of the curse that he bears. He describes this as follows:

> Spirits of earth and air,
> Ye shall not thus elude me: by a power,
> Deeper than all yet urged, a tyrant-spell,
> Which had its birth-place in a star condemn'd,
> The burning wreck of a demolish'd world,
> A wandering hell in the eternal space;
> By the strong curse which is upon my soul,
> The thought which is within me and around me,
> I do compel ye to my will. —Appear![17]

The stirring images of a "burning wreck of a demolish'd world" and a "wandering hell in the eternal space" evoke the power of nature and the finitude of human existence. Manfred emphasizes the natural aspect of humans, portraying them as tiny suffering beings in the vastness of space and time. With this evocation, the spirits of nature appear: the spirits of the air, the mountain, the ocean, the earth, the winds, the night, and the star of Manfred's fate. As they arrive, they introduce themselves, and in their introductions, almost all these forces explain their work in their designated spheres to be destructive to human life. The spirit of the mountain is responsible for earthquakes. The spirit of the wind is responsible for hurricanes. The spirit of the night represents death. In each case, the brute facts of nature are causes of human misery and threats to life. The natural forces thus have no regard for the fates of mortal beings and the human suffering that they cause. The natural world simply runs its own course according to its own laws.

Manfred tells the spirits of his wish for "forgetfulness" and "oblivion."[18] They say that they cannot help him. They control the forces of nature and can give him some power over these, but they cannot erase his memory: "It is not in our

---

[17] Byron, *Manfred, A Dramatic Poem*, p. 9, Act I, Scene I [lines 41–49].
[18] Byron, *Manfred, A Dramatic Poem*, p. 14, Act I, Scene I [lines 136 and 145].

essence, in our skill."[19] Manfred's existence is a bitter burden to him since he languishes with the knowledge of what he has done. His life, which seems now to drag on for an eternity, is for him completely meaningless.[20] His acquired knowledge of the occult, which allows him to summon the spirits, does not help him to relieve his inner torment.

The spirits, however, note that he can of course die. To his question of whether death will then erase his memory, the spirits remind him of immortality: "We are immortal, and do not forget; / We are eternal; and to us the past / Is, as the future, present."[21] There is an ambiguity in the use of "we" here. Since this is spoken by one of the spirits of nature, it might refer to them as the basic forces of the universe that can never perish. But since this is spoken in response to Manfred's question, it seems also to include human beings and to suggest a doctrine of immortality. Manfred picks up on the ambiguity and becomes upset, thinking that they are trying to trick him. He himself insists on the power of the human mind over nature: "The mind, the spirit, the Promethean spark, / The lightning of my being, is as bright, / Pervading, and far-darting as your own, / And shall not yield to yours, though coop'd in clay!"[22] Unlike Klingemann, Byron sees something noble in the human spirit vis-à-vis nature. It is the human mind that can bring nature under control and make it the slave to human purposes. In this insistence on the freedom of the mind and the will over nature, Manfred anticipates an important motif in existentialism. But as will be seen later, he sees this as a dialectical relation by recognizing his finitude and limitations to change the basic facts of nature by his own will. He demands a straight answer to his question about whether death will bring forgetfulness. The spirits respond by affirming the interpretation that the "we" is intended also to include humans. The suggestion is then that just like the forces of nature, humans are immortal, even though they experience death. The implication seems to be that he will retain his memory and continue to suffer even in the afterlife.

Manfred thus laments that the spirits are unable to help him escape his torments. They renew their offer of giving him certain things that humans normally desire: "Kingdom, and sway, and strength, and length of days."[23] But Manfred scorns these things, indicating that he lives outside the normal system of human values. In contrast to Faust, who is tempted by the promises of Mephistopheles, Manfred rejects what the spirits of nature can offer. He desires no worldly wealth, power, or even a long life. Everything has become indifferent for him, and life is only an everlasting torment. When Manfred asks the

---

[19] Byron, *Manfred, A Dramatic Poem*, p. 14, Act I, Scene I [line 147].
[20] Byron, *Manfred, A Dramatic Poem*, pp. 28f., Act II, Scene I [lines 50–58].
[21] Byron, *Manfred, A Dramatic Poem*, p. 14, Act I, Scene I [lines 149–151].
[22] Byron, *Manfred, A Dramatic Poem*, pp. 14f., Act I, Scene I [lines 154–157].
[23] Byron, *Manfred, A Dramatic Poem*, p. 15, Act I, Scene I [lines 168].

3.1 THE PURSUIT OF KNOWLEDGE IN BYRON'S *MANFRED* 105

spirits to appear to him, and they ask what form they should take, he replies, "there is no form on earth / Hideous or beautiful to me."[24] Just as he has become indifferent to all human values, so also has he become indifferent to questions of aesthetics. This is confirmed again at the beginning of Act II, when Manfred looks at mountains and says they hold no beauty for him.[25] He has fully given up on the value and meaning of life.

Manfred conjures forth the witch of the Alps perhaps in the hope that she might be able to help him. When she appears, he recounts how he spent years studying the occult arts and managed to understand profound things. But then he stops short: "with my knowledge grew / The thirst of knowledge, and the power and joy / Of this most bright intelligence, until –."[26] Like the zealous youth in Schiller's poem, Manfred's thirst for knowledge led him to his downfall. When the youth begins to learn, he develops an insatiable appetite for knowing, which he cannot repress. Manfred tells the witch of his great love for his sister Astarte. He explains that she too shared his zeal for the secrets that knowledge can bring: "She had the same lone thoughts and wanderings, / The quest of hidden knowledge, and a mind / To comprehend the universe."[27] The hidden knowledge mentioned presumably includes the incest that they committed. This is a kind of knowledge that should best be left unknown and uninvestigated. In Sophocles' *Oedipus the King*, the people who know the truth about Oedipus's identity and about his incestuous relation with his mother plead with him to stop his investigation to uncover the person responsible for the plague afflicting Thebes. But driven by his vanity to show his great knowledge, he insists on continuing, only to learn the truth that he is the one who is being sought. This truth leaves him blind and languishing for the rest of his days.

Manfred confesses to the witch that he truly loved Astarte and was inadvertently responsible for her death. Although he did not kill her in the strict sense, she died of a broken heart, apparently realizing that they could never live as husband and wife, and that their forbidden love must be confined to the shadows. The witch again returns to the issue of knowledge. She says, seemingly reproaching Manfred, "thou dost forgo / The gifts of our great knowledge, and shrink'st back / To recreant mortality."[28] Due to his experience, he realized the destructive nature of knowledge and discontinued his studies.

Manfred stands in danger not only because of his sin of incest but also because of his communion with the supernatural forces. The abbot of the monastery in St. Maurice comes to him to ask about this since he has heard disturbing rumors about Manfred's nocturnal activities. He tells Manfred,

---

[24] Byron, *Manfred, A Dramatic Poem*, p. 16, Act I, Scene I [lines 184–185].
[25] Byron, *Manfred, A Dramatic Poem*, p. 20, Act I, Scene II [lines 9–12].
[26] Byron, *Manfred, A Dramatic Poem*, p. 33, Act II, Scene II [lines 93–95].
[27] Byron, *Manfred, A Dramatic Poem*, p. 33, Act II, Scene II [lines 109–111].
[28] Byron, *Manfred, A Dramatic Poem*, p. 36, Act II, Scene II [lines 124–126].

"'Tis said thou holdest converse with the things / Which are forbidden to search of man."[29] The abbot knows that occult knowledge can lead to destruction, just like the hierophant in Schiller's poem, who warns the youth against raising the veil of the goddess and discovering her secrets. There is a good reason why this knowledge is forbidden; namely, it can only bring suffering just like eating from the tree of knowledge.

Towards the end of the work, Manfred's servants speculate about the nature of his secretive studies in his tower. Suspicion is raised by a room, which none of them has been allowed to enter. The curious servant Herman ruminates how much he would like to know what it contains. To this the older and more experienced servant Manuel says, "'Twere dangerous; / Content thyself with what thou knowest already."[30] Once again, the implication is that there are some things, such as nihilism, that it is better for humans not to know. Just as science can be a benefit, so also can it be a curse.

The theme of the relation of knowledge and happiness is revisited when the first spirit of Destiny describes the sufferings of Manfred. She says that he has learned that "knowledge is not happiness, and science / But an exchange of ignorance for that / Which is another kind of ignorance."[31] This captures well the dilemma of nihilism. Modern science replaces the older religious conception of the universe and the role of humans in it. It thus sets aside the former superstitious "ignorance" for the new scientifically grounded worldview. But when the implications of this new conception of the universe are worked out, it quickly becomes evident that humans are utterly insignificant, and nihilism arises. The new "ignorance" that replaces the old is that, with the scientific worldview, we have no way to replace the former value system that gave human existence a meaning. Now we are finite and meaningless, adrift in endless space. We are utterly ignorant of what meaning we could possibly have.

3.2 Suffering as the Fate of Humans

The burden of Manfred's curse is too much to bear, and he contemplates suicide.[32] Although he wishes death, he is prevented from acting on this by fear. This illustrates the suffering of human existence, which is another central motif in the work. Our lives are a constant struggle, haunted by the ever-present anxiety of our mortality. The uncertainty of what will happen to us after death makes things even worse. At no point can we truly rest. This motif in *Manfred* can be seen as an echo of Hamlet's "To be, or not to be" soliloquy. Hamlet reflects on the infinite troubles of life that lead one to suicidal thoughts:

---

[29] Byron, *Manfred, A Dramatic Poem*, p. 56, Act III, Scene I [lines 34–35].
[30] Byron, *Manfred, A Dramatic Poem*, p. 65, Act III, Scene III [lines 10–11].
[31] Byron, *Manfred, A Dramatic Poem*, p. 47, Act II, Scene IV [lines 61–63].
[32] Byron, *Manfred, A Dramatic Poem*, pp. 20f., Act I, Scene II [lines 16–21].

3.2 SUFFERING AS THE FATE OF HUMANS

> To be, or not to be, that is the question:
> Whether 'tis nobler in the mind to suffer
> The slings and arrows of outrageous fortune,
> Or to take arms against a sea of troubles
> And by opposing end them. To die—to sleep,
> No more; and by a sleep to say we end
> The heart-ache and the thousand natural shocks
> That flesh is heir to: 'tis a consummation
> Devoutly to be wish'd.[33]

While death might seem to be an easy answer, there remains the uncertainty about exactly what it is. Hamlet expresses the same concern as Manfred, namely, what if after death we retain our consciousness? As long as we are conscious, we risk having terrifying thoughts and dreams. Likewise, if we retain our memories in death, nothing would really be resolved since one would still be vexed by the same thoughts that tormented one's life. Hamlet continues:

> ... to die, to sleep;
> To sleep, perchance to dream—ay, there's the rub:
> For in that sleep of death what dreams may come,
> When we have shuffled off this mortal coil,
> Must give us pause ...[34]

Hamlet concludes that we choose to endure the troubles of life since we are uncertain of what death holds for us, and this fear is what prevents us from resorting to suicide:

> Who would fardels bear,
> To grunt and sweat under a weary life,
> But that the dread of something after death,
> The undiscovered country, from whose bourn
> No traveller returns, puzzles the will,
> And makes us rather bear those ills we have
> Than fly to others that we know not of?
> Thus conscience doth make cowards of us all.[35]

The fear of what awaits after death forces us to endure the sufferings of this world as best we can. The vague responses of the spirits of nature leave Manfred in doubt about what death really is. This can be understood to mean that we can gain no insight about the experience of death or an afterlife from the sciences or empirical observations.

---

[33] Shakespeare, *Hamlet*, Scene 8, lines 57–65, p. 2040 (in editions that divide the play into acts, this appears in Act 3, Scene 1).
[34] Shakespeare, *Hamlet*, Scene 8, lines 65–69, p. 2040 (in editions that divide the play into acts, this appears in Act 3, Scene 1, lines 1757–1761).
[35] Shakespeare, *Hamlet*, Scene 8, lines 77–84, pp. 2040f. (in editions that divide the play into acts, this appears in Act 3, Scene 1).

Manfred's lack of knowledge of whether his consciousness will survive death stops him from ending his life voluntarily. He reasons along lines similar to Hamlet. Contemplating casting himself from the cliff, he explains an ambivalence in himself: "There is a power upon me which withholds / And makes it my fatality to live."[36] His fear of death thus prevents him from jumping. He seems destined to live out a long life of misery. As he considers his death, he strikes a nihilistic tone by noting his indifference to even his own actions:

> This barrenness of spirit, and to be
> My own soul's sepulchre, for I have ceased
> To justify my deeds unto myself—
> The last infirmity of evil.[37]

As long as one continues to try to justify one's actions to oneself and others, one is still within the sphere of human values and ethics, for whatever transgressions one might be guilty of. However, the person who ceases to do this and becomes indifferent to the evil he is responsible for falls outside the realm of the ethical sphere. Such a person is like the animals or nature itself with no sense of right or wrong. Manfred decides to go ahead with jumping from the cliff and is only held back at the last minute by a passing chamois hunter. His nihilistic indifference to life is subsequently reflected in his answers to the hunter, who is curious to know who he is and where he is going. Manfred simply replies indifferently, "It imports not" and "No matter."[38] He regards his role in the world with a nihilistic apathy. Moreover, the hunter repeatedly speaks of Manfred as a madman.[39] Like Klingemann's Kreuzgang, the nihilist appears to be mentally disturbed when judged by the standards of mainstream society.

Byron also uses metaphors from nature to indicate the continuity between the fate of humans and that of other living things. For example, Manfred compares himself with a dead tree that he sees in the mountains:

> Grey-hair'd with anguish, like these blasted pines,
> Wrecks of a single winter, barkless, branchless,
> A blighted trunk upon a cursed root,
> Which but supplies a feeling to decay—
> And to be thus, eternally but thus,
> Having been otherwise![40]

---

[36] Byron, *Manfred, A Dramatic Poem*, p. 21, Act I, Scene II [lines 23–24].
[37] Byron, *Manfred, A Dramatic Poem*, p. 21, Act I, Scene II [lines 26–29].
[38] Byron, *Manfred, A Dramatic Poem*, p. 26, Act II, Scene I [line 5], and p. 27, Act II, Scene I [line 16].
[39] Byron, *Manfred, A Dramatic Poem*, p. 25, Act I, Scene II [line 110]; p. 27, Act II, Scene I [line 31]; p. 29, Act II, Scene I [line 59].
[40] Byron, *Manfred, A Dramatic Poem*, p. 23, Act I, Scene II [lines 66–71].

3.2 SUFFERING AS THE FATE OF HUMANS

Like the withered tree, Manfred has been prematurely aged by the difficulties of life. This is a source of further suffering when he contemplates his better days prior to his sin, when he was still full of vigor. Manfred knows that his fate will be, like the tree, to decay and die. With a different image, Manfred's bleak picture of human existence is reflected in the natural world devoid of meaning or purpose: it is like a desert, "Barren and cold, on which the wild waves break, / But nothing rests, save carcasses and wrecks, / Rocks, and the salt-surf weeds of bitterness."[41] While natural images predominate, the use of the term "bitterness" at the end connects these to the human sphere. The rocks and the weeds in the water cannot be bitter with their meaningless role in the universe. Instead, it is the human mind that struggles with this.

In his discussion with the witch of the Alps, Manfred explains his sense of alienation from other human beings:

> From my youth upwards
> My spirit walk'd not with the souls of men,
> Nor look'd upon the earth with human eyes;
> The thirst of their ambition was not mine,
> The aim of their existence was not mine;
> My joys, my griefs, my passions, and my powers,
> Made me a stranger; though I wore the form,
> I had no sympathy with breathing flesh ...[42]

This might well be another autobiographical reference to Byron as an outsider in the bourgeois society that he was raised in. The normal human value system is something foreign to him. Manfred claims that when he regards other humans, he feels degraded. He believes that the world consists only of narrow-minded people pursing their trivial lives.[43] He sees himself as something different and set apart from them. His special knowledge raises him above the crowd. For this reason, he prefers his solitude to being with others. But having a special genius means that he is also exposed to special suffering as well.

According to Manfred, human existence is just a deception that makes us think that we can achieve happiness. But in fact we have been duped:

> We are the fools of time and terror: Days
> Steal on us and steal from us; yet we live
> Loathing our life, and dreading still to die.
> In all the days of this detested yoke—
> This vital weight upon the struggling heart,
> Which sinks with sorrow, or beats quick with pain
> Or joy that ends in agony or faintness...[44]

---

[41] Byron, *Manfred, A Dramatic Poem*, p. 29, Act II, Scene I [lines 56–58].
[42] Byron, *Manfred, A Dramatic Poem*, p. 33, Act II, Scene II [lines 50–57].
[43] Byron, *Manfred, A Dramatic Poem*, p. 33, Act II, Scene II [lines 77–78].
[44] Byron, *Manfred, A Dramatic Poem*, p. 38, Act II, Scene II [lines 164–171].

The use of the first-person plural, "we," seems to suggest that Manfred's condition is meant to represent the human condition in general. Our lives are a torment, full of sorrow. There are few days in which we do not yearn for death.[45] Even our brief moments of happiness only end in pain. The deceptive element in happiness is also emphasized when one of the spirits of nature appears to Manfred in the form of a beautiful woman, whom he takes to be his beloved Astarte. But when she vanishes, he is devastated.[46] The expression "the struggling heart" seems to suggest that we naturally seek love, but this always ends in sorrow. This recalls the melancholy story of Kreuzgang in *The Nightwatches* who could not resist the power of cupid and allowed himself to love Ophelia. But his brief amorous affair ended with the death of his lover in childbirth. Byron's description of Manfred, like Klingemann's account of Kreuzgang, implies that our moments of happiness are just fleeting illusions that soon pass and leave us feeling sad and disappointed. The ephemeral time of joy makes our melancholy all the more bitter when we recall what we have lost. True lasting happiness simply does not exist.

In Act II of *Manfred*, the spirits of Destiny come together for a festival. They are clearly modeled on the Fates from Greek mythology, who are represented as three old women who weave the tapestry of life and fix the fate of everything. Their power cannot be undermined even by the gods. As each of the Destinies arrives, they, like the forces of nature before, introduce themselves by telling of the pain they have caused human beings. They are completely apathetic to human suffering and only help people when it serves their own purposes. The speech of the First Destiny is as follows:

> The city lies sleeping;
>   The morn, to deplore it,
> May dawn on it weeping:
>   Sullenly, slowly,
> The black plague flew o'er it—
>   Thousands lie lowly;
> Tens of thousands shall perish—
>   The living shall fly from
> The sick they should cherish;
>   But nothing can vanquish
> The touch that they die from.
>   Sorrow and anguish,
> And evil and dread,
>   Envelope a nation—
> The blest are the dead,

---

[45] Byron, *Manfred, A Dramatic Poem*, p. 39, Act II, Scene II [lines 174–175].
[46] Byron, *Manfred, A Dramatic Poem*, p. 16, Act I, Scene I [lines 188–191].

> Who see not the sight
> Of their own desolation.—
> This work of a night—[47]

She emphasizes the point that she is responsible for a plague that kills many people. She seems to take pride in the fact and shows no sign of sympathy or mercy. She explains that this is what she has done throughout history and will continue to do in the future.[48] This can be understood as a metaphor for human life, where we will all die sooner or later, and it is just a matter of time. We are unable to escape death or the pains caused by the Fates. Again, this statement of the First Destiny is not about Manfred and his life specifically, but rather it is about the human condition in general.

In Job we read the famous lines, "The Lord gave and the Lord has taken away."[49] In an allusion to this, Byron has the three Destinies sing together:

> Our hands contain the hearts of men,
> Our footsteps are their graves;
> We only give to take again
> The spirits of our slaves![50]

As long as the Destinies are associated with the Greek Fates, they can be readily dismissed as simple mythology. But, for Byron's contemporary reader, the allusion to Job and the Judeo-Christian tradition suddenly makes the problem more vexing. Byron in effect raises the question of God's benevolence and mercy. Instead of possessing these accustomed divine traits, perhaps God is, like the Fates, cruel and indifferent. Byron thus indirectly raises the question of the consistency of suffering with the existence of an all-powerful and benevolent God. When one observes the endless suffering in the world, it is difficult to see evidence of a loving God who could stop this suffering in an instant but chooses not to do so. This is a nihilistic world without hope and comfort. The Destinies are joined by the goddess Nemesis, who also describes the meaninglessness of human existence.[51] Kingdoms come and go, and people take great care with their projects, which in time all end in nothing.

The Destinies and Nemesis meet in the Hall of the god Arimanes. In Zoroastrianism Ahriman is the god of darkness and evil who stands in an eternal struggle with his counterpart Ormuzd, the god of light and the good.[52]

---

[47] Byron, *Manfred, A Dramatic Poem*, pp. 42f., Act II, Scene III [lines 33–51].
[48] Byron, *Manfred, A Dramatic Poem*, p. 43, Act II, Scene III [line 54].
[49] Job 1:21.
[50] Byron, *Manfred, A Dramatic Poem*, p. 43, Act II, Scene III [lines 54–57].
[51] Byron, *Manfred, A Dramatic Poem*, p. 44, Act II, Scene III [lines 62–71].
[52] See Cochran, "*Manfred* and Zoroastrianism," in his *Manfred: An Edition of Byron's Manuscripts and a Collection of Essays*, pp. 136–143; Maurice J. Quinlan, "Byron's *Manfred* and Zoroastrianism," *Journal of English and German Philology*, vol. 57, no. 4, 1958, pp. 726–738.

However, Byron's twist here is that in *Manfred* there is only mention of Arimanes and little sign of any benevolent or caring god. All the other supernatural spirits are somewhere between indifferent and malevolently disposed towards humans. Arimanes is portrayed as the all-powerful god, to whom all the other spirits pay homage. The Destinies and Nemesis do his bidding. He controls all the elements of nature. The spirits sing of his infinite powers: "planets turn to ashes at his wrath."[53] So, for Manfred, it is clear that the forces of darkness are great. Death and suffering are fundamental to the world. Since Arimanes is the basic principle of the universe, the spirits further sing, "Life is his, / With all its infinite of agonies – / And his the spirit of whatever is!"[54] In Genesis it is said that God breathed the spirit of life into Adam, and from this comes the doctrine that all human beings contain something of the divine in themselves. In Byron we see a perverse mirror image of this. The spirit or breath that we have in ourselves is that of evil.

Manfred asks the spirits to conjure up the ghost of his beloved Astarte so that he can ask her about the nature of death in order to learn if it is a relief from life or a further torment. When the ghost appears, Manfred seems to forget his original question and wants to know instead if she has forgiven him for what he has done and for being responsible for her death. Despite repeated commands from the spirits and even Arimanes himself, Astarte mysteriously remains silent. Only at Manfred's own pleading does she speak. But instead of answering his question, she reveals that he will die the next day.[55] Surprisingly unphased by this knowledge, he implores her again by asking if she has forgiven him and if she still loves him, but she leaves him hanging and disappears. Knowing that he will soon die, Manfred attains the calm and peace that he has wanted for so long. Although he enjoys this only for a brief time before death, he is happy to have known it.

The abbot comes and tries to persuade Manfred to repent and ask God for forgiveness. This discussion brings out the dilemma of the secular scientific worldview. Without a belief in salvation and immortality, humans still have a need to find some way to give themselves peace and comfort. But this is but a self-deception: "'Tis strange – even those who do despair above, / Yet shape themselves some phantasy on earth, / To which frail twig they cling, like drowning men."[56] But once one has rejected the idea of God's salvation with the scientific view, it seems impossible to find anything else that can serve as a replacement for this. Manfred rejects the abbot's consolation and has no intention of confessing. When the abbot makes an appeal to hope, Manfred acknowledges that he did have such ideas in the naïveté of youth. But when

---

[53] Byron, *Manfred, A Dramatic Poem*, p. 45, Act II, Scene IV [line 12].
[54] Byron, *Manfred, A Dramatic Poem*, p. 45, Act II, Scene IV [lines 14–16].
[55] Byron, *Manfred, A Dramatic Poem*, p. 52, Act II, Scene IV [line 152].
[56] Byron, *Manfred, A Dramatic Poem*, p. 59, Act III, Scene I [lines 101–103].

he grew older, he realized that these were deceptions.[57] The suggestion is that no mature, thinking person can maintain such ideas. Since most people subscribe to traditional religious views, Manfred holds them in disdain and tries to avoid them. The etymology of the name "Manfred" combines man + peace. But throughout the work, the character is struggling in vain to find peace or anything that will calm his troubled conscience. Life is a tormented constant movement and not a static state of happiness and satisfaction.

3.3 Byron's Philosophical Anthropology

Manfred contemplates the nature of human beings and sketches a well-known dualist position, whereby the human is a mixture of two basic elements. He says,

> Half dust, half deity, alike unfit
> To sink or soar, with our mix'd essence make
> A conflict of its elements, and breathe
> The breath of degradation and of pride,
> Contending with low wants and lofty will
> Till our mortality predominates,
> And men are—what they name not to themselves
> And trust not to each other.[58]

While we have a rational element that we share with the divine, we have a natural element that inescapably connects us with nature. We are "half dust" and driven by base desires or "low wants," just like the animals. Although we sometimes have noble thoughts and a "lofty will," in the end there is no escape from death. This is presumably the word that people avoid mentioning that completes the sentence "Till our mortality predominates, / And men are *dead*." While we take pride in the illusion that we are masters of the forces of nature, in fact we are at their mercy, like all other created beings. We have no way to stop hurricanes, avalanches, earthquakes, plagues, and so on. While Manfred asserts his free spirit, he is also aware of his finitude and vulnerability.

Later in the work, the abbot makes the same observation about the confused nature of human beings. Specifically, he says the following about Manfred:

> This should have been a noble creature: he
> Hath all the energy which would have made
> A goodly frame of glorious elements,
> Had they been wisely mingled; as it is,
> It is an awful chaos—light and darkness—
> And mind and dust—and passions and pure thoughts,
> Mix'd, and contending without end or order ...[59]

---

[57] Byron, *Manfred, A Dramatic Poem*, p. 59, Act III, Scene I [lines 104–115].
[58] Byron, *Manfred, A Dramatic Poem*, p. 21, Act I, Scene II [lines 40–47].
[59] Byron, *Manfred, A Dramatic Poem*, p. 62, Act III, Scene I [lines 160–166].

The point of the abbot's comment seems to be that there are natural dialectical relations in the world of creation, with light and darkness, life and death, holding each other in a regular balance. This is the norm for human life, but unfortunately in Manfred the equilibrium has been upset. In his case death and darkness have gained the upper hand. While one might take this description to be confined to the troubled Manfred, it can also be understood as a general picture of the human condition itself. Humans are a mixture of reason and passion, or, in the Aristotelian sense, humans are rational animals.[60] Thus the human spirit is always necessarily in conflict with itself. Our rational will struggles with our animal desires. There is no harmony of elements leading to happiness. The human soul is thus a churning "chaos." This recalls Klingemann's portrayal of the universe as chaotic instead of orderly. God's creation has gone wrong and resulted in a "miscarried system."[61] Human beings are part of the confusion of creation.

Byron emphasizes that one of Manfred's problems is that he is unable to sleep due to the fact that his mind always forces him to think about his crime. It is thus the human mind with its knowledge that causes the problem, something that animals are free from. At the very beginning of the work Manfred laments,

> My slumbers—if I slumber—are not sleep,
> But a continuance of enduring thought,
> Which then I can resist not: in my heart
> There is a vigil, and these eyes but close
> To look within ... [62]

As is often the case with insomnia, an overactive brain prevents the body from sleeping. One's own thoughts thus work against the body. Reflection or looking within oneself is a form of thought. For this reason, Manfred wants above all forgetfulness so that the constant thinking and gloomy remembering will stop. His insomnia is a part of his torment and suffering.

3.4 The Rejection of Religion

After his failure to resolve his problem with the help of the spirits of nature, at the beginning of Scene II of Act I, Manfred decides, "I lean no more on superhuman aid."[63] He has also long since become disenchanted with his studies of the occult, which have failed to help him with his tormented conscience.

---

[60] See Aristotle, *Nicomachean Ethics* 1.13.
[61] [Klingemann], *Nachtwachen. Von Bonaventura*, Penig: bey F. Dienemann und Comp. 1805, p. 94 (English translation: *The Nightwatches of Bonaventura*, trans. by Gerald Gillespie, Chicago and London: University of Chicago Press 2014, p. 41). See Chapter 2, Sect. 2.1, p. 67.
[62] Byron, *Manfred, A Dramatic Poem*, p. 7, Act I, Scene I [lines 3–7].
[63] Byron, *Manfred, A Dramatic Poem*, p. 20, Act I, Scene II [line 4].

3.4 THE REJECTION OF RELIGION

He maintains this posture throughout the work. For example, he rejects the prayers of the sympathetic and caring chamois hunter, saying that he has no need for them.[64] With a Faustian theme, the witch of the Alps claims that she can help him with his tormented soul on the condition that he will swear allegiance to her. In contrast to Faust, Manfred categorically rejects this.[65]

When Manfred enters the Hall of Arimanes, the god's powerful spirit followers disdain him as a lowly mortal and command him to bow down before their master.[66] Intrepid, Manfred defies them and remains standing, despite their threats. He explains that he knows full well the power of Arimanes. Moreover, he is aware of his own limitations and weaknesses. He has already bowed before "despair" and "desolation" many times.[67] The spirits insist that the entire world recognizes and bows before Arimanes,[68] which seems to suggest that it is a fundamental part of human existence that we suffer pain and anxiety, since we are subject to forces of evil beyond our control. But Manfred rejects the idea that these great powers have any authority over him. He radically asserts his own individual freedom against the spirits. Even in the face of pain and suffering, there is still room to act freely and with integrity.

More significantly, he rejects the renewed attempts of the persistent abbot to get him to repent and confess to God. Manfred treats the abbot kindly and respectfully, but he refuses to have anything to do with organized religion. He tells the abbot, "whate'er / I may have been, or am, doth rest between / Heaven and myself.— I shall not choose a mortal / to be my mediator."[69] Manfred recognizes no human authority above himself. But he is vague about his own conceptions of God. Manfred becomes irritated with the abbot and claims that there is nothing that the church or prayer can do to relieve the deep sense of guilt and inner pain of someone like himself. Only the individual can manage to come to terms with his or her own soul. His rejection of the abbot's efforts to get him to be reconciled with the church clearly shows an abandonment of traditional religion and again supports an autobiographical reading of the work. Byron's exact religious views have proven difficult to determine unambiguously, and he has been assigned different places on the spectrum of religious belief.[70] However, it seems clear that he rejected the institutionalization of religion.

The final scene of the work begins with a soliloquy by Manfred, who is alone in his tower as twilight approaches. When contemplating the setting sun on his final day, Manfred reflects on how in early times humans worshipped the

---

[64] Byron, *Manfred, A Dramatic Poem*, p. 30, Act II, Scene I [line 90].
[65] Byron, *Manfred, A Dramatic Poem*, p. 38, Act II, Scene II [lines 157–159].
[66] Byron, *Manfred, A Dramatic Poem*, p. 46, Act II, Scene IV [lines 33–35].
[67] Byron, *Manfred, A Dramatic Poem*, p. 46, Act II, Scene IV [lines 41 and 42].
[68] Byron, *Manfred, A Dramatic Poem*, p. 46, Act II, Scene IV [line 44].
[69] Byron, *Manfred, A Dramatic Poem*, p. 57, Act III, Scene I [lines 52–55].
[70] See Christine Kenyon Jones, "Religion," in *Byron in Context*, ed. by Clara Tuite, Cambridge: Cambridge University Press 2019, pp. 101–108.

sun as a great god, but then when science revealed that it was in fact a physical object governed by natural laws, it lost its mystique and ceased to be an object of religious reverence.[71] The older views are revealed to be mere superstition that the modern mind cannot accept. Yet Manfred still seems to want to retain a special place for the sun, referring to it as a "material God."[72] The sun's great influence on human life can be regarded as divine in many ways, even if it is only a great mass of gases floating in space.

The evening brings him to recall a memory of his youth when he made a nocturnal visit to the Colosseum in Rome. He observes the many broken monuments and stones that have been overgrown with ivy. In contrast to this, he thinks of the glory of the great Romans and what they achieved. He notes the following contrast: "But the gladiators' bloody Circus stands, / A noble wreck in ruinous perfection! / While Caesar's chambers, and the Augustan halls, / Grovel on earth in indistinct decay."[73] This seems to testify to the vanity of positive human accomplishment and the triumph of suffering and death.

Finally, when a spirit arrives and calls Manfred to come with him since it is his time to die, Manfred refuses to go.[74] He is not afraid to die and would gladly go to his death, but he claims that he owes nothing to the spirit and will not go with him. He asserts his individual freedom to go to his death alone. Just as he rejected the mediation of the abbot, so also he refuses the mediation of the supernatural spirits. The drama ends with a gesture of defiance and rebellion. In an important deviation from Faust, Manfred rejects owing any allegiance or debt to the supernatural powers of evil. He never made any compact with them. He claims that all his powers came from the acquisition of knowledge that he gained alone and with the help of previous scholars and scientists:

> ... my past power
> Was purchased by no compact with thy crew,
> But by superior science—penance—daring—
> And length of watching—strength of mind—and skill
> In knowledge of our fathers ...[75]

Manfred is proud of his accomplishments, which he achieved himself. He asserts his free will against the spirits who act as if he were beholden to them. Here at the end, the theme of the danger of knowledge thus reappears. Manfred was never tempted by the spirits to research the occult arts. He did this all on his own initiative. He thus argues that the human mind itself is responsible for its own evil.[76] He further claims that the mind is immortal but leaves the details

---

[71] Byron, *Manfred, A Dramatic Poem*, p. 63, Act III, Scene II [lines 3–10].
[72] Byron, *Manfred, A Dramatic Poem*, p. 63, Act III, Scene II [line 14].
[73] Byron, *Manfred, A Dramatic Poem*, p. 69, Act III, Scene IV [lines 27–30].
[74] Byron, *Manfred, A Dramatic Poem*, p. 72, Act III, Scene IV [lines 85–87].
[75] Byron, *Manfred, A Dramatic Poem*, p. 74, Act III, Scene IV [lines 113–117].
[76] Byron, *Manfred, A Dramatic Poem*, p. 74, Act III, Scene IV [lines 129–131].

3.4 THE REJECTION OF RELIGION

vague. In the end Manfred manages to get the evil spirits to retreat, thus demonstrating the success of his defiance. He dies thereafter on his own terms.

This final scene emphasizes the freedom of the individual to live as one wishes, which includes taking responsibility for one's own sins. No one else has any right to interfere in this since it is a matter for each individual and their own conscience. This seems to undermine any universal values by which everything can be judged by the same standard. Instead, it lies with the conscience of everyone to judge their life and actions on their own. This, of course, opens the door for relativism since inevitably there will be very different judgments. While some, like Manfred, will have a guilty conscience and will be plagued by their sins, others will be indifferent to them or even deny them.

When read as an autobiographical reflection, *Manfred* suggests that Byron fully accepts the responsibility for his incestuous relation with his half-sister. He does not seek excuses for it by claiming that it was the forces of nature or evil spirits that tempted him. Instead, he acted on his own free volition and must live with the consequences. This anticipates the analyses in the existential tradition of the many attempts that people use to escape their freedom and eschew responsibility by appealing to some external factor or circumstance that made them do what they did. This is what Sartre calls the escape to facticity.[77] Manfred also asserts his individual freedom even in the face of the spirits of evil. In this regard, *Manfred* can be seen as an anticipation of existentialism. The work might be regarded as the first existential drama *avant la lettre*, with Manfred himself as an existential hero. All of this demonstrates that the key issue of nihilism, with its many concomitant themes, was already explored long before the development of the existentialist movement.

With regard to the question of nihilism, Byron's *Manfred* represents a third position that offers interesting points of contrast to Jean Paul and Klingemann. Manfred rejects the traditional religious belief of Jean Paul. Moreover, he refuses to be frightened by the forces of nature and the threat of death. While *The Valley of Campan* is full of characters crying with emotion, there is none of this in the sober Manfred. Rather, he insists on maintaining his dignity and asserting his personal freedom even when he knows that this will not change the facts of the universe, including pain and suffering. From this perspective, Jean Paul's Karlson looks naïve when he willingly abandons himself to the apparently irrational belief in immortality for the sake of his own comfort and peace of mind. As much as Manfred yearns for this kind of inner calm, he knows full well that it cannot be achieved with self-deception.

---

[77] See, for example, Sartre, "La mauvaise foi," in his *L'Être et le Néant, essai d'ontologie phénoménologique*, Paris: Gallimard 1981 [1943], pp. 82–107 (English translation: "Bad Faith," in his *Being and Nothingness: An Essay on Phenomenological Ontology*, trans. by Hazel E. Barnes, New York: Philosophical Library 1956, pp. 47–70).

He insists on his freedom and taking responsibility for himself without relying on the help of other people or ungrounded beliefs.

Like Klingemann's Kreuzgang,[78] Manfred favors rebellion against the world, despite its lack of effectiveness. This is the only way to maintain true human dignity. However, it is more difficult for Kreuzgang to make this kind of argument since he has a completely jaded view of human nature. For him, humans never had any dignity to start with. The message of the ostensibly crazy, yet sane world creator is that humans are so morally depraved that they are not worthy of redemption even if there were a god to offer it.[79] Byron's drama is a serious work, and the question of human integrity and freedom is important. For Manfred, the self-assertion of the individual in the face of a meaningless universe is the solution to nihilism, to the degree that there is one.

Byron's approach is quite different from Jean Paul's attempts to terrify people into rejecting nihilism and thus convince them to return to traditional belief in God, immortality, and so on. It is also quite different from Klingemann's presentation of a meaningless universe with no proposal at all beyond just seeing it for what it is. For Manfred, Kreuzgang would represent a disposition of resignation that fails to grasp the importance of human freedom and individual choice. Kreuzgang shows no self-assertion at the end, and the reader is left with the repetition of the closing word "nothing."[80] Although we cannot change the fact that we are subject to the forces of nature and that we will endure suffering and eventually die, there are great differences in the way that we can live our lives in the face of this. To be sure, Manfred has shortcomings, but his integrity and fearless defiance of the spirits of nature make him a considerably more attractive model to follow than Kreuzgang.

3.5 The Vanity of Human Accomplishment in Shelley's "Ozymandias"

As was the case with Byron, the work of Shelley has also been treated with an eye towards the issue of nihilism.[81] Less than a year after the publication of *Manfred*, Shelley published the sonnet "Ozymandias" on January 11, 1818, in the London-based journal *The Examiner*.[82] It originally appeared under the enigmatic pseudonym Glirastes. As is evident from letters, Shelley's pet name for

---

[78] This is discussed above in Chapter 2, Sect. 2.6, p. 93. See [Klingemann], *Nachtwachen*, pp. 60, 202, 228, 295 (*The Nightwatches of Bonaventura*, pp. 27, 87, 97, 126).
[79] See above Chapter 2, Sect. 2.3, pp. 76–77.
[80] See above Chapter 2, Sect. 2.6, p. 93; [Klingemann], *Nachtwachen*, p. 296 (*The Nightwatches of Bonaventura*, p. 126).
[81] See, for example, Ross Woodman, "Shelley's Void Circumference: The Aesthetic of Nihilism," *English Studies in Canada*, vol. 9, no. 3, 1983, pp. 272–293; Evan Gottlieb, "Shelley, Nihilism, and Speculative Materialism," in his *Romantic Realities: Speculative Realism and British Romanticism*, Edinburgh: Edinburgh University Press 2016, pp. 143–187.
[82] Shelley [Glirastes], "Ozymandias," *The Examiner*, no. 524, January 11, 1818, p. 24.

3.5 THE VANITY OF HUMAN ACCOMPLISHMENT

his soon-to-be wife Mary Godwin was dormouse. The pseudonym is formed by the combination of the Latin *gliridae*, a plural noun that is the zoological designation for dormice, and the Greek *erastes* (ἐραστής), that is, "a lover" (specifically, the elder of two lovers). When these words are put together to form Glirastes, the name means the lover of the dormouse, an affectionate inside joke for the amusement of Mary. The sonnet was republished a year later in Shelley's *Rosalind and Helen, A Modern Eclogue; with Other Poems*.[83] The appearance of the poem in this collection decisively resolved all questions about its authorship that the pseudonym left open.

The poem takes as its point of departure a passage from Diodorus of Sicily's *The Library of History*, where a funeral monument in Egypt with a massive statue is described in some detail. Diodorus refers to the account in the lost work of the Greek historian Hecataeus of Abdera entitled *Aegyptiaca* or *On the Egyptians*:

> Ten stades from the first tombs, he [sc. Hecataeus of Abdera] says … stands a monument of the king known as Osymandyas. At its entrance there is a pylon, constructed of variegated stone, two plethra in breadth and forty-five cubits high; passing through this one enters a rectangular peristyle, built of stone, four plethra long on each side; it is supported, in place of pillars, by monolithic figures sixteen cubits high, wrought in the ancient manner as to shape; and the entire ceiling, which is two fathoms wide, consists of a single stone, which is highly decorated with stars on a blue field. Beyond this peristyle there is yet another entrance and pylon, in every respect like the one mentioned before, save that it is more richly wrought with every manner of relief; beside the entrance are three statues, each of a single block of black stone from Syene, of which one, that is seated, is the largest of any in Egypt, the foot measuring over seven cubits, while the other two at the knees of this, the one on the right and the other on the left, daughter and mother respectively, are smaller than the one first mentioned. And it is not merely for its size that this work merits approbation, but it is also marvelous by reason of its artistic quality and excellent because of the nature of the stone, since in a block of so great a size there is not a single crack or blemish to be seen.[84]

The title of Shelley's poem thus comes from the mentioned Egyptian king Osymandyas (Ὀσυμανδύας), or with an orthographical variation, Ozymandias (Ὀζυμανδίας). This is the Greek name for the Pharaoh Rameses II from the thirteenth century BC. Hecataeus clearly conveys the impression that the statue was awe-inspiring for anyone who saw it. Diodorus continues the description

---

[83] Shelley, *Rosalind and Helen, A Modern Eclogue; with Other Poems*, London: C. and J. Ollier 1819, p. 72. I quote from this reprinted version.
[84] *Diodorus of Sicily*, vols. 1–12, trans. by C.H. Oldfather et al., Cambridge, MA: Harvard University Press and London: William Heinemann 1933–57 (*Loeb Classical Library*, vol. 279), vol. 1, pp. 167f. (Book I, chapter 47).

as follows: "The inscription upon it runs: 'King of Kings am I, Osymandyas. If anyone would know how great I am and where I lie, let him surpass one of my works.'"[85] Hecataeus' account goes on to describe various paintings and reliefs that portray the king's great achievements. Among other things, his glorious military exploits are represented artistically on great walls.

Strangely, the king is depicted in battle accompanied by a lion. Diodorus cannot allow this description from Hecataeus to stand without explanation, and so he adds the following gloss:

> Of those who have explained the scene some have said that in very truth a tame lion which the king kept accompanied him in the perils of battle and put the enemy to rout by his fierce onset; but others have maintained that the king, who was exceedingly brave and desirous of praising himself in a vulgar way, was trying to portray his own bold spirit in the figure of the lion.[86]

With the story of the lion and the inscription on the monument, one gets the impression of a very vain pharaoh. He appears to have spared no expense in glorifying himself.

Upon reading this account in Diodorus, Shelley was inspired to write his famous poem. Hecataeus provides a detailed description of what he has seen in his work, which Diodorus subsequently uses. Shelley imagines himself, in the first person, to be like Diodorus listening to Hecataeus telling him about this sculpture. His poem begins as follows:

> I met a traveller from an antique land
> Who said, Two vast and trunkless legs of stone
> Stand in the desert. Near them, on the sand,
> Half sunk, a shattered visage lies, whose frown,
> And wrinkled lip, and sneer of cold command,
> Tell that its sculptor well those passions read,
> Which yet survive, stamped on these lifeless things,
> The hand that mocked them and the heart that fed.[87]

Like Hecataeus, Shelley cites the inscription on the work. While Shelley changes the wording, he retains the meaning:

> And on the pedestal these words appear:
> "My name is *Ozymandias*, King of Kings:
> Look on my works, ye Mighty, and despair!"
> Nothing beside remains. Round the decay
> Of that colossal wreck, boundless and bare,
> The lone and level sands stretch far away.[88]

---

[85] *Diodorus of Sicily*, vol. 1, p. 169 (Book I, chapter 47).
[86] *Diodorus of Sicily*, vol. 1, p. 171 (Book I, chapter 48).
[87] Shelley, "Ozymandias," p. 72.
[88] Shelley, "Ozymandias," p. 72.

In line with the account of Hecataeus, the great king overwhelms the onlooker with his massive monument and disdainfully dares anyone to try to surpass his deeds.

The poem presents a contrast between the haughty claims of the king at the height of his powers and the sad reality of his statue having fallen into disrepair and his kingdom into oblivion. The sculpture has turned into a ruin, with the head detached and laying in the sand. The ruins of the statue and the surrounding empty desert seem to mock the words of the king. Try though he might, he could not stop the passage of time and the end of his fame and fortune. The moral to the story seems to be that even the greatest of human achievements end in ruin. There is nothing left of this great king or his kingdom but a few carved fragments surrounded by desert. The three final lines are crucial since they convey a sense of barrenness and desolation in the infinity of the vast desert.

The king's arrogant and condescending disposition blinds him to his limitations as a finite, mortal human being. The poem can be read as a warning against a hubris that believes that human actions and projects are ultimately of any lasting valuable. Everything is ephemeral and will end in ruins and dust. The motif recalls the end of Byron's poem, where Manfred, on the last evening of his life, contemplates the ruins of the Colosseum of Rome in the twilight. The Romans achieved many remarkable things, but now what is left is broken pedestals and foundations overrun with foliage.

While Shelley was doubtless inspired by his reading of Diodorus, he was presumably also familiar with images of the pharaoh. European interest in Egypt was in a frenzy after Napoleon's Egyptian campaign (1798–1801). Ancient Egyptian culture and religion were much discussed due to the subsequent publications made by scholars who accompanied Napoleon on his campaign.[89] These publications contained abundant pictures of, among other things, the monuments and art works that were found. With Napoleon defeated, the colorful Italian adventurer Giovanni Battista Belzoni (1778–1823), during his explorations in Egypt, obtained a giant bust of Rameses II for the British in 1816 (Figure 3.1). The British Museum's plans to acquire the piece were sensational news. Due to the logistical problems of transporting the large bust from Egypt to England, it only arrived in London in 1821. But Shelley presumably saw depictions of it in the press in anticipation of its arrival.

In the wake of the fall of Napoleon, Shelley's poem might be taken to be a kind of political commentary on the imperial ambitions of the French general. There was great hope among the generation of young people in Europe at the aspirations of the French Revolution. When Napoleon became dictator,

---

[89] These scholars published the expansive series *Description de l'Égypte, ou Recueil des observations et des recherches qui ont été faites en Égypte pendant l'expédition de l'armée française*, vols. 1–23, Paris: L'Imprimerie Imperiale 1809–22. This work is widely regarded as the foundation of the modern field of Egyptology.

Figure 3.1 Colossal bust of Rameses II, the "Younger Memnon" (1250 BC) at the British Museum

his abuses were overlooked due to the hope that he would spread the new freedoms of the Revolution throughout the Continent. Enthusiasts for Napoleon included Hegel, Beethoven, Schelling, Goethe, Hölderlin, and Klopstock. But after Napoleon's fall and the Congress of Vienna from 1814 to 1815, it could easily seem as if he had achieved almost nothing for all his efforts. More than a decade of war in Europe had brought no great empire of freedom and human rights. Seen in the light of this disappointment, there might well have been a temptation to regard Napoleon as yet another arrogant, cruel, power-hungry ruler, whose work only brought death and suffering to countless people.

The poem draws our attention to human finitude and our small place in the universe. With the passage of time, we will all be forgotten, and all human achievement rendered meaningless. To be vain about one's accomplishments reveals a lack of perspective. It is necessary always to keep in mind the larger picture, which shows the miniscule role of humans in the grand scheme of things. In this sense Shelley's poem can be understood as an expression of nihilism and despair. If the achievements of one of the greatest of Egyptian kings with vast power, fame, and wealth amount to nothing, then it seems that the activities of the rest of us are hopelessly trivial.

Shelley adds an extra dimension to the discussion of nihilism by using it as a tool for ethical or moral criticism. The meaninglessness of one's life should give one a new perspective. The awareness of nihilism should undermine any sense of pride or vanity in one's accomplishments. We should always bear in mind that this will all come to nothing in the end. Nihilism thus comes with a kind of ethical message about the proper disposition to life. This dimension was not present in the previous discussions, perhaps with the exception of Byron's *Manfred*. For Jean Paul, it is impossible for anyone to live with nihilism, and so there is no real ethical lesson to be learned from it. One should simply abandon it as soon as possible and return to traditional views about meaning. Klingemann's *The Nightwatches* does offer some general social satire that criticizes people for their many follies, including arrogance. However, his protagonist Kreuzgang seems hardly to be a moral crusader. On the contrary, he himself, as an outsider, displays certain aspects of arrogance or pride about his life in contrast to that of the mainstream. Byron's Manfred comes the closest to Shelley, but the message is quite different. For Shelley, nihilism and meaninglessness should teach us humility. However, for Manfred, the message is that one should assert oneself and rebel against the gods of nature, insisting on one's own autonomy. This disposition of stubborn rebellion is almost the opposite of Shelley's humility.

3.6 The Scientific and Nihilistic Views in *Manfred* and "Ozymandias"

Manfred and "Ozymandias" show clearly that the question of nihilism and meaninglessness was one that concerned both Byron and Shelley. They demonstrate that nihilism was not an issue that was confined to the German tradition at this time. We have seen from the other works studied so far that the advances in the sciences played an important role in the rise of nihilism by showing the vastness of the universe and rejecting the explanations of traditional religion. This also seems to be true in the case of Byron and Shelley. The Romantics are often characterized as being suspicious of reason and science. However, this view is oversimplified.

While Byron is keen to show the limitations of human knowing and instead appeals to the supernatural, this can be interpreted in a symbolic manner. The nature spirits, the witch of the Alps, and the Destinies are all personified, but they are meant to represent the forces of nature: the air, the mountain, the ocean, the earth, the winds, the night, the Alps, and so on. Thus, what appear as supernatural deities are in fact poetic representations of nature. The point is that these are unable to help Manfred in any meaningful way. He is left to languish on his own. In fact, it is emphasized that these forces of nature are destructive to human life and happiness. So, while Byron takes poetic license with these characters, in the end the picture that he presents is based on a sobering scientific view. But Byron is far from uncritical concerning science. He sees in it the dangerous roots of nihilism.

Likewise, Manfred's consistent rejection of traditional religion and any form of allegiance to the spirits suggests that no solution or solace can be found here either. Instead, the individual is alone and must cope with the crises of life with his or her own mental and physical resources. To place one's faith in religion or superstition would be the same as giving up one's freedom and trying to pawn off the responsibility for one's actions on someone else. Here *Manfred* clearly anticipates some of the key motifs of twentieth-century existentialism, which tries to think through consistently a picture of the world without God or the false hope of immortality. Thinkers such as Camus, Sartre, and de Beauvoir also end up by focusing on the freedom of the individual as the solution. They too reject what they regard as being satisfied with easy solutions such as religion or political ideology.

Shelley's "Ozymandias" likewise offers no hint of supernatural assistance. It too takes a purely scientific perspective, according to which everything follows a natural course of birth, life, and death. While Byron's religious views are more complex, Shelley was an ardent atheist and an opponent of the doctrine of immortality. This led him to pursue the consequences of the scientific worldview, and this in turn naturally led him to the issue of nihilism.

In his youth Shelley was deeply interested in science and performed scientific experiments as a student at University College, Oxford. There he authored a pamphlet, entitled *The Necessity of Atheism* in 1811, where he argues against the belief in God based on empirical science and rationalism.[90] This led to his expulsion from Oxford. Shelley later reprinted this work in the form of notes to his long poem *Queen Mab*, in 1813.[91] In this reprinted version Shelley added a few longer quotations from works of authors that he had perhaps read in the interim and that were relevant to the topic. One of these is the magnum opus of the French Enlightenment philosopher, Paul Henri Thiry d'Holbach, entitled *Système de la Nature, ou des Loix du Monde Physique et du Monde Morale*, which was published under the pseudonym J.B. Mirabaud.[92] Shelley cites a long passage from the first chapter, "Origine de nos idées sur la Divinité."[93] In his selection of the passage to be quoted, Shelley shows how important the natural sciences are for his view of the world. There is no reason to cite the entire passage, but its spirit is captured by a single sentence: "*Si l'ignorance de la nature donna la naissance*

---

[90] [Percy Bysshe Shelley], *The Necessity of Atheism*, Worthing: C.&W. Philipps 1811.
[91] Percy Bysshe Shelley, *Queen Mab; A Philosophical Poem with Notes*, London: Printed by P. B. Shelley 1813.
[92] [Paul Henri Thiry d'Holbach], *Système de la Nature, ou des Loix du Monde Physique et du Monde Morale. Par M. Mirabaud*, nouvelle édition, vols. 1-2, London: n.p. 1781. Note that this is a reprint of the London edition of 1770, hence the designation "nouvelle édition."
[93] Altogether Shelley cites three passages from this work, namely, *Système de la Nature*, vol. 2, pp. 13–15, p. 22, pp. 249–254. See the useful discussion in the commentary apparatus in *The Complete Poetry of Percy Bysshe Shelley*, ed. by Donald H. Reiman and Neil Fraistat, Baltimore and London: The Johns Hopkins University Press 2004, vol. 2, pp. 629–632.

aux Dieux, la connaissance de la nature est faite pour les détruire."[94] This perfectly captures Shelley's view of the role of Enlightenment science towards traditional belief. As long as people were ignorant of science, they believed in the gods since there seemed to be no other explanation for the mysteries of the world around them. But now with the Enlightenment, knowledge of the sciences has destroyed the gods since they have now been rendered superfluous.

In harmony with the scientific view, the poem "Ozymandias" sees the universe as endless in space and time, a place where human actions, regardless of how significant they might appear at the moment, have no real meaning. In time everything and everyone decays, dies, and is forgotten. Chronos was the most powerful of the early Greek gods. The meaning of this is clearly that time has the ultimate power over everything. Time will outlast the other natural powers of the ocean, the mountains, the sun, and so on. Time is also responsible for the death of every living thing. While people suffer from many different ailments, in the end they die due to the passage of time. The infinity of time renders human action meaningless. Compared to the universe, the periods in which we as individuals live are fleetingly short. It will be recalled that Jean Paul used the image of the short lifespans of insects as a comparison.

Likewise, by referring to the vast desert sands, Shelley also alludes to the infinity of space. In comparison to the unimaginable size of the universe, the space we occupy in our lives is tiny. The theater of all human history is a mere pinpoint compared to our solar system or our galaxy, without even mentioning the colossal distances to other galaxies. This again emphasizes the meaninglessness of human existence. The focus on both time and space in Shelley's poem evidences a scientific worldview, which brings with it the problem of nihilism. Our natural limitations confine us to a condition of utter cosmic insignificance.

---

[94] D'Holbach, "Chapitre Premier. Origine de nos idées sur la Divinité," in his *Système de la Nature*, vol. 2, p. 22. Shelley prints this in the original French in the first edition, but then an English translation is added to the reprint. Percy Bysshe Shelley, *Queen Mab*, London: R. Carlile 1822, "Notes. VII. Page 61. There is no God!" p. 132: "If ignorance of nature gave birth to gods, a knowledge of nature is calculated to destroy them."

4

Schopenhauer's Theory of Human Suffering and Lack of Meaning

Arthur Schopenhauer (1788–1860) was an eccentric and idiosyncratic figure in the history of German philosophy.[1] Born in Danzig (today, Gdańsk, Poland), he traveled throughout Europe and lived in different places in his younger years. This allowed him to learn foreign languages and exposed him to the literature of the world. In his youth he lived in Weimar, where his mother had a literary salon, which hosted well-known figures such as Goethe. The young Schopenhauer entered the University of Göttingen in 1809 and studied medicine but after a year switched to philosophy. He transferred to the University of Berlin in 1811, where he continued his studies in both fields. There he attended the lectures of Fichte and Schleiermacher. He became a convinced atheist and open critic of religion. In 1813 Schopenhauer left Berlin during the chaos of Napoleon's French Army retreating from Moscow with many wounded filling the hospitals and spreading disease. He went back to Weimar and later to the nearby Rudolstadt, where he wrote his dissertation.[2] He was awarded his degree by the neighboring University of Jena as an external student. In Weimar he renewed his acquaintance with Goethe, who was put off by his arrogance, while at the same time acknowledging his academic abilities. During this time Schopenhauer became interested in Hinduism and Buddhism, elements of which he incorporated into his thinking. Like many of his contemporaries, he was caught up in the new and expanding research in the field that would come

---

[1] For Schopenhauer's life, see Patrick Bridgewater, *Arthur Schopenhauer's English Schooling*, London and New York: Routledge 1988; David E. Cartwright, *Schopenhauer: A Biography*, Cambridge: Cambridge University Press 2010; Vivian J. McGill, *Schopenhauer: Pessimist and Pagan*, New York: Haskell House Publishers 1971; Rüdiger Safranski, *Schopenhauer and the Wild Years of Philosophy*, trans. by Ewald Osers, London: Weidenfeld and Nicholson 1989; William Wallace, *Life of Arthur Schopenhauer*, London: Walter Scott 1890; Helen Zimmern, *Arthur Schopenhauer: His Life and Philosophy*, London: Longmans Green & Co. 1876.

[2] Arthur Schopenhauer, *Ueber die vierfache Wurzel des Satzes vom zureichenden Grunde. Eine Philosophische Abhandlung*, Rudolstadt: in Commission der Hof- Buch- und Kunsthandlung 1813. (English translation: *On the Fourfold Root of the Principle of Sufficient Reason*, trans. by E. F. J. Payne, La Salle: Open Court 1974.)

to be known as Asian studies.[3] He is known as one of the first thinkers to introduce Asian philosophical thinking to the West. Schopenhauer's attraction to Buddhism aligns with the general understanding at the time that this was a religion of nihilism that worshiped nothingness or emptiness.[4]

In 1814 Schopenhauer relocated to Dresden, where he wrote *The World as Will and Representation*, which is the definitive statement of his philosophy.[5] The book, which appeared in 1819, did not enjoy a broad reception, thus disappointing Schopenhauer's high hopes and expectations. After extensive travels in Italy, he tried to begin an academic career at the University of Berlin. Hegel had arrived there in 1818 and was already regarded as the star of the philosophy department. Schopenhauer arrogantly scheduled his lectures at the same time as Hegel's, and then, after thus setting himself up for failure, was disappointed

---

[3] See Walter Leifer, *India and the Germans: 500 Years of Indo-German Contacts*, Bombay: Shakuntala Publishing House 1971; Wilhelm Halbfass, *India and Europe: An Essay in Understanding*, Albany, NY: State University of New York Press 1988; Philip C. Almond, *The British Discovery of Buddhism*, Cambridge: Cambridge University Press 1988; Stephen Batchelor, *The Awakening of the West: The Encounter of Buddhism and Western Culture: 543 BCE–1992*, London: Harper Collins 1994; Richard King, *Orientalism and Religion: Postcolonial Theory, India, and "The Mystic East,"* London and New York: Routledge 1999; Raymond Schwab, *The Oriental Renaissance: Europe's Rediscovery of India and the East, 1680–1880*, trans. by Gene Patterson-Black and Victor Reinking, New York: Columbia University Press 1984; Urs App, *The Birth of Orientalism*, Philadelphia: University of Pennsylvania Press 2010; Douglas T. McGetchin, *Indology, Indomania, and Orientalism: Ancient India's Rebirth in Modern Germany*, Madison, NJ: Farleigh Dickinson University Press 2009; Susanne Sommerfeld, *Indienschau und Indiendeutung romantischer Philosophen*, Zürich: Rascher Verlag 1943; Bradley L. Herling, *The German Gita: Hermeneutics and Discipline in the German Reception of Indian Thought, 1778–1831*, New York: Routledge 2006; A. Leslie Willson, *A Mythical Image: The Ideal of India in German Romanticism*, Durham, NC: Duke University Press 1964; Nicholas A. Germana, *The Orient of Europe: The Mythical Image of India and Competing Images of German National Identity*, Newcastle upon Tyne: Cambridge Scholars Publishing 2009; Helmuth von Glasenapp, *Das Indienbild deutscher Denker*, Stuttgart: K.F. Koehler 1960.

[4] See, for example, Roger-Pol Droit, *The Cult of Nothingness: The Philosophers and the Buddha*, trans. by David Streight and Pamela Vohnson, Chapel Hill, NC and London: The University of North Carolina Press 2003; Urs App, *The Cult of Emptiness: The Western Discovery of Buddhist Thought and the Invention of Oriental Philosophy*, Rorschach and Kyoto: University Media 2012; Christopher Ryan, *Schopenhauer's Philosophy of Religion: The Death of God and the Oriental Renaissance*, Leuven: Peeters 2010; Henk Oosterling, "Avoiding Nihilism by Affirming Nothing: Hegel on Buddhism," in *Hegel's Philosophy of the Historical Religions*, ed. by Bart Labuschagne and Timo Slootweg, Leiden and Boston: Brill 2012, pp. 51–77; Urs App, "The Tibet of the Philosophers: Kant, Hegel, and Schopenhauer," in *Images of Tibet in the 19th and 20th Centuries*, vols. 1–2, ed. by Monica Esposito, Paris: École française d'Extrême-Orient 2008, vol. 1, pp. 7–60 (see pp. 22–42); Heinrich Dumoulin, "Buddhism and Nineteenth-Century German Philosophy," *Journal of the History of Ideas*, vol. 42, no. 3, 1981, pp. 457–470.

[5] Arthur Schopenhauer, *Die Welt als Wille und Vorstellung: Vier Bücher nebst einem Anhange, der die Kritik der Kantischen Philosophie enthält*, Leipzig: F. A. Brockhaus 1819.

when only a handful of students showed up for his classes. Giving up the idea of university teaching for the time being, Schopenhauer subsequently spent three years traveling in the German states and Italy before returning to Berlin, where he tried to restart his academic career at the university. Once again disappointed and having no success in his queries at other universities, he definitively abandoned the idea of pursuing a career as a university professor.

He ultimately left Berlin in 1831 and moved to Frankfurt am Main. With the exception of a few trips and a short stay in Mannheim, Schopenhauer would spend the rest of his life there as an independent scholar. In 1844 he published the second edition of *The World as Will and Representation*, which was expanded with an additional volume.[6] The second edition adds new arguments and examples to the position that he set forth in 1819, but his general view did not to change at all in the intervening years. He published his last major work, *Parerga and Paralipomena*, in 1851.[7] This work consists of scattered essays that cover some of the same ground as his previous works, yet again with new arguments and insights. In 1859 he published a third edition of *The World as Will and Representation*, in which he continued to modify and enlarge the text.[8] Schopenhauer only enjoyed academic fame towards the end of his life as his works began to be read and discussed more widely. He died in 1860 at his home in Frankfurt am Main. It can truly be said that he dedicated his life to a single, unwavering worldview.

Schopenhauer regarded himself as a Kantian who wanted to revise and develop Kant's transcendental philosophy further. On his reading, Kant had discovered some key elements about the world and human thinking with his theory of transcendental idealism and the split between representations and things-in-themselves. On his reading, German idealism reached its highpoint with Kant, and it had been downhill ever since in the works of subsequent thinkers such as Fichte, Schelling, and Hegel. Schopenhauer displayed a polemical tendency even at a fairly early age. In his works he frequently rails without abandon against these post-Kantian thinkers in a manner that is purely ad hominem. Often surrounded by personal conflicts, he was a conceited and difficult person by all accounts. He is also infamous for his overt misogyny.

---

[6] Arthur Schopenhauer, *Die Welt als Wille und Vorstellung*, vols. 1–2, 2nd revised and enlarged edition, Leipzig: F. A. Brockhaus 1844.

[7] Arthur Schopenhauer, *Parerga und Paralipomena: kleine philosophische Schriften*, vols. 1–2, Berlin: A. W. Hayn 1851 (English translation: *Parerga and Paralipomena*, vols. 1–2, trans. by E. F. J. Payne, Oxford: Clarendon Press 1974).

[8] Arthur Schopenhauer, *Die Welt als Wille und Vorstellung*, vols. 1–2, 3rd improved and significantly enlarged edition, Leipzig: F. A. Brockhaus 1859 (English translation: *The World as Will and Representation*, vols. 1–2, trans. by E. F. J. Payne, New York: Dover 1969; *The World as Will and Presentation*, vols. 1–2, trans. by Richard Aquila in collaboration with David Carus, New York: Longman 2007–2010; *The World as Will and Representation*, vols. 1–2, trans. by Judith Norman, Alistair Welchman, and Christopher Janaway, Cambridge: Cambridge University Press 2010–2018).

Schopenhauer is well known for his pessimism and nihilism, and therefore it is natural that some account of him should be presented in a book on nihilism in the nineteenth century. Many overviews of his works have been given, and there is of course a long tradition of Schopenhauer scholarship.[9] In this chapter we want to look specifically at Schopenhauer's conception of nihilism in the contexts of the other works that we have previously explored from German literature. The analysis will focus on the original edition of *The World as Will and Representation* from 1819 since we wish to see the text in its proper historical context. However, making an exception to the first edition rule, I am referencing the second edition due primarily to practical purposes. Specifically, the second edition conveniently provides section numbers that are absent in the first edition, thus rendering it considerably easier to orient oneself in the text. Moreover, with regard to the first volume, the text of the second edition contains only minor emendations and is thus virtually the same as the first edition.[10]

4.1 The Theory of the Will

In § 56 of the first volume of *The World as Will and Representation*, Schopenhauer gives a useful overview of his theory of striving and the will. He argues that everything that exists strives without ever reaching a goal or end. This includes physical objects of nature, plants, animals, and human beings. For natural phenomena, he points out how the principle of gravity causes everything to be in motion or to try to get to a central point of mass. He claims that such natural phenomena can be understood as striving, even though the physical objects are not conscious.[11] Both plant and animal life need nourishment, water, sunlight, and so on. Striving continues for as long as a thing exists or as long as a biological being is alive. This constant restless activity is the basic principle of the entire universe, although we are used to thinking of this

---

[9] See Patrick Gardiner, *Schopenhauer*, Baltimore: Penguin 1963; Robert Wicks, *Schopenhauer*, Oxford: Blackwell 2008; Robert Wicks, *Schopenhauer's The World as Will and Representation: A Reader's Guide*, London: Continuum 2011; Julian Young, *Willing and Unwilling: A Study in the Philosophy of Arthur Schopenhauer*, Dordrecht: Martinus Nijhoff 1987; Bryan Magee, *The Philosophy of Schopenhauer*, Oxford: Clarendon Press 1983; Christopher Janaway, *Schopenhauer*, Oxford: Oxford University Press 1994; John E. Atwell, *Schopenhauer on the Character of the World*, Berkeley: University of California Press 1995; Frederick Copleston, *Arthur Schopenhauer: Philosopher of Pessimism*, London: Barnes and Noble 1946.

[10] For a useful overview of the changes made in the different editions, see Norman, Welchman, and Janaway, "Variants in Different Editions," in *The World as Will and Representation*, vols. 1-2, trans. by Norman, Welchman, and Janaway, vol. 1, pp. 567–603; vol. 2, pp. 664–680.

[11] Schopenhauer, *Die Welt als Wille und Vorstellung*, 2nd revised and enlarged edition, vol. 1, § 56, p. 348. As noted, in what follows reference will be made to both volumes in this

striving as something that is confined to humans or highly developed animals. Schopenhauer designates this striving in human beings and advanced animals "the will."[12] But he hastens to add that this can also be extended to everything in the universe, even to nonliving things, albeit to lesser degrees.[13]

Schopenhauer describes the will and its striving as a never-ending inward discord in every living thing. He explains, "Thus a constant struggle is carried on between life and death, the main result whereof is the resistance by which that striving, which constitutes the innermost nature of everything, is everywhere impeded. It presses and urges in vain; yet, by reason of its inner nature, it cannot cease."[14] Humans constantly work to satiate their needs for food, drink, sex, sleep, and so on. But sometimes this is not so easy, and this causes us pain and discomfort. We spend our entire lives catering to our drives, which, once satisfied, always return after a short time. This constant striving is what Schopenhauer calls "suffering."[15] He argues as follows:

> For all striving springs from want or deficiency, from dissatisfaction with one's own state or condition, and is therefore suffering so long as it is not satisfied. No satisfaction, however, is lasting; on the contrary, it is always merely the starting point of a fresh striving. We see striving everywhere impeded in many ways, everywhere struggling and fighting, and hence always as suffering. Thus that there is no ultimate aim of striving means that there is no measure or end of suffering.[16]

Humans are thus condemned to a life of suffering since at no time do they ever reach a point when they can simply sit back satisfied and relax.

Schopenhauer claims that there is a long hierarchy of beings that suffer in this way. He states that, at the lower end of the scale, insects can feel pain. He further argues that the capacity for suffering increases the more the nervous system is developed, and the more intelligent the animal becomes. From this it follows that human beings experience maximum suffering. Among humans, those who have developed the ability to learn and have accumulated the most knowledge

---

second edition and not to the first edition of 1819 (*The World as Will and Representation*, vol. 1, § 56, pp. 308f.). Here and below I refer to the Payne translation of *The World as Will and Representation*.

[12] Schopenhauer, *Die Welt als Wille und Vorstellung*, vol. 1, § 56, p. 349 (*The World as Will and Representation*, vol. 1, § 56, p. 309).

[13] Schopenhauer refers to nonliving things as "the world-without-knowledge" and "nature-without-knowledge"; *Die Welt als Wille und Vorstellung*, vol. 1, § 56, p. 349 (*The World as Will and Representation*, vol. 1, § 56, p. 309).

[14] Schopenhauer, *Die Welt als Wille und Vorstellung*, vol. 1, § 56, p. 349 (*The World as Will and Representation*, vol. 1, § 56, p. 309).

[15] Schopenhauer, *Die Welt als Wille und Vorstellung*, vol. 1, § 56, p. 349 (*The World as Will and Representation*, vol. 1, § 56, p. 309).

[16] Schopenhauer, *Die Welt als Wille und Vorstellung*, vol. 1, § 56, p. 349 (*The World as Will and Representation*, vol. 1, § 56, p. 309).

are at the very top of the hierarchy of suffering. Here Schopenhauer cites the famous words of Ecclesiastes that were mentioned in the Introduction: "For in much wisdom is much vexation, and those who increase knowledge, increase sorrow."[17] He gives an interesting interpretation of this sentence, seeing it as a support for his view that those who know the most, suffer the most. This is a more general claim than the one that seems to be made in Schiller's poem, "The Veiled Statue at Sais."[18] For Schiller, the idea seems to be that some specific sort of knowledge, such as the insight gained by nihilism, makes one despair and leads to unhappiness and death. By contrast, for Schopenhauer, this suffering is a general condition for all humanity that is heightened by the fact that humans are highly developed creatures capable of knowing and learning.

Schopenhauer thus reaches the conclusion at the end of § 56 that "all life is suffering,"[19] which seems to follow from his conception of the never-ending striving of the will. In this bleak conclusion we can see evidence of Schopenhauer's background in medicine and the natural sciences. He sees humans not as being special or separate from nature but, on the contrary, as a continuous part of the natural world, which differs only by degree from plants and animals. Humans are physical beings who have arisen from nature. There is no talk of being the special creations of God or of having an immortal soul. Like the other objects of nature, humans are finite and perishable. This is the beginning of his pessimism or nihilism. Schopenhauer thus believes that he is developing a philosophy that is founded on hard science.

4.2 The Human Condition: The Dialectic of Pain and Boredom

In § 57 Schopenhauer goes on to emphasize the nature of human beings as finite and always on the way to death. He argues that time and space are infinite, in comparison to which the human being is a tiny, insignificant thing that occupies only a small, limited space and a short period of time. Schopenhauer claims that our past can generally be a matter of indifference to us since we do not need to trouble ourselves with the pains or times of stress that we have experienced previously. On the contrary, our primary focus is on the present and immediate needs and desires that require our attention at any given moment. But the present is continually slipping into the past. Schopenhauer refers to this as a "constant dying,"[20] whereby, second by second, we die a little bit as the span of time in which we have left to live becomes ever shorter and shorter.

---

[17] Ecclesiastes 1:18. See Introduction, Sect. 0.5, p. 26. Schopenhauer, *Die Welt als Wille und Vorstellung*, vol. 1, § 56, p. 350 (*The World as Will and Representation*, vol. 1, § 56, p. 310).
[18] See Introduction, Sect. 0.5, pp. 26–28 and Chapter 1, Sect. 1.3, p. 51.
[19] Schopenhauer, *Die Welt als Wille und Vorstellung*, vol. 1, § 56, p. 350 (*The World as Will and Representation*, vol. 1, § 56, p. 310).
[20] Schopenhauer, *Die Welt als Wille und Vorstellung*, vol. 1, § 57, p. 351 (*The World as Will and Representation*, vol. 1, § 57, p. 311).

Our lives can only end in one way, with death. Like the past, the future does not exist. It is the place where human illusions are born, but it has no actuality.

In the previous § 56, Schopenhauer concluded that all life is suffering in the sense that it is the nature of the will constantly to strive to fulfill its desires and needs, which return quickly after they have been momentarily satisfied. As we have seen, this never-ending need to satisfy our desires he understands as a condition of pain. Human existence consists of this pain and the constant occupation with our needs. Now he introduces a new element into this equation. Once a person has reached a prosperous condition where their basic needs are immediately met and the striving is somewhat reduced, this leads to boredom. The tedium of our lives induces people to cultivate ever refined tastes in search of something new. This sense of boredom is also a motif that is found in Ecclesiastes, where it is written, "What has been is what will be, and what has been done is what will be done; there is nothing new under the sun."[21] There are only the constant repetitions of nature. But without anything truly novel and exciting, our lives become tedious. Or similarly, Shakespeare points out the boredom in human life at the beginning of Macbeth's soliloquy, "Tomorrow, and tomorrow, and tomorrow, / Creeps in this petty pace from day to day, / To the last syllable of recorded time."[22] The repetition of the word "tomorrow" underscores the lack of anything novel or interesting and the boredom of our existence. We quickly fall into the tedium of our daily routines and struggle to find something that can entertain or amuse us until we die. The result of boredom is the refinement of ever more sophisticated tastes, for example, in food, wine, or other such kinds. The more people refine their palettes for such things, the more they have to struggle to find satisfaction since there are fewer and fewer things that will actually satisfy them by meeting their high standards. Such connoisseurs must go to great lengths to find something new that they can take pleasure in.

Schopenhauer believes that boredom is an underestimated phenomenon since people who are bored become aggressive and dangerous to the social order. With too much time on their hands in situations of isolation, they are given the opportunity to consider their problems and voice them overtly. Thus the Romans realized that the attention of the people must constantly be diverted, and they must continually be given some kind of entertainment, bread and circuses (*panem et circenses*), to keep them occupied, or else a rebellion might start. Schopenhauer argues that human life "swings like a pendulum to and fro between pain and boredom."[23] People struggle with the pain of constant striving to meet their basic desires, and when these are too easily satisfied, they quickly lapse into the despair of boredom.

---

[21] Ecclesiastes 1:9.
[22] Shakespeare, *Macbeth*, Act 5, Scene 5, lines 18–20, p. 2561.
[23] Schopenhauer, *Die Welt als Wille und Vorstellung*, vol. 1, § 57, p. 352 (*The World as Will and Representation*, vol. 1, § 57, p. 312).

Schopenhauer argues that what enables people "to endure this wearisome battle [sc. of life] is not so much the love of life as the fear of death."[24] Here he seems to be influenced by Hamlet's "To be or not to be" speech, which, as we have seen,[25] likewise argues that for the most part people endure all the difficulties and injustices that life throws at them and thus choose to continue living instead of committing suicide.[26] The reason for this, Hamlet says, is that we are all cowards, fearing that something even worse might come after we are dead.

Schopenhauer is known for his pessimistic philosophy, but here he hints at a partial solution to the nihilistic picture of the human condition that he presents. He claims that a degree of happiness can be achieved if one can manage to find the optimal balance between the pain, where it is difficult to satisfy all our drives and needs, and boredom, where they are too easily satisfied. Human happiness is momentarily possible if one can manage to have one's needs satisfied fairly easily and draw out the moments of satisfaction, but not for so long that this leads to boredom. Schopenhauer seems to draw on the Aristotelian ideas of the golden mean and the life of philosophical contemplation as his model.

He also emphasizes the pleasure of viewing art as a solution to the problem of nihilism: "What might otherwise be called the finest part of life, its purest joy, just because it lifts us out of real existence, and transforms us into disinterested spectators of it, is pure knowledge which remains foreign to all willing, pleasure in the beautiful, genuine delight in art."[27] His idea is that we always have a natural vested interest in satisfying our needs. When we look at things in the world, we immediately interpret them for how they might be used to our advantage. Is this something that I can eat, drink? Is this a place where I can find shelter or be safe, and so on? But this is not the case when we look at a work of art. Since the objects portrayed in a painting or a sculpture are not real, they do not awaken in us this sense of desire or personal interest. We can thus relax and study works of art in a disinterested manner, detached from our needs and desires. This, for Schopenhauer, gives us a sense of pleasure or a feeling of happiness that breaks the cycle of pain and boredom. The same holds true when we do philosophy and discuss abstract concepts that in no way help us to satisfy our natural desires. This is a pleasure that also allows us to forget our immediate needs and drives, as when professors get carried away and lecture

---

[24] Schopenhauer, *Die Welt als Wille und Vorstellung*, vol. 1, § 57, p. 352 (*The World as Will and Representation*, vol. 1, § 57, pp. 312f.).
[25] Chapter 2, Sect. 2.4, p. 79; Sect. 2.5, p. 82; Chapter 3, Sect. 3.2, pp. 106–108.
[26] Shakespeare, *Hamlet*, Scene 8, lines 57–91, pp. 2040f. (in editions that divide the play into acts, this appears in Act 3, Scene 1).
[27] Schopenhauer, *Die Welt als Wille und Vorstellung*, vol. 1, § 57, p. 354 (*The World as Will and Representation*, vol. 1, § 57, p. 314). See also *Die Welt als Wille und Vorstellung*, vol. 1, § 68, p. 440 (*The World as Will and Representation*, vol. 1, § 68, p. 390).

for so long that they do not realize that they have become thirsty or hungry. Unfortunately, these higher pleasures are intellectual and thus presuppose a highly developed intellect, which is, according to Schopenhauer, not possible for the vast majority of people, who are condemned to the sad dialectic of pain and boredom. This seems to be Schopenhauer's proposal for how to escape nihilism, at least partially.

One might argue that aesthetic contemplation is just one distraction among many that people use to divert themselves from their pain and suffering. When we watch sporting events or enjoy leisure activities, is this not the same kind of thing? These examples seem very much like aesthetic contemplation in that they offer us a brief break from our daily struggles. Schopenhauer's point still seems to hold, but it might be argued that it can be expanded to many other areas as well. However, it would be inconsistent to criticize people for self-deception when they engage in these other activities, while applauding them when they become absorbed in great works of art.

Ultimately, there is no escape since sooner or later the desires return in force, and sooner or later even great intellects or art lovers will die and become nothing. Schopenhauer's position does, however, imply that a nihilistic view of the world does not have to end in depression and misery, as Jean Paul seems to think. For Gione in *The Valley of Campan*, this is the crux of the argument with Karlson. She pities him because he must live his life in depression and sadness since he refuses to abandon his scientific worldview and accept the idea of human immortality. Schopenhauer shows here that this is not necessarily the consequence of such a view. It is possible to maintain a scientific and nihilistic disposition yet still attain a degree of happiness, which Gione and the others apparently think impossible.

Schopenhauer also offers another form of consolation to which Jean Paul seems blind. He points out that when we accept his nihilistic view of the human condition and understand that we are necessarily condemned to suffering, then we can take a degree of comfort in the fact that we know what we are up against and entertain no illusions about being able to change things. We are often most vexed when we have difficulties satisfying our desires since we mistakenly think that these are just contingent, accidental, and temporary, and if things were different, we would not have these problems. But we tend to be less vexed by things that we know are inevitable and that we can never escape, such as old age. People also tend to have a kind of tunnel vision with regard to the satisfaction of their needs. When a specific need or desire becomes acute, its satisfaction is the only thing that people can think about. They live in the illusion, for example, that if they only could buy the desired item, then all their other problems would disappear. But, as experience teaches, the satisfaction of the purchase of the desired thing is short-lived, and the thing is never quite as great as one believed it would be, and thus one is soon looking for something even better. Schopenhauer's point is that when we reach this realization that our ever-recurring needs and desires are also necessary, and there is nothing we can do but live with them, then this can fortify us with a degree of Stoic detachment.[28] When we realize that the complete and permanent satisfaction of all of our needs is simply not possible, then we can assume a realistic disposition towards them instead of living in an illusion that only causes more suffering since it increases the intensity of the need and frustrates us when we fail to attain the desired permanent satisfaction, which is unattainable. A part of this is the illusion that our pain and suffering is the result of something external, which, once removed, will leave us to our happiness. But we fail to see that in fact it is a necessary part of our very being and is thus unavoidable. We cannot eliminate it without ceasing to exist ourselves.[29]

4.3 Satisfaction as a Negation

In § 58 Schopenhauer advances the thesis that satisfaction is negative.[30] It only comes about from a desire or need, which is a want or a lack. We can only appreciate the sense of satisfaction when we compare it to the previous condition of the need we felt. But once the need is satisfied, this is quickly forgotten, and we mistakenly take the briefly satisfied condition to be the normal one that is the desired baseline for our existence against which all else is measured. This means that satisfaction is not something positive but simply the absence of a specific need or desire.

Schopenhauer argues that this fact can be found reflected in art. In epic poetry, the heroes struggle through great difficulties to attain their goals. Then once these are attained, the story ends. This gives the impression that life is about struggling to reach some final goal or satisfaction, which, once attained, will ensure one's subsequent happiness. The poets conveniently end their works at this point since to continue the story would mean the protagonists would soon become dissatisfied or bored with their condition and need to address a new set of challenges and difficulties. This is also typical of love stories, where the entire plot and action are focused on the difficulties involved in the lovers finding each other, discovering their mutual love, and consummating it. Then the story ends with a happy event such as a wedding. But this is, of course, only a part of the story since it fails to address the equally difficult challenges of living together in harmony over an extended period when new conflicts and challenges will inevitably arise. This part of the story is conveniently

---

[28] Schopenhauer, *Die Welt als Wille und Vorstellung*, vol. 1, § 57, pp. 355f. (*The World as Will and Representation*, vol. 1, § 57, p. 315).
[29] Schopenhauer, *Die Welt als Wille und Vorstellung*, vol. 1, § 57, pp. 358f. (*The World as Will and Representation*, vol. 1, § 57, pp. 317f.).
[30] Schopenhauer, *Die Welt als Wille und Vorstellung*, vol. 1, § 58, p. 360 (*The World as Will and Representation*, vol. 1, § 58, p. 319).

omitted since it is less glamourous. This again demonstrates the illusion of the idea that an enduring happiness can ever be attained. It shows that our sense of happiness only endures briefly from the momentary satisfaction of a need, but, on its own, happiness is nothing.

We discussed in the previous chapters how Jean Paul seems to regard the idea of nihilism as a tragedy to be avoided. By contrast, Klingemann's Kreuzgang regards it as a comedy that exposes the absurdity of human existence and the ridiculous delusions from which people suffer. Schopenhauer now brings these two positions together and says that the life of individuals in the nihilistic universe is both a tragedy and a comedy:

> The never-fulfilled wishes, the frustrated efforts, the hopes mercilessly blighted by fate, the unfortunate mistakes of the whole life, with increasing suffering and death at the end, always give us a tragedy. Thus, as if fate wished to add mockery to the misery of our existence, our life must contain all the woes of tragedy, and yet we cannot even assert the dignity of tragic characters, but, in the broad detail of life, are inevitably the foolish characters of a comedy.[31]

Schopenhauer thus recognizes both sides of the issue. This is anticipated by the references in Klingemann to his work being tragicomic.[32]

Schopenhauer goes on to give a brief analysis of the origin of religion that anticipates the work of thinkers such as Feuerbach and Bruno Bauer. He claims that humans have created the gods as a kind of distraction for themselves. Religion gives them something with which to occupy themselves instead of dwelling on their own misery and the meaninglessness of life:

> The result of this is that the human mind, still not content with the cares, anxieties, and preoccupations laid upon it by the actual world, creates for itself an imaginary world in the shape of a thousand different superstitions. Then it sets itself to work with this in all kinds of ways, and wastes time and strength on it ... Man creates for himself in his own image demons, gods, and saints; then to these must be incessantly offered sacrifices, prayers, temple decorations, vows and their fulfilment, pilgrimages, salutations, adornment of images and so on.[33]

Religion thus fills people with illusions of hope with regard to their own suffering and finitude. It functions as a support for them in their constant striving

---

[31] Schopenhauer, *Die Welt als Wille und Vorstellung*, vol. 1, § 58, p. 364 (*The World as Will and Representation*, vol. 1, § 58, p. 322).
[32] [Klingemann], *Nachtwachen. Von Bonaventura*, Penig: bey F. Dienemann und Comp. 1805, p. 60 (English translation: *The Nightwatches of Bonaventura*, trans. by Gerald Gillespie, Chicago and London: University of Chicago Press 2014, p. 27).
[33] Schopenhauer, *Die Welt als Wille und Vorstellung*, vol. 1, § 58, p. 364 (*The World as Will and Representation*, vol. 1, § 58, pp. 322f.).

and suffering. Moreover, religion also serves as a kind of diversion and occupation that prevents them from lapsing into boredom.

Schopenhauer's nihilism comes out clearly in the following assessment of the human condition:

> It is really incredible how meaningless and insignificant when seen from without, and how dull and senseless when felt from within, is the course of life of the great majority of men. It is weary longing and worrying, a dreamlike staggering through the four ages of life to death, accompanied by a series of trivial thoughts. They are like clockwork that is wound up and goes without knowing why. Every time a man is begotten and born the clock of human life is wound up anew, to repeat once more its same old tune that has already been played innumerable times, movement by movement and measure by measure, with insignificant variations. Every individual, every human apparition and its course of life, is only one more short dream of the endless spirit of nature, of the persistent will-to-live, is only one more fleeting form, playfully sketched by it on its infinite page, space and time; it is allowed to exist for a short while that is infinitesimal compared with these, and is then effaced, to make new room.[34]

Our tiny and insignificant existence is not even one of joy but rather of pain and suffering, which is the price of existing at all. Humans are like machines, mass-produced by nature with a fixed expiration date. They all go through the same motions and then finally die. The lives of humans are preprogrammed for suffering and death, and thus there is nothing that we can do about it.

4.4 The Empirical Evidence of Striving and Suffering

In § 59 Schopenhauer, using Kant's language, explains that what he has done so far is to have demonstrated his thesis about the striving of the will and the suffering of human existence based on pure a priori reasoning, that is, on a conceptual analysis. This shows that suffering is something that is necessary. Now he proposes to continue in an a posteriori fashion by demonstrating the truth of his thesis based on concrete empirical examples. Such a discussion could go on forever since there are seemingly an infinite number of cases of suffering, human or otherwise. But nonetheless he proposes to touch on a few of these and appeals to the reader's own experience and intuition to fill in the blanks.

Schopenhauer claims that when any honest and reflective person looks at their life, they are inevitably compelled to reach the conclusion that it is a "history of suffering,"[35] despite the fact that people try to hide this from others and

---

[34] Schopenhauer, *Die Welt als Wille und Vorstellung*, vol. 1, § 58, p. 363 (*The World as Will and Representation*, vol. 1, § 58, pp. 321f.).
[35] Schopenhauer, *Die Welt als Wille und Vorstellung*, vol. 1, § 59, p. 366 (*The World as Will and Representation*, vol. 1, § 59, p. 324).

pretend that they have lived happy and fulfilled lives. Schopenhauer refers to Herodotus's portrayal of the dialogue between the Persian King Xerxes and his uncle Artabanus. Upon a review of his massive assembly of troops preparing to cross the Hellespont and invade Greece, Xerxes falls into a philosophical reflection: "I was musing on how short is human life, and the pity of it pierced me through. All these multitudes here, and yet, in a hundred years' time, not one of them will be alive."[36] To this Artabanus replies,

> But we mortals experience many other causes of suffering that better merit your compassion. Brief though the span of human life may be, yet there is no man here—no, nor anywhere else either—to whom nature grants such happiness that he will not ... wish for death rather than to continue living. So numerous the misfortunes that befall us, and so terrible the diseases that afflict us, that life in all its brevity still seems long. Death, to a man whose existence is a burden, provides an escape very much worth choosing. That god should grant us merely the briefest taste of how sweet life can be serves to demonstrate just how much he begrudges us it.[37]

Schopenhauer believes Artabanus's reply is an accurate assessment of the human condition. The problem is not so much the brevity of life, as Xerxes believes, but rather the continual suffering that life itself consists of.

Schopenhauer argues that we tend to keep unpleasant things out of sight, but if we were only to open our eyes, they are perfectly clear for all to see and cannot be denied. He claims,

> If we were to conduct the most hardened and callous optimist through hospitals, infirmaries, operating theatres, through prisons, torture-chambers, and slave-hovels, over battlefields and to places of execution; if we were to open to him all the dark abodes of misery, where it shuns the gaze of cold curiosity, and finally were to allow him to glance into the dungeon of Ugolino where prisoners starved to death, he too would certainly see in the end what kind of a world is this *meilleur des mondes possibles*.[38]

Here Schopenhauer refers to two motifs that were also found in *The Nightwatches*. First the image of Ugolino starving to death in Dante's *Inferno* (Canto 33),[39] and then Leibniz's theory that our world must be the best of all possible worlds.[40] Although these are common motifs, this might nonetheless be taken as evidence that Schopenhauer read Klingemann's book and was in part inspired by it. With respect to Dante, Schopenhauer goes on to add that, in

---

[36] Herodotus, *The Histories*, trans. by Tom Holland, with notes by Paul Cartledge, London: Penguin 2013, Book VII, chapter 46, p. 466.
[37] Herodotus, *The Histories*, Book VII, chapter 46, pp. 466f.
[38] Schopenhauer, *Die Welt als Wille und Vorstellung*, vol. 1, § 59, pp. 366f. (*The World as Will and Representation*, vol. 1, § 59, p. 325).
[39] [Klingemann], *Nachtwachen*, pp. 140f. (*The Nightwatches of Bonaventura*, p. 61).
[40] [Klingemann], *Nachtwachen*, pp. 238f. (*The Nightwatches of Bonaventura*, p. 102).

the world around us, the Italian poet had a broad range of material from which to draw in his portrayal of Hell. But then when he tried to portray Heaven he could only do so ineffectively and unconvincingly since there were no models for him to use in the normal sphere of earthly existence, where everything is suffering. Here he elaborates on Jean Paul's assessment of Dante that was mentioned above.[41]

Schopenhauer shares an element of Kreuzgang's social criticism in claiming that people are hypocrites and liars in that they try to repress the fact that they live in deep anxiety and suffering. Instead, they are keen to put on a face of confidence and certainty, denying that they have any existential concerns at all. People work to convince others that they are happy and fortunate even when they are not. In the social sphere this becomes a kind of competition in the way people try to outdo one another with regard to their wealth or the size of their house or the make of their car. But behind the facade lies pain, anxiety, and suffering.

Schopenhauer notes that when people find themselves in times of great distress, they appeal to the gods for help by means of, for example, sacrifices and prayers. But this is all in vain. No god ever comes to anyone's aid, and nor can they since the cause of the suffering is a part of the fundamental nature of our being. It comes from within us, and so we cannot be saved by something external. Despite all our prayers, we are left to suffer and die. This can be regarded as a criticism of Jean Paul and the traditional religious view of things. In *The Valley of Campan*, Gione and the others get Karlson to change from his scientific worldview to a more religious one that involves immortality and perhaps a belief in God. He capitulates since he recognizes that he cannot go on refusing to believe in these things. Without these traditional beliefs, his life will always be miserable. The idea is that once Karlson comes around to the comforting view, then all is well, and he can live happily ever after. But as Kierkegaard points out, being a Christian and believing in basic dogmas such as immortality and the existence of God does not mean that one can simply escape the fundamental anxiety and despair of life. This is also Schopenhauer's point. Even if Karlson can say that he is now converted to the theistic view of the others, he will, like the others, also still be plagued by moments of uncertainty, anxiety, and pain. This is inescapable since it lies in the very nature of the human condition. Even the most convinced religious believer still has some doubts and suffers. Schopenhauer concludes the discussion by claiming that it is optimism rather than pessimism that is the cynical and wicked view that mocks the true state of things and leads people to illusions that can only end in disappointment and more pain and suffering.[42]

---

[41] See Chapter 1, Sect. 1.2, p. 45.
[42] Schopenhauer, *Die Welt als Wille und Vorstellung*, vol. 1, § 59, p. 368 (*The World as Will and Representation*, vol. 1, § 59, p. 326).

4.5 Asceticism as the Solution to Nihilism

Schopenhauer goes on to explain the implications of his theory for ethics. While Kant believes that there is a thing-in-itself corresponding to every representation, Schopenhauer argues that, on Kant's own premises, this is impossible. Since space and time are forms of the human cognition and perception that allow us to discern individual objects as representations, they cannot be ascribed to things as they are in themselves apart from our ways of knowing and perceiving. This means that in such a realm there is no way to distinguish discrete objects in space and time. The principle of individuation, which Schopenhauer frequently refers to with the Latin term *principium individuationis*, thus only applies to representations since nothing can be individuated as a thing-in-itself. The only possible conclusion is, then, that there is only one underlying reality or thing-in-itself. This stands in contradiction to Kant's view, which implied that there was a thing-in-itself for every representation. For Schopenhauer, this one underlying reality is what he has described as the will, which is a feature of everything in the universe.

This insight is important for ethics since it tells us that we are fundamentally the same as everything in the universe, including other people. This means that when we hurt or wrong other people, we are ultimately hurting and wronging ourselves. Thus, ethics enjoins us to eliminate the distinction between us and others and to treat everyone with love, kindness, and fairness. Egoists are those who are focused primarily on their own will-to-live and fail to grasp their necessary connection with others in the world. Egoists see themselves as separate individuals who need only be concerned with themselves. But this is an illusion based on representations. Schopenhauer also frequently refers to the will, qua the truth that lies behind all reality, as being hidden by the veil of Maya.[43] It cannot be immediately seen by means of perception, which is a distortion and an illusion. Ethics demands that we see the sufferings of others as our own. Only in this way can we empathize with others. This is the basis of Schopenhauer's ethics, which, he believes, is possible for everyone to practice.

While Schopenhauer is known as a hardened atheist and critic of Christianity, his theory of ethics in fact overlaps considerably with Christian ethics. Like the ethics taught by Jesus, Schopenhauer also enjoins people to love others, even their enemies, and passively to accept and endure injustice and violence against themselves. One should have sympathy and mercy towards others. One should live in poverty. Although his metaphysics, in comparison to Christianity, constitutes a completely different point of departure, he comes to many of the same

---

[43] For example, Schopenhauer, *Die Welt als Wille und Vorstellung*, vol. 1, § 68, pp. 428, 429 (*The World as Will and Representation*, vol. 1, § 68, pp. 378, 379).

4.5 ASCETICISM AS THE SOLUTION TO NIHILISM

conclusions in the sphere of ethics. In fact, he even makes use of religious terms to describe his view of the denial of the will such as, "salvation," "conversion," and "sanctification."[44]

Schopenhauer then in § 68 expands his account of ethics to another, higher level by exploring the disposition of asceticism, which can be seen as his proposal to the solution of the constant suffering and striving of the human condition. When one has reached the point where one recognizes the basic principle that the entire universe is the will and that the struggle to fulfill the needs of the will is a never-ending circle, then one is ready for asceticism. One strives to attain "the state of voluntary renunciation, resignation, true composure, and complete willlessness."[45] This is what Schopenhauer calls the denial of the will-to-live. Those who affirm the will-to-live are egoists and hedonists since they embrace their drives and desires and are always focused on satisfying them. But this is the life of an animal that ends in meaninglessness and death. By contrast, the ascetics try to make themselves numb to their desires and thus break the cycle by denying their will. They renounce their own inner nature, which is the source of suffering. They train themselves to ignore their natural drives in order to reach a state of inner peace and happiness. This can be conceived as a kind of self-sacrifice. The ascetics are chaste, live in poverty, engage in fasting, and self-torture as a part of the disciplinary practices aimed at extinguishing the will and the suffering that comes with it. Moreover, the ascetics welcome death happily when it comes since it is a relief and deliverance from the pain and struggle of life. Schopenhauer provides a long list of saints and ascetics as examples of people who have worked to reach this ideal. He takes these examples, drawn from different contexts and traditions, to be a confirmation of his general metaphysical view.

By renouncing the urging of the will, the ascetics are in a better position to endure the suffering and injustices imposed on them by others. Here Schopenhauer's theory overlaps with Christianity, which he usually is rather critical of. He writes,

> As he himself denies the will that appears in his own person, he will not resist when another does the same thing, in other words, inflicts wrong on him. Therefore, every suffering that comes to him from outside through chance or the wickedness of others is welcome to him; every injury, every ignominy, every outrage. He gladly accepts them as the opportunity for giving himself the certainty that he no longer affirms the will, but gladly

---

[44] For example, Schopenhauer, *Die Welt als Wille und Vorstellung*, vol. 1, § 68, pp. 443, 445, 447, 449 (*The World as Will and Representation*, vol. 1, § 68, pp. 393, 395, 397, 398).

[45] Schopenhauer, *Die Welt als Wille und Vorstellung*, vol. 1, § 68, pp. 428f. (*The World as Will and Representation*, vol. 1, § 68, p. 379). See also his definition of asceticism: *Die Welt als Wille und Vorstellung*, vol. 1, § 68, p. 442 (*The World as Will and Representation*, vol. 1, p. 392).

sides with every enemy of the will's phenomenon that is his own person. He therefore endures such ignominy and suffering with inexhaustible patience and gentleness, returns good for all evil without ostentation, and allows the fire of anger to rise again within him as little as he does the fire of desires.[46]

In this we can see Christ's principles of turning the other cheek[47] and loving one's enemies.[48] For Schopenhauer, the key is to see the other, qua enemy, as a part of oneself and not as a separate person.

Schopenhauer thus recommends asceticism as a path to overcoming the suffering caused by the will. But this demands a constant struggle to stifle the will with its drives and desires. Schopenhauer clearly concedes this:

> However, we must not imagine that, after the denial of the will-to-live has once appeared through knowledge that has become a quieter of the will, such denial no longer wavers or falters, and that we can rest on it as on an inherited property. On the contrary, it must always be achieved afresh by constant struggle .... We therefore find in the lives of saintly persons that peace and bliss we have described, only as the blossom resulting from the constant overcoming of the will; and we see the constant struggle with the will-to-live as the soil from which it shoots up; for on earth no one can have lasting peace.[49]

One might critically ask if this is really a solution that leads to joy, peace, and serenity, given that the ascetic must also continue to struggle with the will just like everyone else, even if the ascetic with practice and discipline is better or more successful at it than others. Schopenhauer seems to undermine his own point by conceding that even the great saints, yogis, and ascetics are in constant struggle with their drives and desires. If this is true, then his proposal of asceticism does not really seem to be very useful. In the end even the most rigorous ascetic never achieves the peace or happiness that Schopenhauer claimed previously.[50]

Schopenhauer argues that the life of the ascetic in any form that involves the denial of the will comes from a knowledge of the will's "inner conflict and its essential vanity, expressing themselves in the suffering of all that lives."[51] In short, the ascetic must realize the truth of Schopenhauer's philosophy. This knowledge then functions as a "quieter of the will" that frees one from suffering

---

[46] Schopenhauer, *Die Welt als Wille und Vorstellung*, vol. 1, § 68, p. 431 (*The World as Will and Representation*, vol. 1, § 68, p. 382).
[47] Matthew 15:39; Luke 16:29.
[48] Matthew 15:44.
[49] Schopenhauer, *Die Welt als Wille und Vorstellung*, vol. 1, § 68, pp. 441f. (*The World as Will and Representation*, vol. 1, § 68, p. 391).
[50] Schopenhauer, *Die Welt als Wille und Vorstellung*, vol. 1, § 68, p. 440 (*The World as Will and Representation*, vol. 1, § 68, pp. 389f.).
[51] Schopenhauer, *Die Welt als Wille und Vorstellung*, vol. 1, § 68, p. 448 (*The World as Will and Representation*, vol. 1, § 68, p. 397).

and leads to salvation.[52] Evil comes from not recognizing this knowledge and continuing to believe that one is separate from others and the world. This leads one to follow slavishly the demands of the will.

There are two ways or paths to reach the conclusion of the need for the denial of the will: one is with knowledge and the other is with personal experience of suffering. Schopenhauer himself has shown the first way; namely, through philosophical thinking one understands the truth of the universe as suffering and its solution in the denial of the will-to-live. However, not everyone is reflective or philosophical. In order to come to this conclusion, most people must first themselves experience great suffering, which motivates them to try to repress the will. One sees this when people experience some great trauma in their lives such as the loss of a loved one or a divorce or a serious health problem. Such crises can change people, and when they come out of it, they seem to be transformed and to have a new disposition towards the world. This is the kind of thing that Schopenhauer is talking about. Such a crisis can have an enduring effect on some people for the rest of their lives. But for others, as soon as the immediate crisis is over, they simply go back to their old ways, none the wiser for the experience. This was illustrated by the episode in *The Nightwatches* when Kreuzgang falsely announces that the Last Judgment is imminent.[53] When they no longer feel any acute pain, people no longer see the point in repressing the will.

4.6 Schopenhauer's Nihilism

In the final paragraph (§ 71) of the first volume of *The World as Will and Representation*, Schopenhauer takes up a possible objection to his position. He sketches this as follows: "after our observations have finally brought us to the point where we have before our eyes in perfect saintliness the denial and surrender of all willing, and thus a deliverance from a world whose whole existence presented itself to us as suffering, this now appears to us as a transition into empty *nothingness*."[54] The idea seems to be that Schopenhauer cannot escape the nihilism of his view that in the end everything dies and disappears into nothingness. This means that his philosophy, despite everything that he has said, has nothing positive to offer.

This induces him to take up a metaphysical discussion about the nature of nothingness.[55] He distinguishes two senses of it. In the first sense, which comes from Kant and Hegel, nothingness only exists in necessary relation to

---

[52] Schopenhauer, *Die Welt als Wille und Vorstellung*, vol. 1, § 68, p. 448 (*The World as Will and Representation*, vol. 1, § 68, p. 397).
[53] This was treated in Chapter 2, Sect. 2.1, pp. 66–71.
[54] Schopenhauer, *Die Welt als Wille und Vorstellung*, vol. 1, § 71, p. 460 (*The World as Will and Representation*, vol. 1, § 71, pp. 408f.).
[55] Schopenhauer, *Die Welt als Wille und Vorstellung*, vol. 1, § 71, pp. 460f. (*The World as Will and Representation*, vol. 1, § 71, p. 409).

something positive: being. Being and nothing thus both depend on one another conceptually. One cannot have the one without the other. Schopenhauer designates this notion of nothingness the *nihil privativum*. In this sense nothingness is conceived as the negation or privation of being. It is always understood relatively in relation to something else that is positive. The other notion conceives of nothingness as absolute, on its own, independent of anything else. Schopenhauer designates this *nihil negativum*. But he claims that such a notion is unthinkable since to think anything, one must always see it in relation to other things. This is true of everything in the realm of representation and human understanding. A thing entirely on its own is thus inconceivable to the human mind. Any attempt to think the *nihil negativum* collapses into the *nihil privativum*.

Schopenhauer reminds us then that all being in the universe, including ourselves, is representation, that is, the will. This is everything that appears in space and time. When we deny the will, we then simultaneously deny the being of the world as representation. But unfortunately, we cannot have knowledge about the nature of the nothingness that we are left with since this is not a representation. We can only *know* this nothingness negatively, just as we can only *know* negatively what is outside space and time, that is, as what has no space or time – but we cannot imagine what this looks like. Per analogy we can only know that the nothingness of our being is that which is deprived of the will and the accompanying suffering of existence.[56] But beyond this we cannot have any insight as long as we are confined to the world of existence and life in bodies with wills. The absolute nothingness is inconceivable or unthinkable.

Schopenhauer, however, claims that some vague idea of such a state of nothing can be achieved by ascetics who successfully deny the will. This state "is denoted by the names ecstasy, rapture, illumination, union with God, and so on."[57] He hastens to add that this is not knowledge but a kind of ineffable inward experience. But he concedes that, from a strictly philosophical view, all that we are left with is nothingness:

> If, therefore, we have recognized the inner nature of the world as will, and have seen in all its phenomena only the objectivity of the will; and if we have followed these from the unconscious impulse of obscure natural forces up to the most conscious action of man, we shall by no means evade the consequence that, with the free denial, the surrender, of the will, all those phenomena also are now abolished. That constant pressure and effort, without aim and without rest, at all grades of objectivity in which and through which the world exists; the multifarious forms succeeding

---

[56] Schopenhauer, *Die Welt als Wille und Vorstellung*, vol. 1, § 71, pp. 461f. (*The World as Will and Representation*, vol. 1, § 71, p. 410).

[57] Schopenhauer, *Die Welt als Wille und Vorstellung*, vol. 1, § 71, p. 462 (*The World as Will and Representation*, vol. 1, § 71, p. 410).

one another in gradation; the whole phenomenon of the will; finally, the universal forms of this phenomenon, time and space, and also the last fundamental form of these, subject and object; all these are abolished with the will. No will: no representation, no world.[58]

We fear and resist this idea of nothingness since the will-to-live is a part of our very nature as a living being in the universe. But if we cease to exist, then all of our representations will cease to exist, which means everything in the universe as we know it.

In the end Schopenhauer seems to grant that even those great ascetics who manage to quiet the will with the knowledge that the universe is meaningless suffering cannot, in the end, avoid the common human fate of disappearing into nothing. In the final words of volume 1 of *The World as Will and Representation* he writes, "we freely acknowledge that what remains after the complete abolition of the will is, for all who are still full of the will, assuredly nothing. But also conversely, to those in whom the will has turned and denied itself, this very real world of ours with all its suns and galaxies, is – nothing."[59] So, ultimately if one is a disciplined ascetic or an undisciplined hedonist, it all amounts to the same thing in the end. Everything ends in death and nothingness. This is Schopenhauer's nihilistic or pessimistic conclusion. Like Klingemann, Schopenhauer emphasizes his point by ending the work with the word "nothing."[60]

It should be noted that Schopenhauer tries to think through a consistent vision of the world based on the sciences. In this respect he is not so different from Karlson. It will be recalled that Schopenhauer first studied medicine and the natural sciences. It is thus the new worldview based on the sciences that produces the problem of nihilism, as was the case for Jean Paul and Klingemann. Schopenhauer does not use the term "nihilism" explicitly, but the idea is clearly central to his thinking.

As noted, Schopenhauer's *Parerga and Paralipomena* returns to many of the same themes concerning nihilism that we have seen in *The World as Will and Representation*. While he provides some new quotations and examples in *Parerga and Paralipomena*, he basically reaffirms and illustrates his earlier views instead of presenting new ones. He once again argues that suffering is the basis of all human existence. Further, he explores a handful of Christian

---

[58] Schopenhauer, *Die Welt als Wille und Vorstellung*, vol. 1, § 71, pp. 462f. (*The World as Will and Representation*, vol. 1, § 71, pp. 410f.).
[59] Schopenhauer, *Die Welt als Wille und Vorstellung*, vol. 1, § 71, p. 464 (*The World as Will and Representation*, vol. 1, § 71, pp. 411f.).
[60] It should of course be noted that while this is the end of his main discussion, it is not the end of the book, strictly speaking, since Schopenhauer adds an appendix entitled "Criticism of the Kantian Philosophy"; *Die Welt als Wille und Vorstellung*, vol. 1, pp. 465–599 (*The World as Will and Representation*, vol. 1, pp. 413–534).

doctrines, such as original sin, eternal damnation, and so on, which, he claims, are both alienating and indeed terrifying for common sense. In an anticipation of Nietzsche, he argues that Christianity is ultimately detrimental to cultural and scientific development. As we will see in Chapter 9, Nietzsche praised Schopenhauer on many points and hailed him as a great source of inspiration. However, he was also ultimately critical of Schopenhauer's strategy for overcoming nihilism.

4.7 The Positive Side of Schopenhauer

Schopenhauer represents an important voice in the nineteenth-century discussion of nihilism. The critical side of his philosophy is aimed at those who fail to recognize the problem of human existence, specifically the constant struggle of the will and the meaninglessness of life. Here he anticipates the concept of authenticity found in later thinkers. Although the picture of the universe presented by the sciences is an uncomfortable and frightening one, we must accept it. If we fail to do so, then we end up living in illusions, which only perpetuate the suffering. Only when the problem of nihilism is recognized can real solutions be sought. In this sense Schopenhauer would be highly critical of Jean Paul's solution of retreating to traditional beliefs even though they have been completely undermined by science. On his view, the figure of Karlson would be no positive model to be followed. Instead, he is simply a fool who allows himself to be seduced by the promise of a happiness based on the lie of immortality. This is all an illusion, and a man of science should know better than to go along with this kind of superstition. Schopenhauer might note that it is typical that Jean Paul ends *The Valley of Campan* where he does, that is, shortly after Karlson's capitulation and conversion to traditional belief. If Jean Paul were compelled to continue the story, he would be obliged to describe how over time Karlson would continually return to the issue and be troubled by it. Despite his ostensible conversion, he would still be haunted by doubts about the immortality of his beloved Gione. The image of the complete destruction of the individual and the world would invariably return to him as it would to any reflective person. In the end Jean Paul's conception of a happy, carefree life of faith is simply implausible. Life is forever a struggle, whether we want to admit it or not.

It might appear that Schopenhauer has more in common with Klingemann's Kreuzgang. They share a tone of cynicism and are merciless in their criticism of human weakness, vice, and hypocrisy. The shared ending of *The Nightwatches* and *The World as Will and Representation* with the word "nothing" seems to confirm their common nihilistic worldview. But ultimately their approaches to nihilism are quite different. Klingemann ends with the negative message: the universe is a frightening and meaningless place, full of pain and suffering. If we fail to see this, then we are like the vain and stupid townspeople that Kreuzgang describes. Schopenhauer can follow him so far, but he would argue that this negative message is not enough. Instead, he tries to offer a positive suggestion for the best way of coping with the terrifying fact of nihilism. Schopenhauer's Buddhist-inspired program of asceticism is intended as a practical response to nihilism. If the will can be quieted, then the suffering caused by it will gradually disappear. As was discussed, it is debatable whether this can be seen as a successful solution, but the point is that Schopenhauer, in contrast to Klingemann, feels the need to develop and present a solution to the problem that he has so carefully articulated. While Schopenhauer seems himself to concede that his proposal does not ultimately solve the problem of nihilism, he would argue that he at least has tried to find a solution, which is very different from Klingemann, who simply presents his readers with the problem and then ends the story.

In this sense Schopenhauer seems to have more in common with Byron, who is primarily concerned with maintaining the integrity of humanity in the face of death and a meaningless universe. Manfred is a figure who rebels against the gods, that is, against the terms of existence that the universe presents. He is fully disabused of illusions. There is a certain nobility about him in the fact that, although he is frequently tempted by both the spirits and the abbot, he stubbornly refuses to give in and go along with the easy solutions that they urge. In contrast to Karlson, Manfred will not capitulate to threats, the pressure of others, or the frightening image of a nihilistic universe. Even though he knows that his demise is imminent, Manfred insists on dying on his own terms. While Schopenhauer is not so concerned with the concept of rebellion, he does share with Byron the sense that salvation can be found in oneself alone. With the control of the will, the individual is perfectly able to work on one's own spiritual shortcomings by oneself. There is no need to prop oneself up on an illusory belief system. Both Schopenhauer and Byron attempt to give their readers a sense of personal empowerment in the face of the feeling of helplessness that accompanies the nihilistic worldview. They both, however, acknowledge that this is not easy. Manfred is constantly plagued by a guilty conscience, and Schopenhauer admits that even the most disciplined and experienced ascetics feel the sufferings caused by the will. But they agree that these struggles concern the individual alone. There is thus something positive in their message.

Finally, Schopenhauer shares with Shelley the idea that the fact of nihilism should lead to a change in one's self-image and moral disposition. A recognition of one's tiny and meaningless role in the universe should lead to a sense of humility and a tempered view of one's own accomplishments. Shelley's poem criticizes Ozymandias for his vanity and arrogance that lead him to disdain others. If the king had known that all his accomplishments would be forgotten over time, this would presumably have led to some kind of reform of his character. Shelley, of course, does not develop this into a full-blown theory of ethics in his poem, but this is an important element that he believes follows from the new perspective of nihilism. Along the same lines, Schopenhauer also tries to derive the basic principles of an ethical system based on this same view. Given that everything in the universe is will, this means that we are not ultimately separate individuals, as the principle of individuation would suggest. Instead, we are a small part of the universe as a whole and with it all of humanity. We should therefore treat others with love and kindness since we are a part of them, just as they are a part of us. Schopenhauer thus proposes an ethics of solidarity based on our commonality. In the case of both Shelley and Schopenhauer, the realization of the meaninglessness of the universe has clear ethical consequences. Here again we can see an attempt to take the apparently terrifying nihilistic worldview and turn it into something positive. This separates these two thinkers from Jean Paul, for whom nihilism can only be something negative and disturbing. Despite the humorous and satirical depictions in *The Nightwatches*, Klingemann also seems to regard nihilism as a terrible fact of the universe. While Schopenhauer ends his book with the word "nothing," this does not mean that his view has no positive side.

5

Büchner's Account of the Reign of Terror as a Mirror of Human Existence

The German author Georg Büchner (1813–37) is another important figure for the discussion of nihilism in the nineteenth century. He was a radical thinker who, together with his better-known younger brother Ludwig (1824–99), has often been associated with the Young Germany movement. Georg followed in the footsteps of his father and studied medicine, first at the University of Strasbourg in 1831, and then at the University of Giessen in 1833.[1] In addition to supplying him with many metaphors and similes from, for example, the field of anatomy, Büchner's scientific background was important for his naturalistic worldview.

---

[1] For Büchner's biography, see "George Büchner," in *Georg Büchner's Sämmtliche Werke und handschriftlicher Nachlaß. Erste kritische Gesammt-Ausgabe*, ed. by Karl Emil Franzos, Frankfurt am Main: J.D. Sauerländer's Verlag 1879, pp. i–clxxvi; Gerhard P. Knapp, *Georg Büchner*, 2nd ed., Stuttgart: J.B. Metzler 1984; Julian Hilton, *Georg Büchner*, London: Macmillan 1982; Jan-Christoph Hauschild, *Georg Büchner. Biographie*, Stuttgart and Weimar: J.B. Metzler 1993; Jan-Christoph Hauschild, *Georg Büchner. Studien und neue Quellen zu Leben, Werk und Wirkung*, Königstein: Athenäum 1985; Hans Mayer, *Georg Büchner und seine Zeit*, Frankfurt am Main: Suhrkamp 1972. For Büchner's work, see Henri Poschmann, *Georg Büchner. Dichtung der Revolution und Revolution der Dichtung*, Berlin, Weimar: Aufbau 1983; Maurice B. Benn, *The Drama of Revolt: A Critical Study of Georg Büchner*, Cambridge: Cambridge University Press 1976; Reinhold Grimm, *Love, Lust and Rebellion: New Approaches to Georg Büchner*, Madison: University of Wisconsin Press 1985; Herbert Lindenberger, *Georg Büchner*, Carbondale: Southern Illinois University Press 1964; John Reddick, *Georg Büchner: The Shattered Whole*, Oxford: Clarendon Press 1994; David G. Richards, *Georg Büchner and the Birth of the Modern Drama*, Albany: State University of New York Press 1977; J.P. Stern, "A World of Suffering: Georg Büchner," in his *Reinterpretations: Seven Studies in Nineteenth-Century German Literature*, London: Thames and Hudson 1964, pp. 78-155; J.P. Stern, "Georg Büchner: Potsherds of Experience," in his *Idylls and Realities: Studies in Nineteenth-Century German Literature*, London, Methuen 1973, pp. 33-48; Gerhard Jancke, *Georg Büchner. Genese und Aktualität seines Werkes. Einführung in das Gesamtwerk*, Kronberg: Scriptor-Verlag 1975; Friedrich Sengle, "Georg Büchner," in his *Biedermeierzeit. Deutsche Literatur im Spannungsfeld zwischen Restauration und Revolution 1815-1848*, vols. 1–3, Stuttgart: J.B. Metzler 1971-80, vol. 3, pp. 265-331; Wolfgang Wittkowski, *Georg Büchner. Persönlichkeit, Weltbild, Werk*, Heidelberg: Carl Winter Universitätsverlag 1978; Roland Borgards and Burghard Dedner (eds.), *Georg Büchner und die Romantik*, Berlin: J.B. Metzler 2020; Patrick Fortmann and Martha B. Helfer (eds.), *Commitment and Compassion: Essays on Georg Büchner. Festschrift für Gerhard P. Knapp*, Amsterdam and New York: Rodopi 2012.

Like many of the other authors studied here, the success of the sciences in the Enlightenment played a role in the development of the nihilistic dimension of his thought. Büchner became active in radical revolutionary politics by founding the Society of Human Rights in Giessen. He attracted the attention of the police when he coauthored the pamphlet *The Hessian Messenger* in 1834.[2] This brought him into conflict with the local authorities, and he was forced to flee in order to escape arrest. Less fortunate, his coauthor, Friedrich Ludwig Weiding (1791–1837) was captured and committed suicide after two years of incarceration.

In 1836 Büchner received his doctoral degree in medicine from the University of Zürich. He was subsequently offered a lectureship at the same university and seems to have had a promising career ahead of him. But at the beginning of the following year, he contracted typhus and died shortly thereafter at the age of 23. Alongside his study of medicine, Büchner also wrote a handful of dramas, *Leonce and Lena*, *Woyzeck*, and *Danton's Death*, the last of which was the only one to be published in his lifetime. Due to his short life, he left behind a rather small literary corpus, including a number of letters. Given the paucity of published works, Büchner's fame was long in coming. He only began to receive the attention of literary scholars towards the end of the nineteenth century, after the publication of his collected works.[3] Today Büchner is hailed as an important forerunner of twentieth-century trends in drama and the arts.

In the present chapter I will focus on his drama *Danton's Death*.[4] This work was originally published in 1835 in a strongly censored version in the journal

---

[2] Georg Büchner and Friedrich Ludwig Weidig, *Die Hessische Landbote. Texte. Materialien. Kommentar*, ed. by Gerhard Schaub, Munich: Carl Hanser Verlag 1976; Georg Büchner and Friedrich Ludwig Weidig, *Der Hessische Landbote. Texte, Briefe, Prozeßakten*, edited with commentary by Hans Magnus Enzensberger, Frankfurt am Main: Insel 1965. The text of this pamphlet appears in English in Georg Büchner, *Complete Plays, Lenz and Other Writings*, trans. by John Reddick, London: Penguin 1993, pp. 167–179.

[3] *Georg Büchner's Sämmtliche Werke und handschriftlicher Nachlaß. Erste kritische Gesammt-Ausgabe*, ed. by Karl Emil Franzos, Frankfurt am Main: J.D. Sauerländer's Verlag 1879. For modern editions, see Georg Büchner, *Sämtliche Werke und Briefe. Historisch-kritischen Ausgabe mit Kommentar*, ed. by Werner R. Lehmann, Munich: Hanser 1979; Georg Büchner, *Werke und Briefe. Nach der historisch-kritischen Ausgabe von Werner R. Lehmann. Kommentiert von Karl Pörnbacher, Nachwort von Werner R. Lehmann*, Munich: Hanser 1980; Georg Büchner, *Sämtliche Werke*, ed. by Henri Poschmann, Frankfurt am Main: Insel 2002; Georg Büchner, *Sämtliche Werke und Schriften. Historisch-kritische Ausgabe mit Quellendokumentation und Kommentar*, vols. 1–10, ed. by Burghard Dedner and Thomas Michael Mayer, Darmstadt: Wissenschaftliche Buchgesellschaft 2000–2012; Georg Büchner, *Schriften, Briefe, Dokumente*, ed. by Henri Poschmann, Frankfurt am Main: Deutscher Klassiker Verlag 2006; Georg Büchner, *Complete Works and Letters*, ed. by Walter Hinderer and Henry J. Schmidt, New York: Continuum 1986.

[4] In the following I refer to the edition of Georg Büchner, *Danton's Tod. Ein Drama*, ed. by Thomas Michael Mayer, in *Georg Büchner: Dantons Tod. Die Trauerarbeit im Schönen*, ed. by Peter von Becker, Frankfurt am Main: Schauspiel Frankfurt 1980, pp. 13–74. (English translation: *Danton's Death* in *Complete Plays, Lenz and Other Writings*, trans. by

Phönix. Frühlings-Zeitung für Deutschland.[5] Later the same year the piece appeared in book form. To appease the censors, the subtitle, *Dramatic Scenes from France's Reign of Terror*, was added.[6] The publication of the work was facilitated by the radical Karl Gutzkow (1811–78), who wrote a review of it in the same journal where it originally appeared.[7] Due to the circumstances of the publication of *Danton's Death*, the philological aspect of the work is somewhat complicated. Modern editions try to establish the text based on the two published versions and Büchner's handwritten manuscript, but there is little consensus about this.

5.1 The Vision of Nature and the Human Condition

Büchner's historical drama *Danton's Death* is relevant for the topic of nihilism.[8] The work concerns the trial and execution of the French revolutionary Georges Danton (1759–94) and his comrades. The piece is set during the period of the French Revolution when the Committee of Public Safety represented the provisional government. The play begins with the execution of Jacques-René Hérbet on March 24, 1794 and ends thirteen days later with the execution of Danton and his followers on April 5. The leading figures of the Committee were the infamous Maximilien Robespierre (1758–94) and Louis Antoine Léon de Saint-Just (1767–94). While Danton had been a hero of the Revolution and even a member of the Committee himself, his attempts to restrain the political assassinations during the Reign of Terror brought him into the disfavor of the Jacobinic faction headed by Robespierre. Pleading for moderation and reconciliation, he was condemned for betraying the Revolution and sent to the guillotine. Danton was known for his outstanding oratorical skill and was criticized by his followers for not using it in their hour of need to try to win the support of the people, who might have been able to help them escape political persecution. In writing the

---

John Reddick, London: Penguin 1993; all English references are made to this translation). See Dorothy James, *Georg Büchner's "Dantons Tod": A Reappraisal*, London: Modern Humanities Research Association 1982; Alfred Behrmann and Joachim Wohlleben, *Büchner: Dantons Tod. Eine Dramenanalyse*, Stuttgart; Ernst Klett 1980; Walter Hinderer, *Büchner-Kommentar zum dichterischen Werk*, Munich: Winkler 1977; Riitta Pohjola-Skarp, *Dantons Tod von Georg Büchner. Revolutionsdrama als Tragödie*, Frankfurt am Main: Peter Lang 2014.

[5] Georg Büchner, *Danton's Tod*, in *Phönix. Frühlings-Zeitung für Deutschland*, nos. 73–77, 79–83, March 26–April 7, 1835, pp. 289–290, 293–295, 297–298, 301–302, 305–306, 313–315, 317–318, 321–322, 326–327, 330.

[6] Georg Büchner, *Danton's Tod. Dramatische Bilder aus Frankreichs Schreckensherrschaft*, Frankfurt am Main: J.D. Sauerländer 1835.

[7] [Karl Gutzkow], "*Danton's Tod*, von Georg Büchner," in *Phönix. Frühlings-Zeitung für Deutschland*, no. 162, *Literatur-Blatt*, no. 27, July 11, 1835, pp. 645–646.

[8] See Charles I. Glicksberg, *The Literature of Nihilism*, Lewisburg: Bucknell University Press 1975, pp. 322–327.

play, Büchner made a careful study of the French Revolution, and all the main figures who appear in the work correspond to real historical people.

By choosing this episode from history as his background, Büchner sets the stage for a questioning of the meaning of human existence. The reader knows from the start that most all the main characters in the piece will end up on the guillotine. It is a cruel and inhuman world, where love and loyalty play little role. The threat of death is everywhere, and suicide is a frequent theme. The lead character Danton is portrayed as having a proclivity towards philosophical reflection and can be seen as representing the voice of nihilism. He despairs of the lack of meaning in human existence and meets his death with a kind of indifference or even relief. Similar to that of Klingemann, Büchner's picture of human society is one of dishonesty, hypocrisy, corruption, vice, and misery.

Büchner foreshadows the subsequent executions of Robespierre and his Jacobinic followers only a few months after Danton is sent to his death. Although these events are not portrayed in the drama, Büchner could assume that his contemporary reader was familiar with them. This suggests the fruitlessness of human activity, where violence follows upon violence with nothing ever being accomplished. This motif appears more explicitly in the speech of a nameless citizen who recalls how the suffering people have demanded one political faction after the next to be executed, but despite this, the general condition of the poverty of the people has not changed at all.[9] The insatiable bloodlust of the common people seems to confirm Danton's disenchanted view of human nature.

At the outset of the drama, we see Danton in dialogue with his beloved wife Julie. He laments the fate of humans who are ultimately never able to know one another. While we, of course, are familiar with the superficial things, we are unable to know the deeper, inner person of one another. He explains, "Thick-skinned elephants, that's what we are; we stretch out our hands to each other, but it's a waste of time, hide grating on hide, that's all – we're on our own, completely on our own."[10] This is a sobering picture of human relations and the social order. It is especially striking that Büchner has Danton say this not in the context of a political debate but rather in a private conversation with his wife. This seems to suggest that, even with the people who are closest to us, we remain fundamentally separated. To reassure his wife, he says to her surprise that he loves her "like the grave."[11] She is shocked by this, like most people would be, since death is usually something to be feared and avoided. Danton hastens to explain his point to her by giving death a positive spin:

> People say there's peace in the grave, and that peace and the grave are the selfsame thing. If that's the case, then I'm dead and buried here in your lap.

[9] Büchner, *Dantons Tod*, pp. 23f. (*Danton's Death*, p. 10); see also Lacroix's statement: *Dantons Tod*, p. 30 (*Danton's Death*, p. 17).
[10] Büchner, *Dantons Tod*, p. 14 (*Danton's Death*, p. 5).
[11] Büchner, *Dantons Tod*, p. 14 (*Danton's Death*, p. 5).

5.1 THE VISION OF NATURE AND THE HUMAN CONDITION 153

> You sweet grave, your lips are passing-bells, your voice my death knell, your breast my burial mound, your heart my coffin.[12]

It is only with his wife that he can find peace, presumably by being away from the tumultuous world of political intrigue. This peace resembles the final peace of death. This passage at the very beginning of the work of course foreshadows Danton's death at the end, but it also signals the importance of the motif of nihilism. The message is that there is no real peace in the world. As Schopenhauer claims, human existence is suffering. Death thus comes as a relief from the heavy burden of life.

Danton is one who takes full enjoyment in the pleasures of life with food, drink, and women. According to his view, this is the sole consolation in life. Danton claims, "We are all Epicureans" who "do what we do because it does us good."[13] This is also seen in the speech by Danton's friend Camille Desmoulins, who refers to the "divine" Epicurus and likewise celebrates the pleasures of the senses.[14] Danton's free indulgence in these pleasures is what permits his enemies to single him out as a kind of secret aristocrat who gets fat and rich, while the poor starve. Robespierre leads the life of puritan abstinence, which, in the eyes of the common people, puts him in a positive light, in contrast to Danton with his alleged decadence. This gives Robespierre the political leverage he needs to persecute Danton and his equally decadent followers. In a speech, Robespierre rails against vice as a political crime and an attack on freedom.[15]

The conception of nature is important in the play, and the power of the natural drives is also emphasized. The prostitute Marion tells the story of her first lover. She explains how, when she was young, nature changed her body. Unashamed by the ethical code of society, she could not see any difference between sexual pleasure and other sorts of pleasures that were socially condoned. She claims that those who condemn others for such things are hypocrites, often hiding behind the veil of religious piety. They too indulge in pleasure but just of a different kind. This is a cutting social criticism of the sexual mores of the day. Lacroix – that is, Danton's friend Jean François Delacroix (1753–94) – follows up on this when he enters the scene by comparing a brothel with a nunnery. Referring to his friend Louis Legendre (1752–97), he says,

> Legendre and I have done the rounds of nearly all the cells in this holy establishment, the Little Sisters of the Revelation of the Flesh clung to our coattails and begged for our blessing. Legendre is inflicting a penance on one of them right now, but it means he'll go hungry for a month. I've brought two of them with me, these votaries of the body.[16]

---

[12] Büchner, *Dantons Tod*, p. 14 (*Danton's Death*, p. 5).
[13] Büchner, *Dantons Tod*, p. 35 (*Danton's Death*, p. 24).
[14] Büchner, *Dantons Tod*, p. 22 (*Danton's Death*, p. 7).
[15] Büchner, *Dantons Tod*, p. 27 (*Danton's Death*, p. 15).
[16] Büchner, *Dantons Tod*, p. 32 (*Danton's Death*, p. 19).

The comparison supports Marion's provocative claim that all humans, whether prostitutes or nuns, are basically the same in their pursuit of pleasure. Danton later echoes this view in his pleas with Robespierre to stem the violence: "People tart themselves up just as well as they can, and it's pleasure they're after, each in his own special way."[17] Those who condemn others for pursuing their pleasure are simply sanctimonious and self-righteous, like the puritan Robespierre. The pursuit of pleasure is hardly a crime; on the contrary, it is a natural human impulse. There is no fundamental difference between human beings apart from the object of their pleasure, and in this "Everyone behaves according to his nature."[18] Büchner's universe is in this sense the same as Schopenhauer's: everything is a part of an all-powerful will that drives people to fulfill their desires. But, for Schopenhauer, one should try to repress the never-ceasing will in order to minimize the suffering that comes from the lack of fulfillment. By contrast, Danton sees no problem with engaging in the will with all its desires and drives since this is something that comes from nature itself. There is no reason to be prude or ashamed of this since it is simply the way we have been created.

At the end of the discussion, Marion explains, "I know no pause, no change. I am ever the same. A ceaseless yearning and holding, an ardent fire, a swirling stream."[19] This is the human condition that allows us no rest. Büchner thus emphasizes the natural side of human beings and not their rational capacity, which thus stands in stark contrast to the Enlightenment's dogmas about the power of reason. In this context Danton's yearning for the peace of death is understandable. The picture presented here is very much in the spirit of the diagnostic part of Schopenhauer's account of the inescapable yearning of the will that dominates our lives.

5.2 Robespierre's Nihilism

On the outside Robespierre seems to be completely certain about his cause and his methods. When Danton asks him if he ever has the feeling that he is lying to himself, Robespierre immediately replies that he has a clean conscience.[20] But beneath the surface, Robespierre is in fact vexed by the doubts and uncertainties that all human beings have. Our dreams often make us conscious of these. Alone, he ruminates to himself,

> I don't know which bit of me is lying to the rest. The night snores above the earth, tossing and turning in terrible dreams. Thoughts and wishes, scarcely sensed, confused and formless, that dared not face the light of day, now take on shape and substance, and steal into the silent house of

---

[17] Büchner, *Dantons Tod*, p. 35 (*Danton's Death*, p. 23).
[18] Büchner, *Dantons Tod*, p. 35 (*Danton's Death*, p. 24).
[19] Büchner, *Dantons Tod*, p. 31 (*Danton's Death*, pp. 18f.).
[20] Büchner, *Dantons Tod*, p. 35 (*Danton's Death*, p. 23).

dreams. They open doors and stare from windows, become half flesh in the murmur of lips, the sudden stir of sleeping limbs.—And even our waking life, is it not but a dream in brighter light? Don't we always sleepwalk? Are our actions not like those in a dream, just a little more distinct, more precise, more complete?[21]

On the face of it, this can be interpreted as Robespierre's guilty conscience, which foreshadows his own death on the guillotine. However, it can also be interpreted in a more general manner as a representation of natural human *Angst* in the face of death and suffering. In the light of day, this is something that we try to repress in part by lying to ourselves. But we cannot fully escape it since these dark thoughts always return to us periodically. We cannot fully put it out of our minds that we are finite creatures who will one day die. Our life in the world is nothing more than a fleeting dream, an echo of Pindar's "shadow of a dream."[22] We are so insubstantial that we live for only a short time and then die only to be forgotten forever.

Robespierre seems to see the world as purely the work of nature, where things happen due to strict laws without any higher meaning. He suggests that human actions are all done by chance and are not dictated by rational calculation or will. Like everything else, we are just atoms in the void, sometimes coming into contact with others and sometimes not.[23]

Hoping to spur Robespierre to action, Saint-Just shows him a copy of the journal *Le Vieux Cordelier*, in which a perverse comparison is made between Jesus and Robespierre, with the latter being referred to as "the bloody Messiah."[24] The journal is published by Robespierre's and Danton's friend Camille Desmoulins. Irritated by this criticism, Robespierre, again alone, reflects to himself, expanding on the comparison:

> Yes, indeed: "bloody Messiah, not sacrificed himself but sacrificing others."—He redeemed them with his blood, I redeem them with their own. He made them sin, I take sin upon myself. He had the ecstasy of pain, I have the agony of the executioner. Who denied himself the more—him or me?[25]

Robespierre seems to put on a par the victim and the executioner, suggesting a kind of parity or even indifference, as if in the end the roles do not really matter. He sees himself as a redeemer insofar as he is purging people of their sins by executing those, like Danton, who are morally reprobate. He is himself a martyr since he has to bear the weight of doing this for humanity in general. He must live with the

---

[21] Büchner, *Dantons Tod*, p. 36 (*Danton's Death*, p. 25).
[22] Pindar, *The Odes*, trans. by Maurice Bowra, London: Penguin 1969, "Pythian VIII," p. 237. Quoted in full above in the Introduction, Sect. 0.1, p. 3.
[23] Büchner, *Dantons Tod*, p. 36 (*Danton's Death*, p. 25).
[24] Büchner, *Dantons Tod*, p. 37 (*Danton's Death*, p. 26).
[25] Büchner, *Dantons Tod*, p. 38 (*Danton's Death*, p. 27).

blood of so many on his hands. But then, Robespierre reflects again and modifies his view to a more sobering one: "Why do we always look to this one man? Verily the son of man is crucified in all of us; we writhe in blood and sweat in the Garden of Gethsemane, but none of us redeems the others with his wounds."[26] Finally, he realizes that no one is redeemed, not even with the help of Jesus. Human existence is only "blood and sweat" with no salvation at the end. There is no higher meaning to be found in all the pain and sacrifices of humanity.

Robespierre regrets that, at the urging of Saint-Just, he must also execute his own friend Desmoulins: "Camille, dear Camille! They're all going from me – all around is emptiness and desolation – I'm utterly alone."[27] This, of course, is an example of Büchner's foreshadowing the death of Robespierre himself. But once again there is a deeper existential point to this. After one begins executing one's own friends, life loses its meaning, and it becomes impossible to know right from wrong. Robespierre can see only "emptiness and desolation," a nihilistic world of suffering with no meaning or purpose.

5.3 Danton's Nihilism

At the beginning of Act II, after the danger has become apparent, Danton appears to be world-weary and resigned. As with Ecclesiastes, Shakespeare's Macbeth, and Schopenhauer, he reflects on the repetitive nature of life that leads to boredom:

> How boring life is: day after day we put on our shirts and pull up our trousers, crawl into bed in the evening and out again in the morning, place one foot relentlessly in front of the other, with nothing to suggest things will ever be different. It's terribly sad. And that millions before us have done just the same and millions in the future will do so again; on top of all that, we consist of two halves that ape one another, so everything happens twice over. It's terribly sad.[28]

He seems to suggest that for all the things that humans do, nothing meaningful is ever accomplished. When Lacroix asks Danton why he did not act earlier to prevent the danger that they all now face, he responds, "The truth is, in the end I found it all so boring. Traipsing around forever in the self-same coat with the self-same creases. It's pathetic. To be such a dismal instrument yielding a single note on a single string."[29] Danton has been active in politics for a long time, and he confesses that he is now tired and indifferent to it all. The affairs of the world have ceased to hold any interest for him, although he was once a

---

[26] Büchner, *Dantons Tod*, p. 38 (*Danton's Death*, p. 27).
[27] Büchner, *Dantons Tod*, p. 38 (*Danton's Death*, p. 27).
[28] Büchner, *Dantons Tod*, p. 38 (*Danton's Death*, p. 28).
[29] Büchner, *Dantons Tod*, p. 39 (*Danton's Death*, p. 28).

5.3 DANTON'S NIHILISM

passionate revolutionary. The motif of boredom here seems to fit precisely with Schopenhauer's analysis. Danton spends his life satisfying his sensual drives, but after a while this leads to repetition and boredom.

We saw how at the outset of the work Danton used the image of two elephants grating each other's hides as a metaphor for human relations. Here he continues to develop this negative picture of humans as irrational, cruel beings:

> I would rather be guillotined than guillotine others. I've had enough, what's the point of us humans fighting each other? We should sit down together and be thoroughly at peace. A mistake crept in when we were made, there's something missing, I don't know what it is, we'll never discover it by groping around in each other's guts, so why smash open each other's bodies to try to find it? Let's face it, we're lousy alchemists.[30]

He seems to suggest that he is happy to sacrifice himself since he cannot be like Robespierre, constantly sending others to their death, which is apparently what the Revolution demands of those in power. He observes that this aggressive and cruel aspect of human nature is a sign that there is some fundamental defect in human beings. We have been created with no love or sympathy for others, and for this reason we are constantly fighting with each other as we pursue our own petty interests. This is evidence that we have been created by an indifferent nature and not by God.

Danton's followers, who know him as a passionate and engaged revolutionary, are surprised at his current detached disposition to their situation. His friend Pierre Nicolas Philippeaux (1756–94) asks him if he will just give up France to Robespierre and the other executioners. In response, Danton gives a long speech full of nihilistic elements: "What difference does it make? People are very well off the way things are. They're in the depths of misfortune: what a perfect opportunity to be noble or witty, sentimental or virtuous – above all, to avoid being bored!"[31] Despite his former beliefs in his principles, he now says that none of it matters, and again that the only reason that people do anything is just because otherwise they would find life tedious. Further, he explains that since we will all die sooner or later, it does not really matter when it happens:

> What difference does it make whether they die because of the guillotine, or from disease or old age? It's better to skip into the wings with sprightly limbs and a cheery wave and the applause of the audience ringing in your ears. How killingly jolly, how perfectly apt: we prance on the stage throughout our lives—even if, in the end, we are killed for real.[32]

Like Shakespeare and Klingemann, Büchner uses a metaphor from drama to describe the human condition as a piece for the stage in order to emphasize

---

[30] Büchner, *Dantons Tod*, p. 39 (*Danton's Death*, p. 29).
[31] Büchner, *Dantons Tod*, p. 39 (*Danton's Death*, p. 29).
[32] Büchner, *Dantons Tod*, pp. 39f. (*Danton's Death*, pp. 29f.).

the meaninglessness of life. Even the grim prospect of being executed on the guillotine does not faze Danton. It is just one more act in the pathetic drama of human life. He concludes by saying, "it's all too much bother, life isn't worth all the effort it costs just to keep it going."[33] This sounds similar to Schopenhauer's view of the suffering of human existence. It is a condition of life that one must continue to struggle to satisfy the natural drives and desires, but this satisfaction is only temporary, and one must constantly work to keep them under control. The condition of enduring unfulfilled passions is one of suffering. But if one manages to satisfy them too easily, then, according to Schopenhauer, as we have seen, boredom is the result. Danton appears to have experienced both sides of the dilemma. The triviality and insignificance of one's life make the price needed to pay for it too high. There is no point in living if life is merely a painful struggle or vapid boredom. Humans need something meaningful and valuable to believe in, but Danton has reached the point that he no longer believes in anything.

Danton's bleak worldview is echoed in the next scene, where a man proudly announces that his wife has born him a son, who will grow to be a great revolutionary and fight for France. As he discusses this with an unnamed citizen, a street singer plays a song in the background that seems to be a sad commentary on this. The song goes as follows: "Tell me, tell me, if you can / What is true bliss for every man? / From dawn to dusk he loves to slave / Nursing his sorrows from cradle to grave."[34] The song is then taken up by a beggar, "A clutch of earth / A scrap of moss… / Is all that's left / When life is lost!"[35] These songs resonate in the background of the purported serious discussions of others and seem to undermine them. Like Kreuzgang, the street singer and the beggar are outsiders and represent a segment of society that does not follow the norms of the mainstream. They can thus speak the harsh truth of life directly without having to conform to the common self-delusions of the majority. While the one man celebrates the birth of his son, the street singer undermines the atmosphere of joy by reminding the audience of the suffering of every human life.

The beggar is in a discussion with two well-dressed gentlemen who argue for the virtues of honest labor that allows one to make a living and acquire things. The beggar, however, calls this into question by noting how the things that one buys are generally superfluous and the labor that one undertakes for them wears down the body. His song focuses on death, which implies that a life spent on constant work is meaningless. One dies and disappears forever. Life is thus a meaningless pursuit of illusory wealth and accumulation of useless goods.

With his new apathy, Danton himself in a sense slips into the role of an outsider and social critic like Kreuzgang. He says, "I can't see why people don't

---

[33] Büchner, *Dantons Tod*, p. 40 (*Danton's Death*, p. 30).
[34] Büchner, *Dantons Tod*, p. 40 (*Danton's Death*, p. 31).
[35] Büchner, *Dantons Tod*, p. 41 (*Danton's Death*, p. 31).

5.3   DANTON'S NIHILISM

stop in the street and laugh and laugh in each other's faces, they should laugh from their windows and laugh from their graves, the heavens should burst and the earth convulse with helpless laughter."[36] From the perspective of the outsider, all strivings, beliefs, and activities are the stuff of comedy or, to use Balzac's designation for his *oeuvre*, the human comedy. The nihilism of the world is not the subject for seriousness and despair but rather for laughter. In this Büchner seems at first glance to side with Klingemann against Jean Paul. However, there is something grim about Büchner's piece that makes it a tragedy, despite Danton's attempts to laugh it off. As Schopenhauer noted, both elements of comedy and tragedy are present in the nihilistic view.

When Danton learns that an arrest warrant has been issued for him, he again oddly expresses his indifference: "So they want my head: that's fine by me. I'm fed up with this botching and bungling. Let them take it. What difference does it make? I'll die with courage, it's easier than living."[37] Like Socrates after his condemnation, Danton seems not to care that he will soon die and even regards it in some ways as something positive. He is tired of playing the role of an actor in the comedy of life.

Danton walks out into the countryside with the idea of fleeing to a hiding place. But upon reflection, he decides to turn back to the city. He reasons that if he saves his life by fleeing, he will still be plagued by his memory. However, in death he will lose all memory and become nothing. Here we can see a motif that was found in Byron's *Manfred*, who struggled with the memories of his sin of incest. Danton's sin here refers to his role in the massacres that took place when he was the Minister of Justice. On Büchner's depiction, Danton suffers from a guilty conscience and regret. For this reason, Danton wants to erase his memory. He judges death to be the preferable option over preserving his life and with it his memory. He concludes, "I can't help laughing about the whole damn business. There's this feeling inside me: nothing's going to change, tomorrow will be just like today, and so will the next day and all the days that follow. It's sheer bravado; they're trying to frighten me; they'd never dare."[38] There is an ambivalence in this. On the one hand, he seems to take the prospect of death very seriously, but then, on the other, a part of him seems to think that Robespierre is just bluffing, and things will not come to a head. But this can also be seen at a deeper level as a part of Danton's indifference, *Lebensmüdigkeit*, and nihilism. He returns to the motif of the repetition of the daily routines of life that are devoid of any meaning. Everything will continue as it has always been, and nothing meaningful will ever come from it.

In the next scene, Danton suffers again from the pangs of conscience: "Is it never going to stop? Will the glare never pale, the roar never die? Will it never

---

[36] Büchner, *Dantons Tod*, p. 42 (*Danton's Death*, p. 33).
[37] Büchner, *Dantons Tod*, p. 43 (*Danton's Death*, p. 35).
[38] Büchner, *Dantons Tod*, p. 45 (*Danton's Death*, p. 36).

be dark and still, so we're no longer forced to see and hear our horrible sins?"[39] He seems to regard his own impending death as a just and overdue punishment for his earlier actions. He explains to his wife the nightmare that he had:

> Yes, I was dreaming, but it was something else, I'll tell you right now, my poor frail head, right now, there, that's it, I've got it! Beneath me the earth's whole sphere, roaring and snorting in headlong flight, with me astride it like on a wild stallion, clutching its mane and gripping its flanks with giant limbs, my head bent low, my hair streaming out above the infinite abyss. And so I was swept along. I screamed in terror, and woke.[40]

The dream reveals a feeling of helplessness, a sense of being swept along by larger forces of the world. The "infinite abyss" of the universe gives the dream a tone of despair. The earth is rushing through space at such a great speed, carrying along everyone with it, yet in a sense it is going nowhere since all around it is the abyss. It is not heading towards some important goal or conclusion. It is just hurtling through space obeying natural laws. Danton later extends this idea to human life as well: "Puppets, that's all we are, made to dance on strings by unknown forces; ourselves we are nothing, nothing – mere swords in the hands of warring spirits, the hands themselves cannot be seen, that's all, like in some child's fairy-tale."[41] This vision of a mechanistic universe that also rules over human beings chimes with Robespierre's view. We live in the illusion of free will and rationally calculated projects, but in the end we are just following the natural forces that control everything. This resembles Schopenhauer's idea that there is no escaping the will-to-live, the fundamental principle of the universe, which dictates the lives of everyone. Given this, Danton's resigned disposition starts to make some sense. If one believes that there is nothing that one can do to change anything, then there is nothing left but resignation. This explains the fact that at the end of the discussion Danton says that he is finally truly happy. While this might seem odd at first, it makes perfect sense that once he has reached the point of acceptance and resignation and has realized that there is nothing left to be done, he can finally relax in this knowledge. He no longer needs to fight against what are in fact the basic laws of the universe.

In a speech to the National Convention justifying the arrest of Danton and his followers, Saint-Just refers to nature's apathy towards human desires and hopes. He too presents a cold universe that proceeds by natural laws with no regard to humanity. He argues,

> Nature follows her own laws, calmly, irresistibly; man is destroyed wherever he comes into conflict with them. A change in the composition of the air, a burst of subterranean fire, a shift in the equilibrium of a mass of

---

[39] Büchner, *Dantons Tod*, p. 45 (*Danton's Death*, p. 37).
[40] Büchner, *Dantons Tod*, pp. 45f. (*Danton's Death*, p. 38).
[41] Büchner, *Dantons Tod*, p. 46 (*Danton's Death*, p. 38).

water—and an epidemic, a volcanic eruption, a flood kills thousands. And what is the outcome? An insignificant, scarcely perceptible ripple on the surface of the physical world that would almost have disappeared without trace were it not for the jetsam of corpses.[42]

From this he tries to argue that human society obeys or should obey the same set of rules of nature. He has a Hegelian conception of world-spirit moving forward in history at a very slow pace. While it makes progress, it demands innumerable victims along the way. He claims, "The world-spirit acts through us in the realm of ideas just as, in the physical realm, it acts through floods or volcanoes. What difference does it make whether people die of an epidemic or the revolution?"[43] In a sense this sounds like a nihilistic claim, and from the point of view of the individual it is. But contrary to Danton, Saint-Just retains a sense of truth and meaning in the universe with the idea of historical progress. According to his view, the victims of the Revolution are necessary sacrifices in the name of this progress. This is of course easy to say so long as one is not among those regarded as the necessary sacrifices. But Saint-Just fails to realize that he will soon become a victim as well. This seems to vindicate the nihilistic perspective since, from the point of view of the victim, there is little consolation in the idea of historical progress. For the victim, the reality of the situation is that they are condemned to die not in the service of some grand ideal but rather due to the arbitrary cruelty of others, which leads to the conclusion that there is no rhyme or reason in the universe.

While awaiting execution in prison, Danton expresses a nihilistic view about his entire life, which now, despite everything he has accomplished as a revolutionary, seems completely meaningless in the face of death:

> Will the clock never rest? With every tick it pushes the walls around me that bit closer, like a coffin. I read a story like that as a child: my hair stood on end. Yes, "as a child"! What a waste of time it was feeding me up and keeping me warm, just to make work for the gravediggers![44]

From this perspective, there was no point being born and growing up since life always ends in death. Life itself is a great struggle, and it would have been better not to have been born at all. Danton compares death with birth as two natural processes that mirror each other: "Death is a parody of birth: we die helpless and naked, like newborn infants. We even get swaddled – but in a shroud. Anyway, it makes no difference. We'd cry in the grave as we cried in the cradle."[45] Birth and death are dialectical opposites, which seem at first glance to be completely different, but upon closer examination are in fact the mirror image of one another.

---

[42] Büchner, *Dantons Tod*, p. 49 (*Danton's Death*, p. 42).
[43] Büchner, *Dantons Tod*, p. 49 (*Danton's Death*, p. 42). Translation slightly modified.
[44] Büchner, *Dantons Tod*, p. 65 (*Danton's Death*, p. 64).
[45] Büchner, *Dantons Tod*, p. 65 (*Danton's Death*, p. 64).

5.4 Life as Suffering

Scene Three begins with Danton and his followers imprisoned and awaiting their hearing. The famous revolutionary Thomas Paine (1737–1809) is seen explaining a philosophical argument against the existence of God to a fellow revolutionary, Pierre-Gaspard Chaumette (1763–94). This discussion might seem forced, but it plays an important role in the nihilistic view of the work by making explicit the denial of God, with which the road to nihilism begins. Among his arguments, Paine raises the issue of God's perfection, asking how a perfect God could create such a deeply imperfect world. He argues, "Evil you can deny, but not pain. Only the intellect can prove the notion of God, all the emotions rebel against it. Mark this …: why do I suffer? That is the rock of atheism. The tiniest spasm of pain, be it in a single atom, and divine creation is utterly torn asunder."[46] In a sense this can be regarded as the opposite of Jean Paul's argument for immortality. It will be recalled that, for Jean Paul, the intellect or reason treats the concepts of God and immortality flippantly and with detachment as if there were very little at stake. But when one is confronted with pain, suffering, and death, then, according to Jean Paul, one's emotions force one into becoming a believer. Karlson gives up his rational scientific view and allows himself to be convinced by his emotions of love and affection for Gione and the prospect of her death. Here Paine makes the opposite claim: the emotion or feeling of pain demonstrates that God does not exist since it is a clear sign of an imperfect universe that God in his perfection could not have created.[47] In both cases it is emotions and not reason that are the basis for the argument.

Paine goes on and states his view on ethics. He claims that his position does not destroy ethics, which do not necessarily require the existence of absolute ethical rules. Instead, he argues,

> I behave according to my nature: whatever is appropriate to my nature is good for me, and I do it; whatever is opposed to my nature is bad for me, if it crosses my path I ward it off. You can remain true to so-called virtue and hostile to so-called vice without necessarily despising those of a different persuasion—a pathetic attitude if ever there was one.[48]

There can be a kind of morality that derives from nature itself. We are the products of nature, which has endowed us with certain natural drives. So when we fulfill these, we are acting in accordance with nature and doing what is good for ourselves. Paine is critical of the mainstream bourgeois morality that condemns this and demands that everyone live up to some fictional universal moral standard. This is unnecessary since nature itself provides its own standard for morality.

---

[46] Büchner, *Dantons Tod*, p. 51 (*Danton's Death*, pp. 45f.).
[47] As was noted above (Introduction, Sect. 0.1.3, p. 9), the fact of suffering has long been an argument against the existence of God.
[48] Büchner, *Dantons Tod*, p. 51 (*Danton's Death*, p. 46).

5.4 LIFE AS SUFFERING

When Danton and his friends are led into the jail cell, astonishment is expressed that he has been apprehended so quickly. Danton explains that he knew that he would be arrested soon since he was warned ahead of time that the authorities were coming for him. In astonishment Lacroix asked him why he did not do anything, such as try to hide or escape once he was warned. Danton's reply again highlights his nihilism: "Why bother? The best kind of death is a sudden stroke. Or do you prefer the slow, lingering sort? .... Better to take it easy under the earth than dash around on top getting corns. I'd rather use it as a pillow than a footstool."[49] He suggests that life is too much trouble to be lived and the quiet of death is preferable. This echoes his statements to his wife at the beginning of the work, where he yearns for the quiet and calm of the grave. At this point he seems completely resigned to his death. When he addresses the Revolutionary Tribunal, he remains defiant with respect to the charges raised against him, but at the same time he shows an indifference to his fate: "the void will soon be my refuge. My life is a burden: go ahead, snatch it from me, I can't wait to get rid of it."[50] Danton in a later scene reiterates his need for peace. When asked if he means peace in God, he responds,

> In nothingness. What offers more peace, more oblivion, than nothingness? And if ultimate peace is God, then doesn't that mean that God is nothingness? But I'm an atheist! How I curse the dictum that "something can't become nothing"! And I am something, that's the misery of it! Creation's so rank and rampant that no void is left, there's a seething and swarming wherever you turn. Nothingness has killed itself, creation is its wound, we are the drops of its blood, the world the grave in which it slowly rots.[51]

He wishes for death to be a complete annihilation and not just the loss of consciousness and the slow decay of the body. As with *The Nightwatches*, the work contains many references and allusions to the decomposition of the body after death.

Camille Desmoulins refers to the medieval myth of the Wandering Jew, whose name, Cartaphilus, Ahasver, and so on, varies in the different sources.[52] According to one version of the legend, the Jew did not allow Jesus, on the way to his crucifixion, to rest for a moment at his house. According to a different version, he taunted or even struck Jesus on his way to the crucifixion. As punishment, the Jew was condemned to wander the earth until Christ returns. This intriguing story, which was a favorite of Kierkegaard,[53] is interesting since one might think that death would be an appropriate punishment, but instead

---

[49] Büchner, *Dantons Tod*, p. 52 (*Danton's Death*, p. 47).
[50] Büchner, *Dantons Tod*, p. 54 (*Danton's Death*, p. 50).
[51] Büchner, *Dantons Tod*, p. 61 (*Danton's Death*, p. 58).
[52] Büchner, *Dantons Tod*, p. 61 (*Danton's Death*, p. 58).
[53] See Joseph Ballan, "The Wandering Jew: Kierkegaard and the Figuration of Death in Life," in *Kierkegaard's Literary Figures and Motifs*, tome II, *Gulliver to Zerlina*, ed. by Katalin Nun and Jon Stewart, Aldershot: Ashgate 2015 (*Kierkegaard Research: Sources, Reception and*

the punishment is enduring life on earth. It implicitly acknowledges that life itself is suffering and constitutes a punishment on its own terms. This story highlights Danton's world-weary disposition, where continuing life is such a burden that death is preferable.

5.5 The Power of Love

Yet Danton seems to have a change of heart when he thinks of his poor wife who must carry on alone after his death. It is not for his own sake that he thinks it is worth fighting for life but rather for hers:

> O Julie! If I had to go on my own! If she left me all alone! Even if I utterly dissolved, utterly disintegrated, became but a handful of tortured dust—every last atom could only find peace with her. I cannot die, no, I cannot die. We must rage and roar, they'll have to squeeze the life from my body drop by drop.[54]

This outburst seems somewhat out of character given his previously stated view that we are all ultimately alone in life. This serves to fortify Danton for his final speech to the Revolutionary Tribunal, where he tries to prove his innocence. In any case, Büchner here explores the possibility of love in conquering the cold nihilistic view, which was examined previously with Jean Paul's Karlson and Klingemann's Kreuzgang. While Jean Paul accepted this view, Klingemann rejected love as an illusion in the face of nihilism.

Büchner portrays the great affection between Camille Desmoulins and his wife Lucile. When Camille goes to talk with Robespierre, she has a premonition of his death:

> These are evil times. It's the way things are. What can anyone do? Be brave and accept it.
>
> > Who had the heart
> > To make lovers part
> > And part and part and part?
>
> Why *that*, of all things? For that to come into my head on its own: it's bad. As he went away, I had this feeling he could never turn back and would have to go further and further away from me—further and further. How empty the room is; the windows agape as though a corpse had lain here. I can't bear it.[55]

Resources, vol. 16), pp. 235–247. George Pattison, "'Cosmopolitan Faces': The Presence of the Wandering Jew in 'From the Papers of One Still Living,'" in *Early Polemical Writings*, ed. by Robert L. Perkins, Macon, GA: Mercer University Press 1999 (*International Kierkegaard Commentary*, vol. 1), pp. 109–130; Knud Jensenius, *Nogle Kierkegaardstudier*. "De Tre Store Ideer," Copenhagen: Nyt Nordisk Forlag Arnold Busck 1932, pp. 64–124; Peter Tudvad, *Stadier på antisemitismens vej. Kierkegaard og jøderne*, Copenhagen: Rosinante 2010, pp. 55–165.

[54] Büchner, *Dantons Tod*, p. 61 (*Danton's Death*, p. 59).
[55] Büchner, *Dantons Tod*, p. 44 (*Danton's Death*, pp. 35f.).

5.5 THE POWER OF LOVE

The motif of the necessity of lovers parting reflects a world that crushes human hopes and desires. There is no point in complaining about it or fighting against it. One must simply accept it as the way the world is.

As Danton and his friends await their execution in jail, Camille's thoughts return to his wife. He is concerned that the Committee for Public Safety will also condemn her for treason after he is gone. Like Jean Paul's Karlson, he cannot accept the idea of the death of his beloved:

> They can't touch her, they mustn't. The radiant beauty that streams from her body so sweet can never be quenched. It's impossible. The earth would not dare to devour her, it would rise up vault-like all around her, the sepulchral dank would sparkle like dew upon her lashes, crystals would sprout like flowers around her limbs, pellucid springs would whisper her to sleep.[56]

He hopes that the laws of nature will make an exception with regard to his wife. Since she is so beautiful and loving, he cannot imagine how nature could be so cruel as to make her mortal. Her body surely could not decompose to dust. But this hope is just an illusion. As was the case with Kreuzgang's reluctant love for Ophelia, love affairs always end in pain and suffering. Due to his love, Camille still finds beauty in the world in contrast to Danton, who seems indifferent about his immanent death.

Like her husband, Lucile also seems to be in denial about death. She sits alone outside the prison and imagines her beloved Camille inside. She sings a song about two stars in the sky, suggesting some kind of imaginary immortality for lovers.[57] Verging on madness, she calls on her husband to come to her and is sad and frightened when he fails to appear. She recounts that she has heard others talking about the execution and death of her husband, but she acts as if she does not know what this portends: "'Die'! What does that *mean*? Tell me, Camille! 'Die'! I want to think about that. There, there it is! I'll run after it. Come, my darling, help me catch it. Come on, come on!"[58] On the face of it, she poses the philosophical question of the meaning of death given that it is something we never immediately experience until we actually die. She foreshadows her own end by saying that she will actively pursue death instead of waiting for it to catch her. As she runs off, Camille, from his prison cell, shouts her name after her, but she fails to hear him. This seems to symbolize the fragility of the love relation in the face of the inevitability of death. In the next scene Camille reflects on Lucile's madness, which he sadly accepts as another cold fact about the world. He only wishes that her madness is not of the tormenting but rather of the blissful sort.[59]

---

[56] Büchner, *Dantons Tod*, p. 64 (*Danton's Death*, p. 63).
[57] Büchner, *Dantons Tod*, p. 67 (*Danton's Death*, p. 66).
[58] Büchner, *Dantons Tod*, p. 67 (*Danton's Death*, p. 67).
[59] Büchner, *Dantons Tod*, p. 68 (*Danton's Death*, p. 67).

When Danton tries to console himself and the others that posterity will remember their actions, Camille gives a speech intended to emphasize the vanity of such ideas:

> It's a waste of effort to pout and prink and talk all posh. It's time we removed our masks: we'd think ourselves in a hall of mirrors—wherever we looked we'd see only the same ass's head, no more, no less: primeval, infinite, indestructible. The differences between us are not that great. We're all of us angels and villains, idiots and geniuses, all at the same time: there's plenty of room in a single body for all four things, they're none of them so big as we might imagine.[60]

Here, very much in the spirit of Kreuzgang, Camille points out that whatever differences there appear to be in society are due to the masks that we all wear in our social roles. But behind it all, we are ultimately the same. We are subject to the same drives and desires and the same fate. This fits well with the value of equality that was so important for the French revolutionaries, but once again, there is also a deeper point here. Humans are complex and ambiguous creatures. The masks we wear are all attempts to hide this from ourselves and others. We want to present an unambiguous positive image of ourselves to the world. We interpret things one-sidedly in our favor and disregard and deny anything about ourselves that can be interpreted negatively. In this way we carefully avoid thinking about the sad truths of death and the meaninglessness of life. But with impending death, it is easier to acknowledge the vanity of life. It seems somewhat out of character for Camille to be thinking along these lines since before he wanted to hold on to life due to his love for his wife. But now, he seems to have accepted his fate and capitulated to the nihilistic view.

The inability of love as an answer to nihilism is confirmed at the end of the work with two suicides. First, Danton's wife Julie takes a vial of poison as Danton is being carried off to his execution.[61] Then, Camille's beloved Lucile is the final victim of the piece. After her husband's death, she, still in the grips of madness, returns to further ruminations about the nature of death, which she apparently had not considered previously:

> There's something in it after all, something serious. I do want to think about it. I'm beginning to understand such things. Words like "die," "die."
> —Everything else is allowed to go on living, this tiny insect here, that bird. Why not him? The stream of life should stop aghast if even a single drop is spilt. The earth should show a gaping wound from such a blow. Everything's astir: clocks tick, bells ring, folk pass, water flows, everything continues just as before, forever and forever. —But no! It mustn't happen, no!

---

[60] Büchner, *Dantons Tod*, p. 68 (*Danton's Death*, p. 68).
[61] Büchner, *Dantons Tod*, p. 70 (*Danton's Death*, p. 70).

> I shall sit on the ground and scream, so everything stops, shocked into stillness, not a flicker of movement. It makes no difference. Things are just as they were. The houses, the street. The wind blows, the clouds drift. — Perhaps we just have to bear it.[62]

She is troubled by the banality of death. Despite the traumatic experience, the world goes on indifferent to it. She is inclined to revolt against the universe where this is the state of things. But when she sees that this has no effect, her conclusion is that this is just something that we have to accept.

As the crowds subside, she returns to the Place de la Révolution, where the executions took place. She sits on the steps of the guillotine where her husband has just been executed. Contemplating the guillotine, she sings to herself, "There is a reaper, Death by name, / Whose power from God Almighty came.... / Countless are the myriad lives / That fall beneath his sweeping scythe."[63] She recognizes that death is a natural and necessary part of the universe that God himself created. There is nothing that can be done about it, and all resistance or rebellion is in vain. As she sits there in her misery a police patrol comes by, and she in effect commits suicide by shouting "Long live the King!"[64] Since she is a radical revolutionary and obviously not a royalist, it is clear that her intention is not to make an expression of her political views but rather to die. She is immediately arrested and led off. As was the case with Julie, Lucile ends in misery and resignation. Once she realizes the full cruelty and meaninglessness of human existence, she can no longer bear to continue her life in such a world. Here one can see the triumph of nihilism over love. This conclusion seems completely in line with the tragic result of Kreuzgang's affair with Ophelia. Love, like life itself, is only fleeting and can stand no chance against the great forces of an indifferent universe.

5.6 The Nihilistic Tone of the End of the Work

It is difficult to draw conclusions about Büchner's ultimate message with *Danton's Death*. However, some general observations can be made. There can be little doubt that nihilism is an important motif in the work. The immediate situation of the prisoners awaiting their execution can be regarded as a metaphor for human life in general. Once we are born, we are all destined for death. While each of the characters reacts to this somewhat differently, at the end there is no sign of redemption, reconciliation, or a peace in an afterlife. On the contrary, their deaths are as meaningless as life itself. Their works in life, like their deaths, serve no larger purpose. The world is a cruel and inhuman place, where we suffer merely to survive. Seen from this perspective, *Danton's Death* appears to use the Reign of Terror as a mirror of human existence. Life is

---

[62] Büchner, *Dantons Tod*, p. 71 (*Danton's Death*, p. 72).
[63] Büchner, *Dantons Tod*, p. 72 (*Danton's Death*, p. 73).
[64] Büchner, *Dantons Tod*, p. 72 (*Danton's Death*, p. 73).

fragile, and death could come at any time. It is a constant struggle just to keep going in life.

In their final discussion in prison before Danton and his comrades are summoned by the jailer to get into the carts that will carry them to the guillotine, the different characters give their final assessment of human existence. Philippeaux tries to strike a positive note by arguing that although it is impossible to see from our limited human perspective, God has created the world with a plan and a design, and their deaths must be a part of this. He claims, "My friends, we don't have to stand very far above the earth to lose all sight of its fitful, flickering confusion, and feast our eyes on the grand simplicity of God's design. There is an ear for which the riotous cacophony that deafens us is but a stream of harmonies."[65] Although we cannot know what God's plan is, we must believe that such a plan exists since the thought is too difficult to bear that life is a "riotous cacophony" with no rhyme or reason. This acoustic metaphor seems to echo Macbeth's words about life as full of "sound and fury, / Signifying nothing."[66] Philippeaux's reasoning also seems very much in line with that of Jean Paul. We must believe in God and immortality since the alternative is simply too horrifying to consider.

But Danton rejects this optimistic view. He claims that there is no deeper truth or meaning beyond the noise of human existence. Keeping with the acoustic metaphor, he argues, "But we are the poor musicians, and our bodies the instruments. The ugly sounds scratched out on them: are they just there to rise up higher and higher and gently fade and die like some voluptuous breath in heavenly ears?"[67] There is no beauty in the world of human beings. It is only violence, suffering and cruelty. These are the "ugly sounds" of life. There is no point to any of it since all our tears and sufferings will be forgotten forever in the infinity of time and space.

In the ensuing dialogue, there is the suggestion that the higher powers even take a sadistic pleasure in watching our suffering. The world thus seems to be created not by a loving and caring god but rather by a pitiless and evil demon. From a scientific point of view, this seems to be what the empirical evidence supports. Hérault de Séchelles asks, "Are we suckling-pigs, whipped to death with rods to make their meat more tasty for a princely feast?"[68] To this Danton responds, "Are we children, roasted in the fiery arms of a Moloch world, tickled to death with tongues of flame so the gods can delight in our laughter?"[69] To this Camille adds, "Are the heavens with their winking eyes of gold a bowl of golden carp that stands on the table of the blessed gods, and the blessed gods

---

[65] Büchner, *Dantons Tod*, p. 69 (*Danton's Death*, p. 69).
[66] Shakespeare, *Macbeth*, Act 5, Scene 5, lines 26–27, p. 2561
[67] Büchner, *Dantons Tod*, p. 69 (*Danton's Death*, p. 69).
[68] Büchner, *Dantons Tod*, p. 69 (*Danton's Death*, p. 69).
[69] Büchner, *Dantons Tod*, p. 69 (*Danton's Death*, p. 69).

laugh forever and the fish die forever and the gods delight forever in the dancing colours of their dying agony?"[70] In each of these images humans are portrayed as innocently suffering for the pleasure of more powerful beings. If there is a meaning in life, then it is a bleak one: our suffering serves only the need of perverse amusement for the higher powers.

All these statements are couched in the form of questions, and so it might be argued that Büchner wants to leave the door open for the possibility of a higher purpose. But in the final sentence of the dialogue Danton draws a definitive line when he states, "The world is chaos, nothingness its due messiah."[71] This can perhaps be regarded as the slogan for the entire work. As was the case with Kreuzgang, the only truth in the world for Danton is the nothingness. Everything else is a facade, and hope is a self-delusion. Like Klingemann's *The Nightwatches*, Büchner's *Danton's Death* seems to offer no positive strategy for overcoming nihilism. The suffering and lack of meaning in life are simply the hard facts of human existence that must be accepted on a scientific view of nature.

5.7 Danton as a Symbol of Acceptance and Resignation

Like Jean Paul, Büchner presents a terrifying picture of a nihilistic world. But unlike Jean Paul, his goal is not to frighten his reader into believing in immortality or God. Büchner, like Klingemann and Schopenhauer, would regard this as naïve. Instead, his comparison of humans with fish swimming in a bowl, suffering and dying for the amusement of the gods, indicates a much more pessimistic view of the universe. Büchner presents a cold world of human relations that contrasts strongly with the gushing emotions found in Jean Paul's characters such as Gione, Nadine, and even Karlson. Danton presents the picture of elephants chafing each other's hides.[72] Büchner's drama depicts a materialist view of the world, derived from the sciences. Humans are just biological beings seeking the satisfaction of their own basic desires. In this sense Büchner seems to be in agreement with Schopenhauer that most all of our actions are dictated by our natural needs. There is something base about Büchner's characters who are portrayed as being intoxicated, visiting brothels, and so on. There is little perception of the higher faculties of human beings that transcend the merely physical or biological.

Büchner's harsh image of society seems to have more in common with Kreuzgang's satirical and unforgiving descriptions of people in *The Nightwatches*. But there is also an important difference here. Humor is a significant element in Klingemann's social criticism, whereas Büchner's work is completely sober. Throughout the work there is the constant threat of death. While Danton seems to recognize the absurd aspect of nihilism and says that people should be

---

[70] Büchner, *Dantons Tod*, p. 69 (*Danton's Death*, p. 69).
[71] Büchner, *Dantons Tod*, p. 69 (*Danton's Death*, p. 69).
[72] Büchner, *Dantons Tod*, p. 14 (*Danton's Death*, p. 5).

laughing all the time at their predicament,[73] this statement seems almost like an outburst of delirium in a moment of desperation. To be sure, the work contains many socially critical comments concerning human beings, referring to their fickleness with regard to political trends, their readiness to assign blame and victimize innocent people, their unthinking cruelty and bloodlust, and so on. When Kreuzgang criticizes people, he usually does so in the tone of the straight man, in a neutral, matter-of-fact way. He is unmoved by either the suicide of the writer or the sight the corpse of his father. By contrast, Büchner's critique is much more direct and fueled by invective. The message seems to be that the Reign of Terror was no exception to the usual course of the world, but rather it merely brought out the ugly reality of human nature that is usually carefully concealed behind the facade of social life and rules of politeness and etiquette.

A key motif in Büchner's drama is Danton's tortured conscience and nightmares. He is obsessed with his sins of the past, which leave him no rest. This is very similar to the troubled mind of Manfred in Byron's work. Both protagonists are vexed by their own self-consciousness. The awareness of nihilism can only come about when the mind is mature and reflective. It requires the ability to abstract from our immediate circumstances and surroundings and to see ourselves in the broader perspective of the universe as a whole, which makes us look so small and insignificant. The idea of nihilism would perhaps never arise if, like children, we did not have the ability to abstract in this way. Both Danton and Manfred seek a solution to their own self-consciousness, and both ultimately realize that this can only come with death itself. But here the similarities stop. Manfred is a Promethean symbol of human rebellion against the gods, that is, against the universe. He insists on the freedom of his mind, despite the limitations of his physical strength and capabilities. He maintains human dignity even in the moment of death. By contrast, Danton seems just to give up and welcome his fate. He more fully embraces nihilism by suggesting that there was no point in his being born and that it does not matter when he dies. He thus accepts the grim reality of nihilism. We can see the same thing in the character of Lucile, who struggles to understand how everything can go on as usual despite the death of the individual. Initially, her inclination is to scream and shout in revolt against the world.[74] But after a moment's reflection, she realizes that this is fruitless and resigns herself to it. In the end, she in effect commits suicide by intentionally getting herself arrested. This shows that she has completely given up on everything, including herself. For Byron, these characters would represent a cowardly betrayal of the human spirit. They fail to recognize the true power of freedom that individuals can wield even in extreme situations.

With these examples we can see a clear anticipation of some of the discussions in twentieth-century existentialism. Sartre insisted on the fact that humans are

[73] Büchner, *Dantons Tod*, p. 42 (*Danton's Death*, p. 33).
[74] Büchner, *Dantons Tod*, p. 71 (*Danton's Death*, p. 72).

always free, regardless of their external circumstances. In the context of the Second World War and the French Resistance, he was keen to create a philosophical theory that would hold people strictly responsible for their actions and would provide the ethical leverage to condemn the collaborators. Likewise, Camus's discussion of the importance of rebellion overlaps with the example of Manfred. These existentialist thinkers, along with Byron, would presumably be critical of Büchner's Danton for his spinelessness and his denial of his own freedom. The desperation of the situation leads him to surrender his human dignity. One might be inclined, like the critics of the existentialists, to defend Danton, claiming that he really had no choice, and his resignation is perfectly understandable given the circumstances. Being condemned to the guillotine, he could not change his fate by a spontaneous act of will. But, in the spirit of Byron and the existentialists, one could counter this by saying that Danton in fact had the chance to make a reasonably easy escape and was even on his way to doing so. Moreover, even when imprisoned and sentenced to death, he could still have dealt with this in a way that maintained human freedom and dignity, even if he could not change the outcome.

Shelley's message was that the realization of nihilism should cause a change in our perspective and self-image in such a way that we become humbler and kinder to others. By contrast, in Büchner's *Danton's Death*, there is no sense that the characters develop morally. With their awareness of nihilism, they seem to remain the same people that they always were. The only real change can be seen in their increased sense of desperation, which leads in some cases to resignation and in others to suicide. Nobody is improved ethically by this new perspective. Nobody becomes more loving or forgiving. Rather, the same struggles and conflicts continue as before, and ultimately the idea of nihilism seems to crush them. Büchner would presumably find Shelley's notion naïve and idealistic. There is no possibility of improving human nature, which is purely self-interested and cruel.

Despite Büchner's agreement with Schopenhauer that life is a constant struggle with constant suffering, there are some important differences in their views. The character Danton would clearly disagree with Schopenhauer's solution that one should try to make oneself indifferent to the demands of the will by means of asceticism. On the contrary, Danton embraces the pleasure of the senses, with the idea being that we should take brief moments of enjoyment where we can find them, given that everything else is suffering. Danton and his friends openly advocate an Epicureanism that is the very opposite of Schopenhauer's view. Büchner and Schopenhauer thus draw quite different conclusions from their agreed first premise of the universal suffering of human existence. It can be argued that Büchner's view here is a reflection of his disposition of resignation. Given that we can do nothing to change the basic nihilistic facts of the universe, it is best that we just enjoy whatever we can during our short and meaningless lives.

Given what is known about Büchner's radical politics, it is fair to ask what his message is with regard to the political context of the work. Did he select the Reign of Terror as his setting simply due to its violence and cruelty, or was there also a specific political point to this? Despite Büchner's own political engagement, his drama seems to bespeak a sense of meaninglessness in politics. As a part of his general resignation and disenchantment, Danton gives up his desire to work to improve things. The motifs of repetition and boredom suggest that while political parties and politicians come and go, nothing fundamental really changes. The foreshadowing of the death of Robespierre seems to confirm this. There is something important about this indifferent view of politics since it flies in the face of the very idea of a revolution of any kind, namely, to make a change. How can this be explained? The French Revolution had many German supporters who shared its ideals from a distance. But then the Reign of Terror compelled many people to rethink these ideas. They asked themselves if this was a natural result of undermining the old system of privilege and allowing people too much freedom. Many who were originally supporters of the Revolution thus became disenchanted. Such a shift in one's belief system could easily lead to a cynical, nihilistic resignation concerning politics.

Given all of this, it is difficult to see in Danton a positive proposal for how to deal with nihilism. Instead, Büchner uses his Danton to illustrate the sad nihilistic universe, where humans live, struggle, suffer, and die with no meaning. For both Klingemann and Büchner, this seems to be a problem with no real solution. The best one can do is to realize the sad truth of nihilism and accept it. Like Schopenhauer, Büchner does at least have a suggestion about how best to cope with nihilism, but his recommendation just to enjoy the pleasures of the senses seems to ring hollow.

6

Poul Martin Møller's Criticism of Hegelianism and the Danish Discussion of Nihilism

An important work in the discussion of nihilism in the nineteenth century was the article by the Danish philosopher, poet, and writer Poul Martin Møller (1794-1838), "Thoughts on the Possibility of Proofs of Human Immortality with Regard to the Latest Literature on the Subject," published in 1837.[1] This article represents the most substantial treatment of nihilism in Danish philosophy.[2] Møller is best known today as an important mentor of the young Søren Kierkegaard.[3] He studied theology at the University of Copenhagen and developed a love for Greek and Latin.[4] After completing his studies, he worked for

---

[1] Poul Martin Møller, "Tanker over Muligheden af Beviser for Menneskets Udødelighed, med Hensyn til den nyeste derhen hørende Literatur," *Maanedsskrift for Litteratur*, vol. 17, 1837, pp. 1-72, 422-453. All quotations below are from this first printing of the work (English translation: *Poul Martin Møller's "Thoughts on the Possibility of Proofs of Human Immortality" and Other Texts*, ed. and trans. by Finn Gredal Jensen and Jon Stewart, Leiden and Boston: Brill 2022 (*Texts from Golden Age Denmark*, vol. 8)).

[2] See Jon Stewart, *A History of Hegelianism in Golden Age Denmark*, tome II, *The Martensen Period: 1837-1842*, Copenhagen: C.A. Reitzel 2007 (*Danish Golden Age Studies*, vol. 3), pp. 37-53; Jørgen K. Bukdahl, "Poul Martin Møllers opgør med 'nihilismen,'" *Dansk Udsyn*, vol. 45, 1965, pp. 266-290; K. Brian Söderquist, "The Closed Self: Kierkegaard and Poul Martin Møller on the Hubris of Romantic Irony," in *Kierkegaard and the Word(s): Essays on Hermeneutics and Communication*, ed. by Poul Houe and Gordon D. Marino, Copenhagen: C.A. Reitzel 2003, pp. 204-214; Peter Thielst, "Poul Martin Møller: Scattered Thoughts, Analysis of Affectation, Struggle with Nihilism," *Danish Yearbook of Philosophy*, vol. 13, 1976, pp. 66-83 (reprinted in *Kierkegaard and His Contemporaries: The Culture of Golden Age Denmark*, ed. by Jon Stewart, Berlin and New York: Walter de Gruyter 2003 (*Kierkegaard Studies Monograph Series*, vol. 10), pp. 45-61).

[3] See Finn Gredal Jensen, "Poul Martin Møller: Kierkegaard and the Confidant of Socrates," in *Kierkegaard and His Danish Contemporaries*, tome I, *Philosophy, Politics and Social Theory*, ed. by Jon Stewart, Aldershot: Ashgate 2009 (*Kierkegaard Research: Sources, Reception and Resources*, vol. 7), pp. 101-167; Bernd Henningsen, *Poul Martin Møller oder Die dänische Erziehung des Søren Kierkegaards*, Frankfurt am Main: Akademische Verlagsgesellschaft 1973.

[4] For Møller's biography, see Frederik Christian Olsen, "Poul Martin Møllers Levnet," in *Efterladte Skrifter af Poul M. Møller*, vols. 1-3, ed. by Christian Winther, F.C. Olsen, and Christen Thaarup, Copenhagen: C.A. Reitzel 1839-43, vol. 3, pp. 1-115 (reprinted as a separate monograph: *Poul Martin Møllers Levnet*, Copenhagen: Bianco Luno 1843 [2nd ed., 1850; 3rd ed., 1856]); Vilhelm Andersen, *Poul Møller. Hans Liv og Skrifter efter trykte og*

many years as an instructor of classics at schools in Copenhagen. In 1826 he received an appointment as lecturer in philosophy at the Frederik's University of Christiania (today the University of Oslo).[5] During this time he became one the first Danish thinkers to develop an interest in Hegel's philosophy. In 1831 Møller returned to Copenhagen after having received an appointment as professor of philosophy at the university there. When his young wife Betty Berg died in 1834, Møller was devasted, and this stimulated his reflections on the issue of human immortality that ultimately resulted in his article.

As the title of the article indicates, Møller reviews some of the then recent works of German literature about the issue of whether Hegel's philosophy contained a theory of immortality.[6] This was an unresolved question in Hegel's thought at his death in 1831, and debates about it played an important role in the formation of the schools of right and left Hegelianism.[7] Keen to show that Hegel was a Christian, the right Hegelians insisted that he had a theory of immortality. By contrast, the left Hegelians wanted to read Hegel as critical of Christianity, and as evidence of this they pointed out what they took to be an absence of a theory of immortality in his writings and lectures. Some of Hegel's students pursued projects that were perceived to be critical of the traditional dogmas of Christianity. It was feared that this would lead others down the road

---

utrykte Kilder i Hundredaaret for hans Fødsel, Copenhagen: G.E.C. Gad 1894; Johannes Brøndum-Nielsen, *Poul Møller Studier*, Copenhagen: Gyldendalske Boghandel, Nordisk Forlag 1940; Frederik Rønning, *Poul Martin Møller. En Levnedsskildring med et Udvalg af hans Arbejder*, Copenhagen: G.E.C. Gad 1893, pp. 7–72; Carl Henrik Koch, "Poul Martin Møller," in his *Den danske idealisme 1800–1880*, Copenhagen: Gyldendal 2004, pp. 249–269; Uffe Andreasen, *Poul Møller og Romanticismen*, Copenhagen: Gyldendal 1973.

[5] See Andersen, *Poul Møller, hans Liv og Skrifter*, pp. 302–316; Ludvig Daae, "Fra Poul Møllers Liv som Professor i Christiania," *Historiske Samlinger*, ed. by Den Norske Historiske Kildeskriftkommission, vol. 3, no. 1, 1908, pp. 1–20; Ole Koppang, *Hegelianismen i Norge. En Idéhistorisk Undersøkelse*, Oslo: H. Aschehoug & Co (W. Nygaard) 1943, pp. 38–40. See also *Breve til og fra F.C. Sibbern*, vols. 1–2, ed. by C.L.N. Mynster, Copenhagen: den Gyldenalske Boghandel 1866, vol. 1, pp. 156–159; *Nogle Blade af J.P. Mynster's Liv og Tid*, ed. by C.L.N. Mynster, Copenhagen: den Gyldendalske Boghandel 1875, pp. 223–226.

[6] For the Danish discussions of the issue, see the outstanding work of István Czakó: *Geist und Unsterblichkeit: Grundprobleme der Religionsphilosophie und Eschatologie im Denken Søren Kierkegaards*, Berlin, and Boston: Walter de Gruyter 2014 (*Kierkegaard Studies Monograph Series*, vol. 29); István Czakó, "Heiberg and the Immortality Debate: A Historical Overview," in *Johan Ludvig Heiberg: Philosopher, Littérateur, Dramaturge, and Political Thinker*, ed. by Jon Stewart, Copenhagen: Museum Tusculanum Press 2008 (*Danish Golden Age Studies*, vol. 5), pp. 95–138; István Czakó, "Unsterblichkeitsfurcht. Ein christlicher Beitrag zu einer zeitgenössischen Debatte in Søren Kierkegaards 'Gedanken, die hinterrücks verwunden – zur Erbauung,'" *Kierkegaard Studies Yearbook*, 2007, pp. 227–254.

[7] See Wilhelm Stähler, *Zur Unsterblichkeitsproblematik in Hegels Nachfolge*, Münster: Universitas-Verlag 1928; Jon Stewart, "Hegel's Philosophy of Religion and the Question of 'Right' and 'Left' Hegelianism," in *Politics, Religion and Art: Hegelian Debates*, ed. by Douglas Moggach, Evanston, IL: Northwestern University Press 2011, pp. 66–95.

of nihilism. Møller takes this to be an essential question since if Hegel in fact was lacking a theory of immortality, as some critics claimed, then he could not properly be said to support a Christian point of view. At bottom, the question that was posed was whether Hegel's philosophy helped to resolve the problem of modern nihilism or was in part responsible for it.

Traumatized by the early death of his young wife, Møller understandably regarded the question of immortality as a very personal issue. Although he had previously been positively disposed towards Hegel, when he reached the conclusion that Hegel's system lacked a theory of immortality, his views began to shift, and he became a critic of the German philosopher. In his article Møller concludes that in fact the charges are justified, and there is no meaningful theory of immortality in Hegel. Møller's criticism, however, cuts even deeper than this. Not only does Hegel's philosophy not have a theory of immortality, but, absent such a theory, it leads to nihilism. This is at face value not immediately evident. Hegel's philosophy is couched in the form of a dogmatic system, and, indeed, this has traditionally been a point of criticism. So the question is why Møller believes that Hegel's thought leads to nihilism, despite the fact that it abounds in positive, dogmatic statements and thus represents a system of fixed doctrines.

Møller is clearly in agreement with Jean Paul that no one can deny the immortality of the soul without lapsing into nihilism. But he goes beyond Jean Paul's views and sees the many broad implications of the nihilistic perspective, which he believes would be destructive not just for the individual but for many larger institutions of society in general. In contrast to the authors we have already examined, Møller identifies this issue explicitly with the term "nihilism."[8] He is thus among the first to use the term to characterize the issue of the meaninglessness of the world in the face of human finitude and mortality.

After the publication of his article, which was ultimately his most important philosophical work, Møller became ill. He languished for some time before dying at the age of 44 on March 13, 1838. The article was discussed by several important thinkers in Denmark over the years, and many of the views presented in it can be said to anticipate some of the ideas later developed by Kierkegaard.[9] In his account of nihilism Møller refers directly to figures such as Jean Paul and Schopenhauer, and thus his article can be regarded as a reaction to the German discussions that have been examined in the previous chapters.

Nihilism has an established place in the history of philosophy. However, the contribution of the tradition of Danish philosophy to this narrative has never

---

[8] E.g., Møller, "Tanker over Muligheden af Beviser for Menneskets Udødelighed," p. 51 (*Poul Martin Møller's "Thoughts on the Possibility of Proofs of Human Immortality" and Other Texts*, p. 108).

[9] For an overview, see Finn Gredal Jensen, "Poul Martin Møller: Kierkegaard and the Confidant of Socrates," in *Kierkegaard and his Danish Contemporaries*, tome I, *Philosophy, Politics and Social Theory*, pp. 101–167.

been recognized. In this chapter on Møller and the next on Kierkegaard, it will be clear that the theme of nihilism was an absolutely central element in what was widely perceived to be the cultural crisis of the period that we know today as the Danish Golden Age.[10] This fact often goes unrecognized since the various thinkers explored this issue under different names, for example, subjectivism, irony, autonomy, perspectivism, historicism, acosmism, and even Buddhism. I hope to demonstrate that this issue was such a prevalent part of the academic agenda of so many different Danish thinkers that it can fairly be said, at least in part, to characterize the period as a whole.

6.1 The Problem of the Method for Demonstrating Immortality

At the beginning of the article, Møller refers to the first volume of the book by Friedrich Richter (1807–56), *Die Lehre von den letzten Dingen*, which argued that the idea of immortality was a foolish prejudice from a prescientific age.[11] Richter makes use of Hegel to support his claim. This use provoked a reaction from the right Hegelians, who argued that Hegel was never critical of the idea of immortality.[12] Observing this debate, Møller explains that at no previous time in human history has there ever been such an "open denial" of the belief in immortality as in his own day, and Richter's view, rightly or wrongly, thus captures something about the spirit of the age.[13] With regard to the time frame, he claims that society has been wallowing in this denial "for almost forty years," that is, well before the time of Hegel's main works.[14] Møller reveals his own Hegelian roots by claiming that any argument will necessarily produce its

---

[10] In a recent work, I have tried to point out the importance of the motif of a cultural crisis in Golden Age Denmark. See Jon Stewart, *The Cultural Crisis of the Danish Golden Age: Heiberg, Martensen and Kierkegaard*, Copenhagen: Museum Tusculanum Press 2015 (*Danish Golden Age Studies*, vol. 9). See also Jon Stewart, *Søren Kierkegaard: Subjectivity, Irony and the Crisis of Modernity*, Oxford: Oxford University Press 2015; *The Crisis of the Danish Golden Age and Its Modern Resonance*, ed. by Jon Stewart and Nathaniel Kramer, Copenhagen: Museum Tusculanum 2020 (*Danish Golden Age Studies*, vol. 12).

[11] Friedrich Richter, *Die Lehre von den letzten Dingen. Eine wissenschaftliche Kritik aus dem Standpunct der Religion unternommen*, vol. 1, *welcher die Kritik der Lehre vom Tode, von der Unsterblichkeit und von den Mittelzuständen enthält*, Breslau: In Joh. Fried. Korn des älteren Buchhandlung Julius Hebenstreit 1833; vol. 2, *Die Lehre von jüngsten Tage. Dogma und Kritik*, Berlin: Richter'sche Buchhandlung 1844.

[12] See, for example, Carl Friedrich Göschel, *Von den Beweisen für die Unsterblichkeit der menschlichen Seele im Lichte der spekulativen Philosophie*, Berlin: Duncker und Humblot 1835.

[13] Møller, "Tanker over Muligheden af Beviser for Menneskets Udødelighed," p. 6 (*Poul Martin Møller's "Thoughts on the Possibility of Proofs of Human Immortality" and Other Texts*, p. 67).

[14] Møller, "Tanker over Muligheden af Beviser for Menneskets Udødelighed," p. 63 (*Poul Martin Møller's "Thoughts on the Possibility of Proofs of Human Immortality" and Other Texts*, p. 118).

6.1 THE METHOD FOR DEMONSTRATING IMMORTALITY 177

opposite, namely, a rebuttal that represents the opposite position. This is the natural way in which ideas arise from one another. With this in mind, he explains the goal of his article:

> In what follows, I hope to demonstrate clearly that, due to its special nature, the doctrine of immortality more than any other thetic proposition, when once shaken in its foundation, can never again dominate the human consciousness as it ought, unless the negation develops itself freely in all its consequences so that it becomes evident whether humanity will be able to live with the worldview consistent with the negation.[15]

It is important for Møller to allow the voices of atheism and the deniers of immortality to have their say without restrictions. Only then will it be possible to address them fully and effectively. He thus wants to develop and examine the worldview of those who deny immortality in order to see if it can be applied to real life and lived consistently.

Møller believes that the loss of faith in immortality has come about due to the shift in philosophy away from a conception of unity to plurality, which he sees represented in the systems of Spinoza and Leibniz, respectively. He explains this as follows:

> ... the result of the previous considerations is that in the now displaced metaphysics as well as in its popular echoes the unity of all things had only dimly been recognized, and since an altered worldview is now asserting itself, the old faith in immortality, which was mostly due to the assumption that it was ontologically and physically impossible that souls existing in themselves could perish, is now tottering. The new mode of thought, replacing the other, is dominated by an opposite one-sidedness, since the conviction that one life permeates all has degenerated into a base pantheism in which the finite personality has almost lost its reality.[16]

Leibniz's view of things as individual monads lent itself to a view of immortality in the form of the indestructability of the human soul. However, this contradicted the naturalistic, scientific view, according to which individual things are born and die due to natural causes. But an attempt was made by the Hegelians to restore some version of Spinoza's pantheism with the claim that something like spirit in general is present everywhere. Therefore, insofar as individual humans participate in this, they are immortal. But as Møller points out, this offers little comfort since it seems to imply that the individual perishes and only the whole of humanity or spirit lives on. The problem, for Møller, is that the

---

[15] Møller, "Tanker over Muligheden af Beviser for Menneskets Udødelighed," p. 4 (*Poul Martin Møller's "Thoughts on the Possibility of Proofs of Human Immortality" and Other Texts*, p. 65).
[16] Møller, "Tanker over Muligheden af Beviser for Menneskets Udødelighed," p. 16 (*Poul Martin Møller's "Thoughts on the Possibility of Proofs of Human Immortality" and Other Texts*, p. 76).

pantheistic view fails to recognize the individual personality of God and each human being.

According to Møller, the uncertainty about immortality at the time has led people to yearn for some definitive proof of the issue. They mistakenly believe that such a proof can take the form of a kind of mathematical demonstration, independent of anything else. Møller tells an amusing anecdote about an accountant who demands of his friend, a student of theology, to explain to him the best proofs for immortality that the latter had learned in his studies at the university.[17] The accountant seems to regard such a demonstration as a simple and straightforward matter that can be expedited while he shaves, dresses, and prepares for a lunch appointment. The theology student protests that such matters cannot be explained so quickly and easily. Møller's commentary on this anecdote is that it is impossible to produce a proof for the existence of immortality or any other supersensuous reality based on the methodology of mathematics. While geometry can tell us the necessary truths about the nature of, for example, a triangle, it cannot tell us whether any triangles actually exist. Thus, the truths of mathematics are all in a sense hypothetical since they must assume the existence of the objects that they treat. But mathematics cannot supply the empirical evidence that can confirm the existence of such objects in the real world. In other words, if triangles exist, then they have the properties of having three sides, and so on. But geometry can never prove that they really exist. We never see or experience a perfect triangle in the world. Similarly, since we have no firsthand experience of life after death, we cannot demonstrate its existence empirically. By contrast, a demonstration of immortality can only take place as a part of "a complete philosophical system."[18] It is impossible to extract specific claims about God or immortality and demonstrate them individually and in isolation. Instead, such beliefs constitute parts of a broader worldview that needs demonstration.

Møller turns to the question of whether Hegel's speculative dialectics might be a method that can prove human immortality.[19] He agrees with the left Hegelians when he claims that, while Hegel never explicitly rejected the theory of immortality, he also never explicitly argued for it. Moreover,

> whoever is somewhat able to read between the lines in Hegel's writings will easily reach the inevitable conclusion that this philosopher holds the concept of personal immortality to be a notion with no reality at all.

[17] Møller, "Tanker over Muligheden af Beviser for Menneskets Udødelighed," pp. 18–21 (*Poul Martin Møller's "Thoughts on the Possibility of Proofs of Human Immortality" and Other Texts*, pp. 78–81).

[18] Møller, "Tanker over Muligheden af Beviser for Menneskets Udødelighed," p. 21 (*Poul Martin Møller's "Thoughts on the Possibility of Proofs of Human Immortality" and Other Texts*, p. 81).

[19] Møller, "Tanker over Muligheden af Beviser for Menneskets Udødelighed," pp. 23–28 (*Poul Martin Møller's "Thoughts on the Possibility of Proofs of Human Immortality" and Other Texts*, pp. 83–87).

Consequently, speculative dialectics can never bring forth any proof of immortality if one asks the discoverer of the method himself.[20]

Møller's attack is then primarily against the right Hegelians, who try to argue that there is in fact such a view in Hegel's system and that it is grounded in his speculative approach. For Møller, there is no doubt that Hegel's *Science of Logic*, the foundation of his metaphysics, contains no account of the concept of immortality. This work represents an a priori system that demonstrates the necessary relations among the concepts. But, like mathematics, since it is a priori, the *Science of Logic* cannot prove that there is any actual object in the world that corresponds to the concepts. Therefore, Hegel's speculative philosophy cannot establish a priori the existence of immortality. Once again, the "actually existing world can be known only through experience."[21] The situation with Hegel's a priori ontology thus stands in the same relation to the actual objects in the world as mathematics. Møller concludes by arguing that an a priori proof of immortality is simply impossible.

6.2 Møller's Conception of a Worldview

Having rejected mathematics and Hegelian speculation, Møller then raises the question of whether any kind of proof at all can be given to demonstrate human immortality.[22] Here he develops his idea of a worldview (*Verdensanskuelse*) that is both empirical and a priori. The truth of such a worldview can only be assessed when the worldview is developed completely, and it is clear what it contains. An important part of a worldview grows out of a tradition that one is born into. Feral children who grow up without any such tradition are not capable of reaching abstract thoughts concerning, for example, law or religion. It is only by virtue of the fact that we live together in communities and states that we are able to develop fully our rationality and our views of higher things.[23] Here again we can see a residual element of Hegel's philosophy in Møller's thinking. Hegel also argued that as humans emerge from nature, they only become fully free in the context of the state, where they attain the full consciousness of spirit.

---

[20] Møller, "Tanker over Muligheden af Beviser for Menneskets Udødelighed," p. 25 (*Poul Martin Møller's "Thoughts on the Possibility of Proofs of Human Immortality" and Other Texts*, p. 84).

[21] Møller, "Tanker over Muligheden af Beviser for Menneskets Udødelighed," p. 26 (*Poul Martin Møller's "Thoughts on the Possibility of Proofs of Human Immortality" and Other Texts*, p. 86).

[22] Møller, "Tanker over Muligheden af Beviser for Menneskets Udødelighed," p. 28 (*Poul Martin Møller's "Thoughts on the Possibility of Proofs of Human Immortality" and Other Texts*, p. 87).

[23] Møller, "Tanker over Muligheden af Beviser for Menneskets Udødelighed," pp. 30f. (*Poul Martin Møller's "Thoughts on the Possibility of Proofs of Human Immortality" and Other Texts*, p. 89).

For Møller, the Christian tradition and its notion of a realm beyond our experience, *the supersensuous*, represent an important element in a complete worldview.[24] This is related to his claim that a worldview contains both an empirical and an a priori aspect. But, again in a Hegelian fashion, he introduces a third element that combines these two parts, namely, "the higher experience in which the supersensuous confronts us at a definite time and place in actuality."[25] He explains this as "the presence of the supersensuous in the sensuous as the object of an experience of a higher nature."[26] This is a reflection of Hegel's idea that we can find the universal incarnated in the world of actuality. The concepts do not represent an abstract realm on their own but are in fact connected to the mundane sphere.

In the spirit of Hegel, Møller suggests that the Christian tradition represents the highest product of collective humanity or spirit.[27] While there are always detractors and philosophical systems that criticize Christianity, these will in time wither away and become forgotten. The Christian worldview, by contrast, will forever maintain its validity, although it too changes and develops over time. Møller argues that there are only two ways to refute the Christian conception of immortality: either the critic "must emphasize facts of the world of experience that cannot be brought into harmony with the doctrine of immortality, something which no one has hitherto been able to do, or he must present a convincing worldview in which immortality is entirely superfluous."[28] Concerning the first possibility, one might say that everything we know from the world of nature tells us that every living entity eventually dies. But this is not a proof that there is no form of life after death since this goes beyond our experience in this world. For Møller, the second possibility is the most interesting one philosophically. Is it possible to have a worldview that lacks a conception of immortality but is more convincing and plausible than the Christian worldview, which does? The suggestion of the left Hegelians is that Hegel's philosophy represents just such a secular worldview that challenges the Christian one.

---

[24] Møller, "Tanker over Muligheden af Beviser for Menneskets Udødelighed," pp. 32f. (*Poul Martin Møller's "Thoughts on the Possibility of Proofs of Human Immortality" and Other Texts*, p. 91).

[25] Møller, "Tanker over Muligheden af Beviser for Menneskets Udødelighed," p. 33 (*Poul Martin Møller's "Thoughts on the Possibility of Proofs of Human Immortality" and Other Texts*, p. 91).

[26] Møller, "Tanker over Muligheden af Beviser for Menneskets Udødelighed," p. 32 (*Poul Martin Møller's "Thoughts on the Possibility of Proofs of Human Immortality" and Other Texts*, p. 91).

[27] Møller, "Tanker over Muligheden af Beviser for Menneskets Udødelighed," p. 33 (*Poul Martin Møller's "Thoughts on the Possibility of Proofs of Human Immortality" and Other Texts*, p. 91).

[28] Møller, "Tanker over Muligheden af Beviser for Menneskets Udødelighed," p. 33 (*Poul Martin Møller's "Thoughts on the Possibility of Proofs of Human Immortality" and Other Texts*, p. 92).

6.2 MØLLER'S CONCEPTION OF A WORLDVIEW 181

But Møller claims that any worldview that excludes immortality will always eventually fail. Once such a worldview is explored in detail, its consequence will always show that one cannot reasonably maintain it. Møller insists that the only possible proof for immortality is this indirect one. As has been noted, the doctrine cannot be demonstrated directly on its own as an isolated claim. Instead, the truth of immortality can only be seen as a part of a complete worldview that contains many other beliefs as well.

Møller argues against what he regards as the pantheistic worldview of Hegel's followers. This view takes itself to represent the true scientific conception of the world. According to this conception, an abstract concept is manifested "in an infinite number of perishable essences."[29] Thus, there is no possibility of a personal immortality of the individual, although the abstract concept of spirit can be conceived as enduring. But this is little consolation to the individual, who will completely cease to exist with death. The scientific view does not leave open the possibility that there might be something that transcends human knowledge and that cannot be grasped. It does not even entertain the possibility of personal immortality as something unknown. Møller rejects Hegelian pantheism as incompatible with the worldview of the Christian tradition, despite Hegel's own claims to offer scientific support of Christianity.

Møller further argues that the role of feeling in our knowing is vastly underestimated in philosophy. By contrast, Christianity recognizes the importance of feeling with regard to key issues such as God and immortality.[30] While a person might well come to a rational understanding of religion after some training and education, the person's initial approach as a child is invariably that of feeling. So, feeling and emotion represent in many ways the basis for the Christian worldview. This means that any rival worldview that disregards or downplays the importance of emotion, like that of Hegel, is destined for failure. The idea of immortality is accompanied by a pleasant feeling that must be recognized in a complete worldview. One cannot take a disinterested view towards such things as one can towards the truths of mathematics.[31] Any "life-view that outrages humanity's feeling of truth," as based on emotion, can never be successful.[32]

---

[29] Møller, "Tanker over Muligheden af Beviser for Menneskets Udødelighed," p. 34 (*Poul Martin Møller's "Thoughts on the Possibility of Proofs of Human Immortality" and Other Texts*, p. 93).
[30] Møller, "Tanker over Muligheden af Beviser for Menneskets Udødelighed," p. 43 (*Poul Martin Møller's "Thoughts on the Possibility of Proofs of Human Immortality" and Other Texts*, p. 101).
[31] Møller, "Tanker over Muligheden af Beviser for Menneskets Udødelighed," p. 45 (*Poul Martin Møller's "Thoughts on the Possibility of Proofs of Human Immortality" and Other Texts*, p. 102).
[32] Møller, "Tanker over Muligheden af Beviser for Menneskets Udødelighed," p. 45 (*Poul Martin Møller's "Thoughts on the Possibility of Proofs of Human Immortality" and Other Texts*, p. 103).

Note that Møller's notion of a worldview is very close to Jean Paul's idea in *The Valley of Campan*. To live one's life in peace and without anxiety, one needs a worldview that contains the idea of immortality. Without this, one will always be unhappy. This is the argument that is made to Karlson by Gione and that causes him to embrace the idea of an afterlife. She appeals to his emotions, and it is precisely this that moves Karlson since he harbors such strong feelings for her. Møller mentions Jean Paul explicitly in order to make his own agenda clear:

> It is not my intention to present ... the conditions of life where the loss of hope in immortality becomes most revolting to the natural feeling. This has been done rather often, for example, by Jean Paul, and it is the only way to render intelligible the truth that the doctrine of mortality is unable to satisfy human feeling.[33]

Here Møller might well have in mind Jean Paul's *The Valley of Campan* or "The Dead Christ," both of which aim to evoke a sense of despair that is generated by the terrifying thought of a world without God and immortality. While Møller agrees with Jean Paul's conclusion, his strategy for demonstrating it is quite different.

6.3 The Results of Nihilism for the Different Spheres

Møller goes far beyond Jean Paul by identifying several spheres that would be negatively affected by the denial of immortality. This denial would render human existence impossible. After the discussion of worldviews, Møller explains that his goal is to develop "the thesis that every system that implies the denial of immortality refutes itself by its consequences."[34] Møller's argumentative strategy is to use a *reductio ad absurdum* to refute the view that denies immortality. To begin, he assumes the correctness of this view and tries to explore further what precisely it would mean to hold it. Then from this he deduces negative consequences, which demonstrate that the view must be abandoned as contradictory.

6.3.1 The Individual

Møller first takes up the results of the denial of immortality for the life of the individual. He dubs the denial of immortality "the doctrine of annihilation" (*Tilintetgjørelseslæren*), that is, the belief that the individual is destroyed or

---

[33] Møller, "Tanker over Muligheden af Beviser for Menneskets Udødelighed," p. 47 (*Poul Martin Møller's "Thoughts on the Possibility of Proofs of Human Immortality" and Other Texts*, p. 104).
[34] Møller, "Tanker over Muligheden af Beviser for Menneskets Udødelighed," p. 47 (*Poul Martin Møller's "Thoughts on the Possibility of Proofs of Human Immortality" and Other Texts*, p. 104).

6.3 THE RESULTS OF NIHILISM FOR THE DIFFERENT SPHERES

annihilated with death.[35] He argues that only if humans are immortal or believe that they are immortal, will they take life seriously and be motivated to act in constructive ways. But if humans truly believe that their existence is finite and contingent, then they will be robbed of all motivation for doing anything whatsoever. They will wallow in a nihilism with no solution. He writes, "When a human being, convinced of the transitoriness of his individual life, properly arranges his realm of consciousness, his life loses every essential meaning."[36] Here Møller agrees with Jean Paul that immortality is the key issue since, without it, life is rendered meaningless.

He argues that belief in immortality is essential for any real self-relation, and, without it, there could be no self-respect or self-love.[37] Møller thinks that truly to value oneself as an individual, one must believe that one's individuality is eternal. He makes a somewhat odd epistemological argument for this: "All knowledge has perpetual being as its object, but in the true knowledge the cognizing subject knows itself to be part of perpetual being."[38] When one denies one's immortality and claims that one has no enduring existence, then one cannot regard oneself as the object of truth. This undermines the feeling of self-love that is necessary for one to lead a normal life.

Møller points out that those who deny immortality interpret self-love only in terms of the natural drive for self-preservation that is found in all animals.[39] However, there is much more to it than this. For Møller, self-love involves holding oneself in esteem and regarding oneself as something important and significant. The implication is that this is only possible when one believes oneself to be immortal. It would be difficult to regard oneself as having value and dignity if one thought of one's existence as only finite and transitory. No one can truly believe in themselves or their projects in life if they think that they are but a mere speck of dust in the universe.

Møller argues that anyone who says that they can live with the idea of their own finitude and insignificance is simply in denial. Such ideas lead to anxiety

---

[35] Møller, "Tanker over Muligheden af Beviser for Menneskets Udødelighed," p. 47 (*Poul Martin Møller's "Thoughts on the Possibility of Proofs of Human Immortality" and Other Texts*, p. 105).
[36] Møller, "Tanker over Muligheden af Beviser for Menneskets Udødelighed," p. 48 (*Poul Martin Møller's "Thoughts on the Possibility of Proofs of Human Immortality" and Other Texts*, p. 105).
[37] Møller, "Tanker over Muligheden af Beviser for Menneskets Udødelighed," p. 48 (*Poul Martin Møller's "Thoughts on the Possibility of Proofs of Human Immortality" and Other Texts*, p. 105).
[38] Møller, "Tanker over Muligheden af Beviser for Menneskets Udødelighed," p. 49 (*Poul Martin Møller's "Thoughts on the Possibility of Proofs of Human Immortality" and Other Texts*, p. 106).
[39] Møller, "Tanker over Muligheden af Beviser for Menneskets Udødelighed," pp. 49f. (*Poul Martin Møller's "Thoughts on the Possibility of Proofs of Human Immortality" and Other Texts*, p. 106).

throughout one's life. Møller refers to Friedrich Richter, whom he mentioned before: "he admits without hesitation that certainty of the individuals' perishability is the greatest of all the misfortunes which are inseparably connected with the conditions of mankind, and that this is a misfortune for which there is no satisfying consolation."[40] Even the deniers of immortality must concede that this is a difficult view to accept and live with. Again, this was precisely the problem for Jean Paul's Karlson. His scientific worldview told him that immortality was impossible, but emotionally he could not bring himself to maintain this idea. For Møller, this is a powerful argument for his indirect proof of immortality based on the idea of a complete worldview. It is impossible to embrace a worldview that one finds completely repellent to one's emotions. Møller's dubious assumption is that the truth cannot "be revolting to human feeling."[41] But, of course, the nihilist could easily call this premise into question. If the world arose due to natural forces without any God or intelligence, then what reason would there be to think that it must conform to our wishes, hopes, and feelings? Given all the tragedy and suffering in the world, there is precious little empirical evidence that it does. In the views of Klingemann's Kreuzgang, Schopenhauer, and Büchner's Danton, the universe is indifferent at best and hostile at worst to human interests, despite the fact that we would wish it otherwise.

6.3.2 Groups of People and Political Life

Møller then moves to his second argument, which concerns the significance of nihilism not for the individual but rather for groups of people. Just as no meaningful sense of oneself as an individual is possible without the idea of immortality, so also no meaningful conception of other people is possible. Møller argues,

> no true social interest can have permanence when human beings are assumed to be mere temporary beings that constantly come into existence and disappear from existence forever. All striving for human welfare and for the organization of states will necessarily cease if human beings, convinced of each other's absolute transitoriness, properly think over the inanity of their plans.[42]

---

[40] Møller, "Tanker over Muligheden af Beviser for Menneskets Udødelighed," p. 50 (*Poul Martin Møller's "Thoughts on the Possibility of Proofs of Human Immortality" and Other Texts*, p. 107).

[41] Møller, "Tanker over Muligheden af Beviser for Menneskets Udødelighed," p. 50 (*Poul Martin Møller's "Thoughts on the Possibility of Proofs of Human Immortality" and Other Texts*, p. 107).

[42] Møller, "Tanker over Muligheden af Beviser for Menneskets Udødelighed," p. 50 (*Poul Martin Møller's "Thoughts on the Possibility of Proofs of Human Immortality" and Other Texts*, p. 107).

6.3 THE RESULTS OF NIHILISM FOR THE DIFFERENT SPHERES

If everything is regarded as contingent and finite, people would have no interest in improving society, creating civil institutions, or establishing states. There would be no point in this if people were convinced that in the end everyone would die and perish forever.

For Møller, the only way to avoid this consequence would be to engage in a "voluntary illusion" and pretend that what one was doing in such contexts really had an importance, while at the same time knowing full well that it did not.[43] One sees people who bury themselves in work to the point that they are so busy that they never have any time to reflect on the issue of their own mortality. But this is just a form of self-distraction that keeps their deepest fears at a safe distance. Møller believes that this cannot be maintained over the long run. He argues, "No serious striving for the well-being of others, no sympathy for their anguish can be maintained by a thoughtful individual who regards their existence merely as a passing phantasmagoria."[44]

The nihilism, which Møller believes necessarily accompanies the denial of immortality, would thus completely undermine our sense of ethics. If nothing matters due to human finitude, then there is no point in trying to act morally towards others. Whatever crimes or injuries one committed against other people would over time be completely forgotten. This is what Møller refers to as a "practical nihilism," which is the first time he uses the term "nihilism" in the work as a label for the problem of meaninglessness.[45]

A further negative consequence of the denial of immortality is the desire for suicide. Without the hope offered by immortality, people lapse into despair, and this can result in suicide. Møller claims, "A life-view that leads to practical nihilism easily passes over to a positive striving for self-annihilation."[46] In the absence of this meaning people lose their desire to live. He offers a few historical examples, which he believes testify to the truth of this claim. Drawing on his knowledge of classical studies, Møller refers the followers of Cyrenaic and the Cynic philosophy. He mentions explicitly Hegesias of Cyrene (ca. 300 BC) who was dubbed Πεισιθάνατος (Peisithanatos), that is, the "death-persuader." He argued that it was impossible to be happy in life since happiness consists in pleasure that cannot be attained in any sustained manner. From this perspective, death can appear to be a desirable refuge from

---

[43] Møller, "Tanker over Muligheden af Beviser for Menneskets Udødelighed," p. 51 (*Poul Martin Møller's "Thoughts on the Possibility of Proofs of Human Immortality" and Other Texts*, p. 107).

[44] Møller, "Tanker over Muligheden af Beviser for Menneskets Udødelighed," p. 51 (*Poul Martin Møller's "Thoughts on the Possibility of Proofs of Human Immortality" and Other Texts*, pp. 107f.).

[45] Møller, "Tanker over Muligheden af Beviser for Menneskets Udødelighed," p. 51 (*Poul Martin Møller's "Thoughts on the Possibility of Proofs of Human Immortality" and Other Texts*, p. 108).

[46] Møller, "Tanker over Muligheden af Beviser for Menneskets Udødelighed," p. 51 (*Poul Martin Møller's "Thoughts on the Possibility of Proofs of Human Immortality" and Other Texts*, p. 108).

the suffering of human existence.[47] It was claimed that Hegesias's teachings caused many people to commit suicide, which ultimately led king Ptolemy II Philadelphus to prohibit him from lecturing on this issue in Alexandria. Møller claims that the naturalistic worldview of the modern age has also led to many suicides for the same reason, namely, that it teaches the finitude and meaninglessness of human existence. For Møller, one could hardly ask for a clearer demonstration of a worldview that is impossible to live with.

He further claims that it is impossible for someone to deny immortality and at the same time nourish a love for humanity. He sketches the contradiction that this leads to as follows:

> Those who nonetheless, without human esteem having any ground in their life-view, allow the benevolent feelings to occupy a large space in their consciousness, thereby concede to the natural feelings a power which their understanding cannot approve of. In general, it is also the drive to know determinate human individuals as imperishable objects of their love which leads doubting or infidel thinkers back to the Christian worldview.[48]

It will be noted again that this is exactly what happens to Jean Paul's Karlson. Although he cannot convince his reason that immortality is possible, his natural feeling of love for Gione forces him on this point to reject the scientific view and accept the Christian one, or at least a view that has a place for immortality.

For Møller it is impossible truly to love someone and at the same time regard them as perishable. Instead, the object of true love is only that which is eternal. In what might be interpreted as an autobiographical remark, he notes that many scholars who had previously embraced a Hegelian pantheism with its denial of individual immortality, later came to abandon this once they had experienced the loss of a loved one.[49] Once again, it is impossible to live with the thought of human finitude and mortality, not only in the case of oneself but also in the case of others.

6.3.3 Art

After having discussed the implications of nihilism for the individual and others, Møller now turns to what might be regarded as larger institutions. He argues that all art, philosophy, and religion would be impossible without a belief in

---

[47] See Diogenes Laertius, *Lives of Eminent Philosophers*, vols. 1–2, trans. by R.D. Hicks, Cambridge, MA: Harvard University Press and London: William Heinemann 1925 (*Loeb Classical Library*, vol. 184), vol. 1, p. 223, 2.94.

[48] Møller, "Tanker over Muligheden af Beviser for Menneskets Udødelighed," p. 52 (*Poul Martin Møller's "Thoughts on the Possibility of Proofs of Human Immortality" and Other Texts*, pp. 108f.).

[49] Møller, "Tanker over Muligheden af Beviser for Menneskets Udødelighed," p. 52 (*Poul Martin Møller's "Thoughts on the Possibility of Proofs of Human Immortality" and Other Texts*, p. 109).

immortality. In a sense this might be regarded as an analogy to the final triad in the Hegelian system, namely, absolute spirit, which contains these three parts, and which Hegel takes to be the highest form of culture. Møller begins his account of the consequences for art.[50] He states his thesis as follows: "Here I set forth the claim without any hesitation that doubt of the immortality of individuals is the cancer of art, and the conviction of their perishability is the grave of art."[51]

Møller argues that artists attain a perfect harmony of universal and particular when they produce genuine works of art, that is, when their particular work corresponds with the universal concept of beauty. He claims that this is the same as immortality when the individual becomes eternal. In our normal mundane life, we only get a sense for this sporadically through the higher things, such as art. When our individual will corresponds to the universal will, we can grasp this feeling of the artist.

Møller thus claims that art or true beauty is a representation of the immortal sphere, or in his words, "True art is an anticipation of the blessed life."[52] This idea is also taken up by Kierkegaard in *The Concept of Anxiety*.[53] Art in a sense gives us a preview of the immortal life. It provides a fleeting glimpse of the bliss that awaits us in the beyond. This is not to say that every artist necessarily is aware of this consciously, but this is what gives art its power and significance for us. The claim is that if there were no view of immortality, then it would be impossible for artists to create beautiful works. Artistic creations cannot be simply the representation of finite, transitory objects. Instead, they must reveal something higher. But when people no longer believe that there is anything

---

[50] Møller, "Tanker over Muligheden af Beviser for Menneskets Udødelighed," pp. 53–57 (*Poul Martin Møller's "Thoughts on the Possibility of Proofs of Human Immortality" and Other Texts*, pp. 109–113).

[51] Møller, "Tanker over Muligheden af Beviser for Menneskets Udødelighed," p. 53 (*Poul Martin Møller's "Thoughts on the Possibility of Proofs of Human Immortality" and Other Texts*, p. 110).

[52] Møller, "Tanker over Muligheden af Beviser for Menneskets Udødelighed," pp. 53f. (*Poul Martin Møller's "Thoughts on the Possibility of Proofs of Human Immortality" and Other Texts*, p. 110).

[53] *Søren Kierkegaards Skrifter*, vols. 1–28, K1–K28, ed. by Niels Jørgen Cappelørn, Joakim Garff, Jette Knudsen, Johnny Kondrup and Alastair McKinnon, Copenhagen: Gad Publishers 1997–2012, vol. 4, p. 452 (English translation: *The Concept of Anxiety*, trans. by Reidar Thomte, Princeton, NJ: Princeton University Press 1980, p. 153): "This conception has found definite expression in the statement: Art is an anticipation of eternal life, because poetry and art are the reconciliation only of the imagination, and they may well have the *Sinnigkeit* of intuition but by no means the *Innigkeit* of earnestness." See also Johan Ludvig Heiberg, "Om Malerkunsten i dens Forhold til de andre skjønne Kunster," *Perseus, Journal for den speculative Idee*, no. 2, 1838, p. 121 (reprinted in Heiberg's *Prosaiske Skrifter*, vols. 1–11, Copenhagen: C.A. Reitzel 1861–62, vol. 2, p. 274). See Lasse Horne Kjældgaard, *Sjælen efter døden. Guldalderens moderne gennembrud*, Copenhagen: Gyldendal 2007, pp. 83–112; Stewart, *A History of Hegelianism in Golden Age Denmark*, tome II, *The Martensen Period: 1837–1842*, pp. 49f.

higher, then art would simply disappear: "When faith in immortality has completely left an age, true art will disappear more and more, and the feeble artistic production that remains behind will largely attach itself to the ruins of the works of earlier times."[54] It is thus impossible for someone to want to maintain art and abandon the worldview that contains the doctrine of immortality. This creates a necessary tension that cannot be resolved, and eventually such a position would lead to the abandonment of art entirely.

It will be noted that Møller's view is in a sense analogous to Schopenhauer's understanding of the value of art. Although Schopenhauer rejects the idea of immortality, he does believe that through a complete immersion in the experience of art, one can gain a momentary liberation from the demands of the will and attain a short-term happiness. Møller believes that this feeling constitutes proof of immortality. Similarly, for Jean Paul, the sublime experience of ascending above the earth in a hot-air balloon at the end of *The Valley of Campan* provides a foretaste of the afterlife. Schopenhauer is more guarded in his conclusion. The experience of art offers only a brief respite from the suffering of life caused by the will, but there is no evidence that this has anything to do with immortality.

Møller notes how in his own time, when religion was beginning to lose its grip on people, there was an increasing number of writers who did not believe in an afterlife, yet they still could not avoid including certain supernatural elements in their works. He mentions the current fad of ghost stories, which end up with an anticlimax by some natural explanation. He also mentions authors who make use of figures or stories from mythology, which they themselves do not believe in. Møller frowns on these efforts since they do not take the supersensuous as something serious but instead merely play with it flippantly. To take art in such a "trifling manner" is a complete misconception, according to Møller.[55] It is a kind of willful self-deception that cannot be taken seriously. This kind of art can never retain people's interest for long and will soon disappear. It is of a completely different sort from the art produced by poets such as Homer, who still maintain a living belief in the gods and goddesses that they portray.

As an example of this contradiction, Møller criticizes poets such as Heinrich Heine and those associated with the Young Germany movement for celebrating the finite and abandoning anything beyond the immediate world of sense. Despite their celebration of the senses and the flesh, they nonetheless remain in a "secret melancholy."[56] This would seem to be a good description of Büchner's

---

[54] Møller, "Tanker over Muligheden af Beviser for Menneskets Udødelighed," p. 55 (*Poul Martin Møller's "Thoughts on the Possibility of Proofs of Human Immortality" and Other Texts*, p. 111).

[55] Møller, "Tanker over Muligheden af Beviser for Menneskets Udødelighed," p. 56 (*Poul Martin Møller's "Thoughts on the Possibility of Proofs of Human Immortality" and Other Texts*, p. 112).

[56] Møller, "Tanker over Muligheden af Beviser for Menneskets Udødelighed," p. 57 (*Poul Martin Møller's "Thoughts on the Possibility of Proofs of Human Immortality" and Other Texts*, p. 113). See also Kierkegaard's references to the Young Germany movement in *The*

Danton, who fully embraces the momentary sensual pleasures but at the same time suffers from nightmares and depression. The self-proclaimed secularism of the advocates of the Young Germany movement produces its opposite, a yearning for the divine: "It is in such phenomena that the world-historical dialectic becomes evident; as its language becomes distorted, nihilism appears as its own involuntary accuser and, thus, clears the way for the restitution of the positive worldview."[57] The young radicals stand in contradiction to their own nihilistic position, and their art is degraded. This analysis anticipates Kierkegaard's account of the inevitability of despair without Christianity in *The Sickness unto Death*. For art to exist, a view of immortality is necessary since the very nature of art itself is connected to it.

6.3.4 Philosophy and Science

Møller now turns to the consequences of nihilism for science.[58] Just as was the case with art, he claims that the nihilistic view without a doctrine of immortality leads to the destruction of science. It should be noted here that by "science" Møller means, strictly speaking, not just the natural sciences but rather philosophy. Specifically, he has in mind what he takes to be Hegel's pantheistic system, which he believes is the dominant view of educated people in philosophy of the day. His claim is that such a philosophical view without a doctrine of immortality will inevitably lose its power and influence.

Møller is critical of the idea that all knowledge is found in the immanent sphere as an object of consciousness. As is well known, Hegel rejects the idea of the transcendent in the sense of something beyond consciousness.[59] Møller criticizes the conception of science that results from this view. In short, he claims that in any simple description of the empirical, there is always something missing, and complete knowledge can never be achieved by human perception in the mundane sphere since the realm of the empirical is inexhaustible. No matter how many empirical things one has perceived in the world, there will always be more that one has not perceived. If one can talk about a complete system of knowledge, then this can only refer to the abstract conceptual structures.

Concept of Irony: Søren Kierkegaards Skrifter, vol. 1, pp. 311n, 321, 325 (English translation: *The Concept of Irony; Schelling Lecture Notes*, trans. by Howard V. Hong and Edna H. Hong, Princeton, NJ: Princeton University Press 1989, pp. 275n, 286, 290).

[57] Møller, "Tanker over Muligheden af Beviser for Menneskets Udødelighed," p. 57 (*Poul Martin Møller's "Thoughts on the Possibility of Proofs of Human Immortality" and Other Texts*, p. 113).

[58] Møller, "Tanker over Muligheden af Beviser for Menneskets Udødelighed," pp. 56–60 (*Poul Martin Møller's "Thoughts on the Possibility of Proofs of Human Immortality" and Other Texts*, pp. 113–116).

[59] For an interesting discussion of this issue, see Philip T. Grier, "On Divine Transcendence and Non-Transcendence," *The Owl of Minerva*, vol. 52, nos. 1–2, 2021, pp. 73–88.

But no such a priori system can ever refer to the infinity of individual empirical objects in the universe. While science struggles to discover new things, it will always fall short of knowing everything.

Moreover, the understanding of the objects of empirical perception, which are the subject matter of conceptual structures, is always changing in the course of the history of science. Absolute knowing is impossible here since it lies in the nature of science constantly to develop new schemes and laws that make sense of the different phenomena as they appear. Science is always working to incorporate the individual objects of the empirical sphere in new and better conceptual systems. So, for Møller, it is absurd to think that this process would ever be complete.[60] Møller argues,

> But all *a priori* or, if one prefers, immanent thinking that is to elucidate the fundamental relations of existence (by which I mean God's relation to the universe) must proceed from an obscure intuition of these fundamental relations and strive toward a clearer, immediate knowledge of them. However, inasmuch as no one can attain an adequate intuition of all things in the present order of things, no scientific thinking under any conditions known to us can lead to the completion of knowledge.[61]

Humans in their mundane existence will never be able to have God's knowledge of everything. Our knowledge is finite and limited due to the limitations of our conceptual schemes and theories. These will always be imperfect and in need of improvement.

For Hegel's immanent view, since the empirical is ultimately transitory, it cannot be true in the end. Therefore, if there are some empirical things that humans have never perceived, then this does not matter since the truth lies in the realm of the conceptual. Provided that we have the correct understanding of the necessary relations of the concepts, humans can in fact have absolute knowing without having knowledge of every particular entity in the universe. But, for Møller, it is absurd to deny that these objects can have any truth value just because they cannot all be known.[62] He argues that science must be able to grasp not just the abstract concepts and theories but also the empirical particulars as such for science to claim to be complete. Paradoxically, Møller proposes a Hegelian solution to the dichotomy between the empirical knowledge

---

[60] Møller, "Tanker over Muligheden af Beviser for Menneskets Udødelighed," p. 58 (*Poul Martin Møller's "Thoughts on the Possibility of Proofs of Human Immortality" and Other Texts*, p. 114).

[61] Møller, "Tanker over Muligheden af Beviser for Menneskets Udødelighed," p. 59 (*Poul Martin Møller's "Thoughts on the Possibility of Proofs of Human Immortality" and Other Texts*, p. 115).

[62] Møller, "Tanker over Muligheden af Beviser for Menneskets Udødelighed," pp. 59f. (*Poul Martin Møller's "Thoughts on the Possibility of Proofs of Human Immortality" and Other Texts*, pp. 115f.).

of experience and the conceptual knowledge of reason by arguing for a combination of the two:

> There must be a third and higher knowledge which is neither restricted to the region of pure concepts nor confined to the abstractions of empirical thought, but in which the universal, in a sense that surpasses human concepts, is known in such a way that the particular (the single) does not disappear in it. Such knowledge would be an intellectual intuition in the true sense of the term, but this true "*tertium cognitionis genus*" is unattainable under the conditions of present life.[63]

The combination of the universal and the particular is precisely what Hegel's calls "speculative thinking," and it is what defines his entire methodology. Møller's special twist on this is that he seems to believe that we are not capable of this in our worldly existence. Instead, this kind of knowledge can only be conceived if humans are immortal and can enter a blessed state after death.

The force of Møller's argument is that, without the presupposition of the state of immortality, science would disappear since it would have to give up the claim of ever attaining complete truth. Scientists and philosophers are motived by the search for the truth, even though they are resigned to the fact that they will never fully achieve it in their lifetimes. But if they did not believe that it was even possible in principle, then there would no longer be any motivation to pursue the search for truth, which of course involves many difficulties and requires great sacrifices. Nihilism would thus undermine scientific study entirely.

6.3.5 *Religion and Truth*

Møller finally turns to religion.[64] Although it hardly requires any argument, he points out the obvious: nihilism destroys religion. In line with what he said previously about the sciences, he associates nihilism directly with pantheism, and claims that this undermines the idea of a personal God. The divine must be conceived not just as an abstract idea in the minds of individuals; rather, God must also be a single, self-conscious entity. This is a higher conception than the pantheistic secular view that accepts one's own destruction and disappearance into the universal at death. Individual immortality is thus connected to the idea of a personal God. For immortality to make sense, the individual must survive death as the same person one was in life. Likewise, for the conception of God to make sense, the divinity must be conceived as a personal deity and not simply

---

[63] Møller, "Tanker over Muligheden af Beviser for Menneskets Udødelighed," p. 60 (*Poul Martin Møller's "Thoughts on the Possibility of Proofs of Human Immortality" and Other Texts*, p. 116).

[64] Møller, "Tanker over Muligheden af Beviser for Menneskets Udødelighed," pp. 60–63 (*Poul Martin Møller's "Thoughts on the Possibility of Proofs of Human Immortality" and Other Texts*, pp. 116–118).

the whole of nature or the universe. On the pantheistic view, humans are merely regarded as "illuminating flashes that in turn are extinguished forever."[65] For this reason, Møller believes that it is necessary to accept the worldview of the Christian tradition, which contains these conceptions of the individual and of God. This is the only worldview that can be consistently thought.

Moreover, the nihilistic view eliminates any lasting sense of truth, which only a personal God can guarantee. Møller calls the view that he wishes to criticize an "oriental fable" and a "mythology," which he believes the majority of scholars in his time subscribe to.[66] The reference to the Orient is made clear when he goes on to mention Schopenhauer, whose philosophy, as noted,[67] was largely inspired by Hinduism and Buddhism.[68] Møller points out that Schopenhauer explicitly embraces atheism and "endorses greatly the Brahminic doctrine of the abode of the blessed after death because it is spoken of as 'Niban,' which actually means 'nothing.'"[69] Thus, this Hindu doctrine or Niban, better known as Nirvana, becomes associated with nihilism.

Møller believes that Schopenhauer's work represents a case in point that confirms his own argument about the consequences of nihilism. Møller

---

[65] Møller, "Tanker over Muligheden af Beviser for Menneskets Udødelighed," p. 61 (*Poul Martin Møller's "Thoughts on the Possibility of Proofs of Human Immortality" and Other Texts*, p. 117).

[66] Møller, "Tanker over Muligheden af Beviser for Menneskets Udødelighed," p. 61, p. 62 (*Poul Martin Møller's "Thoughts on the Possibility of Proofs of Human Immortality" and Other Texts*, p. 117).

[67] See Chapter 4 and the Introduction.

[68] See Douglas L. Berger, *"The Veil of Maya": Schopenhauer's System and Early Indian Thought*, Binghamton, New York: Global Academic Publishing 2004; Heinz Bechert, "Flucht in den Orient?," *Schopenhauer Jahrbuch*, vol. 62, 1981, pp. 55-65; Wilhelm Halbfass, "Schopenhauer im Gespräch mit der Indischen Tradition," in *Schopenhauer im Denken der Gegenwart*, ed. by Volker Spierling, Munich and Zürich: Piper Verlag 1987, pp. 55-71; Helmuth von Glasenapp, *Das Indienbild deutscher Denker*, Stuttgart: K.F. Koehler 1960, pp. 68-101; Arthur Hübscher, "Schopenhauer und die Religionen Asiens," *Schopenhauer Jahrbuch*, vol. 60, 1979, pp. 1-16; Susanne Sommerfeld, *Indienschau und Indiendeutung romantischer Philosophen*, Zürich: Rascher Verlag 1943, pp. 91-106; René Gérard, "Schopenhauer," in his *L'Orient et la pensée romantique allemande*, Nancy: Georges Thomas 1963, pp. 215-251; *Schopenhauer and Indian Philosophy: A Dialogue between India and Germany*, ed. by Arati Barua, New Delhi: Northern Book Centre 2008; Peter Abelsen, "Schopenhauer and Buddhism," *Philosophy East and West*, vol. 43, no. 2, 1993, pp. 255-278; Urs App, "Schopenhauers Begegnung mit dem Buddhismus," *Schopenhauer Jahrbuch*, vol. 79, 1998, pp. 35-56.

[69] Møller, "Tanker over Muligheden af Beviser for Menneskets Udødelighed," pp. 62f. (*Poul Martin Møller's "Thoughts on the Possibility of Proofs of Human Immortality" and Other Texts*, p. 118). See Roger-Pol Droit, *The Cult of Nothingness: The Philosophers and the Buddha*, trans. by David Streight and Pamela Vohnson, Chapel Hill and London: The University of North Carolina Press 2003; Urs App, *The Cult of Emptiness: The Western Discovery of Buddhist Thought and the Invention of Oriental Philosophy*, Rorschach and Kyoto: University Media 2012; Jon Stewart, *Hegel's Interpretation of the Religions of the World: The Logic of the Gods*, Oxford: Oxford University Press 2018, p. 92.

6.3 THE RESULTS OF NIHILISM FOR THE DIFFERENT SPHERES 193

explains, specifically with reference to the first volume of *The World as Will and Representation*:

> This nihilistic aspect of modern pantheism is hardly carried out more forcefully and consistently anywhere else than in a work by *Arthur Schopenhauer*, professor in Berlin, which, although the work was published in the year 1819, is still rarely and only cursorily mentioned by philosophers today. The author himself most openly describes his philosophy as anti-Christian and nihilistic. Thus he regards several Indian myths as superior to the dogmas of Christianity .... Were this work, which has certainly not by accident been relegated to literary obscurity, better known, it would unquestionably contribute a great deal to make the nihilism, to which one-sided pantheism leads, more understandable to people of this age.[70]

Møller thus holds out Schopenhauer as a kind of *Schreckbild*. It is no accident, he thinks, that *The World as Will and Representation* has remained a little-known book since it holds little attraction for people with its denial of God and immortality. It represents a secular worldview that cannot be maintained consistently. Schopenhauer clearly articulates this when he claims that the "surrender of 'the will to live' is the emancipation of the human race."[71]

The reference to Buddhism was taken up shortly after Møller's death by the Danish philosopher Frederik Christian Sibbern (1785–1872) in his *Remarks and Investigations Primarily Concerning Hegel's Philosophy with Regard to Our Age*.[72] This work began as part of a long review of a new journal entitled *Perseus*, which was edited by the Danish poet, dramatist, and philosopher Johan Ludvig Heiberg (1791–1860).[73] Sibbern's text treats key issues in Hegel's philosophy and Heiberg's optimistic assessment of its value. Heiberg had previously sketched what he regards as the crisis of the age, namely, nihilism and relativism. Then he argues that the solution to this can be found in Hegel's philosophy.[74] In response, Sibbern tries to demonstrate that Hegel's system does not

---

[70] Møller, "Tanker over Muligheden af Beviser for Menneskets Udødelighed," pp. 62f. (*Poul Martin Møller's "Thoughts on the Possibility of Proofs of Human Immortality" and Other Texts*, p. 118).

[71] Møller, "Tanker over Muligheden af Beviser for Menneskets Udødelighed," p. 66 (*Poul Martin Møller's "Thoughts on the Possibility of Proofs of Human Immortality" and Other Texts*, p. 121).

[72] Frederik Christian Sibbern, *Bemærkninger og Undersøgelser, fornemmelig betreffende Hegels Philosophie, betragtet i Forhold til vor Tid*, Copenhagen: C.A. Reitzel 1838 (English translation: *Sibbern's Remarks and Investigations Primarily concerning Hegel's Philosophy*, ed. and trans. by Jon Stewart, Copenhagen: Museum Tusculanum Press 2018 (*Texts from Golden Age Denmark*, vol. 7)).

[73] Johan Ludvig Heiberg (ed.)., *Perseus, Journal for den speculative Idee*, no. 1, 1837 (English translation: *Heiberg's Perseus and Other Texts*, ed. and trans. by Jon Stewart, Copenhagen: Museum Tusculanum Press 2011 (*Texts from Golden Age Denmark*, vol. 6)).

[74] Johan Ludvig Heiberg, *Om Philosophiens Betydning for den nuværende Tid. Et Indbydelses-Skrift til en Række af philosophiske Forelæsninger*, Copenhagen: C.A. Reitzel

live up to the high claims that Heiberg has made about it. Much of *Remarks and Investigations* thus amounts to a detailed criticism of different aspects of Hegel's thought. Like Møller, Sibbern also wants to show what he takes to be the negative results of Hegel's philosophy for his own day.

What is important for the present purposes is that Sibbern follows Møller in the criticism that Hegel's philosophy leads to a form of nihilism. He writes,

> I have been concerned not with Hegel in and for himself, but with Hegel in relation to our age and in relation to the worldview which should satisfy us. I have in mind also the entire spirit of the age and the manner of thinking among so many people, this Buddhism, if I may call it so, which has spread so far in certain circles among us in Denmark as to have become almost self-sustaining and firm. I cannot see anything other than that this simultaneously fulfilling and enervating view of life finds nourishment and support in Hegelianism.[75]

Sibbern states clearly that nihilism is a widespread phenomenon in the Danish cultural life of the age. Like Møller, Sibbern sees Hegel's philosophy not as the *solution* to the problem of relativism and nihilism as Heiberg had claimed, but rather as the *cause* of it. While it is not clear whether Sibbern believes that Hegel himself is responsible for this, he seems convinced in any case that this is one of the negative results of the reception of Hegelian philosophy at the time.

It is noteworthy that Sibbern uses the term "Buddhism" to describe the problem of the age. Here he picks up on Møller's reference to Schopenhauer's use of Asian philosophy. In this usage, both Sibbern and Møller were following a long tradition of the European reception of Asian religion. The attempt of the Buddhists to eliminate the passions and to focus on nothing became associated with nihilism and conceived as the worship of nothingness. This was coupled with the lack of a deity in Buddhism, which was also taken to be a part of the nihilistic view. In the *Lectures on the Philosophy of History*, Hegel explains that "the fundamental dogma" of this religion is "that nothingness is the principle of all things – that all proceeded from and returns to nothingness."[76] Hegel himself was drawing on earlier accounts from the eighteenth century, which characterize Buddhism as a religion of nihilism.[77]

1833, p. 4 (English translation: *Heiberg's On the Significance of Philosophy for the Present Age and Other Texts*, ed. and trans. by Jon Stewart, Copenhagen: C.A. Reitzel 2005 (*Texts from Golden Age Denmark*, vol. 1), p. 87).

[75] See Sibbern, *Bemærkninger og Undersøgelser*, pp. 76f. (*Remarks and Investigations*, p. 128).
[76] Hegel, *Vorlesungen über die Philosophie der Geschichte*, ed. by Eduard Gans, in *Georg Wilhelm Friedrich Hegel's Werke. Vollständige Ausgabe*, vols. 1–18, Berlin: Duncker und Humblot 1832–45, vol. 9 (1837), p. 140 (English translation: *The Philosophy of History*, trans. by J. Sibree, New York: Willey Book Co. 1944, p. 168).
[77] See Johann Joachim Schwabe (ed.), *Allgemeine Historie der Reisen zu Wasser und zu Lande; oder Sammlung aller Reisebeschreibungen*, vols. 1–21, Leipzig: Heinrich Merkus 1747–74, vol. 6, p. 360; Joseph de Guignes, *Histoire générale des Huns, des Turcs, des Mogols, et des*

In this discussion, it is easy to overlook the key points about the nature of nihilism during the Danish Golden Age since this is characterized under the rubric of Buddhism. In any case, Sibbern shared Møller's concern about Hegel's philosophy and the cultural state of the time. The two men were thus clearly allied against Heiberg in this regard, although Møller had previously been associated with Heiberg's Hegelian campaign. But all three men seem to agree on the nature of the then current cultural crisis: the age is suffering from an increasing feeling of nihilism. Where they differ is in their assessment of its origins and solutions.

6.4 Møller's Conclusions

This completes Møller's series of *reductio ad absurdum* arguments against nihilism and the denial of immortality. He thus surveys the different spheres of human life and activity and shows how the denial of the idea of immortality undermines them all. In a sense Møller's claim can be regarded as an enhanced version of Ivan Karamazov's famous statement, mentioned above,[78] that if God does not exist, then "everything is allowed."[79] For Dostoevsky, ethics and the moral sphere are undermined if God does not exist. Without God, there would be no right and wrong and no meaning in the world. This is a well-known version of nihilism. Møller makes a similar argument with respect to the doctrine of immortality. But, for Møller, the consequences are much more serious. According to him, all art, science, and religion are undermined. Truth itself must be abandoned. The matter of reinstating the doctrine of immortality is thus an urgent one in Møller's eyes. This is particularly pressing since he takes pantheism to be "the prevailing belief of European scholars" in his time.[80]

After this account of how the denial of immortality leads to nihilism, which in turn leads to the destruction of art, science, and religion, Møller casts a glance at the current state of things in society with regard to the issue. After the above-mentioned spheres of human undertaking are undermined, life loses its meaning: "But under these concepts everything can be included that is capable of filling the human consciousness, and when a person loses interest in the entire

---

autres Tartares occidentaux, vols. 1–4, Paris: Desaint & Saillant 1756–58, vol. 1, part 2, pp. 224, 226; Jean-Baptiste Alexandre Grosier, *Description générale de la Chine, ou Tableau de l'état actuel de cet empire*, vols. 1–2, Paris: Moutard 1785–87, vol. 1, pp. 581–582; Johann Gottfried Herder, *Ideen zur Philosophie der Geschichte der Menschheit*, vols. 1–4, Riga and Leipzig: Johann Friedrich Hartknoch 1784–91, vol. 3, p. 28. See also Stewart, *Hegel's Interpretation of the Religions of the World*, pp. 95–103.

[78] See Introduction, Sect. 0.1.5, p. 14.
[79] Fyodor Dostoevsky, *The Brothers Karamazov*, vols. 1–2, trans. by David Magarshack, Harmondsworth: Penguin 1958, vol. 2, p. 691.
[80] Møller, "Tanker over Muligheden af Beviser for Menneskets Udødelighed," p. 62 (*Poul Martin Møller's "Thoughts on the Possibility of Proofs of Human Immortality" and Other Texts*, p. 117).

contents of his life, he can no longer continue his vacuous existence without self-contradiction."[81]

But Møller believes there are signs that people are beginning to react to this nihilism negatively and are tentatively looking to restore the view of immortality.[82] The time has come when people have begun to realize that it is impossible to live consistently with the nihilistic view. Although even educated people try to hide this from themselves, they cannot help but become aware of the contradiction that their lives represent. Such people are only the pawns of the spirit of the time, which allows them to develop the view of nihilism to the extreme in order to prepare for the dialectical reaction to it, as the pendulum swings back.[83] Once everyone becomes aware of the negative consequences of nihilism, they will abandon it and embrace what Møller calls "the true worldview," that is, the one that contains God and immortality and subsequently truth and meaning.[84] Møller refers to the poem by Schiller mentioned in the Introduction:

> That science in the course it has taken will end up with a nihilistic result was expressed with remarkable premonitions by *Schiller* in his well-known poem, "The Veiled Image at Sais." This poem, which possibly neither the contemporary readers nor the poet himself fully understood, has in our day found an enlightening commentary in the history of science. It tells of a daring youth who lifted the veil of truth but then saw a vision that deprived him of all the zest for life, so that from that time on he walked about like a living dead. What he saw, or rather what *Schiller* saw with his prophetic eye, we are not told, but it was the advancing nihilism, the *Niban* of the Brahmins.[85]

Møller thus sees Schiller as anticipating the growth of nihilism in the modern secular age, which seeks the solution to everything in the sciences. The scientific worldview leads to the denial of immortality and thus meaning, and this results in nihilism, which is impossible to live with. Once the youth, zealous for knowledge, discovered this, he fell into a languishing state and died. The poem thus clearly spells out the necessary result of nihilism.

---

[81] Møller, "Tanker over Muligheden af Beviser for Menneskets Udødelighed," p. 64 (*Poul Martin Møller's "Thoughts on the Possibility of Proofs of Human Immortality" and Other Texts*, p. 119).

[82] Møller, "Tanker over Muligheden af Beviser for Menneskets Udødelighed," p. 63 (*Poul Martin Møller's "Thoughts on the Possibility of Proofs of Human Immortality" and Other Texts*, p. 118).

[83] Møller, "Tanker over Muligheden af Beviser for Menneskets Udødelighed," p. 64 (*Poul Martin Møller's "Thoughts on the Possibility of Proofs of Human Immortality" and Other Texts*, p. 119).

[84] Møller, "Tanker over Muligheden af Beviser for Menneskets Udødelighed," p. 64 (*Poul Martin Møller's "Thoughts on the Possibility of Proofs of Human Immortality" and Other Texts*, p. 120).

[85] Møller, "Tanker over Muligheden af Beviser for Menneskets Udødelighed," pp. 64f. (*Poul Martin Møller's "Thoughts on the Possibility of Proofs of Human Immortality" and Other Texts*, p. 120). See Introduction, Sect. 0.5, pp. 26–28.

6.4 MØLLER'S CONCLUSIONS

Since the modern age is beginning to grasp the contradiction between nihilism and life, Møller predicts that it will soon reject the nihilistic view. He returns to the question about which methodology is best to refute this view. He explains,

> it can hardly be denied that the conviction that it is only by self-deception and self-oblivion that an individual can live with a belief in nihilism, is a very forceful *argumentum ad hominem* against its validity. But the complete proof of immortality must be the scientific exposition of the true worldview in which the doctrine of immortality is a principal part.[86]

The first kind of argument against nihilism, which Møller refers to as ad hominem, is in effect what Jean Paul employs against his character Karlson. It is shown that Karlson cannot continue to have a happy and meaningful life unless he embraces the doctrine of immortality. Møller seems to think that this might be useful in individual cases, but it is far more important to have a refutation that will be valid for society as a whole. For this, Møller believes that his idea of a worldview is the answer. This explains why he was so concerned to explore the negative consequences of nihilism for so many different spheres of human activity. All of these play a role in a general worldview.

But Møller believes that his brief analyses in the article are only indications of the direction that should be followed, but the true worldview "is in a process of development in many respects," and "it is only in its early beginning as long as it is only the endeavor of particular individuals."[87] This can be seen as a criticism of Jean Paul's approach to illustrate the dangers of nihilism only in the case of a single fictional person.

While Møller thinks that a belief in an afterlife can be compatible with science, he rejects the then current claims to be able to know what this afterlife will look like. For example, the Swedish mystic Emanuel Swedenborg (1688–1772) gave a detailed account of how after death people will see again the great cities, such as London and Paris, in which they lived.[88] Møller regards ideas like

---

[86] Møller, "Tanker over Muligheden af Beviser for Menneskets Udødelighed," p. 66 (*Poul Martin Møller's "Thoughts on the Possibility of Proofs of Human Immortality" and Other Texts*, p. 121).

[87] Møller, "Tanker over Muligheden af Beviser for Menneskets Udødelighed," p. 66 (*Poul Martin Møller's "Thoughts on the Possibility of Proofs of Human Immortality" and Other Texts*, p. 121).

[88] See Emanuel Swedenborg, *Continuatio de ultimo Judicio, et de mundo spirituali*, Amsterdam: n.p. 1763, § 42, p. 14: "42. There are two great cities similar to London, into which many of the English enter after death: these cities, it was given me to see, as well as to walk through. The middle of the one city answers to that part of the English London, where there is a meeting of merchants, called the Exchange; there dwell the governors. Above that middle is the east; below it is the west; on the right side of it is the south; on the left side of it is the north. They who pre-eminently have led a life of charity, dwell in the eastern quarter, where there are magnificent palaces. The wise, among whom there is much

this as simply fantasies and fairy tales, which are a natural negative reaction to the hegemony of scientific explanation.[89] Møller is thus clearly making a plea not for superstition but rather for what he believes to be a rationally grounded conviction in a life after death in a different condition. This is based on a general worldview that contains this idea and many others as well that all stand in harmony with one another. His argument is dialectical in the Hegelian sense that he takes himself to be combining two one-sided views into a higher truth:

> When the present life is regarded as a fragment of a greater whole, it becomes evident that neither the one-sided idea of a here nor the one-sided idea of a hereafter can lead to a true consciousness of the infinity of existence. By accepting the present life as a part of an eternity, the individual lives already in one sense of the word an infinite life, and only in experiencing the decisive aspects of this life is it possible to form an idea of an intensive infinity of a future life.[90]

The purely scientific view that rejects the idea of immortality as simple fantasy of the imagination, as we have seen, undermines the value and meaning of this life. Likewise, the religious enthusiast who "lives only for the contemplation of eternity for itself, with no thought of its reflection in the present time, leads a life just as empty as the one who keeps to the present, detached from eternity, as the actual reality."[91] For Møller, the correct view lies in the middle, where one maintains a general scientific skepticism about the fantasies of the details of the afterlife but embraces the possibility of it. In this way one can enjoy a meaningful life in the here and now without either falling into despair (like the scientific view) or focusing entirely on the anticipation of the afterlife (like the superstitious view). Life and death are an integrated whole, and we should always keep an eye on both. It is only in this way that "the present human life may regain its lost significance and become an actual life, which it is not, unless man recollects its continuity with eternity."[92]

---

splendor, dwell in the southern quarter. They who foremostly love the liberty of speaking and writing, dwell in the northern quarter. They who make profession of faith, dwell in the western quarter; to the right in this quarter, there is an entrance into, and an exit from the city; they who live wickedly are there sent out of it" (English translation: *A Continuation Concerning The Last Judgment and Concerning the Spiritual World*, New York: American Swedenborg Printing and Publishing Society 1865, § 42, pp. 507f.).

[89] Møller, "Tanker over Muligheden af Beviser for Menneskets Udødelighed," p. 69 (*Poul Martin Møller's "Thoughts on the Possibility of Proofs of Human Immortality" and Other Texts*, p. 124).

[90] Møller, "Tanker over Muligheden af Beviser for Menneskets Udødelighed," p. 71 (*Poul Martin Møller's "Thoughts on the Possibility of Proofs of Human Immortality" and Other Texts*, p. 125).

[91] Møller, "Tanker over Muligheden af Beviser for Menneskets Udødelighed," p. 71 (*Poul Martin Møller's "Thoughts on the Possibility of Proofs of Human Immortality" and Other Texts*, p. 126).

[92] Møller, "Tanker over Muligheden af Beviser for Menneskets Udødelighed," pp. 71f. (*Poul Martin Møller's "Thoughts on the Possibility of Proofs of Human Immortality" and Other Texts*, p. 126).

6.5 Møller and Existentialism

As we have seen, for Møller, the absence of a belief in immortality meant that everything was meaningless since no enduring value could be ascribed to finite, transitory things. In his view, this was something that was disastrous for both the individual and culture in general, and his Danish contemporaries all seemed to agree with him on this point. He also shares this idea with Jean Paul. Møller's unique contribution to the discussion of nihilism can be found in his idea of a worldview, which develops Jean Paul's basic idea in a more substantial manner.

Writers such as Klingemann, Schopenhauer, and Büchner would quickly dismiss Møller's idea of a complete worldview as the solution to nihilism. This would, in their eyes, amount to a grandiose lie to oneself in the same way that Jean Paul's Karlson must lie to himself about immortality, which he knows full well cannot be true. It makes little difference whether it is an isolated belief, as in Jean Paul, or one belief among others in a large worldview, as in Møller. The desire to believe in immortality in order to achieve a view that makes one feel better about life is not an argument for its truth.

Møller does, however, go considerably further than Jean Paul in his depiction of the consequences of nihilism in the different spheres of life. Jean Paul wants to present a horrific image and let the readers draw the conclusion for themselves. By contrast, Møller goes to work systematically and explores one by one all the areas that would be rendered meaningless if nihilism were to be the reigning idea. He tries to think through to the end how things would look if large masses of people really believed nihilism to be true. It would amount to nothing less than the complete collapse of society. While Møller regards this as a rather urgent matter, he nonetheless believes that when individuals reach the point of nihilism, they will themselves see where it leads and will of their own accord simply return to traditional values. As was the case with Jean Paul, nihilism is simply not a realistic alternative to traditional religion and belief.

However, it is worth noting that the first premise of both Møller and Jean Paul can be called into question, namely, that the lack of a belief in immortality leads to nihilism. This is just the opposite of the well-known arguments of other thinkers, including those associated with existentialism, many of whom greet the rise of nihilism as a form of liberation. Here one might recall Schopenhauer's proposal of liberating oneself from the passions and drives as a response to nihilism. As we have seen, Møller rejects this outright as a complete absurdity since it in effect means embracing the nothingness. Likewise, Nietzsche's *Übermenschen* are able to shrug off the repressive ethics of Christianity and create their own system of values based only on their own authority and will to power. Similarly, in *The Myth of Sisyphus*, Camus claims that it is just because human existence is finite that it takes on its infinite value, just like the scarcity of a commodity or resource drives up its value and price. As will be seen in the following chapter, Kierkegaard anticipates this argument.[93] Along the same lines, in a short story, Jorge Luis Borges tries to show that the very premise of immortality would rob life of all meaning.[94] Given the inevitability of death, people are zealous to pursue projects and organize their lives in such a way that they have the time to accomplish the things that they want to do while they are still able to do so. But, according to Borges, with an eternity of time on their hands, people would lose their motivation to do anything. There would be no need to rush to get a degree or make a great career since one would always have time for this tomorrow. Far from saving people from nihilism, the idea of immortality would instead lead them to it. The logic of Borges's story is that nihilism would end in indifference and lethargy. If one could live forever, there would be no point in doing anything today.

Perhaps the difference between Møller and these other thinkers can be best captured by the observation that the threat of nihilism leads the former to try to hold firmly to some version of traditional values and beliefs since the alternative seems so disastrous. By contrast, the other thinkers are keen to move on and regard the retreat to traditional belief as absurd and inauthentic. Here one recalls Camus's criticism of Kierkegaard for seeing the truth of nihilism but nonetheless, due to psychological weakness, lapsing back into what Camus dubs metaphysical "comfort."[95] While Kierkegaard portrays despair as a sickness, his ultimate goal, according to Camus's somewhat questionable interpretation, is to be cured of it.[96] For Camus, the goal should be to embrace the absurdity of nihilism. It should be noted in Kierkegaard's defense that his notion of Christian faith is by no means traditional but rather tries to take into account the challenges of critical reason. Kierkegaard uses the same terms as Camus, "absurdity" or "the absurd," to capture the contradictory nature of Christian faith in contrast to the perspective of rationality. But in any case, Møller and Kierkegaard clearly object to the idea of wallowing in nihilism. They see nihilism as a major threat to every sphere of culture and would presumably be astonished to see thinkers in the twentieth century trying to find ways to affirm and welcome it as a liberation.

---

[93] See Chapter 7, Sect. 7.7, p. 231.
[94] Jorge Luis Borges, "The Immortal," in *Labyrinths, Selected Stories and Other Writings*, ed. by Donald A. Yates and James E. Irby, New York: New Directions 1962, pp. 109–121. See also Jon Stewart, *The Unity of Content and Form in Philosophical Writing: The Perils of Conformity*, London, New Delhi, New York, and Sydney: Bloomsbury 2013, pp. 133–141; Jon Stewart, "Borges on Immortality," *Philosophy and Literature*, vol. 17, no. 2, 1993, pp. 78–82.
[95] Albert Camus, *The Myth of Sisyphus and Other Essays*, trans. by Justin O'Brien, New York: Random House 1975, p. 50. See his analysis of Kierkegaard, pp. 37–41, 49–50.
[96] Camus, *The Myth of Sisyphus*, p. 38.

7

Kierkegaard and the Indefinability and Inexplicability of Death

The Danish thinker Søren Kierkegaard (1813–55) struggled with the issues of human existence from an early age. Nihilism was among his earliest interests, and he returned to it throughout his life. Like his teacher Poul Martin Møller, he was clearly engaged in the discussions about it that were going on in Prussia and the German states as well as his native Denmark. But nihilism was much more than simply an academic problem for him. By the time he was twenty-one, his mother and five of his siblings had already died. All that remained of his family was his father and elder brother. The experience of the deaths of his brothers and sisters must have made for a gloomy childhood, which was also accompanied by the strong Lutheran religiosity of his father. While Kierkegaard is generally known today as a committed religious thinker, he clearly knew and explored the depths of the nihilistic worldview.

In the first half of the nineteenth century Danish culture was closely related to German culture, and Kierkegaard was well versed in the German classics. He read with great interest the works of, for example, Jean Paul and Schopenhauer, who, as we have seen, were important in the discussion of nihilism at the time.[1] Perhaps more importantly was the influence of Møller, whose article on immortality discusses nihilism at length, as was explored in the previous chapter. Kierkegaard followed Møller in rejecting nihilism in favor of a Christian orientation. But his view of Christianity is such that it cannot really be regarded as a *solution* to nihilism in the usual sense. When we talk about a solution to an academic or philosophical problem, we are usually talking about presenting strong evidence or arguments that lead to a conclusion that removes the problem. But, for Kierkegaard, Christian faith is not like this. He characterizes faith with terms such as "paradox," "contradiction,"

---

[1] See Markus Kleinert, "Jean Paul: Apparent and Hidden Relations between Kierkegaard and Jean Paul," in *Kierkegaard and His German Contemporaries*, tome III, *Literature and Aesthetics*, ed. by Jon Stewart, Aldershot: Ashgate 2008 (*Kierkegaard Research: Sources, Reception and Resources*, vol. 6), pp. 155–170; Simonella Davini, "Schopenhauer: Kierkegaard's Late Encounter with His Opposite," in *Kierkegaard and His German Contemporaries*, tome I, *Philosophy*, ed. by Jon Stewart, Aldershot: Ashgate 2007 (*Kierkegaard Research: Sources, Reception and Resources*, vol. 6), pp. 277–291.

and so on.[2] It is not something that can be decisively proven or even argued for based on reason. He frequently talks about "belief by virtue of the absurd."[3] This is counterintuitive for most of us since we like to think that we have good reasons to believe the things that we do. Instead, for Kierkegaard, this is a mistake when it comes to Christianity. He is thus quick to criticize those who rest complacently in Christian faith, as if it were a certain and straightforward matter that was definitively demonstrated once and for all. He is acutely aware of the dark, nihilistic side of the human mind that continues to raise doubts and uncertainties.

Kierkegaard examines the problem of nihilism in several different texts,[4] such as *The Concept of Irony*, *Either/Or*, *Repetition*, "At a Graveside," *A Literary Review*, and *The Sickness unto Death*.[5] Although he almost never uses the term explicitly, he frequently discusses issues such as the meaning of life, death, anxiety, and despair, which are clearly related to nihilism. It is impossible here to do justice to all these treatments. I will instead simply point out a few of the main analyses of the issue in Kierkegaard's corpus and try to connect them with the ongoing discussion about nihilism that we have been following.

---

[2] See Jakub Marek, "Contradiction," in *Kierkegaard's Concepts*, tome II, *Classicism to Enthusiasm*, ed. by Jon Stewart, Steven M. Emmanuel, and William McDonald, Aldershot: Ashgate 2014 (*Kierkegaard Research: Sources, Reception and Resources*, vol. 15), pp. 73–80; Sean Turchin, "Paradox," in *Kierkegaard's Concepts*, tome V, *Objectivity to Sacrifice*, ed. by Jon Stewart, Steven M. Emmanuel, and William McDonald, Aldershot: Ashgate 2015 (*Kierkegaard Research: Sources, Reception and Resources*, vol. 15), pp. 43–48.

[3] See Sean Turchin, "Absurd," in *Kierkegaard's Concepts*, tome I, *Absolute to Church*, ed. by Steven M. Emmanuel, William McDonald, and Jon Stewart, Aldershot: Ashgate 2013 (*Kierkegaard Research: Sources, Reception and Resources*, vol. 15), pp. 5–9.

[4] The sole monograph to date dedicated to a study of nihilism in Kierkegaard's work in general is Mădălina Diaconu's *Pe marginea abisului. Søren Kierkegaard și nihilismul secolului al XIX-lea*, Bucharest: Editura Științifică 1996. See also Jean dos Santos Vargas, "Kierkegaard entre a existência e o niilismo," *Revista do Departamento de Filosofia da Pontifícia Universidade Católica de Minas Gerais*, vol. 6, no. 12, 2015, pp. 657–671; Peter Šajda, "The Struggles of the Individual in a Nihilistic Age: Kierkegaard's and Jünger's Critiques of Modernity," in *Modern and Postmodern Crises of Symbolic Structures: Essays in Philosophical Anthropology*, ed. by Peter Šajda, Leiden and Boston: Brill Rodopi 2021, pp. 22–40.

[5] See Heiko Schulz, "Aesthetic Nihilism: The Dialectic of Repetition and Non-Repetition in Nietzsche and Kierkegaard," in his *Aneignung und Reflexion*, vol. 2, *Studien zur Philosophie und Theologie Søren Kierkegaards*, Berlin and Boston: De Gruyter 2014 (*Kierkegaard Studies Monograph Series*, vol. 28), pp. 130–145; Hubert Dreyfus and Jane Rubin, "Kierkegaard on the Nihilism of the Present Age: The Case of Commitment as Addiction," *Synthese*, vol. 98, 1994, pp. 3–19; George Pattison, "Nihilism and the Novel: Kierkegaard's Literary Reviews," *The British Journal of Aesthetics*, vol. 26, 1986, pp. 161–171; Jane Louise Rubin, "Narcissism and Nihilism: Kohut and Kierkegaard on the Modern Self," in *Self Psychology: Comparisons and Contrasts*, ed. by Douglas W. Detrick and Susan P. Detrick, Hillsdale and London: Analytic Press 1989, pp. 131–150; Geoffrey Clive, "The Sickness unto Death in the Underworld: A Study of Nihilism," *The Harvard Theological Review*, vol. 51, 1958, pp. 135–167.

7.1 The Criticism of Romantic Irony

The Concept of Irony, from 1841, was Kierkegaard's master's thesis at the University of Copenhagen.[6] It is an important early statement of his views. The different forms of Romantic irony that he explores in the second part of that work are all forms of modern relativism, which can be taken as an expression of nihilism.[7] Kierkegaard takes aim at specific figures in German Romanticism such as Friedrich von Schlegel, Karl Solger, and Ludwig Tieck. Like Socratic irony, this modern irony is a negative force that undermines the legitimacy of current institutions, customs, and beliefs. Here Kierkegaard makes use of Hegel's analyses on the subject and offers his own criticism of the form of relativism that he refers to as "irony." Kierkegaard's use of this term, instead of nihilism, has been misleading for readers who understand irony primarily as a literary device. But there can be no doubt from the content of his discussion that he intends this term to reflect a certain way of life that we would today associate with nihilism. The positions that he sketches resemble the figure of Kreuzgang in *The Nightwatches*. Convinced of the meaninglessness of human existence and the vacuity of the accepted values of society, Kreuzgang is unrelenting in his social criticism. Likewise, Kierkegaard has an eye for the hypocrisy and folly of society as people desperately try to create values for themselves and make themselves important with trivial jobs and pursuits.

Kierkegaard's critical point is that the relativists or nihilists offer nothing positive after they have eliminated all truths, customs, and values with their negative critique. The nihilistic view leads to an unbounded freedom that dismisses the world of actuality, which is not thought to have any validity. This fits well with the artistic disposition, which believes that it can create the world itself. Individuals are thus free to imagine themselves in different roles and present different views of themselves in accordance with whatever mood strikes them. Irony comes in when the individual takes a critical stance towards

---

[6] Søren Kierkegaard, *Om Begrebet Ironi med stadigt Hensyn til Socrates*, Copenhagen: P.G. Philipsens Forlag 1841. The original Danish text is reprinted in volume 1 of *Søren Kierkegaards Skrifter*, vols. 1–28, K1–K28, Copenhagen: Gad Publishers 1997–2012 (English translation: *The Concept of Irony; Schelling Lecture Notes*, trans. by Howard V. Hong and Edna H. Hong, Princeton, NJ: Princeton University Press 1989.)

[7] See K. Brian Söderquist, *The Isolated Self: Irony as Truth and Untruth in Søren Kierkegaard's On the Concept of Irony*, Copenhagen: C.A. Reitzel 2007 (*Danish Golden Age Studies*, vol. 1); K. Brian Söderquist, "Kierkegaard's Nihilistic Socrates in *The Concept of Irony*," in *Tänkarens mångfald. Nutida perspektiv på Søren Kierkegaard*, ed. by Lone Koldtoft, Jon Stewart, and Jan Holmgaard, Göteborg and Stockholm: Makadam Förlag 2005, pp. 213–243; George J. Stack, "Kierkegaard and Nihilism," *Philosophy Today*, vol. 14, 1970, pp. 274–292; George J. Stack, "Kierkegaard's Ironic Stage of Existence," *Laval théologique et philosophique*, vol. 25, no. 2, 1969, pp. 192–207; George J. Stack, "Irony and Existence: The Nihilistic Possibility," in his *Kierkegaard's Existential Ethics*, Tuscaloosa, AL: University of Alabama Press 1977, pp. 1–43.

the customs, traditions, and ways of life that the majority of people live by. Irony is used as a tool to undermine the truth of these things. The denial of the truth and validity of the world of actuality leads to relativism.

Kierkegaard believes that irony can perform a beneficial function of undermining traditions that are corrupt, hypocritical, and contradictory. But the mistake that the Romantics make is to universalize the use of irony so that it is employed not just against such things that are deserving of criticism but rather against the entire sphere of actuality. In the end Kierkegaard believes that this relativism or irony needs to be selective in the targets of its critique. He argues that it should be *controlled* so that it can perform its negative and destructive work without leading to a complete negation of everything. Thus, in *The Concept of Irony*, he proposes the concept of *controlled irony* as the solution.[8] Irony, as a form of social criticism, should specifically target those elements of society that are in need of criticism, but not everything is. There are some values or institutions that should be left alone since they are not the result of hypocrisy, self-delusion, and corruption.

In this way Kierkegaard shows an appreciation for the value of the Romantics' criticism of bourgeois culture, without, however, accepting it wholeheartedly. While the Romantics, indeed, have an important point that there is much that needs to be torn down, this only makes sense if the goal is to reach some truth that lies beyond this. Kierkegaard thinks that it is important to go through a phase of rebellion and skepticism about the ways of the world, but this should only be a phase and not an enduring way of life. When one comes out of this, one has a well-developed sense for critical thinking and is better able to evaluate things in the world than someone who never had such a skeptical phase and remains naïve, accepting every foolish thing they were ever told. Kierkegaard alludes to

---

[8] See Jon Stewart, "Heiberg's Speculative Poetry as a Model for Kierkegaard's Concept of Controlled Irony," in *Johan Ludvig Heiberg: Philosopher, Littérateur, Dramaturge, and Political Thinker*, ed. by Jon Stewart, Copenhagen: C.A. Reitzel 2008 (*Danish Golden Age Studies*, vol. 5), pp. 195–216; Richard M. Summers, "'Controlled Irony' and the Emergence of the Self in Kierkegaard's Dissertation," in *The Concept of Irony*, ed. by Robert L. Perkins, Macon, GA: Mercer University Press 2001 (*International Kierkegaard Commentary*, vol. 2), pp. 289–315; Oscar Parcero Oubiña, "'Controlled Irony' ... Are you Serious? Reading Kierkegaard's Irony Ironically," *Kierkegaard Studies Yearbook*, 2006, pp. 241–260; Anders Moe Rasmussen, "Gives der en 'behersket Ironi'?," *Kredsen*, vol. 61, no. 1, 1995, pp. 71–86; Eivind Tjønneland, "Beherrschte Ironie als Vermittlungsbegriff," in his *Ironie als Symptom. Eine kritische Auseinandersetzung mit Søren Kierkegaards Über den Begriff der Ironie*, Frankfurt am Main: Peter Lang 2004, pp. 263–288; Andrew Cross, "Neither Either nor Or: The Perils of Reflexive Irony," in *The Cambridge Companion to Kierkegaard*, ed. by Alastair Hannay and Gordon D. Marino, New York: Cambridge University Press 1998, pp. 125–153; Henri-Bernard Vergote, "L'ironie maîtrisée," in his *Sens et répétition. Essai sur l'ironie kierkegaardienne*, vols. 1–2, Paris: Cerf/Orante 1982, vol. 1, pp. 178–181; Bo Kampmann Walter, "Den beherskede ironi," in his *Øjeblik og tavshed. Læsninger i Søren Kierkegaards forfatterskab*, Odense: Odense Universitetsforlag 2002, pp. 69–73.

the Gospel of John when he says, "Irony as the negative is the way; it is not the truth but the way."[9]

An echo of Kierkegaard's distinction between Romantic irony and controlled irony can be found in Karl Gutzkow's novel *The Ring or the Nihilists* from 1853.[10] The story portrays the development of a group of young people with radical ideas, influenced by the left Hegelians, in the period before and after the Revolutions of 1848. One of the leading characters is Konstantin Ulrichs, who is highly intelligent and full of charisma. He represents a radical form of absolute nihilism that seeks to destroy everything. In Kierkegaard's language, Konstantin is the force of purely destructive Romantic irony, without any real purpose behind it. Gutzkow portrays him unsympathetically as an egoist who is generally indifferent to others. His sister Frida is cut from the same cloth and likewise represents the destructive side of nihilism. Konstantin's friend Eberhart Ott is a far more sympathetic person. He too is a nihilist but not an absolute one. He can be thought to represent Kierkegaard's idea of controlled irony. He realizes that social and political change are not an all or nothing proposition. He is happy to criticize certain things but at the same time to work constructively for new reforms and institutions. Unlike Konstantin, Eberhard realizes that social development is something that requires both time and patience. Konstantin, however, throws overboard every idea of reform since it will not lead to the perfection of society immediately. Like Kierkegaard, Gutzkow's point is to criticize the futility of abstract, fully fledged nihilism and at the same time to recommend a limited form of nihilism that can still serve a constructive function.

7.2 The Portrait of the Aesthete in the "Diapsalmata"

This criticism of nihilism in *The Concept of Irony* is reworked in a more literary form in Kierkegaard's first pseudonymous work, *Either/Or*, from 1843.[11] Kierkegaard wrote most of this book when he was attending lectures at the

---

[9] *Søren Kierkegaards Skrifter*, vol. 1, p. 356 (*The Concept of Irony*, p. 327). See John 14:6.

[10] This work appeared in installments in Gutzkow's journal: *Der Ring oder die Nihilisten*, in *Unterhaltungen am häuslichen Herd*, 1853, no. 37, pp. 577–585; no. 38, pp. 593–601; no. 39, pp. 609–616; no. 40, pp. 628–638; no. 41, pp. 641–651; no. 42, pp. 657–662; no. 43, pp. 673–684. See Michael Allen Gillespie, *Nihilism before Nietzsche*, Chicago: University of Chicago Press 1996, pp. 128–134.

[11] [Victor Eremita], *Enten-Eller. Et Livs-Fragment*, vols. 1–2, Copenhagen: C.A. Reitzel 1843. In what follows reference is made to the reprint of this text in *Søren Kierkegaards Skrifter* (English translation: *Either/Or*, vols. 1–2, trans. by Howard V. Hong and Edna H. Hong, Princeton, NJ: Princeton University Press 1987). See Karsten Harries, *Between Nihilism and Faith: A Commentary on Either/Or*, Berlin and New York: Walter de Gruyter 2010 (*Kierkegaard Studies Monograph Series*, vol. 21); Schulz, "Aesthetic Nihilism," pp. 130–145; Leonardo Lisi, "Diapsalmata: Nihilism as a Spiritual Exercise," in *Entweder/Oder*, ed. by Hermann Deuser and Markus Kleinert, Berlin and Boston: Walter de Gruyter 2017, pp. 75–94; Jean Vargas, "O Tédio como Figura do Nihilismo em Ou-Ou de Kierkegaard," in *Kierkegaard através do tempo*, ed. by Natalia Mendes Teixeira, São Paulo: LiberArs 2021, pp. 253–275.

Royal Friedrich Wilhelm's University in Berlin. His stay in Berlin took place immediately after the completion of his MA thesis and his well-known breakup with Regine Olsen. This period was an important crossroads for the young Kierkegaard – a time to reflect on what direction he wanted to take in life. Different options presented themselves to him, and as he weighed these in his mind, he developed the idea for *Either/Or*, which is a dialogue between two people, each of which represents a certain way of life.

Either/Or purports to be a pseudonymous book, edited by one Victor Eremita, who found the manuscript of the text by accident. The unnamed first author, referred to simply as "A," is an aesthete who represents the life of a bachelor with no social or familial obligations. The aesthete has a certain disdain for people and enjoys laughing at the absurdities of human behavior. This first part of the book contains a series of essays that reflect his way of life. The second part is penned by one Judge Wilhelm, who is referred to as "B." A married man and a loyal civil servant, the judge argues for a more stable, traditional way of life in accordance with the customs and values of society. For him, life is about responsibility and not freedom to do whatever one wants whenever one wants. These two views are thus juxtaposed to one another so that the reader can evaluate which one is the more appealing.

It is the essays from the aesthete that are the most important for our purposes. In these pieces, Kierkegaard gives a penetrating psychological portrayal of the aesthete as a kind of Romantic relativist. In this way the work can be seen as a continuation of the second part of *The Concept of Irony*, where he discussed the German Romantics. But *Either/Or*, in contrast to *The Concept of Irony*, is not an academic text but rather a literary one. Instead of criticizing Romantic irony as a movement, he sketches the relativist, ironist, and nihilist in the figure of the aesthete. In the "Diapsalmata," the first chapter in the book,[12] he gives us a portrait of the modern nihilist and raises the question of what the point of life is if all traditional meaning has been undermined. Are we all doomed to be forever unhappy and to despair? Likewise, with "The Diary of a Seducer" the reader is presented with a character sketch of a person who is wholly self-indulgent and morally reprehensible. Johannes the Seducer has long since ceased to believe in traditional ethics, which he seems to regard as silly bourgeois trivialities or platitudes based on outdated sentimentality. He has no moral scruples at all about manipulating and seducing his naïve young victim.

Kierkegaard's understanding of the aesthetic sphere is largely critical. The point of his character sketch of aesthete A or the seducer is that we are to find these characters repugnant. The seducer is a negative example of the results of nihilism. However, there is a truth in these characters; namely, they serve a negative function of calling us to reflection and of rightly criticizing

---

[12] *Søren Kierkegaards Skrifter*, vol. 2, pp. 25–52 (*Either/Or*, vol. 1, pp. 17–43).

7.2 THE PORTRAIT OF THE AESTHETE IN THE "DIAPSALMATA" 207

bourgeois culture and complacency. Kierkegaard is critical of the view of the bourgeois philistine (*Spidsborger*), which is represented by the judge, and praises the aesthetic realm as a criticism of this. But he is acutely aware of the extremes that the aesthetic view can reach if it is allowed to go its way without any impediment. In order to overcome this problem, one needs religion. Specifically, one needs Christian faith as Kierkegaard understands it. The aesthetic sphere can help us attain this by purging us of our naïve and uncritical views of faith.

The character sketch that Kierkegaard provides for A, the aesthete, in the "Diapsalmata" is useful for how he understands the issue of nihilism. The chapter consists of scattered aphorisms and anecdotes written by A. They are intended to help readers gain some insight into what kind of person they are. A close look reveals that the aesthete has many nihilistic views. The Greek word "diapsalmata" (διάψαλματα) ("diapsalma" (διάψαλμα) in the singular) refers to breaks or pauses in a musical piece. The word is used in connection with the biblical book of Psalms to refer to the end of verses, which provides a kind of refrain. The idea of an aesthete seems to suggest someone who has independent means and is wholly self-indulgent, seeking pleasure when they get bored. But this is oversimplified. The aesthete closely resembles Schopenhauer's description of human existence balancing between suffering and boredom. The aesthete repeatedly mentions his sorrow and suffering along with the failure to find something to relieve his boredom. The topic of boredom is especially highlighted in A's essay "The Rotation of the Crops."

The first indication that the reader gets of this is at the very beginning of the text, where the aesthete provides the following epigram as a kind of motto, but without any commentary or explanation: "*Grandeur, savoir, renomée, / Amitié, plaisir et bien, / Tout n'est que vent, que fumée: / Pour mieux dire, tout n'est rien.*"[13] The poem, entitled simply "Epigram," comes from the pen of the French author Paul Pellisson (1624–93).[14] It recalls motifs from Ecclesiastes, with human activities and goals amounting to "wind" and "smoke." The things that people spend their lives trying to obtain all amount to "nothing." This immediately distinguishes the aesthete as a social outsider who does not share the same goals as others. He can see the hollowness of the ambitious plans and projects of people. Like Kreuzgang in *The Nightwatches*, the aesthete has a cynical view towards other people, whom he keeps at a distance.

---

[13] *Søren Kierkegaards Skrifter*, vol. 2, p. 26 (*Either/Or*, vol. 1, p. 18) ("Greatness, knowledge, renown, / Friendship, pleasure and possessions, / All is only wind, only smoke: / To say it better, all is nothing").

[14] Paul Pellisson, *Oeuvres diverses*, vols. 1–3, Paris: Chez Didot 1735, vol. 1, p. 212. The poem is also cited in "Zerstreute Anmerkungen über das Epigramm," in *Gotthold Ephraim Lessing's sämmtliche Schriften*, vols. 1–32; vols. 1–28, Berlin: Vossische Buchhandlung 1825–27; vols. 29–32, Berlin and Stettin: Nicolaische Buchhandlung 1828, vol. 17, p. 82.

7.3 The Aesthete's View of the Meaninglessness of Existence

Perhaps the most overt nihilistic motif in the "Diapsalmata" is the recurring reflections on the meaninglessness of life. The aesthete writes, "My observation of life is completely meaningless. I suppose that an evil spirit has put a pair of glasses on my nose, one lens of which magnifies on an immense scale and the other reduces on the same scale."[15] The nihilistic view presupposes the juxtaposition of two perspectives. First, one must see the universe on the grand scale like the astronomers. Then, one must compare this to the much smaller scale of human life, which, by comparison, seems completely meaningless and insignificant. If one could just remain unreflective and stick to the smaller perspective, then the issue of nihilism would never arise since it would never occur to one how small we are in the universe. The aesthete imagines an "evil spirit" has caused him to make this comparison by giving him the distorted glasses, which bring the two perspectives together. Similarly, Kreuzgang often refers to the devil as the hidden voice of nihilism that we have in ourselves, which causes us constantly to lapse into despair. In both the case of the aesthete and Kreuzgang, it might be argued that the evil spirit or the devil is the spirit of the natural sciences. Or it can be interpreted as an inner voice that arises in everyone from time to time, when we despair of our mortality and finitude.

The aesthete's nihilism comes out once again when he writes, "My achievement amounts to nothing at all, a mood, a single color."[16] All human works are nothing but a passing triviality. An expansion of this idea comes shortly thereafter: "The best demonstration of the wretchedness of life is that which is obtained through a consideration of its glory."[17] Even when one looks at the greatest achievements of the greatest heroes of human history, as Hamlet does in the gravedigger scene,[18] these all look hollow when we think that they have been reduced to dust. To glorify such deeds is only to perpetuate the illusion, but the truth is the "wretchedness of life." Perhaps the clearest expression of the aesthete's nihilism comes in the following reflection on death:

> How empty and meaningless life is. —We bury a man; we accompany him to the grave, throw three spadefuls of earth on him; we ride out in a carriage, ride home in a carriage; we find consolation in the thought that we have a long life ahead of us. But how long is seven times ten years? Why not settle it all at once, why not stay out there and go along down into the grave and draw lots to see to whom will befall the misfortune of

---

[15] *Søren Kierkegaards Skrifter*, vol. 2, p. 33 (*Either/Or*, vol. 1, p. 24). Translation slightly modified.
[16] *Søren Kierkegaards Skrifter*, vol. 2, p. 37 (*Either/Or*, vol. 1, p. 28).
[17] *Søren Kierkegaards Skrifter*, vol. 2, p. 37 (*Either/Or*, vol. 1, p. 28).
[18] Shakespeare, *Hamlet*, Scene 18, pp. 2081–2088 (in editions that divide the play into acts, this appears in *Hamlet*, Act 5, Scene 1).

7.3 THE MEANINGLESSNESS OF EXISTENCE

being the last of the living who throws the last three spadefuls of earth on the last of the dead?[19]

This in some ways recalls Hamlet's "to be or not to be" speech, Schopenhauer's discussion of suicide, and Manfred's despair. The awareness of the inevitability of death and the suffering of life makes one wonder if it is all worth it. Here we can also find an echo of Büchner's Danton, who regards as meaningless the work of his parents and teachers in raising him since he was only going to die later. The issue of time is irrelevant given the infinitesimally short lifespans of humans in comparison with the universe. Nothing is won by hanging on to life for longer since we are unable to accomplish anything of meaning anyway.

The aesthete critically examines a couple of different responses to the question of the meaning of life and seems unable to come up with a solution to the problem:

> What, if anything, is the meaning of this life? If people are divided into two great classes, it may be said that one class works for a living and the other does not have that need. But to work for a living certainly cannot be the meaning of life, since it is indeed a contradiction that the continual production of the conditions is supposed to be the answer to the question of the meaning of that which is conditional upon their production. The lives of the rest of them generally have no meaning except to consume the conditions. To say that the meaning of life is to die seems to be a contradiction also.[20]

Here he rejects two possible definitions. The first one can be found in Ecclesiastes, where it is written that the best one can do is to find satisfaction in one's work (which is a necessity for procuring the means to live).[21] This might also be seen as a Marxist view *avant la lettre*, whereby one finds one's identity and satisfaction in meaningful labor. But for the aesthete, the meaning of life cannot be something so trivial as just working in order to remain alive. The second is the more scientifically motivated view that there is no afterlife and that humans, as biological beings, are created only to die. This resembles Schopenhauer's view. But for the aesthete, just because death is a necessity for everyone, this does not imply that it is the meaning of our lives in the sense of a goal that we strive all our lives to reach. For the aesthete, neither of these provides any real meaning, which presumably must be sought elsewhere if indeed it exists at all.

The aesthete laments, "My life is utterly meaningless."[22] This remark comes with a reflection on the different periods of his life that seem not to represent any meaningful continuity or direction. He uses the analogy of the German word

---

[19] *Søren Kierkegaards Skrifter*, vol. 2, p. 38 (*Either/Or*, vol. 1, p. 29).
[20] *Søren Kierkegaards Skrifter*, vol. 2, p. 40 (*Either/Or*, vol. 1, p. 31).
[21] Ecclesiastes 2:24; see also 3:13, 22; 5:18.
[22] *Søren Kierkegaards Skrifter*, vol. 2, p. 45 (*Either/Or*, vol. 1, p. 36).

Schnur, which can have a variety of very different meanings. Likewise, life has many different meanings. We all like to believe that our lives constitute a unity with a clear meaning and purpose. But the implication of this diapsalma seems to be that human existence only consists of scattered experiences and impressions with nothing deeper to bind them together. The unity or continuity in our lives is only an illusion that we posit. The proof of this is that the story that we tell about our lives changes over time as we gain new experiences and perspectives.

7.4 The Aesthete's View of the Suffering of Existence

The aesthete also emphasizes the suffering of human existence. He uses a variety of terms to describe this: anxiety, depression, sorrow, loneliness, and so on. In the first diapsalma, the aesthete seems to associate himself with a poet. He defines a poet as an "unhappy person who conceals profound anguish in his heart."[23] The poet verbalizes this anguish in his works, which, due to their beauty, cover over the poet's hidden internal anguish. It might be suggested here that the anguish is caused by the realization of nihilism, which, as Jean Paul, Klingemann, and Schopenhauer have all discussed, leads to pain and despair. The poet wallows in the despair of the nothingness but is hopelessly misunderstood by the people, who are misled by the charm of his work. They cannot perceive his anguish from the outside. Every time the poet recites his work, the pain and anguish return. Later the aesthete refers to the fact that he suffers from depression and sorrow, which can also be taken as signs of the realization of nihilism.[24] In another aphorism, he writes, "Over my inner being broods an oppressiveness, an anxiety, that forbodes an earthquake."[25]

The aesthete describes his inward struggle with nihilism in a way similar to what some of our other authors have described. It is a constantly nagging fear that comes out in the night. During the day we can repress it to a large degree since we are busy with our daily affairs and must keep up appearances. Our routines allow us to slip into the illusion that everything is fine. But then when we are alone in a dark hour, the fear appears:

> I have, I believe, the courage to doubt everything; I have, I believe, the courage to fight against everything; but I do not have the courage to acknowledge anything, the courage to possess, to own, anything .... I complain that in life it is not as in the novel, where one has hardhearted fathers and nisses and trolls to battle, and enchanted princesses to free. What are all such adversaries together compared with the pale, bloodless, tenacious-of-life nocturnal forms with which I battle and to which I myself give life and existence.[26]

---

[23] *Søren Kierkegaards Skrifter*, vol. 2, p. 27 (*Either/Or*, vol. 1, p. 19).
[24] *Søren Kierkegaards Skrifter*, vol. 2, pp. 29, 30 (*Either/Or*, vol. 1, pp. 20, 21).
[25] *Søren Kierkegaards Skrifter*, vol. 2, p. 38 (*Either/Or*, vol. 1, p. 29).
[26] *Søren Kierkegaards Skrifter*, vol. 2, p. 32 (*Either/Or*, vol. 1, p. 23).

7.4 THE AESTHETE'S VIEW OF THE SUFFERING OF EXISTENCE 211

The aesthete does not have the courage to ascribe a positive value to anything but only to criticize and tear down. The cause of his fear is not something that one sees in the external world, such as a villain or a monster, but rather the thought of nihilism that everything is meaningless and that we will all die and turn to dust. In contrast to most of the usual struggles in life, this inward battle is impossible to win since it returns to us again and again. We can never quite be at rest with this idea as long as we live. This seems to suggest that the key issue in human suffering for the aesthete has to do with our reflection about death and the finitude of human existence.

Although Schopenhauer also makes human suffering a key motif, his understanding of this is quite different from that of the aesthete. For Schopenhauer, suffering is primarily caused by the fact that we have natural drives and desires that constantly demand our attention and that cause us pain when they remain unsatisfied. By contrast, for the aesthete, the idea seems to be that suffering is caused by the reflection that leads to the view that we are insignificant and will one day die. This is an idea that at some level haunts everyone, even those who are unreflective and try to repress such thoughts.

It will be recalled that both Jean Paul and Klingemann made use of the motif of dreams or nightmares in which our innermost fears about death and meaninglessness come to the surface. While repressed during our waking life, these fears nonetheless remain with us and appear when we have let our guard down in our sleep. Kierkegaard's aesthete refers to this same phenomenon as follows: "I, too, am bound ... by a chain formed of gloomy fancies, of alarming dreams, of troubled thoughts, of fearful presentiments, of inexplicable anxieties."[27] All three thinkers seem to agree that this is a constant feature of our inward life.

The aesthete comes to sound a bit like Schopenhauer, when he says, "Life for me has become a bitter drink."[28] Human existence is full of pain and suffering, for which there is no solution. It is the price of living. The aesthete continues, "No one comes back from the dead; no one has come into the world without weeping. No one asks when one wants to come in; no one asks when one wants to go out."[29] This seems to emphasize the finitude of human existence and the helplessness of people to do anything to change it. The universe is created with certain rules that also govern human life. It is beyond our power to make them conform with our wishes and hopes. We must simply accept them as they are.

We can find some of the motifs from *The Nightwatches* in the following diapsalma: "I have only one friend, and that is echo. Why is it my friend? Because I love my sorrow, and echo does not take it away from me. I have only one confidant, and that is the silence of night. Why is it my confidant? Because it

---

[27] *Søren Kierkegaards Skrifter*, vol. 2, p. 43 (*Either/Or*, vol. 1, p. 34).
[28] *Søren Kierkegaards Skrifter*, vol. 2, p. 34 (*Either/Or*, vol. 1, p. 26).
[29] *Søren Kierkegaards Skrifter*, vol. 2, p. 34 (*Either/Or*, vol. 1, p. 26).

remains silent."[30] The aesthete portrays himself as a socially isolated and lonely figure like Kreuzgang. The two also have in common the fact that they enjoy the silence of the night. The echo in *The Nightwatches* seemed to represent the emptiness of human existence and the fact that whatever truth or meaning was found was merely put there by humans. The aesthete portrays the echo as a comforter who allows him to continue in his sorrow in contrast to another person, who would naturally try to cheer him up. In both cases there is a clear sense of melancholy and emptiness.

Although apparently a somewhat cynical person like Kreuzgang, the aesthete also has a sensitive side. He writes, "There are particular occasions when one may be most painfully moved to see a person standing utterly alone in the world. The other day I saw a poor girl walking utterly alone to church to be confirmed."[31] While all people are ultimately alone in the world on the nihilistic view, this is a particularly sad scene when it concerns young people or children. We recall the pathos of Jean Paul's "The Dead Christ," when the dead children come out of their graves and appeal to Jesus, who can only answer that we are all orphans in the world.[32] The motif of childhood appears often in the "Diapsalmata." The aesthete seems to appreciate the naïveté, genuineness, and authenticity of children in contrast to adults, who have become conformists corrupted by society. The aesthete offers another moving reflection on the death of children as follows:

> Why was I not born in Nyboder, why did I not die as a baby? Then my father would himself have laid me in a little casket, taken me under his arm, carried me out to the grave on a Sunday morning, would himself have cast the earth on it and in a low voice said a few words understandable only to himself. Only in the happy days of yore could people have the idea of babies weeping in Elysium because they died so prematurely.[33]

For Jean Paul the image of the dead children was one of infinite sadness that no one could possibly accept. Here the aesthete seems to imply that both the Roman conception of a place in Elysium for the souls of children and Jean Paul's notion of an afterlife for children are absurdities stemming from a naïve and unreflective mind. Only in a prescientific age could people really believe in such things in order to comfort themselves. The suffering and death of innocent children is a sad fact of human existence that cannot be changed.

---

[30] *Søren Kierkegaards Skrifter*, vol. 2, pp. 42f. (*Either/Or*, vol. 1, p. 33).

[31] *Søren Kierkegaards Skrifter*, vol. 2, p. 29 (*Either/Or*, vol. 1, p. 21).

[32] Jean Paul, *Blumen-, Frucht- und Dornenstücke oder Ehestand, Tod und Hochzeit des Armenadvokaten F. St. Siebenkäs im Reichsmarktflecken Kuhschnappel*, vols. 1–3, Berlin: In Carl Matzdorff's Buchhandlung 1796–97, pp. 7f. (English translation: *Flower, Fruit, and Thorn Pieces; Or, The Wedded Life, Death, and Marriage of Firmian Stanislaus Siebenkæs*, trans. by Alexander Ewing, London: George Bell and Sons 1897, p. 263).

[33] *Søren Kierkegaards Skrifter*, vol. 2, p. 49 (*Either/Or*, vol. 1, p. 40).

7.4 THE AESTHETE'S VIEW OF THE SUFFERING OF EXISTENCE 213

Also consistent with nihilism, the aesthete is focused on death, as has been apparent in some of the reflections above. He writes directly, "My misfortune is this: an angel of death always walks at my side."[34] This might be taken as an autobiographical reflection since, as noted above, Kierkegaard experienced the premature death of all his siblings with the exception of his elder brother. He was also convinced that he too would die before he became old. This constant presence of death clearly left its mark. The obsession with death is similar to the constant use of it in *The Nightwatches*, where it is referred to in numerous ways with motifs such as skulls, dust, and nothingness. One can read a later diapsalma along the same lines when the aesthete again reflects on his sorrow, which comes from reflecting on the past. He talks about how he only occasionally emerges from his recollection of the past in order to enter into the world of the day and then retreats again to it: "I live as one already dead. Everything I have experienced I immerse in a baptism of oblivion unto an eternity of recollection. Everything temporal and fortuitous is forgotten and blotted out."[35]

The aesthete also gives a reflection on his disposition towards the future. While the concrete nature of his future is unknown, what is absolutely certain is that it will end with death. He draws an analogy with a spider:

> What is going to happen? What will the future bring? I do not know, I have no presentiment. When a spider flings itself from a fixed point down into its consequences, it continually sees before it an empty space in which it can find no foothold, however much it stretches. So it is with me; before me is continually an empty space, and I am propelled by a consequence that lies behind me. This life is turned around and dreadful, not to be endured.[36]

The future ends in the emptiness and nothingness of death. With the analogy of the spider, Kierkegaard follows Jean Paul in his recognition of the importance of the sciences in understanding the world of nature. But it is this scientific view that leads to the undesirable conclusion of nihilism.

Kierkegaard again comes very close to Klingemann in the following passage: "My life is like an eternal night; when I die, I shall be able to say with Achilles: 'You are fulfilled, nightwatch of my life.'"[37] Kreuzgang seems to live his life at night, and there are constant images of darkness and gloom. With the quotation from a fragment of Aeschylus's tragedy *Achilles*,[38] Kierkegaard also refers to life as a dark nightwatch.

---

[34] *Søren Kierkegaards Skrifter*, vol. 2, p. 49 (*Either/Or*, vol. 1, p. 41).
[35] *Søren Kierkegaards Skrifter*, vol. 2, p. 51 (*Either/Or*, vol. 1, p. 42).
[36] *Søren Kierkegaards Skrifter*, vol. 2, pp. 32f. (*Either/Or*, vol. 1, p. 24).
[37] *Søren Kierkegaards Skrifter*, vol. 2, p. 45 (*Either/Or*, vol. 1, pp. 35f.).
[38] See *Søren Kierkegaards Skrifter*, vol. K2, p. 108, where the source is referenced: *Des Aischylos Werke*, trans. by Johann Gustav Droysen, 2nd ed., Berlin: G. Bethge 1842, p. 498.

In a related diapsalma the aesthete again acknowledges his limitation as a created being in the universe: "So I am not the one who is the lord of my life; I am one of the threads to be spun into the calico of life! Well, then, even though I cannot spin, I can still cut the thread."[39] The forces of nature and cause and effect govern our lives. We did not ask to be born, and we are thrown into a world that is not of our own choosing. The point seems to be that while we make up a small part of actuality or existence (like a single thread in a cloth) that we cannot control, we can always opt for suicide (thus cutting the thread, like the Greek Fates) and remove ourselves from the world. The aesthete seems to recall Hamlet in a contemplation of suicide. If life is so miserable and full of suffering, then why do more people not commit suicide? The aesthete explains,

> How strange! With what equivocal anxiety about losing and keeping, people nevertheless cling to this life. At times I have considered taking a decisive step compared with which all previous ones were but child's play—to set out on the great voyage of discovery. As a ship is saluted with a cannonade when it is launched, so I would salute myself. And yet. Is it courage that I lack? If a stone fell down and killed me, that would still be a way out.[40]

The suggestion is that the "decisive step" would be committing suicide and the "voyage of discovery" would be finding out if there is an afterlife that lies beyond death. This is the "undiscovere'd country" in *Hamlet*.[41] The aesthete then turns this morbid reflection into something comic with the idea that he might be killed by something as trivial as a falling stone. The beginning of the diapsalma notes the deep anxiety that people have about death and their desire to remain alive at all costs. This squares with Schopenhauer's notion of the will-to-live as being the fundamental feature of human life and the rest of the universe. The reflection on suicide also recalls the inner struggles of Lord Byron's Manfred and Büchner's Danton, both of whom are tormented by memories of past sins. In these cases, there is a desire to eliminate one's own self-consciousness as the only way to find peace.

Towards the end of the "Diapslamata," the aesthete shows a dialectical proclivity with a longer reflection on the term "either/or," which he borrows from the traditional formulation of the law of excluded middle: A thing must be *either* X *or* not X. This was a topical issue at the time since Hegel argued that this law was mistaken and proposed instead the concept of mediation. This caused a debate on the subject in Denmark, and so Kierkegaard takes this up in a satirical

---

[39] *Søren Kierkegaards Skrifter*, vol. 2, p. 40 (*Either/Or*, vol. 1, p. 31).
[40] *Søren Kierkegaards Skrifter*, vol. 2, p. 46 (*Either/Or*, vol. 1, p. 37).
[41] Shakespeare, *Hamlet*, Scene 8, line 80, p. 2041 (in editions that divide the play into acts, this appears in Act 3, Scene 1).

fashion.[42] The aesthete writes, "Laugh at the stupidities of the world, and you will regret it; weep over them, and you will also regret it. Laugh at the stupidities of the world or weep over them, you will regret it either way."[43] This is one of a series of formulations that follows the same pattern of positing a dilemma and then declaring that whatever one chooses, one will regret it. Here we can see the tragic-comic element in the aesthete, which reflects Schopenhauer's view of the dialectical relation of nihilism.[44] The aesthete repeats this formula many times with different issues in life. The result of this is to provoke a feeling in the reader that it does not matter what one does in life. Everything is meaningless, or everything will end in death anyway. Life is suffering since, although one is constantly confronted with important life decisions, there is no good choice to be had. Whatever decision one makes will end in suffering and regret.

By contrast to most of the rest of society, the aesthete complains, "I have lost all my illusions. In vain do I seek to abandon myself in joy's infinitude; it cannot lift me, or, rather, I cannot lift myself."[45] He is the victim of his own reflection, which has caused him to see through the myths and illusions of the world. After he arrives at the truth of nihilism, there is nothing that he can find pleasure in. He is lost to a constant melancholy. This idea of losing one's illusions leads to another major theme in the "Diapsalmata," namely, the aesthete's social criticism.

7.5 The Aesthete's Social Criticism

Like Kreuzgang, the aesthete is a merciless social critic, mocking the common bourgeois views of society about what is important and meaningful:

> When I was very young, I forgot ... how to laugh; when I became an adult, when I opened my eyes and saw actuality, then I started to laugh and have never stopped laughing since that time. I saw that the meaning of life was to make a living, its goal to become a councilor, that the rich delight of love was to acquire a well-to-do girl, that the blessedness of friendship was to help each other in financial difficulties, that wisdom was whatever the majority assumed it to be, that enthusiasm was to give a speech, that

---

[42] See Jon Stewart, "The Paradox and the Criticism of Hegelian Mediation in *Philosophical Fragments*," *Kierkegaard Studies Yearbook*, 2004, pp. 186–209; Jon Stewart, *A History of Hegelianism in Golden Age Denmark*, tome II, *The Martensen Period: 1837–1842*, Copenhagen: C.A. Reitzel 2007 (*Danish Golden Age Studies*, vol. 3), pp. 289–373; *Mynster's "Rationalism, Supernaturalism" and the Debate about Mediation*, ed. and trans. by Jon Stewart, Copenhagen: Museum Tusculanum Press 2009 (*Texts from Golden Age Denmark*, vol. 5); Jon Stewart, "Hegel, Kierkegaard and the Danish Debate about Mediation," *Bulletin of the Hegel Society of Great Britain*, no. 61, 2010, pp. 61–86.
[43] *Søren Kierkegaards Skrifter*, vol. 2, p. 47 (*Either/Or*, vol. 1, p. 38).
[44] Arthur Schopenhauer, *Die Welt als Wille und Vorstellung*, vols. 1–2, 2nd revised and enlarged ed., Leipzig: F.A. Brockhaus 1844, vol. 1, p. 364 (*The World as Will and Representation*, vols. 1–2, trans. by E.F.J. Payne, New York: Dover 1969, vol. 1, p. 322).
[45] *Søren Kierkegaards Skrifter*, vol. 2, p. 50 (*Either/Or*, vol. 1, p. 41).

courage was to risk being fined ten dollars, that cordiality was to say "May it do you good" after a meal, that piety was to go to communion once a year. This I saw, and I laughed.[46]

He can quickly see through the facade of society. Although the aesthete took the accepted values of society seriously as a child, as an adult he clearly regards them as absurd. People would be able to see this if they had the ability to reflect on them critically. Also like Kreuzgang, he finds the values of society not tragic but comic. He gets pleasure out of laughing at the folly of others who mindlessly follow the requirements of social convention.

Like Kreuzgang, the aesthete has a critical view of his fellow human beings. As we have seen above, he appreciates the naturalness and naïveté of children, whereas he takes adults to be corrupt and self-deluded, playing out their meaningless roles in society. In one diapsalma, A writes, "I prefer to talk with children, for one may still dare to hope that they may become rational beings; but those who have become that – good Lord!"[47] There is something refreshing about the directness of children. They do not stand on rules of etiquette in order to hide their true views. By contrast, adults are much more concerned about what others will think about them, and so they carefully hide their real opinions and feelings. This is a pernicious form of rationality, to which the irrationality of children is much preferable. There is thus a critique here of what society celebrates as the triumphs of reason.

Somewhat in the same spirit, the next diapsalma reads, "How unreasonable people are! They never use the freedoms they have but demand those they do not have; they have freedom of thought – they demand freedom of speech."[48] At the time the Kingdom of Denmark was an absolute monarchy. In the wake of the July Revolution of 1830 in France, there were many political debates about the freedom of the press and the use of censorship. Here Kierkegaard takes a jab at those clamoring for reform. Such people who demand the freedom of speech do not even make use of the freedom of thought that they already have. The humorous point is of course that the aesthete is accusing these reformers of being stupid and unthinking. This can also be connected with *The Nightwatches*, where, as discussed,[49] Kreuzgang as a hoax declares the immanent end of the world.[50] Only when the people think that the Last Judgement is at hand do they start to reflect on their lives and the meaning of their reprehensible actions. However, when the crisis passes, they all return

---

[46] *Søren Kierkegaards Skrifter*, vol. 2, p. 43 (*Either/Or*, vol. 1, p. 34).
[47] *Søren Kierkegaards Skrifter*, vol. 2, p. 27 (*Either/Or*, vol. 1, p. 19).
[48] *Søren Kierkegaards Skrifter*, vol. 2, p. 28 (*Either/Or*, vol. 1, p. 19).
[49] See above Chapter 2, Sect. 2.1, pp. 66–71.
[50] [Klingemann], *Nachtwachen. Von Bonaventura*, Penig: bey F. Dienemann und Comp. 1805, p. 95 (English translation: *The Nightwatches of Bonaventura*, trans. by Gerald Gillespie, Chicago and London: University of Chicago Press 2014, p. 42).

7.5 THE AESTHETE'S SOCIAL CRITICISM

immediately to their usual habits. They learn nothing at all from the experience and lapse back into their unthinking and unreflective ways. The truth of nihilism is too difficult to face, and so they believe it is better to live in a safe illusion.

The aesthete's criticism of the illusions and lack of reflection of most people comes out nicely in the following anecdote:

> The most ludicrous of all ludicrous things, it seems to me, is to be busy in the world, to be a man who is brisk at his meals and brisk at his work. Therefore, when I see a fly settle on the nose of one of those men of business in a decisive moment, or if he is splashed by a carriage that passes him in even greater haste, or Knippelsbro tilts up, or a roof tile falls and kills him, I laugh from the bottom of my heart. And who could keep from laughing?[51]

People who are "brisk" are those who take themselves to be very important. They need to hurry since they believe that they have important jobs to perform. They enjoy social esteem and respect for being such important people. They live in the delusion that their lives are something especially valuable, while they secretly disdain others in society, whom they regard as less important. They put on the facade of being very busy in order to demonstrate their importance to others. But they do not see through the meaninglessness of their own lives. They are completely blind to the fact that they could die at any moment or be killed in the most trivial of accidents. The aesthete regards this as a kind of tragicomedy.

The aesthete criticizes religious superstition in favor of the scientific worldview. He recalls a preacher who claims that when one has a problem, one needs only look to the clouds to see God's helping hand.[52] Then later when taking a walk, the aesthete sees a storm on the horizon with some unusually shaped clouds, apparently a tornado. He perceives the danger and runs to safety. He satirically wonders if the preacher would do the same or if he would regard this terrible and dangerous destructive force of nature as the hand of God. Here the scientific worldview is clearly juxtaposed to the religious. It might surprise some readers that Kierkegaard, who is known as a Christian author, clearly sides with the scientific view here and mocks religious superstition.

Despite his criticism of society, the aesthete makes no point of trying to enlighten people about the sad truth of the world, its misery and lack of meaning. Unlike Kreuzgang, for example, in his false announcement of the end of the world, the aesthete has no interest in moral reform. The aesthete writes, "Should I then communicate my sorrow to the world, make one more contribution to prove how pitiable and wretched everything is, perhaps discover a new, hitherto undetected stain in human life? ... I still prefer to remain silent."[53] He

---

[51] *Søren Kierkegaards Skrifter*, vol. 2, p. 33 (*Either/Or*, vol. 1, p. 25).
[52] *Søren Kierkegaards Skrifter*, vol. 2, p. 36 (*Either/Or*, vol. 1, p. 27).
[53] *Søren Kierkegaards Skrifter*, vol. 2, p. 44 (*Either/Or*, vol. 1, p. 35).

is only too happy to let people continue to live in their folly and ignorance and laugh at it from a distance.

Like Kreuzgang, the aesthete is a misanthrope because he cannot stand the folly, corruption, and hypocrisy of society: "Then when I walk past people, happy-go-lucky as a god, and they envy me because of my good fortune, I laugh, for I despise people, and I take my revenge .... Then when I hear others praised for their faithfulness, their integrity, I laugh, for I despise people, and I take my revenge."[54] He realizes that this in turn causes others to disdain him, but instead of being worried about this, he takes a perverse pleasure in it: "When I see myself cursed, abhorred, hated for my coldness and heartlessness, then I laugh, then my rage is satisfied."[55] To be hated by people that one disdains can be taken as a form of recognition. In an inverted world, it is good to be an outsider and not share the common values of society. This recalls the inversions found in *The Nightwatches*, where those regarded as sane are in fact the insane and vice versa.

Another point of comparison can be found in Kreuzgang's cynical understanding of love, which he struggled against. He regarded it as an illusion that led people to think that they were happy. But this was only a trick of nature to make people forget for a moment that they will die and be forever separated from those they love. The aesthete seems to have a similar view: "I call to mind my youth and my first love – when I was filled with longing; now I long only for my first longing. What is youth? A dream. What is love? The content of the dream."[56] The aesthete seems to concur that love is just an illusion with nothing substantial or enduring. As an illusion, it can only cause pain later when one is separated from one's beloved. This recalls Schopenhauer's view that the world is an illusion hidden beneath the veil of Maya.[57]

The aesthete, like Kreuzgang, criticizes the folly and vanity of academics. He recalls that as a young student at the age of fifteen he wrote "demonstrations for the existence of God and the immortality of the soul, on the concept of faith, and on the meaning of miracles."[58] Later he again wrote two further essays on immortality, which were highly praised. He then notes that when he reached the age of twenty-five, he was no longer able to produce any such proof. The idea seems to be that such proofs are for the young and naïve, but when one gets older and develops a sense of critical thinking, then it becomes apparent that such proofs are impossible. It belongs to the absurdity of academics that they continue to waste their time on such things that cannot be proven. The aesthete, as an adult, has developed a deeper appreciation for the difficulties

---

[54] *Søren Kierkegaards Skrifter*, vol. 2, p. 49 (*Either/Or*, vol. 1, p. 40).
[55] *Søren Kierkegaards Skrifter*, vol. 2, p. 49 (*Either/Or*, vol. 1, p. 40).
[56] *Søren Kierkegaards Skrifter*, vol. 2, p. 51 (*Either/Or*, vol. 1, p. 42).
[57] See Schopenhauer, *Die Welt als Wille und Vorstellung*, vol. 1, § 68, pp. 428, 429 (*The World as Will and Representation*, vol. 1, § 68, pp. 378, 379).
[58] *Søren Kierkegaards Skrifter*, vol. 2, p. 43 (*Either/Or*, vol. 1, p. 34).

involved in religious faith. This anticipates Kierkegaard's later criticisms of the proofs for the existence of God in works such as the *Philosophical Fragments*.[59]

We saw how Kreuzgang was committed to a mental asylum since he purportedly suffered from a malady that made him believe that what was rational was what the world thought was irrational, and vice versa.[60] He thus posited an inverted world, by which the generally accepted values of society are turned on their head. Kierkegaard portrays the aesthete with a similar motif:

> Generally speaking, the imperfection in everything human is that its aspirations are achieved only by way of their opposites. I shall not discuss the variety of formations, which can give a psychologist plenty to do (the melancholy have the best sense of the comic, the most opulent often the best sense of the rustic, the dissolute often the best sense of the moral, the doubter often the best sense of the religious), but merely call to mind that it is through sin that one gains a first glimpse of salvation.[61]

Like Klingemann, Kierkegaard perceives the dialectical opposites in things. Although Kreuzgang appears as a morbid, melancholy man, in fact, he is a humorous figure. Like Schopenhauer, Kierkegaard understands that necessary relation between tragedy and comedy with regard to the issue of nihilism. Later he notes the close connection between laughing and crying.[62] The last sentence in the quotation above emphasizes the necessary relation between sin and salvation. This can be taken to imply that the nihilist, who ostensibly is a sinner since he denies God, immortality, meaning, and so on, is in fact on the way to salvation, since he, in contrast to the rest of society, has realized the truth of the meaninglessness of the world and is no longer living in the typical illusions about it. Thus, according to this view, there is no contradiction between the nihilistic view of the meaninglessness of the world and the religious view.

We saw how the idea of boredom was a central feature of Schopenhauer's philosophical psychology. For Schopenhauer, when we reach a state of material well-being and can fairly easily satisfy our desires, then the natural result is boredom. This motif is also central in the work of the aesthete,[63] who says, "I

---

[59] See *Søren Kierkegaards Skrifter*, vol. 4, pp. 242–252 (English translation: *Philosophical Fragments; Johannes Climacus, or De omnibus dubitandum est*, trans. by Howard V. Hong and Edna H. Hong, Princeton, NJ: Princeton University Press 1985, pp. 37–48).
[60] [Klingemann], *Nachtwachen*, p. 170 (*The Nightwatches of Bonaventura*, p. 73).
[61] *Søren Kierkegaards Skrifter*, vol. 2, p. 28 (*Either/Or*, vol. 1, p. 20).
[62] *Søren Kierkegaards Skrifter*, vol. 2, p. 29 (*Either/Or*, vol. 1, p. 21).
[63] See Roberto Garaventa, "The Aesthetic Way of Life between Boredom and the Search of the Interesting," in *Kierkegaard and the Challenges of Infinitude: Philosophy and Literature in Dialogue*, ed. by José Miranda Justo, Elisabete M. de Sousa, and René Rosfort, Lisbon: Centro de Filosofia da Universidade de Lisboa 2013, pp. 83–92; Laura Liva, "The Abyss of Demonic Boredom: An Analysis of the Dialectic of Freedom and Facticity in Kierkegaard's Early Works," *Kierkegaard Studies Yearbook*, 2013, pp. 143–155; William McDonald,

don't feel like doing anything."[64] He then lists a number of different activities that he is not interested in for one reason or another. The aesthete is bored. His nihilistic point of view has leveled all human activity and determined everything to be meaningless. The sad truth is that we will all die and turn to nothingness, despite what we do in life. In the next diapsalma, the aesthete writes, "There are, as is known, insects that die in the moment of fertilization. So it is with all joy: life's highest, most splendid moment of enjoyment is accompanied by death."[65] Some people might choose to strive for pleasure all their lives, but they cannot escape their own mortality. The reference to the life of insects can be regarded as a hint at a worldview guided by the modern scientific model of things.

The motif of the boredom of existence comes up once again in the following diapsalma: "Wretched fate! In vain do you prink up your wrinkled face like an old prostitute, in vain do you jingle your fool's bells. You bore me; it is still the same, an *idem per idem*. No variation, always a rehash. Come, sleep and death; you promise nothing, you hold everything."[66] The aesthete is keen to find something new and distracting but struggles in vain to do so. As in Ecclesiastes, there is nothing new under the sun, and the aesthete's appetite for amusement is never satisfied. Death is portrayed as a welcome release from the tedium of daily existence.

The aesthete returns to the motif of boredom and meaninglessness: "I lie prostrate, inert; the only thing I see is emptiness, the only thing I live on is emptiness, the only thing I move in is emptiness."[67] His sense of boredom has made him numb to the point that he has no preference for pleasure over pain. In fact, he was thankful for pain since it was at least a distraction from the monotony and boredom of existence.[68] He explains his overwhelming doubt as follows:

> And what could divert me? Well, if I managed to see a faithfulness that withstood every ordeal, an enthusiasm that endured everything, a faith that moved mountains; if I were to become aware of an idea that joined the finite and the infinite. But my soul's poisonous doubt consumes everything. My soul is like the Dead Sea, over which no bird is able to fly; when it has come midway, it sinks down, exhausted, to death and destruction.[69]

This kind of strong faith seems impossible to him. His doubt is overpowering. Like Jean Paul's "The Dead Christ,"[70] the aesthete portrays doubt or atheism as

"Kierkegaard's Demonic Boredom," in *Essays on Boredom and Modernity*, ed. by Barbara Dalle Pezze and Carlo Salzani, Amsterdam and New York: Rodopi 2009, pp. 61–84.

[64] *Søren Kierkegaards Skrifter*, vol. 2, p. 28 (*Either/Or*, vol. 1, p. 20).
[65] *Søren Kierkegaards Skrifter*, vol. 2, p. 28 (*Either/Or*, vol. 1, p. 20).
[66] *Søren Kierkegaards Skrifter*, vol. 2, pp. 38f. (*Either/Or*, vol. 1, pp. 29f.).
[67] *Søren Kierkegaards Skrifter*, vol. 2, p. 46 (*Either/Or*, vol. 1, p. 37).
[68] He says he is "dying death." *Søren Kierkegaards Skrifter*, vol. 2, p. 46 (*Either/Or*, vol. 1, p. 37). This is a reference to the Danish Bible translation of Genesis 2:17, where this formulation (*døe Døden*) appears. See *Søren Kierkegaards Skrifter*, vol. K2, p. 109.
[69] *Søren Kierkegaards Skrifter*, vol. 2, p. 46 (*Either/Or*, vol. 1, p. 37).
[70] Jean Paul, *Blumen-, Frucht- und Dornenstücke*, vol. 1, p. 2 (*Flower, Fruit, and Thorn Pieces*, p. 260).

a kind of poison. Here again we can see the scientific spirit of criticism that does not allow anything to be regarded as true that cannot be proven. This is the view that leads to the aesthete's nihilism. The idea that the sight of such a strong faith would finally be a source of diversion and amusement for him implies that this is a very rare or even unknown thing. This can be taken as a criticism of the thin religiosity of the age that he comes to criticize more vocally in his later works.

One might attribute the aesthete's boredom to an overrefined sense of taste that results from the easy satiation of one's desires. As was noted in connection with Schopenhauer, wine connoisseurs and gourmands become more and more exacting in their palates. The result is that they, in a sense, lose their enjoyment in drinking and eating since their tastes have become so refined that it is both difficult and expensive to satisfy them.

Given all this, there is thus much compelling textual evidence that Kierkegaard intended to portray the aesthete as a nihilist. What is Kierkegaard's point with this portrayal? This must be seen in the context of *Either/Or* as a whole. As was noted in Sect. 7.2, he attempts to sketch two distinct worldviews, or life-views, that of the aesthete in Part I, and that of Judge Wilhelm in Part II. These two are juxtaposed to one another so that the reader can compare and contrast them. Thus, when analyzing the portrayal of the aesthete, we must always bear in mind the intended opposition to Judge Wilhelm.

Hence, Kierkegaard's portrayal of the aesthete as a nihilist cannot be immediately interpreted as a form of recommendation in the same way that one should be cautious about ascribing to Klingemann the views of his character Kreuzgang. Kierkegaard is not recommending the aesthetic view of life any more than he is recommending the bourgeois view of the judge. With the aesthete, Kierkegaard is presumably sketching what he regards as a certain mindset found in his own day. This view is in line with the scientific conception of the world that rejects God, immortality, and meaning. Perhaps like Jean Paul, the point is to present this figure as a kind of *Schreckbild* that will frighten the readers and push them in the opposite direction. Kierkegaard's vision of nihilism in the aesthete is one that he sees some merit in but also wants to criticize. We need to appreciate the critical aspect of this position in order to see through the facade of traditional views. But we cannot dwell in a negative, nihilistic view. Instead, we must make our way to a higher religious conception of life, which he sketches in his many discourses.

In the "Diapslamata," the only real attempt at a solution to the problem of nihilism seems to be a halfhearted recommendation just to conform to society's expectations and avoid thinking more about things: "It takes a lot of naivete to believe that it helps to shout and scream in the world, as if one's fate would thereby be altered. Take what comes and avoid all complications."[71] This recalls the actions of Lucile in Büchner's *Danton's Death*, when she finally comes to

---

[71] *Søren Kierkegaards Skrifter*, vol. 2, p. 42 (*Either/Or*, vol. 1, p. 33).

the full realization of nihilism and says that she will "sit on the ground and scream."[72] But then she simply resigns herself to the situation. In both cases, it is agreed that there is no point in protesting against the universe. By contrast, the message of Byron's *Manfred* seems to be that although there is nothing that we can do to change the world, we should still maintain our individual freedom and human integrity, which we always have control over.

7.6 The Notion of Earnestness in "At a Graveside"

Kierkegaard published the discourse "At a Graveside" on April 29, 1845, in his collection *Three Discourses on Imagined Occasions*.[73] These discourses follow the series of edifying discourses that appeared from 1843 to 1844, which Kierkegaard published in his own name instead of under a pseudonym. His *oeuvre* is thus divided into two parts with the edifying or religious works signed in his own name on the one hand, and the more technical pseudonymous philosophical works on the other. The idea is that the works in the one group should run parallel to the works in the other, with one individual book from the edifying genre corresponding to one in the philosophical genre. The pseudonymous pendant to *Three Discourses on Imagined Occasions* is *Stages on Life's Way*, which was published on April 30, 1845, that is, one day after the *Discourses*. The three discourses are each dedicated to a specific occasion: the first, a confession, the second a wedding, and the third a funeral. Thus, "At a Graveside" is the third of the discourses. These are not real events that Kierkegaard witnessed and then reported on, but rather they are fictional or "imagined" ones that serve as the occasion for him to reflect on key issues concerning human existence. "At a Graveside" focuses primarily on the issue of death and what kind of a disposition one should have to it.[74] In this context it is relevant for the concept of nihilism.[75] This is not a technical philosophical work but rather is intended for less-educated religious believers.

---

[72] Georg Büchner, *Danton's Tod. Ein Drama*, ed. by Thomas Michael Mayer, in *Georg Büchner: Dantons Tod. Die Trauerarbeit im Schönen*, ed. by Peter von Becker, Frankfurt am Main: Schauspiel Frankfurt 1980, p. 71 (in English as Georg Büchner, *Danton's Death* in *Complete Plays, Lenz and Other Writings*, trans. by John Reddick, London: Penguin 1993, p. 72). Quoted in full above in Chapter 5, Sect. 5.5, p. 167.

[73] Søren Kierkegaard, *Tre Taler ved tænkte Leiligheder*, Copenhagen: C.A. Reitzel 1845. In what follows reference is made to the reprint in *Søren Kierkegaards Skrifter* (English translation: *Three Discourses on Imagined Occasions*, trans. by Howard V. Hong and Edna H. Hong, Princeton, NJ: Princeton University Press 1993).

[74] See *Kierkegaard and Death*, ed. by Patrick Stokes and Adam J. Buben, Bloomington and Indianapolis: Indiana University Press 2011.

[75] See Marius G. Mjaaland, "Death and Aporia: Some Reflections on the Problem of Thinking Death in *At a Graveside* (1845)," *Kierkegaard Studies Yearbook*, 2003, pp. 395–418; Michael Theunissen, "Das Erbauliche im Gedanken an den Tod. Traditionale Elemente, innovative Ideen und unausgeschöpfte Potentiale in Kierkegaards Rede. An einem

7.6 THE NOTION OF EARNESTNESS IN "AT A GRAVESIDE"

The discourse begins with a description of a funeral and the next of kin grieving over the dead man. Kierkegaard uses the phrase "Then all is over" as the first words of the discourse and as a kind of mantra throughout.[76] He seems clearly to want to suggest that with death we lose our conscious being. This seems to be supported by the fact that "in the grave there is quiet," and "there is no recollection."[77] In his description of the deceased, Kierkegaard emphasizes the simple piety of the deceased. Since the person knew that it would be impossible to think of God when he was dead, *"he recollected God, while he was living."*[78] In other words, he tried to live a Christian life and to think on or pray to God regularly. In the sketch of the man, there is nothing remarkable. He was a quiet unassuming person who did his job and lived happily with his wife and son. He was not someone famous or important, and his death was hardly noticed by people. The death of such an obscure and humble person seems to emphasize the meaninglessness of human existence. What was the point of the life of such a person?

Although there were no great ceremonies or official days of mourning for the dead man, nonetheless Kierkegaard emphasizes that there was something important about him:

> Yet he still had one more work; in simplicity of heart it was performed with the same faithfulness: he recollected God. He was a man, old, he became aged, and then he died, but the recollection of God remained the same, a guide in all his activity, a quiet joy in his devout contemplation. Indeed, if there were no one at all who missed him in death, yes, if he were not with God now, God would miss him in life and know his dwelling and seek him there, because the deceased walked before him and was better known by him than by anyone else.[79]

The idea seems to be that there is something important about the dead man's relation to God, even if he were the most insignificant person in the world. The implication is that it is here that the man found meaning in his life. Kierkegaard emphasizes the point that the deceased, so to speak, lived with God in every aspect of his life. Like all his edifying discourses, Kierkegaard simply presupposes the existence of God without argument here. This is because these works are intended for Christian readers. But here he does not assume immortality in the same way. Instead, he seems to regard it as an open question with the

---

Grabe," *Kierkegaard Studies Yearbook*, 2000, pp. 40–73 (in English as Michael Theunissen, "The Upbuilding in the Thought of Death: Traditional Elements, Innovative Ideas, and Unexhausted Possibilities in Kierkegaard's Discourse 'At a Graveside,'" in *"Prefaces" and "Writing Sampler" / "Three Discourses on Imagined Occasions,"* ed. by Robert L. Perkins, Macon, GA: Mercer University Press 2006 (*International Kierkegaard Commentary*, vols. 9–10), pp. 321–358).

[76] *Søren Kierkegaards Skrifter*, vol. 5, p. 442 (*Three Discourses on Imagined Occasions*, p. 71).
[77] *Søren Kierkegaards Skrifter*, vol. 5, p. 442 (*Three Discourses on Imagined Occasions*, p. 71).
[78] *Søren Kierkegaards Skrifter*, vol. 5, p. 442 (*Three Discourses on Imagined Occasions*, p. 71).
[79] *Søren Kierkegaards Skrifter*, vol. 5, p. 443 (*Three Discourses on Imagined Occasions*, p. 72).

remark, "if he were not with God now." This implies that it might be the case that he is immortal and with God or that he might not be. Moreover, at the beginning of the discourse, Kierkegaard seems clearly to imply that in death we have no consciousness or feeling, which seems to point in the direction of a skepticism about life after death.

Kierkegaard introduces the concept of the earnestness (*Alvor*) of death, which is central to the discourse.[80] He describes the idea behind this concept as follows: "Death can expressly teach that earnestness lies in the inner being, in thought, can teach that it is only an illusion when the external is regarded light-mindedly or heavy-mindedly or when the observer, profoundly considering the thought of death, forgets to think about and take into account his own death."[81] It is possible to think about death in many ways. It is a sensitive topic that makes people uncomfortable. Kierkegaard's point is that as long as we think of death only when we think of the death of others, then we are not being earnest about it. We only appreciate the full importance and gravity of it when we think of *our own death* honestly and in our "inner being." Only when we personalize the idea as our own death are we able to have the correct perspective. Everything else is a form of distraction, self-deception, repression, or denial.

The death of another and my own death have different meanings. For however sad we might be about the death of a loved one, the situation is fundamentally changed when we consider our own death personally. Death is not the same as sorrow. Sorrow is what happens to the survivors of the death of a loved one. But the dead feel no sorrow. For them "it is over."[82]

For Kierkegaard, true earnestness involves thinking on and appropriating the idea of one's own death. He uses the term "appropriation" (*Tilegnelse*) to emphasize the individual nature of this relation.[83] Along the same lines he uses the term "the single individual" (*den Enkelte*) to underscore the fact that this

---

[80] *Søren Kierkegaards Skrifter*, vol. 5, p. 444 (*Three Discourses on Imagined Occasions*, p. 73). See Michael Theunissen, *Der Begriff Ernst bei Søren Kierkegaard*, Freiburg i. Br. and Munich: Alber 1958; W. Glenn Kirkconnell, "Earnestness or Estheticism: Post 9/11 Reflections on Kierkegaard's Two Views of Death," *Florida Philosophical Review*, vol. 3, 2003, pp. 62–72; Robert J. Widenmann, "Christian Earnestness (Seriousness)," in *The Sources and Depths of Faith in Kierkegaard*, ed. by Marie Mikulová Thulstrup, Copenhagen: C.A. Reitzel 1978 (*Bibliotheca Kierkegaardiana*, vol. 2), pp. 83–99; John Davenport, "Earnestness," in *Kierkegaard's Concepts*, tome II, *Classicism to Enthusiasm*, ed. by Jon Stewart, Steven M. Emmanuel, and William McDonald, Aldershot: Ashgate 2014 (*Kierkegaard Research: Sources, Reception and Resources*, vol. 15), pp. 219–227.

[81] *Søren Kierkegaards Skrifter*, vol. 5, p. 444 (*Three Discourses on Imagined Occasions*, p. 73).

[82] *Søren Kierkegaards Skrifter*, vol. 5, p. 445 (*Three Discourses on Imagined Occasions*, p. 74).

[83] *Søren Kierkegaards Skrifter*, vol. 5, p. 445 (*Three Discourses on Imagined Occasions*, p. 74). See Jon Stewart, "Kierkegaard's Criticism of Abstraction and His Proposed Solution: Appropriation," in his *Idealism and Existentialism: Hegel and Nineteenth- and Twentieth-Century European Philosophy*, New York and London: Continuum International Publishing 2010, pp. 94–119.

concerns every human being on their own.[84] The point of these concepts in this context seems to be that each of us individually must come to terms with the inevitability of our own death. Only you can think of your own death. No one can do it for you. There is no fixed formula for the best way to do this.

It can be said that this was really the key issue in Jean Paul's *The Valley of Campan*. The characters in the novel all struggle with the idea of death and mortality. They are all in a sense searching for the correct disposition towards it. Jean Paul's conclusion was, of course, that we need to have some kind of belief in immortality in order to counter the negative psychological effects of thinking that death means the complete annihilation of our persons. One important difference here, however, is that in the novel, the scientist Karlson capitulates to the belief in immortality not because he is vexed by his own death but rather because he cannot bear the thought of the death of Gione. According to Kierkegaard's view, this is not earnestness since it is not concerned with one's own death. Karlson would, for Kierkegaard, be inauthentic in his newfound belief, which could never offer any certainty or ease one's conscience and nightmares about death anyway. Kierkegaard would thus clearly reject Jean Paul's proposal for a clear-cut solution to the problem of nihilism. This solution is just a form of deception. Here he ultimately sides with Klingemann, Schopenhauer, Büchner, and Byron that there is no real solution, and the best that can be done is to find effective ways of coping.

7.7 The Notion of Mood with regard to Death

Kierkegaard distinguishes between earnestness and mood (*Stemning*).[85] He lists many cases where one feels a sense of sorrow at the death of people whom one knows or does not know. But all of these, he claims, are moods that come and go. They are prompted by concrete events such as seeing a hearse or a grave. Such sights remind us of the inevitability of death, but they do not compel us to think earnestly about it. By contrast, the earnestness of death is not a feeling or a mood, but rather a thought, an idea that never leaves us. The death of another might prompt us to think of our own deaths, but it might not. Earnestness is a secondary level of reflection that goes beyond a mood or feeling of sorrow.

Kierkegaard is well aware of the psychological need to believe in some kind of immortality in the way that Jean Paul is so keen to emphasize. He explains,

> there is a longing for the eternal when death took and took again and now took the last outstanding person you knew; there is a fever heat or cold

---

[84] *Søren Kierkegaards Skrifter*, vol. 5, p. 446 (*Three Discourses on Imagined Occasions*, p. 76). Kierkegaard frequently uses this kind of formulation. See Lydia B. Amir, "Individual," in *Kierkegaard's Concepts*, tome IV, *Individual to Novel*, ed. by Steven M. Emmanuel, William McDonald, and Jon Stewart, Farnham and Burlington, VT: Ashgate 2014 (*Kierkegaard Research: Sources, Reception and Resources*, vol. 15), pp. 1–7.

[85] *Søren Kierkegaards Skrifter*, vol. 5, p. 446 (*Three Discourses on Imagined Occasions*, p. 75).

fire of soul illness when someone becomes so familiar with death and the loss of next of kin that life becomes soul-destroying for him; there is sheer sorrow when the dead person was one of yours; there are the labor pains of immortal hope when it was your beloved; there is the jolting breakthrough of earnestness when it was your one and only guide and loneliness overwhelms you—but even if it was your child, even if it was your beloved, and even if it was your one and only guide, this is still a mood.[86]

This might easily be taken as an autobiographical reflection based on Kierkegaard's own experience with the deaths of his siblings. He is fully aware of how deeply people suffer when their loved ones die and that this can bring with it a psychological trauma that can last a lifetime. He refers to this above as the "fever heat or cold fire of soul illness" and acknowledges that the death of another can be "soul-destroying." But once again he reiterates his point that despite this, earnestness only truly arises when one thinks one's own death.

We have seen the use of dreams in both Jean Paul and Klingemann to explore the human fear of a meaningless universe. Kierkegaard offers his own version of this:

A poet has told of a youth who on the night when the year changes dreamed of being an old man, and as an old man in his dream he looked back over a wasted life, until he woke in anxiety New Year's morning not only to a new year but to a new life. Likewise, to be wide awake and to think death, to think what surely is more decisive than old age, which of course also has its time, to think that all was over, that everything was lost along with life, in order then to win everything in life—this is earnestness.[87]

The "poet" here who is the source of the story is Jean Paul, and the work in question is, his "Die Neujahrnacht eines Unglücklichen" (1789), which constitutes the second part of the "Postscript" to the "Vierter Brief. An Benigna."[88] Frightened by a vision of his life that took the wrong path and was wasted, the protagonist changes his ways and tries to live a virtuous and ethical life starting with the new year. The perspective of imminent death and looking back on a life full of regrets is the kind of thing that Kierkegaard means by earnestness, which can effect a radical change in the person. The thought of one's own death enjoins one to think of one's own life differently.

In a long sentence, Kierkegaard describes the simple person who goes out to the grave of a loved one and recollects them while at the same time thinking earnestly about his own death:

---

[86] *Søren Kierkegaards Skrifter*, vol. 5, p. 446 (*Three Discourses on Imagined Occasions*, p. 75).
[87] *Søren Kierkegaards Skrifter*, vol. 5, pp. 446f. (*Three Discourses on Imagined Occasions*, p. 76).
[88] See *Jean Paul's Briefe und bevorstehender Lebenslauf*, in *Jean Paul's sämmtliche Werke*, vols. 1–60, Berlin: G. Reimer 1826–28, vol. 35, pp. 46–48. See *The Auction Catalogue of Kierkegaard's Library*, ed. by Katalin Nun, Gerhard Schreiber, and Jon Stewart, Farnham and Burlington: Ashgate 2015 (*Kierkegaard Research: Sources, Reception and Resources*, vol. 20), numbers 1777–1799. See *Søren Kierkegaards Skrifter*, vol. K5, pp. 453f.

7.7 THE NOTION OF MOOD WITH REGARD TO DEATH 227

> We surely do agree ... that his recollecting is precious to the deceased, is received with joy in heaven, and that his earnestness is just as laudable, just as well-pleasing to God, just as serviceable to him as that of someone who with rare talent used day and night in practicing in his life the earnest thought of death, so that he was halted and halted again in order to renounce vain pursuits, was prompted and prompted again to hasten on the road of the good, now was weaned of being talkative and busy in life in order to learn wisdom in silence, now learned not to shudder at phantoms and human inventions but at the responsibility of death, now learned not to fear those who kill the body but to fear for himself and fear having his life in vanity, in the moment, in imagination.[89]

The religious side of Kierkegaard comes out here without any real explanation. Before it seemed clear that the dead had no consciousness and were not capable of thought, but now the dead are portrayed as being "in heaven" and being joyful that they are remembered. Moreover, God is pleased by the fact that the grieving person remembers the dead and thinks earnestly about his own death. Kierkegaard gives no evidence or argument for any of this since it is written for Christians, but the vagueness of his view and its apparent contradiction with the more secular picture he presented before raises interpretative problems about where exactly he comes down on the issue of the immortality of the soul.

The question of one's relation to God, for Kierkegaard, is essential for addressing the problem of the apparent meaninglessness of existence. He explains, "The person who is without God in the world soon becomes sad about himself – and expresses this haughtily by being sad about all life, but the person who is in fellowship with God indeed lives with the one whose presence gives infinite significance to even the most insignificant."[90] Without God, the problem of nihilism arises, and one is easily depressed about the fact that there is no meaning. However, if one has a relationship to God, this provides all the meaning that one needs. Even the poorest and most insignificant person can have a great sense of meaning and significance in life in this way. This is completely independent of one's status in society. The belief in God thus seems to be a key element in Kierkegaard's view about the proper disposition towards nihilism. Here his position seems very close to that of Jean Paul, who argues that belief in God and immortality are necessary for one to have meaning and enjoy peace of mind without being constantly vexed by the thought of one's inevitable death.

Kierkegaard reflects on the passage of time as something that we are unable to prevent. During our lives it is impossible to find rest in a deeper sense, due to time. This kind of rest would have to take place outside of time. Here he seems to be in agreement with Schopenhauer about the constant difficulties presented

---

[89] *Søren Kierkegaards Skrifter*, vol. 5, pp. 447f. (*Three Discourses on Imagined Occasions*, p. 77).
[90] *Søren Kierkegaards Skrifter*, vol. 5, p. 448 (*Three Discourses on Imagined Occasions*, p. 78). Translation slightly modified.

in our mundane existence. Time only stops with death: "When death comes, the word is: Up to here, not one step further; then it is concluded, not a letter is added; the meaning is at an end and not one more sound is to be heard – all is over."[91] He refers to this as the decisiveness of death. From the perspective of death, it does not matter what one considers to be important or meaningful in one's life. Death simply acts without interest or emotion. It is a force of nature that cannot be avoided.

Here Kierkegaard was perhaps influenced by the anonymous book with the cumbersome title, *Det menneskelige Livs Flugt, eller Døde-Dands, hvorudi ved tydelige Forestillinger og Underviisningsvers vises, hvorledes Døden uden Personsanseelse dandser af med Enhver, endog ofte uformodentlig, fra Verden til Evigheden; afbildet ved lærerige Stykker, og Samtaler imellem Døden og Personerne.*[92] The title translates as *The Flight of Human Life, or the Death-Dance, in which, by clear Representations and Verses of Instruction, Death is shown to Dance off with Anyone, even often unconsciously, from the World to Eternity; Depicted with instructive Illustrations, and Conversations between Death and the Persons.* The original edition from 1762 was published anonymously. Today it is thought that the poet and translator Niels Prahl (1724–92) was the author of the work, with the publisher Thomas Larsen Borup (1726–70) being the illustrator (see Figure 7.1).[93]

This work is written in verse, and the illustrations show how death, personified as a skeleton, comes for different people in the different social classes. In some cases, such as "The Death of the King," the people facing death plead with him to give them more time and to come back later. But, of course, death is unwavering, as Kierkegaard says, and does not engage in argument. This illustrates what Kierkegaard means by death's decision or the decisiveness of death.[94] Kierkegaard seems to allude to this text later when he writes that for someone

---

[91] *Søren Kierkegaards Skrifter*, vol. 5, p. 449 (*Three Discourses on Imagined Occasions*, pp. 78f.).

[92] [Niels Prahl], *Det menneskelige Livs Flugt, eller Døde-Dands, hvorudi ved tydelige Forestillinger og Underviisnings-Vers viises, hvorledes at Døden uden Persons Anseelse, dandser af med Enhver, endog ofte uformodentlig, fra Verden til Evigheden; Afbildet ved lærerige Stykker, og Samtaler imellem Døden og Personerne, Forlagt og besørgt til sine Landsmænds Nytte og Fornøyelse af Thomas Larsen Borup*, Copenhagen: T.L. Borup 1762. Kierkegaard owned a copy of the third edition: *Det menneskelige Livs Flugt, eller Døde-Dands, hvorudi ved tydelige Forestillinger og Underviisningsvers vises, hvorledes Døden uden Personsanseelse dandser af med Enhver, endog ofte uformodentlig, fra Verden til Evigheden; afbildet ved lærerige Stykker, og Samtaler imellem Døden og Personerne*, [ed. by] Thomas Larsen Borup, 3rd ed., Copenhagen: J.H. Schubothe 1814. See *The Auction Catalogue of Kierkegaard's Library*, ed. by Nun, Schreiber and Stewart, number 1466.

[93] See Harald Ilsøe, *Bogtrykkerne i København og deres virksomhed ca. 1600–1810. En biobibliografisk håndbog med bidrag til bogproduktionens historie*, Copenhagen: Museum Tusculanums Forlag 1992, pp. 150–153.

[94] *Søren Kierkegaards Skrifter*, vol. 5, p. 448 (*Three Discourses on Imagined Occasions*, p. 78).

7.7 THE NOTION OF MOOD WITH REGARD TO DEATH 229

Figure 7.1 [Niels Prahl], *Det menneskelige Livs Flugt, eller Døde-Dands, hvorudi ved tydelige Forestillinger og Underviisnings-Vers viises, hvorledes at Døden uden Persons Anseelse, dandser af med Enhver, endog ofte uformodentlig, fra Verden til Evigheden; Afbildet ved lærerige Stykker, og Samtaler imellem Døden og Personerne, Forlagt og besørgt til sine Landsmænds Nytte og Fornøyelse af Thomas Larsen Borup*, Copenhagen: T.L. Borup 1762, p. 18.

who is suffering "it is supposed to be a relief to reflect that death invites him also to the dance, and in that dance all become equal."[95] Here we find an important motif of death dancing from *The Flight of Human Life, or the Death-Dance*. The title of Figure 7.1, which begins the chapter, is "Death comes to the King." The text reads, "From the King of Kings I have orders to fetch you. / You cannot now expect more days of life. / You know that the final goal for the gods of the earth is / That they shall all die like other humans."

Kierkegaard emphasizes again that "the challenge of earnestness to the living is to think it, to think that all is over, that there comes a time when all is over."[96] The problem is that when one is young and healthy, one tends not to think about one's own death. It seems irrelevant since it will presumably only happen long in the future. However, this notion gives a false sense of security since, of course, death can happen at any time to anyone. Likewise, if one has a position of power or prestige, one believes that one is invulnerable. But all of this is an illusion. Again, perhaps with inspiration from *The Flight of Human Life, or the Death-Dance*, Kierkegaard refers to the deaths of people in different stations of life: a child, a young man, an older man with an unfinished project.[97] All of them seem to have a good argument that they should be granted more time to live, but death is indifferent to their pleas. The point seems to be that thinking earnestly about one's own death means thinking about what this means for one's life. A part of this involves preparing oneself for death. When death comes, one should be able to accept it and be at peace with it instead of pleading for more time or wishing in vain that one could complete one final task or fulfill one final wish. Only thinking earnestly about death can prepare one for it.

We saw aspects of the notion of defiance in the face of death and meaninglessness in the figure of Kreuzgang, who rejected the idea of prayer or begging to God for something better.[98] Byron's Manfred was also a defiant figure in the face of the gods. Kierkegaard, by contrast, is critical of the notion of rebellion or defiance, which he regards as a form of egotism.[99] It is self-delusion to think that one does not fear death. Kierkegaard's rejection of rebellion should be seen against the background of his Christian view. Death is presumably a part of God's plan, and to commit suicide or rebel against it means calling into question God's wisdom. Instead, it is best to trust in God's plan, even though one does not fully understand it and is even frightened by some aspects of it.

Kierkegaard acknowledges that the contemplation of one's own death in earnestness can lead to different conclusions: "Death in earnest gives life force as nothing else does; it makes one alert as nothing else does. Death induces the

---

[95] *Søren Kierkegaards Skrifter*, vol. 5, p. 456 (*Three Discourses on Imagined Occasions*, p. 87).
[96] *Søren Kierkegaards Skrifter*, vol. 5, p. 449 (*Three Discourses on Imagined Occasions*, p. 79).
[97] *Søren Kierkegaards Skrifter*, vol. 5, p. 450 (*Three Discourses on Imagined Occasions*, p. 80).
[98] See Chapter 2, Sect. 2.8, p. 98.
[99] *Søren Kierkegaards Skrifter*, vol. 5, pp. 451f. (*Three Discourses on Imagined Occasions*, pp. 81f.).

sensual person to say: Let us eat and drink, because tomorrow we shall die – but this is sensuality's cowardly lust for life."[100] Hedonism is, of course, a mistaken conception of how to live one's life in the consciousness of death. On the contrary, the thought of death

> gives the earnest person the right momentum in life and the right goal toward which he directs his momentum .... Then earnestness grasps the present this very day, disdains no task as too insignificant, rejects no time as too short, works with all its might even though it is willing to smile at itself if this effort is said to be merit before God, in weakness is willing to understand that a human being is nothing at all and that one who works with all one's might gains only the proper opportunity to wonder at God.[101]

Here again the idea of God seems to be essential as the source of true value and meaning in life.

Kierkegaard observes how the finitude of life makes it more valuable. When one only has a specific period of time to live, then every hour seems to be important. He gives the analogy of a merchant selling his goods for a specific price. When the goods become scarce, the price goes up since they are more difficult to obtain and are thus more in demand. Likewise, death makes our time scarce, and this makes each day infinitely valuable.[102] From the idea of our own death we can derive the value in our lives. Everything becomes meaningful since it is finite and transitory. There is, therefore, a dialectic involved in thinking about one's death and also having the right to enjoy and value one's life. The two are closely and necessarily related: "So, then, let death keep its power, 'that all is over,' but let life also keep the right to work while it is day; and let the earnest person seek the thought of death as an aid in that work."[103] The earnest thought of death sheds light on our lives in a positive manner.

7.8 Death as Indefinable and Inexplicable

Kierkegaard goes on to claim, "Concerning death's decision, the next thing that must be said is that it is *indefinable*. By this nothing is said, but this is the way it must be when the question is about an enigma."[104] The point seems to be that nothing can be known about death, which must always remain at bottom a mystery. Later Kierkegaard returns to this point: "So death is indefinable – the only certainty, and the only thing about which nothing is certain."[105] Nonetheless this does not stop people from engaging in discussions

---

[100] *Søren Kierkegaards Skrifter*, vol. 5, p. 453 (*Three Discourses on Imagined Occasions*, p. 83).
[101] *Søren Kierkegaards Skrifter*, vol. 5, p. 453 (*Three Discourses on Imagined Occasions*, p. 83).
[102] *Søren Kierkegaards Skrifter*, vol. 5, p. 453 (*Three Discourses on Imagined Occasions*, pp. 83f.).
[103] *Søren Kierkegaards Skrifter*, vol. 5, p. 454 (*Three Discourses on Imagined Occasions*, p. 84).
[104] *Søren Kierkegaards Skrifter*, vol. 5, p. 454 (*Three Discourses on Imagined Occasions*, p. 85).
[105] *Søren Kierkegaards Skrifter*, vol. 5, p. 460 (*Three Discourses on Imagined Occasions*, p. 91).

about death, where they speculate, for example, on why a certain person died at a certain time, or whether it was a relief or not. But, for Kierkegaard, all these kinds of speculations lead away from an earnest consideration of death as one's own death. This is precisely what is overlooked in the thoughtless discussions about the meaning of the death of someone else. Kierkegaard points out that people have a difficult time thinking about their own death and accepting the fact that it is inexplicable.[106] They therefore repress thoughts of this kind and prefer to live as if death did not exist. Only God can understand the mystery of death since he created and governs the universe "with wise and omnipresent purpose."[107] Here we can again see Kierkegaard's Christian commitments, which are not always so obvious.

Kierkegaard discusses in some detail how death makes everyone equal. This is an important motif that we also found in *The Nightwatches*.[108] Kierkegaard observes that equality in death can seem to be something attractive, especially to those who suffer in life from the inequalities of society. It can be a motivation for suicide. For Kierkegaard, however, this is not earnestness but rather a form of defiance of God. Instead, the correct view is, with the thought of earnestness about one's own death, to embrace life and to understand equality in the sense that we are all equal before God.[109] This idea allows us to be reconciled with the hardships and injustices of life that are caused by social inequalities. Equality in death is also an important motif in *The Flight of Human Life, or the Death-Dance*. The work is constructed in such a way that death visits people from every different station of society. In life they are all very different, but in death they are all the same. It is presumably a part of the enigma of death that we do not know why death takes people when he does. There seems to be no logic in this. It defies human understanding. A part of the earnestness thus means to be able to live with the uncertainty and enigma of death instead of repressing it or trying to speculate about possible explanations for it. While death itself is certain, what death *means* must remain forever uncertain.

After the discussion of indefinability, Kierkegaard introduces the notion of inexplicability: "Finally, it must be said of death's decision that it is inexplicable. That is, whether or not people find an explanation, death itself explains nothing."[110] Any kind of explanation that can be given to death is simply a reflection of the subjective views and desires of the person doing the explaining. The mere fact of death does not explain anything. It remains a mystery. Why did a certain person die here and now? No one can know. It could always have been different. It is absurd to claim that a person's death was "the supreme good fortune"

---

[106] *Søren Kierkegaards Skrifter*, vol. 5, p. 461 (*Three Discourses on Imagined Occasions*, p. 93).
[107] *Søren Kierkegaards Skrifter*, vol. 5, p. 461 (*Three Discourses on Imagined Occasions*, p. 93).
[108] [Klingemann], *Nachtwachen*, pp. 272f. (*The Nightwatches of Bonaventura*, p. 117).
[109] *Søren Kierkegaards Skrifter*, vol. 5, p. 458 (*Three Discourses on Imagined Occasions*, p. 89).
[110] *Søren Kierkegaards Skrifter*, vol. 5, p. 464 (*Three Discourses on Imagined Occasions*, p. 96).

7.8 DEATH AS INDEFINABLE AND INEXPLICABLE 233

or "the greatest misfortune."[111] There is no evidence that points in either direction. It is simply inexplicable. Both perspectives reflect a certain view of life but have nothing to do with the nature of death. The earnest person is the one who understands this and refrains from trying to give any kind of explanation. All forms of explanation of death are simply "diversion and absentmindedness in intellectual distraction."[112]

With the concepts of indefinability and inexplicability, Kierkegaard seems to want to establish a clear limit to human knowledge. Most talk about death is simply meaningless since in the end nothing can be known about it. It is a mystery. The problem is how we are able to manage to live with such an important thing being a mystery. Kierkegaard clearly thinks that just knowing with certainty that we will die is all we need to know in order to consider our lives carefully. But we must reject any further attempt to extend our knowledge beyond this bare fact to a more concrete picture of death being something positive or negative or something else altogether. The mystery of death is what frightens people, and so it is a difficult challenge to appropriate the earnest thought of one's own death in a way that does not make one constantly anxious and nervous, but we must find a way to do so, presumably with the help of God.

As in many of his other works, Kierkegaard seems to take a Socratic approach to the issue here.[113] As is well known, many of the Platonic dialogues end in *aporeia*. Socrates' interlocutors propose different definitions to his questions about the nature of truth, beauty, or justice, and he refutes each of them. In the end there is no positive conclusion or result. Socrates merely arrives at the point that the only thing that can be said is that one cannot know. It will be recalled that at the end of *The Apology*, after the death sentence has been issued, Socrates says that he does not fear death since he does not know

---

[111] *Søren Kierkegaards Skrifter*, vol. 5, p. 466 (*Three Discourses on Imagined Occasions*, p. 98).
[112] *Søren Kierkegaards Skrifter*, vol. 5, p. 468 (*Three Discourses on Imagined Occasions*, p. 100).
[113] For Kierkegaard's use of Socrates as a model, see Jon Stewart, *Søren Kierkegaard: Subjectivity, Irony and the Crisis of Modernity*, Oxford: Oxford University Press 2015; Benjamin Daise, *Kierkegaard's Socratic Art*, Macon, GA: Mercer University Press 1999; Wilfried Greve, *Kierkegaards maieutische Ethik*, Frankfurt am Main: Suhrkamp 1990; Jens Himmelstrup, *Søren Kierkegaards Opfattelse af Sokrates. En Studie i dansk Filosofis Historie*, Copenhagen: Arnold Busck 1924; Jacob Howland, *Kierkegaard and Socrates: A Study in Philosophy and Faith*, New York: Cambridge University Press 2006; Wolfdietrich von Kloeden, "Sokrates," in *Kierkegaard's Classical Inspiration*, ed. by Niels Thulstrup and Marie Mikulová Thulstrup, Copenhagen: C.A. Reitzel 1985 (*Bibliotheca Kierkegaardiana*, vol. 14), pp. 104–181; Wolfdietrich von Kloeden, *Kierkegaard und Sokrates. Sören Kierkegaards Sokratesrezeption*, Rheinland-Westfalen-Lippe: Evangelische Fachhochschule 1991; Hans Rudolf Schär, *Christliche Sokratik. Kierkegaard über den Gebrauch der Reflexion in der Christenheit*, Frankfurt am Main: Peter Lang Verlag 1977; Sophia Scopetea, *Kierkegaard og græciteten. En kamp med ironi*, Copenhagen: C.A. Reitzel 1995; Jon Stewart and Katalin Nun (eds.), *Kierkegaard and the Greek World*, tome I, *Socrates and Plato*, Aldershot: Ashgate 2010 (*Kierkegaard Research: Sources, Reception and Resources*, vol. 2).

what it is.[114] He mentions a couple of possibilities and concludes that neither of these is something to fear. But he refuses to say that he knows for certain anything about death. Kierkegaard also follows Socrates on this point with the idea of what he calls "the equilibrium of indecisiveness."[115] Even though one would very much like to know with certainty about death, or to pretend to know, for Kierkegaard it is important to maintain and respect the uncertainty about it. We must always keep in mind that we cannot know what death is, whether it is complete annihilation or a blissful afterlife. We must accept this *aporeia* and cease trying to find a way to solve the mystery and say something more about it. The real difficulty is thus to hold on to the uncertainty firmly.

This Socratic motif fits nicely with what Kierkegaard says at the end of the text when he claims that he is not teaching anything with the discourse. He explains,

> The person who has spoken here is, of course, not your teacher, my listener; he is merely letting you witness, just as he himself is doing, how a person seeks to learn something from the thought of death, that teacher of earnestness who at birth is appointed to everyone for a whole lifetime and who in the uncertainty is always ready to begin the instruction when it is requested.[116]

Thus, like Socrates, he claims to have no knowledge of death and to teach nothing. With the discourse Kierkegaard has merely enjoined his reader to reflect on the issue of death and its connection to one's own life. If there is a teacher, it is death itself, which should serve as a wake-up call for the living.

7.9 Kierkegaard's Contribution

While Jean Paul thinks that we need to embrace some form of life after death to be happy, Kierkegaard seems to believe that this is going too far since it makes a claim for something that we simply cannot know. Jean Paul is guilty of trying to define or explain death in some way. Kierkegaard would thus regard this solution as being unpersuasive from an epistemological perspective. Jean Paul would simply be engaging in wishful thinking with regard to life after death. The mere belief in an afterlife cannot really help us to be reconciled with human existence in the way Jean Paul seems to think. For Kierkegaard, it is impossible to rest assured as if in some kind of certainty about life after death.

All of this might seem strange to some readers who would emphasize that Kierkegaard, qua Christian author, should have some definitive view of immortality. His repeated claim that it is all over seems to emphasize the fact that with

---

[114] Plato, *Apology*, 40b–41d.
[115] *Søren Kierkegaards Skrifter*, vol. 5, p. 465 (*Three Discourses on Imagined Occasions*, p. 97).
[116] *Søren Kierkegaards Skrifter*, vol. 5, p. 469 (*Three Discourses on Imagined Occasions*, p. 102).

death all consciousness disappears. This view offers little consolation, which clashes with the key Christian doctrines of hope and an afterlife. Surely, one can say that one believes in an afterlife since death is a part of God's plan, and although we cannot know the meaning of it, God does, and we must trust in his wisdom and power. This then brings us to Kierkegaard's theory of religious faith, which follows much the same lines as his view of the idea of immortality. Kierkegaard repeatedly claims that, according to the scientific approach, belief in God is absurd, contradictory, paradoxical, and irrational. This is precisely the initial view of Jean Paul's Karlson regarding the question of immortality. One can nonetheless choose to believe despite all the evidence to the contrary, as Karlson does in the end. But this kind of belief is by no means an easy task. Even if one affirms that one believes in God and immortality, this will not prevent dark thoughts about death from creeping into one's mind or coming out in dreams when one is in despair. There is still a great uncertainty that can never be overcome. Jean Paul's solution is thus ineffective with regard to the practical side of living a more peaceful and happy life, which was the *desideratum* of the argument made by Gione.

For Jean Paul, the focus is on establishing a belief in immortality, which he thinks solves the problem of the meaninglessness of human existence. By contrast, for Kierkegaard, the focus is on the brute fact of death and what this might mean to us in our lives. He believes that earnest thinking about our own death is what is important. It is the only thing that is really in our power in any case. We can use the fact of the inevitability of our death and the finitude of our life to change how we live. Reflection on our own mortality provides an unaccustomed perspective that is important for every one of us. For Kierkegaard, there is no point in speculating about life after death or giving reasoned arguments for it in the way Jean Paul does (although to the latter's credit none of these arguments works and only an appeal to the irrationality of emotions manages to get Karlson to accede to the belief in an afterlife). For Kierkegaard, what is certain is that we will die. The question then becomes what this means for our lives and how we live them.

Kierkegaard sketches in some detail the despair and sense of meaninglessness that come with a nihilistic view, and in this sense he would certainly understand the grim portrayals found in Klingemann's *The Nightwatches* and Büchner's *Danton's Death*. However, unlike these works, Kierkegaard is clearly not recommending that we all just resign ourselves to the fact of death and annihilation and give up on life. His point seems rather to be that we should be reflective and sober about the inevitability of our own deaths and ask ourselves what this means to us as individuals. His position bears a resemblance to Møller's conception of having a complete worldview that involves a belief in immortality, although it stops short of this conclusion. He agrees with Møller on the need for a coherent worldview, but the difference is that, according to Kierkegaard's version of this, we are not obliged to embrace a doctrine of immortality, but rather we must maintain some open space for dwelling on the indefinability and inexplicability of death.

This position is far more subtle than that of either Jean Paul or Møller. A true follower of Socrates, Kierkegaard enjoins us to keep the question of our mortality in our minds and resist the great temptation to ascribe to it some determinate meaning, either positive or negative. We should dwell in Socratic *aporeia*, although this is uncomfortable for most people. Kierkegaard thus seems to agree with Klingemann and Büchner that there is no ultimate solution to nihilism, but this by no means needs to be something debilitating. As was the case with Shelley's "Ozymandias," the threat of death and the finitude of our existence can teach us something about our own lives if we are brave enough to be receptive to it. The awareness of death and its indefinability and inexplicability give us an unaccustomed perspective that can lead to positive changes in our lives. Shelley's plea was about the need to be humble and kind to others, with king Ozymandias serving as the negative example. Kierkegaard's message is considerably vaguer. He leaves it to the individual readers to interpret for themselves what their mortality means for their lives. In this sense he refrains from any explicit preaching or moralizing. There is, of course, much more that can be said about Kierkegaard and nihilism, but this should suffice to demonstrate that it is an important dimension in his thought and that he has his own unique approach to it that represents an important contribution to the nineteenth-century discussion.

8

Turgenev's Portrait of a Nihilist

While the term "nihilism" existed before in the work of Poul Martin Møller,[1] it was made popular in the second half of the nineteenth century by the Russian nihilist movement, with figures such as Dmitry Pisarev (1840–68) and Nicholas Chernyshevsky (1828–89).[2] This was a cultural and social movement that rejected the values and institutions of the past. The nihilist movement in Russian culture is usually thought to cover the period from around 1855 to around 1870. Although the individual thinkers who constituted the movement are not generally well known today, their spirit comes to life in a series of memorable fictional characters from Russian literature. The movement arose from the developments in the natural sciences and the rise of scientific materialism at the time. In contrast to many of the other examples of nihilism that we have explored above, which concerned specific characters or thinkers regarded as strange, isolated individuals, the Russian nihilist movement was an identifiable group phenomenon that involved several young people.[3] While they were indeed regarded by the mainstream as outsiders with strange ideas, their movement nonetheless can be said to have had a social dimension with a high degree of solidarity among its members. They were not loners and misanthropes like Kreuzgang or Kierkegaard's aesthete.

The Russian writer Ivan Turgenev (1818–83) provided an influential portrait of a nihilist in his character Bazarov from his novel *Fathers and Sons* from 1862.[4]

---

[1] See the discussion of the origin of the word in Johan Goudsblom, *Nihilism and Culture*, Totowa, NJ: Rowman and Littlefield 1980, pp. 3–7.

[2] See "The Nihilists," in *Russian Philosophy*, vol. 2, *The Nihilists, The Populists, Critics of Religion and Culture*, by James M. Edie, James P. Scanlan, and Mary-Barbara Zeldin, Chicago: Quadrangle Books 1965, pp. 1–108 (this work contains valuable source materials for the Russian nihilist movement); Philip Pomper, "The Period of Nihilism, 1855–1869," in his *The Russian Revolutionary Intelligensia*, New York: Thomas Y. Crowell 1970, pp. 59–100; Daniel R. Brower, *Training the Nihilists: Education and Radicalism in Tsarist Russia*, Ithaca, NY and London: Cornell University Press 1975.

[3] See Stepniak [sc. Sergey Mikhaylovich Stepnyak-Kravchinsky], *Underground Russia: Revolutionary Profiles*, New York: Charles Scribner's Sons 1883, pp. 244f.

[4] Ivan S. Turgenev, *Fathers and Sons*, trans. by Bernard Guibert Guerney, New York: Random House 1961. See Michael Allen Gillespie, *Nihilism before Nietzsche*, Chicago: University of Chicago Press 1996, pp. 145–156.

Turgenev portrays the rise of nihilism as a conflict between the older and the younger generation in Russia. The older generation believed itself to represent progressive ideas, for example, supporting the emancipation of the serfs in 1861 under Emperor Alexander II (1818–81) and reading French and German literature from the Enlightenment and the Romantic period. However, for the younger nihilists, the generation of their fathers still embraced a number of reactionary ideas and values. The nihilists wanted a full-scale criticism of everything. A key component of this conception of nihilism was a biting social criticism of the reigning values and institutions, in a way similar to what we saw in *The Nightwatches*, Schopenhauer, and Kierkegaard.

With his character sketch of Bazarov, Turgenev made the Russian nihilist movement famous throughout Europe. The story tells of the homecoming of the young Arkady Kirsanov who just graduated from the University of Saint Petersburg. He brings with him his friend from the university, Bazarov. The novel depicts the conflicts that arise when the two young men stay at Maryino, the rural estate of Arkady's father Nicholai. The disputes break out between the younger generation – Arkady and Bazarov – and the older generation, represented by Nicholai and his brother Pavel. In the course of these disputes, Bazarov, with the support of Arkady, confidently articulates the nihilistic view of things, to the consternation of the brothers. Turgenev thus depicts this as a conflict between the two generations that was characteristic of the times.

8.1 Kropotkin's Characterization of the Nihilist Movement

In his *Memoirs of a Revolutionist*, the Russian anarchist Peter Kropotkin (1842–1921) gives an insightful firsthand account of the nihilist movement and its causes.[5] He explains that after the abolition of serfdom, there nonetheless remained firmly in place most all the previous hierarchical structures that dominated Russian society. These were highly repressive and did not allow for the development of the individual:

> A formidable movement was developing in the meantime amongst the educated youth of Russia. Serfdom was abolished. But quite a network of habits and customs of domestic slavery, of utter disregard of human individuality, of despotism on the part of the fathers, and of hypocritical submission on that of the wives, the sons, and the daughters, had developed during the two hundred and fifty years that serfdom had existed.[6]

The nihilist movement thus tried to attack these long-standing repressive customs and traditions in order to make possible individual freedom. Kropotkin

---

[5] Peter Kropotkin, *Memoirs of a Revolutionist*, vols. 1–2, London: Smith, Elder & Co. 1899, vol. 2, pp. 83–91.
[6] Kropotkin, *Memoirs of a Revolutionist*, vol. 2, p. 83.

8.1 KROPOTKIN'S CHARACTERIZATION OF THE NIHILIST

celebrates this movement as a particularly Russian phenomenon that reached a level of radicalism for which there was no pendant in Western Europe or America. Kropotkin also notes that the movement was closely associated with that of the sciences: the nihilist "in his philosophical conceptions ... was a positivist, an agnostic, a Spencerian evolutionist, or a scientific materialist."[7]

Kropotkin begins by explaining what he takes to be the basic principles of nihilism. He writes,

> First of all, the nihilist declared war upon what may be described as "the conventional lies of civilized mankind." Absolute sincerity was his distinctive feature, and in the name of that sincerity he gave up, and asked others to give up, those superstitions, prejudices, habits, and customs which their own reason could not justify. He refused to bend before any authority except that of reason, and in the analysis of every social institution or habit he revolted against any sort of more or less masked sophism.[8]

Nihilism's goal, on this account, was a kind of liberation that must start by destroying the repressive habits and customs that had been accepted without critical reflection for so long. It takes aim not at the religion or superstitions of the lower classes but rather at the hypocrisy of the upper classes who make use of traditional values and beliefs to their own advantage.

Kropotkin also emphasizes the importance of sincerity, frankness, and authenticity for the nihilists. They disdain the traditional forms of politeness and speak directly what they think. The nihilist "carried his love of sincerity even into the minutest details of everyday life. He discarded the conventional forms of society talk and expressed his opinions in a blunt and terse way, even with a certain affectation of outward roughness."[9] This practice led others to believe that the nihilists were arrogant or conceited, but this is not the case. They were simply disabused of the hypocritical social rules that enjoin people to dissemble their true feelings and views. The nihilists thus stand in opposition to "the smooth amiability" of the older generation, which appears to them as both stupid and naïve.[10] While the older generation revels in high-sounding idealist philosophy and sentimentalism, it nonetheless engages in the most base and cruel forms of oppression in their own household. The aristocrats quickly forget their high ideals when they punish their daughters, wives, and servants, thus denying to them their freedom and individual development.

Kropotkin notes that a part of the nihilist program was a rejection of art as something vain and useless:

> Art was involved in the same sweeping negation. Continual talk about beauty, the ideal, art for art's sake, aesthetics, and the like, so willingly

[7] Kropotkin, *Memoirs of a Revolutionist*, vol. 2, p. 85.
[8] Kropotkin, *Memoirs of a Revolutionist*, vol. 2, pp. 84f.
[9] Kropotkin, *Memoirs of a Revolutionist*, vol. 2, p. 86.
[10] Kropotkin, *Memoirs of a Revolutionist*, vol. 2, p. 85.

indulged in—while every object of art was bought with money exacted from starving peasants or from underpaid workers, and the so-called "worship of the beautiful" was but a mask to cover the most commonplace dissoluteness—inspired him [sc. the nihilist] with disgust.[11]

Here it is clear that the rejection of art is connected to the larger conception of social reform. On this account, the nihilists have sentiments that are close to those of socialists, communists, and anarchists in their desire to improve the lot of the working classes and free them from the tyranny of poverty caused by their being exploited by the upper classes. This seems to stand at variance from the other forms of nihilism that we have explored. While Kreuzgang had sympathy for the poor and the downtrodden, he never really develops this into a plan for social reform as such. He is content merely to make fun of the hypocrites in society who exploit the poor. Likewise, Kierkegaard's aesthete prefers to remain silent instead of engaging in social activism.[12]

Kropotkin also mentions the nihilist women and indicates a clear connection between nihilism and an incipient feminism. He notes how many young women from upper-class families chose to assert their independence instead of following the path planned for them by their parents, who obliged them to get married and remain housewives for the rest of their days. Instead, the "nihilist girl ... put on a black woolen dress of the plainest description, cut off her hair, and went to a high school, in order to win there her personal independence."[13] Likewise, women who were unhappy in their marriages left with their children to live a life of poverty rather than continuing a life of hypocrisy with a man whom they did not love. Here marriage is portrayed as repressive towards women: it makes them slaves to their husbands and prevents them from pursuing education and meaningful work.

The nihilist rejects the hypocrisy of those who claim to be concerned about the sad lot of the poor, while they themselves live in luxury. The nihilist would have no compunction about saying this directly to the face of the hypocrite as honesty would dictate, but which social convention would forbid. In an effort to enlighten women to assert their own individuality, "the nihilist would rebuke the woman who indulged in small talk and prided herself on her 'womanly' manners and elaborate toilette. He would bluntly say to a pretty young person: 'How is it that you are not ashamed to talk this nonsense and to wear that chignon of false hair?'"[14] By contrast, the nihilist was eager to help women

---

[11] Kropotkin, *Memoirs of a Revolutionist*, vol. 2, pp. 85f.
[12] [Victor Eremita], *Enten-Eller. Et Livs-Fragment*, vols. 1–2, Copenhagen: C.A. Reitzel 1843, vol. 1, pp. 21f. (in *Søren Kierkegaards Skrifter*, vols. 1–28, K1–K28, Copenhagen: Gad Publishers 1997–2012, vol. 2, p. 44) (English translation: *Either/Or*, vols. 1–2, trans. by Howard V. Hong and Edna H. Hong, Princeton, NJ: Princeton University Press 1987, vol. 1, p. 35).
[13] Kropotkin, *Memoirs of a Revolutionist*, vol. 2, p. 86.
[14] Kropotkin, *Memoirs of a Revolutionist*, vol. 2, p. 88.

who showed a desire to develop their own abilities and learn new things about the modern world.

In his characterization of nihilism Kropotkin refers explicitly to Turgenev's portrayal of Bazarov in *Fathers and Sons*.[15] He criticizes Turgenev's character as follows:

> We found him too harsh, especially in his relations with his old parents, and, above all, we reproached him with his seeming neglect of his duties as a citizen. Russian youth could not be satisfied with the merely negative attitude of Turgenev's hero. Nihilism, with its affirmation of the rights of the individual and its negation of all hypocrisy, was but a first step toward a higher type of men and women, who are equally free, but live for a great cause.[16]

Kropotkin explicitly singles out the element of social reform in the nihilist movement, which he takes Turgenev to have misrepresented. According to Kropotkin's account, the young nihilists asserted their own individual freedom by breaking with their families. Then they were keen to use their newfound freedom to help the masses. They thus went to the provinces to become doctors or schoolteachers in order to improve the condition of the poor. They gave up their lives in aristocratic families to live with the peasants. Turgenev's Bazarov does have great sympathy for the poor and tries to help them in this way as a doctor. But he denies that he has any kind of social-political agenda or program as Kropotkin believes he should. Kropotkin was himself a political agitator for anarchism, and it might be that his own political investment caused him to place more emphasis on this aspect of the Russian nihilist movement than was actually warranted.

8.2 Bazarov's Materialism and Scientific Spirit

The first thing that we learn about Turgenev's Bazarov at the beginning of *Fathers and Sons* is that he is a student of the natural sciences and is working to be a medical doctor.[17] Bazarov's scientific spirit is a central theme of the work. He is constantly portrayed as exploring the world of nature, collecting plants and insects, examining the trees on the estate of Arkady's father, dissecting animals, studying objects under his microscope, and conducting scientific experiments. Like Jean Paul's Karlson, he believes only in the material world and what science can teach about it. Everything else is regarded as old-fashioned superstition. This is an important aspect of Bazarov's background as a nihilist. As with the other figures we have examined, the scientific advances of the day were highly compelling for the young generation and caused them to call

---

[15] Kropotkin, *Memoirs of a Revolutionist*, vol. 2, pp. 84, 88f.
[16] Kropotkin, *Memoirs of a Revolutionist*, vol. 2, pp. 84, 89.
[17] Turgenev, *Fathers and Sons*, p. 11.

into question the views of their elders, which the former believed were steeped in irrationality. The scientific view led the nihilists to want to destroy society and start again from the ground up.

One interesting example of this can be found in Bazarov's explanation to two peasant boys of his need for frogs for dissection. When they ask why he wants to know what the inside of frogs looks like, Bazarov answers, "so's to avoid mistakes if you should happen to fall sick and it were up to me to treat you."[18] Bazarov thus draws an analogy between human beings and frogs, which is not lost on the boys. One of them responds to his friend, "You hear that ...? The gentleman says you and I are no different than frogs. Sounds funny to me!"[19] This exchange highlights Bazarov's scientific materialism. He is clearly familiar with Darwin's then new theory of evolution by natural selection. He sees no fundamental difference between humans and the animal world, all of which are products of nature. Humans are physical beings just like any other animal. This view stands in sharp contrast to the traditional Christian picture that makes a strict distinction between humans and the animals, claiming that it was God who made humans in his image and only later made the animals to serve them. This is the kind of view that Bazarov believes is mere superstition and needs to be eliminated in favor of the more rational explanation given by science.

An antipathy quickly arises between Bazarov and Arkady's uncle Pavel, who regards the unexpected guest as unkempt, conceited, and lax with regard to social protocol. By contrast, Bazarov finds it laughable that Pavel continues to observe aristocratic habits in the countryside, maintaining meticulously kept nails, a close shave, a perfumed mustache, a tie, and an aristocratic way of dressing as if he were a regular guest at dinner parties given by the elite of Moscow or Saint Petersburg. He is attentive to the correct ways of doing things and the expectations of society. Bazarov thus declares Arkady's uncle to be an "archaic phenomenon."[20] From this it is already clear that Bazarov has no patience for pretension or aristocratic habits. These belong to the past and should be forgotten. There is no need to put on airs in modern society. Pavel's comportment demonstrates the vanity, stupidity, and worthlessness of Russian aristocratic culture.

Bazarov the next day goes out and inspects the farm and the property of the estate, which he, aided by his knowledge of the sciences, finds to be in a poor condition. He meets the two abovementioned peasant boys "with whom he immediately struck up a friendship."[21] Here Bazarov again shows that he is indifferent to class distinctions. He is able to relate immediately to the uneducated boys and to develop a friendly rapport with them. It is not beneath his dignity to have this kind of intercourse with the lower classes. The boys help

---

[18] Turgenev, *Fathers and Sons*, p. 25.
[19] Turgenev, *Fathers and Sons*, p. 25. Translation slightly modified.
[20] Turgenev, *Fathers and Sons*, p. 22.
[21] Turgenev, *Fathers and Sons*, pp. 24f.

Bazarov to collect frogs for dissection, and, as noted, he happily explains to them the scientific value of such a study. In time Bazarov also develops good relations with the servants on the estate who come to regard him as one of their own and not as one of their masters like the others.

Arkady likewise shows a generous and forward-thinking spirit in his discussion with his father. While not as dogmatic or direct as Bazarov, Arkady shares his friend's nihilistic orientation. He reveres Bazarov as a kind of mentor. Arkady learns that his father has had a child with a young servant girl, Theodosia. For Nicholai, this is a matter of some embarrassment given his old-fashioned value system. Arkady hastens to assure him that he finds no problem with the amorous relation or the new child. On the contrary, he rejoices at his father's happiness. In this way, Arkady also shows that he dismisses the ethical views of the past, and that he is indifferent to class distinctions. He is a modern, progressively minded young man with no use for an old-fashioned sense of morality.

Over breakfast, Nicholai and Pavel curiously ask Arkady about his friend Bazarov, and Arkady bluntly declares, "He is a nihilist."[22] The older men ponder what this could mean. Nicholai recognizes the Latin origin of the word and concludes that this must mean that Bazarov is someone who accepts or believes in nothing. More critically, Pavel interprets the word to refer to someone who respects nothing. Arkady corrects them both and defines a nihilist as someone who "regards everything from a critical point of view."[23] This clearly places the focus on the social criticism of the nihilist position. There is no mention of issues such as mortality or the meaninglessness of human existence in the face of the scientific worldview, as we have seen in the earlier authors. Arkady elaborates that the nihilist accepts nothing on authority or faith. Instead, the nihilist exposes everything to the test of critical reason and reflection. On this definition, nihilism follows in the tradition of rationalism. The view resembles Descartes's method of systematic doubt that calls everything into question in order first to determine what can be known without any doubt and then to try to build on this principle. One can ask how it is even possible to subject absolutely everything to critical examination. Surely, we need to assume certain basic things in order to function normally. As Descartes observed, while this kind of thing sounds good as a slogan, in practice it is impossible since, despite one's best efforts, one will always be working with assumptions and unreflective views of certain things. I have to believe that I am sitting here at this moment. Descartes resolves this with the famous idea of the evil deceiver who tricks him about absolutely everything. But this is just a methodological tool that he uses to get started. Yet as a practical matter, the idea seems completely implausible.

Pavel is quick to object that it is important to respect authority and tradition and to take certain things on faith. He finds it absurd to throw out age-old

---

[22] Turgenev, *Fathers and Sons*, p. 29.
[23] Turgenev, *Fathers and Sons*, p. 30.

traditions and customs for no good reason. Such things constitute the very fabric of society. He argues that without these we are left with a "void" or "vacuum."[24] If all the old traditions and institutions were destroyed, there would be nothing left. It would be impossible for people to live together in the social sphere, without that sphere being governed by generally accepted rules. When Bazarov joins them for breakfast, Pavel, now sufficiently provoked, is keen to question him critically. Pavel's mood is described as follows: "He was beginning to feel a secret irritation. Bazarov's utter nonchalance went against the grain of Pavel Petrovich's aristocratic nature. This son of a sawbones was not only not cowed – he actually answered back, curtly and grudgingly, and there was something rude, well-nigh insolent about the tone of his voice."[25] In a discussion of the merits of German culture, Pavel mentions the favorites of his generation, Schiller and Goethe. Bazarov regards this as hopeless sentimentalism. He shocks his interlocutor by claiming, "A passable chemist is twenty times more useful than any poet."[26] In line with Kropotkin's characterization, Bazarov is dismissive of poetry and idealist philosophy since they engage in abstractions. He returns to this again later when Pavel tries to defend the merits of the Italian artist, Raphael. Bazarov boldly states, "According to me ... Raphael isn't worth a sou marquee."[27] For him the only things that have any value are those that are real, that is, the objects that can be studied by the hard sciences or used for some concrete purpose. Everything else is a waste of time. Turgenev's portrayal of the nihilist view of poetry and art is not quite complete with this account. The nihilists tended to be utilitarian, believing that whatever they did should be based on scientific facts and should be for the good of society. Thus, some of the nihilists believed that art could serve the utilitarian function of awakening people to the ills of the day and teaching them the practice of social criticism. If didactical, art could be seen as consistent with the nihilist program. However, as is well known, this kind of art tends quickly to turn into ideology, which differs radically from any of the traditional objectives of art.

What is important here is that Bazarov clearly makes a judgment about what is important and valuable and what is not. This seems to run contrary to the view of nihilism that says that everything is meaningless since humans are completely insignificant in the universe. Yet, even such radical nihilist figures as Kreuzgang and Schopenhauer also do not shy away from value judgments. This is important for their social criticism, which can work only if they assume that the values of society are mistaken and some other values are correct. How can this inconsistency be reconciled? The point seems to be that one is free to posit one's own values based on scientific reason, provided that one

---

[24] Turgenev, *Fathers and Sons*, p. 31.
[25] Turgenev, *Fathers and Sons*, p. 33.
[26] Turgenev, *Fathers and Sons*, p. 35.
[27] Turgenev, *Fathers and Sons*, p. 73.

8.2 BAZAROV'S MATERIALISM AND SCIENTIFIC SPIRIT   245

has thought them through for oneself. The mistake is to accept things merely on faith or cultural authority. So, one can question whether such a view is still really nihilistic since it simply replaces one value system with another one. The more consistent nihilistic position would maintain that everything is meaningless, including all science, reason, and so on, since these things also can be counted as belonging to the many illusions that people try to maintain in the face of the nothingness.

Pavel tries to catch Bazarov in a contradiction. He points out that Bazarov claims to reject all belief and authority, yet he believes in science and accepts its authority.[28] Bazarov rejects this contradiction, again reasserting that he does not believe in anything. With regard to science, he has studied it for himself and has found it rational, and therefore he has given his assent to it. So, there was never any question of simply believing in something blindly. This exchange demonstrates the fundamentally different conceptions of individual freedom that the two men have. For Pavel, freedom means having the ability to do one's duty and receive what one is due. For society to function, we must have some basic beliefs in the system that governs it. With this comes a system of authority that we must simply accept whether we like it or not. But for Bazarov the idea of freedom is all about consent. In society we are born into specific power structures that custom obliges us to obey. But these are not based on reason, and we never gave our consent to them. The structures are repressive and prevent us from developing our freedom. Thus, we are not obliged to take on faith, even the opinion of experts in fields that we do not know much about. We should, of course, listen to their opinions and hear their reasoning for them, but we should never give up our own rational capacity to evaluate this critically and come to our own conclusions. We can never allow someone to exercise authority over us in this way. In this regard his position resembles that of the anarchists Bakunin and Kropotkin.

Pavel becomes bitterly sarcastic about how the people of his generation, despite all of their experience and learning, are callously written off by the self-confident younger generation with their new views. When Nicholai and Pavel depart with a mixture of anger and frustration, Bazarov laments the shallowness of their perspective, which he refers to as "vanity, dandified mannerisms, [and] foppery."[29]

When they are alone later, Arkady tries to defend his uncle against Bazarov's criticisms, asking his friend to show some restraint and recognize that Pavel was born and raised in an earlier age, when education was very different. Bazarov quickly dismisses this: "'Education?' Bazarov caught at the word. 'Every man must educate himself – well, just as I have done, for example.'"[30] The idea is clearly that education is available to anyone at any time since it merely requires the faculty of critical thinking. If a person is unable to develop this faculty, for

---

[28] Turgenev, *Fathers and Sons*, p. 35.
[29] Turgenev, *Fathers and Sons*, p. 36.
[30] Turgenev, *Fathers and Sons*, p. 45.

whatever reason, then they cannot regard themselves as truly educated. The concept of education is thus closely connected to the given definition of nihilism as not accepting anything as true without putting it to one's own critical test. Education at bottom means not accumulating a vast amount of information but rather thinking for oneself.

8.3 The Nihilist View of Love and Marriage

Arkady tries to mitigate Bazarov's negative disposition towards Pavel by telling the story of his uncle, who fell in love with a sophisticated princess and, after a short affair, was rejected by her. This was the defining moment in Pavel's life that he never recovered from. Instead of making Bazarov more sympathetic towards Pavel, Arkady's story simply renders him more disdainful. Bazarov finds Pavel's romantic feelings laughable. For Bazarov, the attraction between the sexes is merely a biological fact of nature, but culture creates a silly mystique around this in the name of love. Bazarov exclaims, "All that is romanticism, twaddle, dry rot, artiness."[31] In this respect Bazarov's view of love is similar to that of Kreuzgang in *The Nightwatches*.[32] Love is just an absurd notion that our culture has drummed into us, but in the end, it is based on simple physiological facts that do not warrant any particular cultural celebration. It should be noted that later in the work, like Kreuzgang, Bazarov seems to repent of this view when he himself falls in love.

Bazarov meets Theodosia who is sitting outside with her child and is keen to win her friendship. When Arkady tells him the story of his father's amorous relation to her, Bazarov salutes her. While traditional morality would condemn her relationship with Nicholai as scandalous due to the differences in their age and social class, Theodosia is not overly ashamed of the situation and does not subscribe to bourgeois ethics about such things. Arkady is keen to show his own progressive views and explains that he thinks that his father should marry her, despite what people might think. But his comment has the opposite of the intended effect since Bazarov reproaches him for having old-fashioned views on the matter: "You still attribute significance to marriage – I didn't expect that of you."[33] Clearly Bazarov regards marriage as an antiquated and oppressive institution in the way that Kropotkin outlined.

Bazarov rejects what he regards as all the mistaken ideas of others who are slavishly following custom and tradition. He claims, "The only important thing is that two times two makes four, while everything else is all bosh."[34] Again he does not hesitate to posit a value judgment. His appeal to mathematics as the only thing that can be known with certainty again aligns him with the

---

[31] Turgenev, *Fathers and Sons*, p. 45.
[32] See Chapter 2, Sect. 2.5, pp. 82–87.
[33] Turgenev, *Fathers and Sons*, p. 57.
[34] Turgenev, *Fathers and Sons*, p. 58.

rationalists. Arkady tries to raise a counterargument by pointing to nature, which he argues should also be regarded as important. But Bazarov likewise rejects this: "And nature, too, is bosh – the way you conceive it. Nature is no temple but a workshop, and man is the worker therein."[35] Here Bazarov is critical of the romantic view of nature, which regards the natural world as an object of beauty and reverence. By contrast, he regards it with the eyes of a natural scientist. It is a "workshop" since it allows humans to observe and understand it. A part of this takes place by means of scientific experimentation. But, for Bazarov, there is nothing in itself beautiful about nature. It is simply a brute fact like that of mathematics. The job of humans is to try to use rational methods to understand it. Then based on this knowledge, people can work to use nature to improve the human condition.

8.4 The Criticism of Aristocracy

When Nicholai inadvertently overhears Bazarov referring to him as behind the times or as a "has-been,"[36] whose day has passed, he does not get offended, but instead seems to acknowledge the criticism and take it to heart, although he does not understand it fully. He brings this up with his brother Pavel and expresses his regret that this stands in the way of him having a closer relationship to his son Arkady. As evidence to back up his claim, Bazarov cites that he saw Nicholai reading Pushkin, which, to his mind, belongs to hopelessly naïve literature that should be immediately discarded. He proposes that Arkady give his father some real instructive reading such as the work by the German philosopher and scientist Ludwig Büchner, entitled *Kraft und Stoff. Empirisch-naturphilosophische Studien* from 1855.[37] As noted above,[38] Ludwig Büchner was the younger brother of Georg Büchner, the author of *Danton's Death*. The book *Kraft und Stoff* is known for its radical materialism, which cost its author his position as lecturer in medicine at the University of Tübingen. Nonetheless it proved to be a popular work that was reprinted several times. Indeed, we are told that Arkady gave his father a copy of the ninth edition of the work.[39] So in effect Bazarov believes that reading this work of a radical materialist will help to enlighten Arkady's father and free him from the prejudices of the past. When Arkady gives his father a copy of the book, Nicholai cannot make any sense of it.

Puzzled, Nicholai struggles to understand the young men since by his own estimate he is himself a very progressively minded person and is so regarded

---

[35] Turgenev, *Fathers and Sons*, p. 58.
[36] Turgenev, *Fathers and Sons*, p. 61.
[37] Ludwig Büchner, *Kraft und Stoff. Empirisch-naturphilosophische Studien. In allgemeinverständlicher Darstellung*, Frankfurt am Main: Meidinger Sohn & Cie 1855.
[38] See the introduction to Chapter 5, p. 149.
[39] Turgenev, *Fathers and Sons*, p. 63.

by others as well. But then in comparison to the standards set by Bazarov and Arkady, he is a reactionary:

> There's only one thing that I can't grasp. I'm doing everything, it seems, not to fall behind the times; I've arranged things for the peasants, I have started a farm—why, they actually style me a Red all over the province; I read, I study, I strive—on the whole—to keep up with the demands of the times, yet they're saying my act is over.[40]

Evidence of their progressive views comes later when Nicholai and Pavel ignore the invitation of a relation who has become an important person in the province and wishes to parade his power and authority as privy councilor.[41] To their credit the brothers find this laughable. The problem is that Nicholai regards himself as progressive based on the views that he was brought up with. However, the new views of the present day are far more radical than this.

The conflict between Bazarov and Pavel comes to a head over evening tea. When Bazarov makes a remark about a mutual acquaintance, whom he dubs a "wretched little aristocrat,"[42] Pavel gives a spirited defense of the aristocratic class. Like his brother Nicholai, Pavel insists that he is "a liberal and a man who loves progress."[43] He refers to the English aristocracy as a source of social progress: "They do not yield an iota of their rights, and therefore respect the rights of others; they demand the fulfillment of the obligations due them, and therefore they themselves fulfill *their* obligations. The aristocracy has given freedom to England, and it supports that freedom."[44] As noted, for Pavel, the concept of freedom means giving each person their due in accordance with the social hierarchy, but it does not include a conception of equality. Each class has its own duties that it is required to fulfill, and the great differences in these duties among the different classes are irrelevant. Pavel goes on to make the claim that for the aristocrats fulfilling one's obligations is a matter of self-respect and an awareness of one's one value. This high sense of personal integrity in the aristocrats is what provides the very foundation of society and allows for progress to take place. The aristocrats do their duty and advance society by working for the public good. Pavel continues in a more direct tone, "I know very well, for example, that it pleases you to find amusement in my habits, my dress – my personal neatness, if it comes to that; all this, however, emanates from a sense of self-respect, from a sense of duty – yes sir, yes sir: duty."[45]

Bazarov objects that Pavel is doing nothing at all to advance the public good by just hanging around at his brother's estate and putting on aristocratic airs.

---

[40] Turgenev, *Fathers and Sons*, p. 62.
[41] Turgenev, *Fathers and Sons*, p. 64.
[42] Turgenev, *Fathers and Sons*, p. 64.
[43] Turgenev, *Fathers and Sons*, p. 65.
[44] Turgenev, *Fathers and Sons*, p. 65.
[45] Turgenev, *Fathers and Sons*, p. 66.

Pavel refuses to answer for his own case but returns to the general question: "All I want to say is that aristocracy is a principle, and it is solely immoral and frivolous people who can live without principles in our time."[46] Bazarov makes it clear that he rejects Pavel's conception of aristocracy, progress, liberalism, and principles, which he claims are good for nothing. These are meaningless abstractions that do not result in any concrete improvements in society.

This is inconceivable to Pavel, who regards it as a direct attack on all forms of civilized life. Highly agitated, he asks how Bazarov can possibly deny principles since they are necessary for one to act in the world at all. The only principle that the nihilists seem to have is the rejection of all authority and everything that does not pass the test of critical reason. Astonished, Pavel continues to question Bazarov about his views, and in the subsequent discussion the nihilist program begins to emerge.

8.5 Nihilism as Negation

Bazarov emphasizes that nihilism is about negation. He argues, "We act by virtue of that which we acknowledge to be useful. At the present time repudiation is the most useful of all."[47] This claim is coupled with the assertion that he negates everything. This seems a bit odd since it is not clear how the negation of everything can be useful to anyone. While Pavel is nonplussed by this, his less combative brother Nicholai raises the obvious objection: "You're repudiating everything, or, to put it more exactly, you're demolishing everything. But then, it is necessary to be constructive as well."[48] The response of both Bazarov and Arkady is that at the present time what is necessary is to clear the ground completely of all reactionary and oppressive customs, traditions, and views since they are standing in the way of any real social progress. This is the immediate need of the time, and the issue of the construction of something different with which to replace these will only come later. This is relevant for Kierkegaard's observation that a general criticism of everything via irony is important for everyone at some point, but this should not be regarded as a solution to anything. Negativity is a means to get to the truth, but it is not the truth itself.[49] This is the intuition behind Nicholai's question. He too can accept some forms of social criticism, but this must be in the service of some clear positive goal, which, to his amazement, Bazarov seems not to have.

It might be claimed that Bazarov's insistence on sheer negativity without any positive program resembles Büchner's Danton, who ends in resignation,

---

[46] Turgenev, *Fathers and Sons*, p. 66.
[47] Turgenev, *Fathers and Sons*, p. 67.
[48] Turgenev, *Fathers and Sons*, p. 67.
[49] *Søren Kierkegaards Skrifter*, vol. 1, p. 356 (*The Concept of Irony*, p. 327). See John 14:6. This was discussed in Chapter 7, Sect. 7.1, pp. 204–205.

completing giving up on politics. But there is an important difference here. While Danton has become so disenchanted with the world that he ultimately gives up, Bazarov, by contrast, still has the zeal of a revolutionary, even though he has no positive plan. Danton is jaded and has no desire or energy to launch a movement aimed at the complete destruction of beliefs, traditions, and institutions. Bazarov, however, still seems to care about some kind of undefined cause, although he denies it, and so he continues his negative campaign. It might be argued that Büchner's character is closer to the original sense of nihilism as a belief in nothing. Since Danton has lost his belief in everything, he no longer has any desire to pursue any particular social-political cause. By contrast, Bazarov still has some intuitions about truth and meaning, despite his ostensible negative stance and lack of any positive social program. It is this that gives him the motivation to carry on. He would thus not, strictly speaking, count as a nihilist when defined as someone who believes in nothing. He clearly does hold dearly certain beliefs about social justice. The true nihilist would be completely indifferent or cynical towards politics, like Danton or even Klingemann's Kreuzgang. It might be claimed that Shelley could also be put in this group since "Ozymandias" seems to suggest the uselessness of any political goals or achievements, which will always be erased by time.

As this negative social program begins to emerge, Pavel objects to the fact that the nihilists have arrogantly set themselves up as judges of the desires and needs of the Russian people. He argues that the people in fact both want and need tradition and faith, both of which the nihilists flatly reject. While Bazarov concedes this point, his counterargument is that the people cling to many absurd superstitions that no thinking person could accept, and so nothing really follows from this. The implication is clearly that the people do not really know themselves what they want or need since they are so steeped in confused, prescientific ideas. Bazarov's position resembles that of Büchner's Danton, who has great empathy for the struggles of the people and at the same time is under no illusions about their poor critical thinking skills, which make them vulnerable to the deceptions of cynical politicians. Bazarov again brings the argument to the personal level by pointing out that he has a far better rapport with the peasants than does Pavel or Nicholai, who regard them with a degree of contempt. The peasants would much more readily accept him than one of the aristocrats. This argument seems intended to support the implied claim that the nihilists know best what the people need; indeed, that they know this even better than the people themselves. Thus, an important element in the argument concerns a sense of Russian nationalism. Both the aristocrats and the nihilists acknowledge that they have some kind of a duty to help improve Russian society at this difficult time of transition. However, they vary greatly on where the problems lie and what the solutions should be.

Given what Bazarov has said, Pavel draws the conclusion that the nihilists are social reformers. But Bazarov is quick to deny this. He claims that reformers

8.5 NIHILISM AS NEGATION

are simply hypocrites who sit around and talk endlessly about social ills and how to combat them. These discussions lead to nothing but "banality and doctrinarism."[50] While the so-called reformers go on discussing highfalutin ideas, the poor continue to be exploited and starve. The needs of the peasants are more basic than any abstract theory of social reform. They simply need obvious things such as education, health care, and food. For this reason, Bazarov believes that the reforms of the government fall well short of the mark and will have little lasting effect on the condition of the poor.

However, for Bazarov, this argument does not lead to any kind of positive social program in contrast to the position of the reformers he criticizes. Instead, he says plainly, "And we resolved not to take on anything .... And to go in for abuse."[51] So instead of doing anything positive to remedy the situation, the nihilists are concerned solely with the negative mission of criticizing and tearing down the older institutions and beliefs that they see as repressive. While social criticism can be important, this seems hardly to be a convincing solution on its own, especially given Bazarov's purported deep concern and sympathy for the poor.

Pavel struggles to understand how the nihilist program of destruction of everything can be conceived as beneficial in any way. Again, he sees this as a direct attack on civilized life, which is based on structures, institutions, and rules: "It is civilization that we hold dear – yes, yes, my dear sir; we hold dear its fruits."[52] This brings into focus the heart of the debate. While the aristocrats regard customs and traditions as valuable since they are the basis of civilization, the nihilists reject this assessment since in their view the reigning customs and traditions create poverty and inequality, which stand in the way of the development of the individual. When the aristocrats make the case for civilization, they are only trying to promote the advantages of their own class, while they are oblivious to the condition of the poor and the disenfranchised. They have thus ideologically associated civilized life with the state of things where they enjoy all the benefits of society.

Pavel further objects that by simply dismissing everything, the nihilists in effect have no motivation to try to understand the way things really work.[53] He argues that in the past young people were concerned about their education and tried to learn as much as they could. But now the nihilists have simply created a formula for ignorance. Since nothing is worth anything, there is no reason to work hard to try to understand it or to master a skill or to do anything at all. The nihilists can simply sit back in a self-satisfied manner with their dogma that nothing is valuable, while they criticize others who are working hard to improve themselves by learning new things and acquiring new skills.

---

[50] Turgenev, *Fathers and Sons*, p. 70.
[51] Turgenev, *Fathers and Sons*, pp. 70f.
[52] Turgenev, *Fathers and Sons*, p. 72.
[53] Turgenev, *Fathers and Sons*, p. 73.

The debate ends in bitterness, and the two sides make their retreat to their own private quarters. Pavel is angry beyond reconciliation. Nicholai is more reflective and, with some sadness and resignation, draws the conclusion that it is simply impossible for the two generations to understand one another.[54] This seems to be an important part of Turgenev's message with the novel. Later in the work it is clear that Bazarov's old parents love him deeply, but they do not understand him, and he does not understand them. The times in which the older generation was raised were radically different from those of the new generation, which had different experiences. While the older generation wanted change in some respects, they were generally proponents of the status quo. They believed that the changes were happening too quickly and that it was thus important to return to the values and traditions that had always given Russian society its stability. By contrast, the younger generation, encouraged by the emancipation of the serfs, believed that this was only the first small step in a radical transformation of society that was soon to come. The young generation was thus impatient for a more fundamental change in society than the older generation could ever have imagined. Thus, the nihilist view of challenging everything and destroying everything seemed a logical conclusion. While it sounds implausible, the nihilists have simply universalized their many individual experiences where they have found specific beliefs and institutions irrational and oppressive. Once this has been done often enough, one can quickly reach the conclusion that there is nothing left that is worth preserving. From this comes the view that everything should be destroyed, although not everything has necessarily been the object of critical examination.

8.6 The Problem of Death

At the end of the work Bazarov returns to the home of his parents. Tired and melancholy due to his failed incipient love affair with the progressive noblewoman Anna Sergheievna Odintsova, Bazarov tries to distract himself by helping his father Vassilii attend to the medical needs of the local peasants. In this context a dying man is brought to them who has been stricken by typhus.[55] There is nothing that can be done for him, and he quickly dies thereafter. A few days after this, Bazarov tells his father that he volunteered to do the autopsy on the dead man. In the course of the procedure, he cut himself and became infected since he was not able to attend to his wound quickly enough. His condition gradually worsens, and his parents become increasingly alarmed. Although he seems sometimes better and sometimes worse, this only serves to give false hope. Bazarov faces his own death in a sober manner. He knows that the kind

---

[54] Turgenev, *Fathers and Sons*, p. 75.
[55] Turgenev, *Fathers and Sons*, p. 258.

8.6 THE PROBLEM OF DEATH

of infection that he has contracted is always terminal. He thus entertains no illusions about it, while his father continues to try to be optimistic, Bazarov tells him directly from his sickbed, "my goose is cooked; I've been infected and in a few days you'll be burying me."[56] His father struggles to grasp this, pretending that Bazarov just has a simple cold. Bazarov patiently shows him the unmistakable symptoms, and this seems to sway his father. Yet Vassilii still refuses to give up hope and starts discussing the possibility of a cure. Bazarov knows that there is no cure, and he dismisses the idea immediately: "Cure me, fiddlesticks! But that's not the point. I didn't expect I'd die so soon. This, to tell you the truth, is a most unpleasant happenstance."[57] Bazarov states this coolly. He does not fall into a deep depression or become angry or full of regret as some might. Instead, he immediately accepts his fate. In fact, he is more concerned for his parents than for himself since he knows that his death will be difficult for them. There seems to be something profoundly absurd about the fact that a trivial incident such as a simple cut could lead to his death, particularly since he was still young and had so much of his life ahead.

Bazarov makes a single request to his father and asks him to send a message to his beloved Anna Sergheievna to inform her that he is dying. When the countess receives this and learns that he is gravely ill, she comes immediately with her German doctor to try to save him. The doctor quickly ascertains that there is nothing that can be done since the disease is already too far advanced. Bazarov asks the others to leave and has his last conversation with Anna. Turgenev portrays this conversation with great pathos. Bazarov says, "Eh, Anna Sergheievna, let's speak the truth. I'm done for. I'm caught under the wheel. And now it turns out that there was no use in thinking of the future. Death is an old trick, yet it strikes everyone as something new. Up to now I have no craven fear of it."[58] He knows that he faces death and annihilation, but there is nothing new in this, given his scientific or materialist view of things. Like all the other animals, he is a product of nature, and all animals die at some point. Even though death is somewhat unexpected for him at the moment, he does not try to pretend that it is possible to escape it. Bazarov thus takes the approach of his own death stoically, which seems in line with his nihilist views.

He is able to embrace the nothingness in a way that Jean Paul would have thought impossible for someone who does not subscribe to some belief in an afterlife. But Bazarov concedes that, as a young man, he himself was not completely free from illusions about his own mortality:

> Just look—what a hideous spectacle: a worm half-crushed but writhing still. And yet, I, too, was thinking: I'd bend so many things to my ends; I wouldn't die—that's not for me! If there's a hard nut to crack—why, that's

---

[56] Turgenev, *Fathers and Sons*, p. 262.
[57] Turgenev, *Fathers and Sons*, p. 263.
[58] Turgenev, *Fathers and Sons*, p. 271.

what I'm a giant for! But now the only hard nut the giant has to crack is how to die decently—although that really doesn't concern anybody.[59]

As a young person, Bazarov dismissed death since it was not an immediate issue for him. Instead, he was on a nihilist mission to improve Russia by means of destroying the old views and ways. But now that death has come, he fully realizes that there is nothing that anyone can do about it. The idea of dying decently was something that we saw in Kierkegaard's "At a Graveside," where it was claimed that thinking earnestly about one's death would help one to die well.[60] But Bazarov has apparently not followed the Kierkegaardian idea of thinking earnestly about death earlier in his life, and he seems not to have given it much thought. Indeed, in the passage just quoted he seems to have brushed off the idea of his own death for a long time.

Bazarov turns to his now ill-fated relation with Anna Sergheievna. He tells her, "Well, what am I to say to you ... I loved you! That had no sense whatsoever even before, and surely it hasn't any more now. Love is a form, and my own form is already decomposing. I'd do better by saying how fine you are! And even now you're standing there so beautiful."[61] This is a powerful passage since they both know now that their love will never be realized. Whatever they had together will be lost forever. Bazarov continues, "And, now, farewell! Live long, that's the best thing of all, and make the most of it while there is time."[62] He continues with some pathos, "You will forget me .... The dead man is no fit companion for one living."[63] This seems to suggest that even the power of love means nothing in the end. As Schopenhauer said and as Kreuzgang experienced, love too is transitory and cannot be regarded as the key to the salvation of anyone. Love dies with our loved ones. As was seen in Büchner, the death of a loved one can drive the surviving lover to complete despair and nihilism. Danton's beloved wife Julie commits suicide, and Camille's wife Lucile goes insane and gives up all hope.

Bazarov regrets that his love for Anna will never be realized and that he did not take advantage of the opportunity that he had with her. He makes a final request of her, "Breathe on a dying image-lamp, and let it go out."[64] Anna kisses him farewell, and he utters his final words, "Now ... darkness."[65] Turgenev's portrayal of the death of Bazarov is an important aspect of the work since, as was seen in the foregoing chapters, the problem of death is often associated with the concept of nihilism, but this is distinctly absent from Bazarov's program. The situation thus forces him to confront it, whether he wants to or

---

[59] Turgenev, *Fathers and Sons*, p. 272.
[60] See Chapter 7, Sect. 7.6, pp. 224–227.
[61] Turgenev, *Fathers and Sons*, p. 271.
[62] Turgenev, *Fathers and Sons*, p. 272.
[63] Turgenev, *Fathers and Sons*, p. 272.
[64] Turgenev, *Fathers and Sons*, p. 273.
[65] Turgenev, *Fathers and Sons*, p. 273.

8.7 BAZAROV AS A DIFFERENT KIND OF NIHILIST 255

not. This then makes it possible to compare his views with those of the others we have studied on this key issue as well. He seems to have a straightforward materialist conception of death as annihilation, but this is in no way a central aspect of his nihilistic view as it was for some of our other authors such as Jean Paul, Klingemann, Schopenhauer, Møller, and Kierkegaard. His concern was far more with improving life in society than with death.

After the death of Bazarov, the novel ends with a final section that constitutes a kind of epilogue in which the author describes what happened subsequently to the other characters. The reader is glad to see that they are all generally happy and thriving. This makes Bazarov's death even more bitter since he is no longer around to share their happiness. A part of this is the report that Anna Sergheievna has in the interim married an important and talented man, but not for love. Instead, the unnamed man is described as "cold as ice,"[66] despite all his many talents and high social standing. It is sad to think of Anna in a loveless marriage after the death of Bazarov, who could have offered her something better.

Perhaps the most moving scene in the book is Turgenev's description of Bazarov's old parents going to his grave and mourning their son many years after his death. The last lines of the work are as follows:

> Can it be that their prayers, their tears are fruitless? Can it be that love, holy devoted love is not omnipotent? Oh, nay! No matter how passionate, how sinful and riotous the heart that has hid itself in the grave, the flowers growing thereon gaze untroubled at us with their innocent eyes; it is not solely of eternal peace that they speak to us, of that great peace of "indifferent" nature; they speak, also, of eternal reconcilement and of life everlasting.[67]

This seems to resemble closely the view of Jean Paul. While Turgenev generally gives a sympathetic sketch of Bazarov, he cannot subscribe to his ideas. Like Jean Paul, he cannot bring himself to accept the idea that death is annihilation. His model is rather Bazarov's simple grieving parents, who believe in something higher than death. It is impossible to imagine or live with the idea of complete annihilation. There must surely be salvation and eternal life.

8.7 Bazarov as a Different Kind of Nihilist

Turgenev's portrayal of Bazarov as typical of the Russian nihilist movement seems in many ways rather different from the other nihilist figures we have explored. The nihilism that Jean Paul describes concerns the lack of meaning in the world and the thought of complete annihilation with death. These are the kinds of things that haunt our dreams and visit us in our moments of darkest

---

[66] Turgenev, *Fathers and Sons*, p. 276.
[67] Turgenev, *Fathers and Sons*, pp. 280f.

despair. This seems also to be the case with Kreuzgang, who is a profoundly troubled character. Byron's Manfred also languishes from an inner anguish that he cannot escape. Likewise, Schopenhauer's philosophy of pessimism reflects this view, when he claims that all of life is suffering. This aspect is also found in the inward struggles and *Lebensmüdigkeit* of Büchner's Danton. Kierkegaard's aesthete also repeatedly refers to his own inward ferment when he doubts the meaning of existence and is disturbed by nightmares.

In contrast to these depictions, Bazarov is not haunted by anything. He is completely convinced of the truth of his view and sees no aspect of it that would cause him dark thoughts or sleepless nights. When he asserts without hesitation that he negates everything, Turgenev adds that he did this "with inexpressible calm."[68] This is not something that he finds vexing or troubling in any way. The key emotions such as despair, anxiety, melancholy, boredom, and so on that accompany the other figures seem completely absent in him. His view of nihilism does not seem to be concerned with the question of the meaninglessness of human existence or the fact of human mortality. When at the end Bazarov is confronted with death, he takes it calmly, but this is not any explicit part of what he regards as his nihilist program.

Turgenev clearly understands the national nihilist movement as being focused on the social-political life of Russia at the time. Although Bazarov rejects the idea that he and the other nihilists are social reformers since they have no clearly defined positive plan, nonetheless it seems clear that he does have some firm intuitions of what a more just and less oppressive society would look like. Bazarov shows a deep sympathy for the peasants and feels the need to help them. He has disdain for the nobles, whom he regards as simple-minded and corrupt. The other nihilists that we have seen so far have lacked this kind of social-political dimension. There is no pendant to this in Jean Paul, and this is far removed from the disposition of the misanthropic nihilists, such as Kreuzgang and Kierkegaard's aesthete. Arguably, it might be claimed that Schopenhauer makes some cautious steps in this direction with his theory of ethics, but this is not really developed into a full-blown social-political theory as such. Moreover, the few things that he does say about this, such as his infamous views on women, seem to point in the direction of a misanthropy rather akin to that of Kreuzgang.

Yet despite these differences between Bazarov and the other nihilists we have explored, there are also some important points of overlap. Perhaps most significant is the fact that Bazarov is a scientist and a doctor. He comes from a rationalist, scientific background, and this strongly defines his character. He shares this in common with Jean Paul's Karlson. Likewise, the modern scientific view was clearly at the heart of Schopenhauer's theory. There were also some elements of science that animated certain aspects of the characters of Kreuzgang and Kierkegaard's aesthete. This scientific worldview leads Bazarov to want to

---

[68] Turgenev, *Fathers and Sons*, pp. 280f.

launch his all-out campaign of negation against tradition values, customs, and institutions. This resembles closely the social criticism of Karlson, Kreuzgang, and the aesthete. So Bazarov shares with the other versions of nihilism a critical perspective towards the world in general, which he develops in a direction that can be regarded as political.

The Russian nihilist movement died out around 1870, by which time its leading figures either died or emigrated to the West. The movement had met with serious opposition primarily among Slavophile intellectuals.[69] For example, Dostoevsky's novel *The Possessed* (also translated as *The Demons*) gives a critical account of nihilism. Yet, as Kropotkin notes, nihilism made an impact on Russian culture, although it gradually was replaced by more decidedly political movements such as socialism, communism, and anarchism. It might be argued that the idea of nihilism became politicized, and this led it away from the questions of meaninglessness and immortality that were central to the initial constellation of problems. It also seems to imply some kind of positive determination of certain *desiderata* with regard to the social order, as Kropotkin depicts it. While Kreuzgang and Kierkegaard's aesthete seem entirely negative, the social side of Bazarov, despite his claims to be solely a negative and destructive force, cannot help but posit certain values implicitly. This positive dimension of his view is at odds with the other conceptions of nihilism that we have explored.

Turgenev's understanding of nihilism as a kind of political movement was passed on to the Anglophone tradition when *Fathers and Sons* first appeared in English in 1867 in a translation by the American scholar Eugene Schuyler (1840–90).[70] In the political context, the nihilist movement was often associated with terrorism. The political dimension of nihilism was made famous by the work *Underground Russia: Revolutionary Profiles*, written by the revolutionary and terrorist Sergey Mikhaylovich Stepnyak-Kravchinsky (1851–95), and published in English under the pseudonym Sergius Stepniak in 1883.[71] Also worthy of mention is the short story "A Night among the Nihilists" by Arthur Conan Doyle from 1881.[72] In this story an English corn merchant on a business trip in Russia is mistakenly taken to be a Russian nihilist and brought to a meeting of their local group. Here again the term is used as a synonym for terrorism or anarchism. This association with revolutionary terrorism is also evident in Oscar Wilde's first drama, *Vera, or the Nihilists*, which was written

---

[69] Charles A. Moser, *Antinihilism in the Russian Novel of the 1860s*, London, The Hague, and Paris: Mouton 1964.
[70] Ivan Turgenev, *Father and Sons: A Novel*, trans. by Eugene Schuyler, New York: Leypold & Holt 1867.
[71] See Stepniak [sc. Stepnyak-Kravchinsky], *Underground Russia*.
[72] The work was published in several different journals in Great Britain and the United States in April and May of 1881. For example, Arthur Conan Doyle, "A Night among the Nihilists," *London Society. An Illustrated Magazine of Light and Amusing Literature for Hours of Relaxation*, vol. 39, April 1881, pp. 337–344.

in 1881 but only published a decade later.[73] This drama is inspired by the life of the Russian radical Vera Ivanovna Zasulich (1851–1919). It gives a portrayal of Vera and the band of nihilists to which she belongs. In these works, nihilism is used primarily as a purely political designation that has little in common with the philosophical understanding of the term as calling into doubt the meaning of human existence. In any case, *Fathers and Sons* had a great impact by disseminating the use of the word into much wider circles than ever before. The dissonance between Turgenev's meaning of the term and the constellation of issues concerning the vanity of human existence and mortality have contributed to the difficulty of defining nihilism as a single specific concept.

[73] Oscar Wilde, *Vera, or the Nihilists*, privately printed 1902.

9

Nietzsche's Vision of the Past and the Future of Nihilism

The concept of nihilism plays an important role in the philosophy of Friedrich Nietzsche (1844–1900), and he is the philosophical figure from the nineteenth century who is most often associated with the term.[1] The issue comes up in different ways in many of his books. His most sustained account of the topic comes in the posthumously published text known as *The Will to Power*. Strictly speaking, this is not a book by Nietzsche but rather a set of notes from his *Nachlass* that has a complex history of publication.[2] Some of this material was originally put together under this title by his friend Heinrich Köselitz (also known as the pseudonym Peter Gast) (1854–1918), along with the brothers Ernst Horneffer (1871–1954) and August Horneffer (1875–1955) and published in 1901 in the context of the first collected works edition of his writings.[3] This edition was initiated by Nietzsche's sister Elisabeth Förster-Nietzsche (1846–1935), who was keen to promote her brother's legacy. The desire to publish more of the *Nachlass* resulted in a new edition of *The Will to Power*. This was published in

---

[1] See, for example, Paul van Tongeren, *Friedrich Nietzsche and European Nihilism*, Newcastle upon Tyne: Cambridge Scholars Publishing 2018. See the relevant articles in the following collections: *Nihilism Now! Monsters of Energy*, ed. by Keith Ansell Pearson and Diane Morgan, Houndmills: Macmillan Press and New York: St. Martin's Press 2000; *Nietzsche and the Rhetoric of Nihilism: Essays on Interpretation, Language and Politics*, ed. by Tom Darby, Béla Egyed, and Ben Jones, Ottawa: Carleton University Press 1989; *Nietzsche, Nihilism and the Philosophy of the Future*, ed. by Jeffrey Metzger, London: Bloomsbury 2009. See also Randal Havas, *Nietzsche's Genealogy: Nihilism and the Will to Knowledge*, Ithaca, NY: Cornell University Press 1995; Bernard Reginster, *The Affirmation of Life: Nietzsche on Overcoming Nihilism*, Cambridge, MA and London: Harvard University Press 2006; Daniel W. Conway, *Nietzsche's Dangerous Game: Philosophy in the Twilight of the Idols*, New York: Cambridge University Press 1997.

[2] See "On the Editions of *The Will to Power*," in *The Will to Power*, trans. by Walter Kaufmann and R.J. Hollingdale, New York: Vintage 1967, pp. xxvii–xxix.

[3] Friedrich Nietzsche, *Nietzsche's Werke*, vols. 1–20, Leipzig: C.G. Naumann 1895–1926, vol. 15, Zweite Abtheilung, Nachgelassene Werke, vol. 7, *Der Wille zur Macht. Versuch einer Umwertung aller Werthe* (1901). This edition is further complicated by the fact that it was published by two different publishing houses. It was published from 1894 to 1913 with C.G. Naumann in Leipzig. Then the rest of the volumes appeared with Alfred Kröner Verlag, also in Leipzig.

1906, and the new material swelled the text to two volumes.[4] Yet more material was introduced in another edition from 1911.[5] This confusing story continues with even more editions. Since Nietzsche never really conceived of *The Will to Power* in the form given to it by these editors, Karl Schlechta (1904–85) criticized the philological work of Förster-Nietzsche and rejected it for his edition of Nietzsche's writings.[6] Likewise, the Italian scholars Mazzino Montinari (1928–86) and Giorgio Colli (1917–79) for similar reasons omitted it from their edition.[7] Instead, they dissolved the material known as *The Will to Power* into individual loose papers, which they presented with the rest of the *Nachlass*. The philological dimension of the work is thus a highly complicated matter since the text changes from edition to edition. Indeed, scholars continue to argue about this to this day. For the sake of simplicity, I refer to the modern edition of the text that is based on that of Köselitz and Elisabeth Förster-Nietzsche from 1906.[8]

The fact that *The Will to Power* is really only notes explains why the text generally has the form of a work-in-progress with incomplete sentences and undeveloped ideas. However, in the notes Nietzsche tries to develop a systematic understanding of the concept of nihilism, its origins, and possible solutions to it. He clearly believes that nihilism is a cultural-historical force in his time that has developed through several phases, which he tries to identify and explain. Despite its philological shortcomings, *The Will to Power* enjoyed a widespread history of reception and thus had a great impact on the understanding of Nietzsche as a thinker on nihilism. For this reason, we are obliged to take it seriously in the present study.

Given that the notes that constitute *The Will to Power* do not always contain fully developed ideas, we are left with the task of piecing together a theory or

---

[4] Friedrich Nietzsche, *Friedrich Nietzsche's Werke. Taschen-Ausgabe in Lieferungen*, vols. 1–11, Leipzig: C.G. Naumann 1906–1913; vol. 9, *Der Wille zur Macht: 1884–1888* (1906); vol. 10, *Der Wille zur Macht: 1884–1888* (1906).

[5] Friedrich Nietzsche, *Nietzsche's Werke*, vols. 1–20, Leipzig: C.G. Naumann 1895–1926; vol. 15, Zweite Abtheilung, Nachgelassene Werke; vol. 7, Zweite völlig neugestaltete und vermehrte Ausgabe, *Der Wille zur Macht. Versuch einer Umwertung aller Werthe. 1. und 2. Buch* (1911); vol. 16, Zweite Abtheilung, Nachgelassene Werke; vol. 8, Zweite völlig neugestaltete und vermehrte Ausgabe, *Der Wille zur Macht. Versuch einer Umwertung aller Werthe. 3. und 4. Buch* (1911).

[6] *Friedrich Nietzsches Werke in drei Bänden*, ed. by Karl Schlechta, Munich: Carl Hanser 1954–56.

[7] Friedrich Nietzsche, *Sämtliche Werke. Kritische Gesamtausgabe*, vols. 1–15, ed. by Mazzino Montinari and Giorgio Colli, Berlin and New York: Walter De Gruyter 1967–77. See also the second edition, *Kritische Studienausgabe*, vols. 1–15, ed. by Mazzino Montinari and Giorgio Colli, Berlin: Walter De Gruyter and Munich: Deutscher Taschenbuch Verlag 1980.

[8] Friedrich Nietzsche, *Der Wille zur Macht*, Stuttgart: Alfred Kröner 1964. For the English translation I use *The Will to Power*, trans. by Walter Kaufmann and R.J. Hollingdale, New York: Vintage 1967.

account of nihilism derived from these and Nietzsche's other occasional, scattered references to nihilism. He seems to think that nihilism names a condition of crisis wherein individuals are no longer able to muster the volitional intensity needed to project their will into the future. Given the death of God and the collapse of traditional values, people are debilitated by a sense of hopelessness and meaninglessness. The condition itself is close to what Kierkegaard calls "despair" and what others, following Schopenhauer, would call "resignation" or "pessimism." This is also what Büchner portrays in the figure of Danton, who gives up on everything and willingly accepts death. Nietzsche's account of nihilism is intrinsically related to his detailed diagnostic account of the European cultural decay that he sees in his own time.

In addition to the notes that are referred to as *The Will to Power*, Nietzsche also discusses the encroachment of nihilism into modern European culture in his *Twilight of the Idols* (1888). There he argues that Christianity and modern rationalism create a metaphysics that is nihilistic in the sense that it denies life and the positive, spontaneous impulses necessary for a flourishing existence. In fact, it can be said that the issue of nihilism in one form or another was central to Nietzsche's thinking throughout his life. It would therefore be impossible here to cover this exhaustively, and for this reason I will limit myself to *The Will to Power*.

9.1 Nietzsche's Definition of Nihilism

At the outset Nietzsche tries to give a basic working definition of nihilism: "What does nihilism mean? *That the highest values devaluate themselves.* The aim is lacking; 'why?' finds no answer."[9] He describes nihilism as "the radical repudiation of value, meaning, and desirability."[10] Here it is clear that nihilism, for Nietzsche, is concerned primarily with values and judgments about things. He often speaks of morality, but this too he seems to understand not simply as ethics but rather in this broader sense of any kind of evaluative claim. This understanding of the problem is somewhat different from what has been seen in the other authors we have explored. Although most of the others did not use the term "nihilism" explicitly, they were clearly familiar with the constellation of problems surrounding it. For Jean Paul and Møller, the main issue was human mortality and the possibility of annihilation with death. The motif of death as a central aspect of nihilism also appears in Klingemann's *The Nightwatches* and Kierkegaard. Perhaps the closest to Nietzsche's view is that of Schopenhauer, who focuses on the meaninglessness of human existence in the universe. All our strivings to satisfy our drives and desires that come from the will-to-live are doomed to failure. It is well known that Nietzsche was strongly

---

[9] Nietzsche, *Der Wille zur Macht*, § 2, p. 10 (*The Will to Power*, § 2, p. 9).
[10] Nietzsche, *Der Wille zur Macht*, § 1, p. 7 (*The Will to Power*, § 1, p. 7).

influenced by Schopenhauer, and so it is no surprise that a part of this influence concerns the notion of nihilism.

Another special aspect of Nietzsche's understanding of nihilism is that he takes it to be a broad phenomenon that has found its way into all the different realms of culture, including science, politics, history, and art.[11] It is thus not confined to the single issue of human mortality or even the existence of God. For Nietzsche, nihilism is related to the sciences since they teach us that human beings occupy only the most peripheral role in the universe and are in no way special. He explains this with reference to Copernicus's revolution from the geocentric to the heliocentric model of the universe that displaced humanity from its privileged central position. He uses the image of humans "rolling from the center toward X,"[12] an image that continued to be fitting when, in 1924, the astronomer Edwin Hubble discovered that the universe consisted not only of the Milky Way galaxy but of innumerable other galaxies, of which the Milky Way is but one. This discovery again pushed humans even further to the periphery of the universe, which raised serious questions about the idea that God created humanity with a special plan. If this were true, it is difficult to understand why God would assign to us such a small and completely insignificant place in the grand scheme of things.

Nietzsche also talks about nihilism in politics.[13] In the past, political leaders seemed to rule by virtue of some special right or privilege such as the divine right of kings. Now, however, in our more democratically minded age, we cannot accept that anyone has any such right to rule over us, and so the result is the unscrupulous use of politics for personal self-interest. We thus tend to think of our leaders as corrupt, mendacious, unscrupulous, and so on. We have largely lost faith in politics since it seems to be a forum where truth is completely absent.

Along the same lines Nietzsche talks about nihilism as having entered the sphere of history writing.[14] Previously the goal of historians was to determine as precisely as possible what happened in the past based on the extant sources and records. Now, however, historians only practice what Hegel calls "pragmatical history,"[15] that is, they want to use history in a practical way in order to advance their own social-political views. In short, history has become a kind of ideology. Such historians are not really interested in what happened in the past. Indeed, they have given up the idea of any historical truths. Hence, the only role

---

[11] Nietzsche, *Der Wille zur Macht*, § 1, pp. 8f. (*The Will to Power*, § 1, pp. 7f.).
[12] Nietzsche, *Der Wille zur Macht*, § 1, p. 8 (*The Will to Power*, § 1, p. 8).
[13] Nietzsche, *Der Wille zur Macht*, § 1, p. 8 (*The Will to Power*, § 1, p. 8).
[14] Nietzsche, *Der Wille zur Macht*, § 1, p. 9 (*The Will to Power*, § 1, p. 8).
[15] Georg Wilhelm Friedrich Hegel, *Vorlesungen über die Philosophie der Geschichte*, ed. by Eduard Gans, in *Georg Wilhelm Friedrich Hegel's Werke. Vollständige Ausgabe*, vols. 1–18, Berlin: Duncker und Humblot 1832–45, vol. 9 (1837), pp. 8–10 (English translation: *The Philosophy of History*, trans. by J. Sibree, New York: Willey Book Co. 1944, pp. 6–7).

left for history to play is to be a source of examples that can be used to support whatever political agenda one wishes to advance, regardless of how much this might distort what is actually found in the historical records and sources.

Finally, Nietzsche prophetically mentions the nihilism found in contemporary art.[16] In the past, art tried to represent the beautiful in certain established forms such as painting and sculpture. These forms required great technical skill and many years of practice to acquire. Now the idea of beauty along with the traditional forms of art have been abandoned. As a result, most anything at all can be regarded as a work of art, a toilet, a can of soup, and so on. This means that there is no longer any premium set on technical expertise. The objects of modern art can in a sense simply be found ready-made, and what makes them art is merely the fact that they are put in an exhibition where they are removed from their usual context in daily life and explicitly designated as objects of art for the viewer's contemplation. It will be recalled that one of the objections of Pavel in *Fathers and Sons* against the young generation of artists was that they arrogantly criticize traditional forms of art, while pursuing shallow artistic projects that require no technical skill or training.[17] In this sense nihilism represents the loss of meaning and ideals in art. The entire field has collapsed into a complete relativism with no one being able to say what is better or worse. The result is that artists simply compete to outdo each other by trying to be increasingly provocative so as to stir up controversy and thus wider attention for their works, hoping to attain importance for them by means of the number of people who can be enticed to discuss them.

9.2 The Origin and Development of Nihilism

Given that nihilism, for Nietzsche, is the repudiation of all values, the question arises about how this situation came about. What happened to make people come to this point that they despair of the value and meaning of things? Nietzsche tries to trace the rise of nihilism through various stages. He believes that initially the Christian worldview provided people with the answers that they needed to understand the big questions. He outlines four positive functions that Christianity served:

> What were the advantages of the Christian moral hypothesis? 1. It granted man an absolute value, as opposed to his smallness and accidental occurrence in the flux of becoming and passing away. 2. It served the advocates of God insofar as it conceded to the world, in spite of suffering and evil, the character of perfection—including "freedom": evil appeared full of meaning. 3. It posited that man had a *knowledge* of absolute values and thus

---

[16] Nietzsche, *Der Wille zur Macht*, § 1, p. 9 (*The Will to Power*, § 1, p. 8).
[17] Ivan S. Turgenev, *Fathers and Sons*, trans. by Bernard Guibert Guerney, New York: Random House 1961, pp. 72f.

adequate knowledge precisely regarding what is most important. 4. It prevented man from despising himself as man, from taking sides against life; from despairing of knowledge: it was a *means of preservation*.[18]

The Christian view elevates humans to a special status and ascribes knowledge to them. This provided a sense of comfort and security in an otherwise changing and uncertain world.

Then with the rise of the natural sciences, all of this was called into question. The scientific worldview seemed irrefutably to reject the traditional Christian notions of God, immortality, the centrality of humans in the universe, and so on. This is what Nietzsche means by the devaluation of the highest values. This left people torn between Christianity, which they wanted to believe, and the new scientific view, which seemed more compelling. Using Kantian language, Nietzsche describes this kind of dilemma as an antinomy.[19] This is the dilemma in which Jean Paul's Karlson finds himself. Karlson is a convinced scientist, yet he cannot bring himself to believe that Gione will be completely annihilated with death, and so he makes room for the belief in an afterlife in his scientific worldview, knowing full well that this is unjustified by scientific reasoning.

Nietzsche explains how the Christian virtue of truthfulness played an important role in undermining the Christian worldview.[20] Christians believe that the traditional dogmas are true and that we should honor the truth. Jesus says, "If you hold to my teaching, you are really my disciples. Then you will know the truth, and the truth will set you free."[21] When the natural sciences began to refute the Christian view, this engrained value of truth encouraged people to take seriously the new scientific view. This then led them to discover many aspects of the Christian view that suddenly appeared to be lies propagated by, for example, the ecclesiastical or political authorities in order to justify their positions of power. The demand for intellectual honesty and truth, which previously had served to support Christianity, was now turned against it, with the result that its critics dismantled the Christian worldview piece by piece. People felt duped or betrayed by Christianity, and their love for the truth, born from Christianity itself, made them increasingly bitter critics of it. Nietzsche explains, "This antagonism – not to esteem what we know, and not to be allowed any longer to esteem the lies we should like to tell ourselves – results in a process of dissolution."[22]

From this point one is unwillingly led to the conclusion that everything is meaningless, and there is no point to human existence. Any form of judgment or moral evaluation seems completely arbitrary. Nietzsche outlines three key

---

[18] Nietzsche, *Der Wille zur Macht*, § 4, pp. 10f. (*The Will to Power*, § 4, pp. 9f.).
[19] Nietzsche, *Der Wille zur Macht*, § 6, p. 11 (*The Will to Power*, § 6, p. 10).
[20] Nietzsche, *Der Wille zur Macht*, § 5, p. 11 (*The Will to Power*, § 5, p. 10).
[21] John 8:31–32.
[22] Nietzsche, *Der Wille zur Macht*, § 5, p. 11 (*The Will to Power*, § 5, p. 10).

9.2 THE ORIGIN AND DEVELOPMENT OF NIHILISM

cosmological values that one is obliged to abandon once one has reached the stage of nihilism.[23] The first of these is that there is any purpose or goal in the universe or in human existence. There is no real progress aiming at anything. On the contrary, the world is just a constant flux of becoming with no *logos* behind it. Here he seems to recall the views of, among others, Kant and Hegel, who see a teleological movement in history that develops towards a final state of perfection. The concept of love plays an important role in many of the works that we have explored. Jean Paul's Karlson, against his better judgment, capitulates to a belief in an afterlife out of love for Gione. The cynical Kreuzgang in *The Nightwatches* also falls victim to love, despite his efforts to resist it. Møller claims that true love cannot exist in a nihilist universe since it would be impossible to take an amorous relationship seriously and invest one's emotions in it. Bazarov's last wish before he dies is to see his beloved Anna. Nietzsche rejects the idea of love as being the final goal of human existence.[24] Like Klingemann and Schopenhauer, he sees that love is just as transitory and mutable as everything else in the universe. The lovers themselves will die and with them their love. In time this will be forgotten forever. In spite of Virgil's oft-quoted line, love does not conquer all.[25]

The second cosmological value that is abandoned by the nihilist is the notion that the universe constitutes some kind of unity or coherent system. This can also be regarded in part as a criticism of the German idealists, Kant and Hegel, who were keen to provide a systematic overview of the sciences. The idea of a unified structure has the benefit that it provides for the location of the life of the individual and the meaning of that life in the bigger picture. But if there is no discernably coherent system, then the individual is just one free atom among countless others with no more meaning than a speck of dust. Nietzsche explains this as follows: "Some sort of unity, some form of 'monism': this faith suffices to give man a deep feeling of standing in the context of, and being dependent on, some whole that is infinitely superior to him, and he sees himself as a mode of the deity."[26] This psychological need can explain the well-known phenomenon of the odd attraction of populist movements among the masses. Once one reaches the stage of nihilism and finds no firm points of orientation in the world after the abandonment of the Christian worldview, it can be a very disorienting and frightening experience. It is difficult in this context to create one's own values since these seem to be arbitrary and insignificant, having no deeper grounding. Thus, it is in a sense natural that large movements, such as nationalism, fascism, communism, or capitalism, appear attractive since they

---

[23] Nietzsche, *Der Wille zur Macht*, § 12, pp. 13–16 (*The Will to Power*, § 12, pp. 12–14).
[24] Nietzsche, *Der Wille zur Macht*, § 12, p. 12 (*The Will to Power*, § 12, p. 12).
[25] See Virgil, *The Eclogues*, trans. by Guy Lee, Harmondsworth: Penguin 1984, Eclogue X, p. 104: "*omnia vincit amor.*"
[26] Nietzsche, *Der Wille zur Macht*, § 12, p. 14 (*The Will to Power*, § 12, p. 12).

offer one a sense of mission and meaning. As Nietzsche explains, "One wants to get around the will, the willing of a goal, the risk of positing a goal for oneself; one wants to rid oneself of the responsibility."[27] People sometimes believe that everything would be so much easier if they were simply told what to do by some higher authority. Mass movements help their members to overcome the feeling that they are alone with the great burden of freedom to decide everything for themselves. Instead, they can appoint a higher authority above themselves as a kind of *Ersatz* for the God of Christianity. People happily surrender their freedom and critical thinking for a sense of meaning and community. Hence, nihilism can be a motivation to affiliate oneself with mass movements. This is what Nietzsche refers to as the social or the herd instinct.[28] This is also thematized in later existentialist writers under headings such as the "flight from freedom" or "bad faith."

This provides another useful point of comparison and contrast with our previous authors. For Jean Paul, Klingemann, Schopenhauer, and Kierkegaard, the question of nihilism seems to be primarily about the individual. Their characters, such as Klingemann's Kreuzgang and Kierkegaard's aesthete, are loners and outsiders. As we saw above, this stands in contrast to Turgenev's understanding nihilism as a kind of social-political movement among the youth of his time. In this respect Nietzsche also seems attentive to the social aspect of nihilism. For him, nihilism is not just some abstract theoretical view held by academics or overly reflective people. On the contrary, it has infected all walks of life and every area of culture. For this reason, it has become a widespread social force that must be addressed.[29] Nietzsche, like Bazarov, believes that one should be active in destroying the distorted values and prejudices that have hindered the development of humanity for so long.

The third cosmic value that is abandoned is the very notion of truth itself.[30] Since the Christian worldview has failed, people cease to believe in any kind of interpretation of the world that can be final. The Christian view was not an accurate representation of the universe itself but instead a reflection of the psychological needs of human beings. Thus, the very idea of any kind of objective truth must be rejected altogether. The only true reality is the constant flux of becoming, and any attempt to find some reason or pattern in this is just a fiction of our imagination projected onto the world for psychological reasons. This is perhaps the most radical form of rejection that nihilism reaches since it leads to the view that every interpretation of the world is just an individual perspective with no deeper grounding.[31] This is what is often referred to as

---

[27] Nietzsche, *Der Wille zur Macht*, § 20, p. 20 (*The Will to Power*, § 20, p. 17).
[28] Nietzsche, *Der Wille zur Macht*, § 20, p. 19 (*The Will to Power*, § 20, p. 17).
[29] Nietzsche, *Der Wille zur Macht*, § 24, pp. 21f. (*The Will to Power*, § 24, p. 18).
[30] Nietzsche, *Der Wille zur Macht*, § 12, p. 14 (*The Will to Power*, § 12, p. 13).
[31] Nietzsche, *Der Wille zur Macht*, § 15, p. 17 (*The Will to Power*, § 15, pp. 14f.).

Nietzsche's theory of perspectivism. Since there is no God to see the world as it really is or to see the thing-in-itself that lies on the other side of our representations, all we have left is our own relative perspectives. The very concept of an external objective truth is a misconception. A *true* or *veridical* understanding of the world does not exist.

The radicality of Nietzsche's version of nihilism will be noted. For Jean Paul the big issue was limited to the question of the immortality of the soul or the existence of God. But by calling into question fundamental beliefs such as progress towards a goal, unity, and truth, Nietzsche has clearly thought through the dilemma of nihilism at a much deeper level. It is not just about a few individual beliefs, which, if maintained, could salvage everything from the destructive force of nihilism. Instead, the concept of nihilism has to do with much more fundamental ways of perceiving the world around us as a whole. The ideas of progress towards a goal, unity, and truth are engrained in our minds as fundamental intuitions. Nietzsche includes, among the group of metaphysical prejudices or false beliefs, the law of contradiction itself, which is often considered to be the very foundation of any kind of rational thought.[32] These metaphysical prejudices constitute the preconditions for science itself. If the universe is not a unitary system where things are in interaction with one another in regular patterns, then science would be impossible. If the world were a chaos, then science would never be able to arise since there would be no laws or patterns in nature to be found. Likewise, if there is no objective truth about things in the world that could ever be attained by the human mind, then science could never get started. Finally, science regularly makes use of the ideas of progress leading to a goal. From biology to astronomy to cosmology, many kinds of quite heterogenous things are said to develop or evolve over time. These different forms of development are thought to run through a natural sequence that can be traced and understood. By rejecting these fundamental ideas as antiquated vestiges of the Christian worldview, the nihilist rejects the validity of science itself.

9.3 The False Inference

Nietzsche tries to trace the logical train of thought that has led to the situation where people have given up on their most treasured values, which have previously given them great comfort and hope. He claims that people have reached the point that they see that they must abandon not merely the idea of God and the afterlife but even the fundamental assumptions of science (progress towards a goal, unity, and truth). After this, nihilism sets in. When these ideas are abandoned, then everything appears meaningless, and there is no way back to traditional belief. We have lived under the illusion of these values for millennia, and now we are left with nothing.

[32] Nietzsche, *Der Wille zur Macht*, § 584, p. 400 (*The Will to Power*, § 584, p. 315).

But Nietzsche suggests that, upon closer examination, this is in fact an invalid inference. He explains, "Nihilism represents a pathological transitional stage (what is pathological is the tremendous generalization, the inference that there is no meaning at all)."[33] He argues that from the rejection of the fundamental values that were previously held, it does not follow that everything is meaningless and there is no point to anything. Instead, it just means that the way in which we had conceived of values previously was mistaken. It was wrong of us to believe that values could ever have any kind of absolute grounding. But once we are disabused of this idea, we are free to try to think of values in a different, more realistic manner.

Nietzsche thus implies that it is possible to move beyond nihilism if we can see the logical problem with this inference. This raises the question of the possibility of creating a new set of values on the strength of one's own authority. But Nietzsche believes that people in his age have not yet emancipated themselves from nihilism to the extent that they can do this. He wonders "whether the productive forces are not yet strong enough, or whether decadence still hesitates and has not yet invented its remedies."[34] His point here is that people have suffered a kind of psychological trauma with the collapse of their long-held traditional belief system. They feel crushed by the prospect of their lives being meaningless. Nietzsche explains, "The most universal sign of the modern age: man has lost *dignity* in his own eyes to an incredible extent."[35] People feel embarrassed and ashamed of having believed in a false view for so long. Once they reach the idea of nihilism, they feel helpless and insignificant. They can see no way out of the dilemma since every value that they posit seems relative and thus meaningless in the big picture of the universe. This leaves them in a psychological situation where they have completely lost faith in themselves. Since the highest values have always come from God, the nihilist fails to hit upon the idea that one can conceive of oneself as value-positing. People are thus in no way in a position to assert themselves and try to establish new values based on their own authority. Nietzsche states, "Just now when the greatest strength of will would be necessary, it is weakest and least confident."[36] This is the state of decadence that the modern world has arrived at.

Nietzsche insightfully analyzes this as a development from an external to an internal authority. He explains,

> The nihilistic question "for what?" is rooted in the old habit of supposing that the goal must be put up, given, demanded *from outside*—by some *superhuman authority*. Having unlearned faith in that, one still follows the old habit and seeks *another* authority that can *speak unconditionally*

---

[33] Nietzsche, *Der Wille zur Macht*, § 13, p. 16 (*The Will to Power*, § 13, p. 14).
[34] Nietzsche, *Der Wille zur Macht*, § 13, p. 16 (*The Will to Power*, § 13, p. 14).
[35] Nietzsche, *Der Wille zur Macht*, § 18, p. 19 (*The Will to Power*, § 18, p. 16).
[36] Nietzsche, *Der Wille zur Macht*, § 20, p. 20 (*The Will to Power*, § 20, p. 17).

9.3 THE FALSE INFERENCE

and *command* goals and tasks. The authority of *conscience* now steps up front.[37]

Throughout human history it was always necessary to obey external authorities who determined how people were to lead their lives. Such authorities were the tribe, the clan, or custom. Then with the rise of Christianity this was replaced with God and his representative, the church. Obedience and compliance were the keys to a happy life. The notion that individuals had some important value on their own, and that they had a rational faculty that would allow them to make choices and decisions for themselves was a foreign concept. The very idea that the individual should have any kind of inalienable rights is a modern invention. But in the modern world with the French Revolution and the subsequent rise of nihilism these external authorities began to lose their grip. Now people, like Turgenev's Bazarov, enjoined others to reject these authorities and traditions.

It will be recalled that figures such as Bazarov, Kreuzgang, and Kierkegaard's aesthete are all merciless social critics. They are forces of negation that are directed against any form of unquestioned custom, tradition, or belief. Their realization of nihilism leads them to feel a sense of superiority over the rest of society, whom they generally regard as mindless, unreflective cattle. They thus put themselves in a position of authority to criticize others. One of the ways in which this is done is represented by Romantic irony in the works of writers such as Friedrich von Schlegel, Tieck, and Solger. As noted, these authors are explored in some detail in Kierkegaard's book *The Concept of Irony*.[38] The Romantics shift the authority from the outer to the inner and find within themselves the critical tools with which to tear down bourgeois culture.

However, this raises the problem posed by Nicholai in *Fathers and Sons*.[39] Once the nihilists succeed in their negative agenda of tearing down everything, what do they propose to replace it with? What is the positive agenda that the nihilists find preferable to traditional values and beliefs? Nicholai is astonished to hear that Bazarov does not really have such an agenda, but instead insists that the nihilist program is purely negative. Klingemann's Kreuzgang and Kierkegaard's aesthete seem to be deprived characters who use the nihilist insight also for purely negative means with no positive or constructive plan. Likewise, the resignation towards life displayed by Büchner's Danton offers no hope or means of coping with nihilism at all. In contrast to these views, Nietzsche suggests that it is possible to posit positive values for oneself. This is the road that leads beyond nihilism.

---

[37] Nietzsche, *Der Wille zur Macht*, § 20, p. 19 (*The Will to Power*, § 20, p. 16).

[38] Søren Kierkegaard, *Om Begrebet Ironi med stadigt Hensyn til Socrates*, in *Søren Kierkegaards Skrifter*, vols. 1-28, K1-K28, Copenhagen: Gad Publishers 1997-2012, vol. 1, pp. 321-352 (English translation: *The Concept of Irony; Schelling Lecture Notes*, trans. by Howard V. Hong and Edna H. Hong, Princeton, NJ: Princeton University Press 1989, vol. 1, pp. 286-323). See above Chapter 7, Sect. 7.1, pp. 203-205.

[39] Turgenev, *Fathers and Sons*, p. 67.

For Nietzsche, the realization of nihilism can lead to a sense of power. Bazarov, Kreuzgang, and the aesthete all feel that they are superior to the others in society who cling to traditional beliefs and customs. These colorful characters feel liberated from such things and can live as they please without being concerned about what bourgeois culture thinks of them. Nietzsche describes this as an increase in power:

> Values and their changes are related to increases in the power of those positing the values. The measure of *unbelief*, of permitted "freedom of the spirit" as *an expression of an increase in power*. "Nihilism" [is] an ideal of the highest degree of powerfulness of the spirit, the over-richest life—partly destructive, partly ironic.[40]

This form of what Nietzsche calls "active nihilism" is contrasted with "passive nihilism."[41] Instead of increasing a feeling of power, passive nihilism decreases it. This is the stage of nihilism, mentioned above, where people feel devastated and incapacitated by the thought that their existence is meaningless. At this stage it is impossible for them to muster the positive power needed to posit their own values. Instead, they simply wallow in a feeling of misery, helplessness, and impotence.

9.4 The Criticism of Schopenhauer

It is well known that Schopenhauer had a great influence on the young Nietzsche. In fact, Nietzsche himself acknowledges this directly in his "Schopenhauer as Educator," the third essay from *Untimely Meditations*.[42] However, over time Nietzsche grew more critical of the main thrust of Schopenhauer's system. He believes that Schopenhauer has fallen victim to the mistaken inference, taking the collapse of all traditional values to mean that everything is worthless. This is why his predecessor's philosophy can be characterized as pessimism.[43] Schopenhauer appears to be the "philosophical nihilist [who] is convinced that all that happens is meaningless and in vain; and that there ought not to be anything meaningless and in vain."[44] He still feels a sense of dismay and desperation at this realization. Schopenhauer has arrived at the stage of nihilism but was unable to go beyond it. By contrast, Nietzsche believes that it is possible to start anew by positing new values. In this way he takes his own philosophy to

---

[40] Nietzsche, *Der Wille zur Macht*, § 14, p. 17 (*The Will to Power*, § 14, p. 14).
[41] Nietzsche, *Der Wille zur Macht*, § 22, p. 20 (*The Will to Power*, § 22, p. 17).
[42] Friedrich Nietzsche, *Unzeitgemässe Betrachtungen. Drittes Stück: Schopenhauer als Erzieher*, Schloss-Chemnitz: Ernst Schmeitzner 1874 (English translation: "Schopenhauer as Educator," in *Untimely Meditations*, trans. by R.J. Hollingdale, Cambridge: Cambridge University Press 1983, pp. 125–194).
[43] Nietzsche, *Der Wille zur Macht*, § 32, p. 26 (*The Will to Power*, § 32, p. 22).
[44] Nietzsche, *Der Wille zur Macht*, § 36, p. 28 (*The Will to Power*, § 36, p. 23).

9.4 THE CRITICISM OF SCHOPENHAUER

have progressed beyond nihilism. According to Nietzsche, one can regard pessimism as a characteristic symptom of the nihilism of the age.[45]

It might be argued that this is not true since Schopenhauer in fact tries to provide a means of escape from nihilism and the suffering of the world. However, Nietzsche objects to Schopenhauer's solution to the problem of nihilism. It will be recalled that for Schopenhauer the root cause of suffering was the constant drives and needs of the will that one had to continue to satisfy. He believed that this was an endless cycle since no sooner has one desire been satisfied than others arise that demand satisfaction as well. Schopenhauer argued that the only solution was the denial of the will-to-live by the repression of these drives and desires. He thus recommends the life of a monk or ascetic, free from the demands of these natural forces within us.

Nietzsche disagrees with this picture, which he regards as negative and life-denying. To repress one's drives and desires is not to overcome nihilism but rather to admit defeat. For Nietzsche, the goal should rather be something positive, namely, an affirmation of one's will. His theory of the will to power is thus intended to mean that we should embrace our desire to accumulate and exercise power, although contemporary Christian morality is critical of this. Nietzsche's concept of the will to power can be regarded as a variant of Schopenhauer's will-to-live. Both thinkers regard these as fundamental metaphysical principles of the universe. A part of Nietzsche's criticism is that Schopenhauer has inadvertently embraced the key features of Christian ethics, despite his outspoken atheism.[46] Like Kant, Schopenhauer posits the thing-in-itself in the form of the will. Again, in contradiction to Schopenhauer's atheism, this is a reflection of the old theistic view that still believes that there is some kind of external, objective reality or absolute principle.[47] By contrast, Nietzsche's own idea of the will to power stands in stark opposition to Christian ethics and is intended to shock our intuitions.

Nietzsche regards Schopenhauer as a "throwback" to the eighteenth century since he still retains certain religious values, such as pity and sympathy.[48] He claims that Schopenhauer represents a weakness of the will. Nietzsche argues that Schopenhauer's conception of the will, that is, the will-to-live, as something that should be suppressed, is a fundamental misconception. Schopenhauer cannot imagine that the will, qua the will to power, can be something positive. Nietzsche likewise rejects his forerunner's praise for Buddhism as offering the solution to nihilism.[49] Instead, with its doctrine of quieting the passions,

---

[45] Nietzsche, *Der Wille zur Macht*, § 38, pp. 29f. (*The Will to Power*, § 38, p. 24).
[46] Nietzsche, *Der Wille zur Macht*, § 17, pp. 17f. (*The Will to Power*, § 17, p. 15).
[47] Nietzsche, *Der Wille zur Macht*, § 17, p. 18 (*The Will to Power*, § 17, p. 15).
[48] Nietzsche, *Der Wille zur Macht*, § 84, p. 63 (*The Will to Power*, § 84, p. 52).
[49] E.g., Nietzsche, *Der Wille zur Macht*, § 19, p. 19; § 23, p. 21 (*The Will to Power*, § 19, p. 16; § 23, p. 18).

Buddhism is, for Nietzsche, a philosophy of resignation. Rather than affirming the will as something positive, it becomes a form of passive nihilism in repressing the natural drives. The goal is to cultivate strength, by allowing one's will to power to flourish. But instead, Buddhism deprives the individual of strength and ends in weakness.

9.5 The Idea of Metaphysical Need

Nietzsche's radicalism comes out clearly in the section of *The Will to Power* entitled "Metaphysical Need."[50] His argument is that after the death of God and the onset of nihilism, it is possible to see that the tradition of Western metaphysics has been thoroughly infected by a certain prejudice towards the concept of being at the expense of change and becoming.[51] The cause for this is our psychological desire to have a world around us that is stable, continuous, and safe. If the world were merely a constant flux of change with nothing that endured, this would be troubling for us. Nietzsche argues that this metaphysical need created a two-world split. What people saw around them in the empirical world was nothing but change and becoming. But to avoid this uncomfortable fact, they posited another world beyond this one, where things were not mutable or inconstant. The focus then shifted from the actual, perceived world, which was regarded as corrupt and erroneous, to a transcendent other world, which was that of truth. According to this view, there is a true world, but it is not the one that we know and live in. This amounts to a reversal of what common sense would seem to dictate concerning what is real and true. But after Christianity adopted this idea of a higher and truer world and spread it to all areas of culture over a long period of time, we have become so accustomed to it that it does not even strike us as strange or counterintuitive.[52]

The need for some other world arose from the dissatisfaction with the shortcomings of the real world. One perceives injustice in this world and reasons that there must be another place where such injustice does not exist. One suffers in this world and reasons that there must be somewhere else where there is no suffering but instead happiness. The idea of "eternal bliss" represents the opposite of our mundane life of suffering.[53] The negative conception seems to imply a positive one as its necessary pendant.[54] Our psychological need for comfort thus leads us to posit fictions that, while making us feel better, have no grounding in the real world.

---

[50] Nietzsche, *Der Wille zur Macht*, §§ 570–586, pp. 389–405 (*The Will to Power*, §§ 570–586, pp. 307–322).
[51] Nietzsche, *Der Wille zur Macht*, § 570, p. 389; § 581, p. 396 (*The Will to Power*, § 570, p. 307; § 581, p. 312).
[52] Nietzsche, *Der Wille zur Macht*, § 572, p. 390 (*The Will to Power*, § 572, p. 308).
[53] Nietzsche, *Der Wille zur Macht*, § 579, p. 394 (*The Will to Power*, § 579, p. 311).
[54] Nietzsche, *Der Wille zur Macht*, § 579, p. 393 (*The Will to Power*, § 579, pp. 310f.).

9.5 THE IDEA OF METAPHYSICAL NEED

In the history of philosophy this resulted in systems such as that of Plato, with the realm of the ideas in contrast to the empirical world, and that of Kant, with the split between representations and things-in-itself.[55] As discussed above,[56] Kant believed that the objects that we see are conditioned by the categories of the human mind and the forms of perception, space, and time. These make it possible for us to discern discrete objects, but since they are a part of the human apparatus of thinking and perceiving, and not of the world, the objects that are produced by them are representations. But a representation naturally implies something that is represented, and so it follows that for each representation there must also be a thing-in-itself, that is, a thing considered from the perspective of something unconditioned by our cognitive apparatus.[57] But since we can never escape our cognitive apparatus in order to see things as they are in themselves, we are forever cut off from this sphere, which only God, as omniscient, has access to. But, for Nietzsche, the idea of a thing-in-itself is simply a fiction, created as something standing in contrast to the appearances.

Another such fiction is the idea of a single unified ego.[58] This refers to Kant's doctrine of the transcendental unity of apperception, which states that in order for us to be able to discern individual objects in the world, there must be a single unified subject that brings together all of the perceptions that we have. In other words, if the many perceptions that we receive from the outside world were divided among a number of people, with each person just receiving a single perception, then it would be impossible for our cognitive apparatus to form determinate objects. It is only when the perceptions of an object are united in a single mind that they can become the representations that make up what we understand as reality. But Nietzsche's objection is that this is but another metaphysical fiction that resulted from our psychological needs. In this case we want to believe that we are all discrete individual subjects. The idea that we are simply an assortment of confused impressions, feelings, perceptions, thoughts, and so on, with no real substance or unity, makes us uncomfortable. If we are nothing but flux and change, then this implies that we will one day decay and die. We thus seek something stable and continuous in our own persons just as we do in the objects in the world around us. Only this can save us from the terrifying thought of death.

Nietzsche argues that the epistemological mistake lies in the fact that philosophers have always considered the one side of the two-world view to be a foundational truth in contrast to the empirical world, which is erroneous or illusory. Instead, he argues that the positing of such a view might be understandable as

---

[55] Nietzsche, *Der Wille zur Macht*, § 572, pp. 389f. (*The Will to Power*, § 572, p. 308).
[56] Chapter 2, Sect. 2.5, pp. 91–92 and Chapter 4, Sect. 4.5, p. 140.
[57] Nietzsche, *Der Wille zur Macht*, § 574, p. 391 (*The Will to Power*, § 574, pp. 308f.).
[58] Nietzsche, *Der Wille zur Macht*, § 574, p. 391; § 581, p. 396; § 585, p. 401 (*The Will to Power*, § 574, p. 309; § 581, p. 312; § 585, p. 316).

serving a purpose for the survival of the species. It is an evolutionary advantage to be able to discern individual objects as unities instead of as a riot of perceptions and impressions. But this is a far cry from an epistemological justification of a metaphysical truth claim that such unities actually exist. To say that I believe something because it is useful to me personally is by no means the same as saying that it is really true: "one would perish if one did not reason according to this mode of reason; but this is no 'proof' of what it asserts."[59] This fits perfectly with Jean Paul's description of Karlson's conversion. Gione argues that Karlson should believe in some form of afterlife since he would be much happier if he does. But this is not to say that there really is an afterlife. Indeed, prior to Karlson's capitulation, all such arguments had been heartily refuted. Yet Karlson gives in, despite his scientific training and disposition. From Nietzsche's perspective, this would be an obvious demonstration of the psychological importance of our metaphysical needs. Karlson needs to believe that Gione will not be completely annihilated when she dies, but this need to believe is not a replacement for a demonstration of the factual truth of the matter.

The result of these two-world views is that people come to disdain the world around them since it can never live up to the standard of the other world, to which one attributes all the positive characteristics such as truth, being, and reality. Both philosophers and ordinary people hate chaos, change, and transitoriness.[60] This disposition also comes to include a hatred for oneself since we are destined to live out our lives in the realm of error and becoming, without ever tasting the fruits of truth and being. Nietzsche refers to this hatred of the world with the French words, *décadence* and *ressentiment*.[61] Nihilism causes people to give up and resign themselves to the fact that they will never reach the truth or have any meaning or significance in the universe. This capitulation leads to *décadence*, which deprives them of their strength and energy to create values for themselves. It also leads to resentment as people come to resent the world and themselves for falling sadly short of the ideal. All of this sounds very much like Büchner's portrayal of Danton. Nietzsche takes the different forms of the denial of this world to be the consequences of nihilism. Since nothing in this world is regarded as having any value, when the belief in the other world disappears with the death of God, one is left with only a negative view of things.[62] Nietzsche also talks about this in terms of a weariness with life.[63] When one has suffered and becomes tired of life, it is natural to complain about

---

[59] Nietzsche, *Der Wille zur Macht*, § 579, p. 394 (*The Will to Power*, § 579, p. 311). See also *Der Wille zur Macht*, § 583, p. 397; § 584, p. 400 (*The Will to Power*, § 583, p. 313; § 584, p. 315).

[60] Nietzsche, *Der Wille zur Macht*, § 576, p. 392; § 585, p. 402 (*The Will to Power*, § 576, p. 309; § 585, p. 317).

[61] Nietzsche, *Der Wille zur Macht*, §§ 40–44, pp. 30–33; § 579, p. 393; § 584, p. 401; § 586, p. 409 (*The Will to Power*, §§ 40–44, pp. 25–27; § 579, p. 311; § 584, p. 316; § 586, p. 322).

[62] Nietzsche, *Der Wille zur Macht*, § 580, p. 395 (*The Will to Power*, § 580, p. 312).

[63] Nietzsche, *Der Wille zur Macht*, § 586, p. 409 (*The Will to Power*, § 586, p. 322).

one's lot and regret the lack of hope that accompanies the death of God. For Nietzsche, nihilism is the result of a lack of the strength of will:

> This same species of man, grown one stage poorer, no longer possessing the strength to interpret, to create fictions, produces *nihilists*. A nihilist is a man who judges of the world as it is that it ought not to be, and of the world as it ought to be that it does *not* exist. According to this view, our existence (action, suffering, willing, feeling) has no meaning.[64]

The nihilist sees the defects with the real world but is unable to retreat to the illusions of God or another world, which have lost their credibility. But this is not an easy position to be in psychologically. It takes great intellectual honesty and inward strength to maintain this: "It is a measure of the degree of strength of will to what extent one can do without meaning in things, to what extent one can endure to live in a meaningless world *because one organizes a small portion of it oneself*."[65] It was precisely on this point that Karlson failed. He did not have sufficient inward strength to live without the illusion of immortality, and so he chose to fall victim to it.

9.6 Nietzsche's Solution to Nihilism

Nietzsche provides a highly insightful analysis of the phenomenon of nihilism and its development in modern culture. But what does he propose as a solution to the problem? He begins by arguing that we must get rid of the two-world view, which has caused so many psychological distortions. He claims, "It is of cardinal importance that one should abolish the *true* world. It is the great inspirer of doubt and devaluator in respect of the world *we are*; it has been our most dangerous attempt yet to assassinate life."[66] The notion of a true world in the beyond has caused us to resent ourselves and this world. It has caused us to repress our passions and drives, or the will to power, which is the fundamental feature of human beings. We want to assert our will to power, but the corrupt and twisted worldview, perpetrated in large part by Christianity, deems such assertions of power negative and wages war on them. We are thus conflicted with our inner will and the rules, laws, and ethics of the external world, which we are obliged to follow even though they contradict this inner will.

Nietzsche also believes that it is necessary for people to begin to posit their own values. People feel incapacitated since the death of God removes any possibility of an objective or absolute value system. This leads them to resignation and weakness. But in time, some people can recover from this shock and begin

---

[64] Nietzsche, *Der Wille zur Macht*, § 585, p. 403 (*The Will to Power*, § 585, pp. 317f.).
[65] Nietzsche, *Der Wille zur Macht*, § 585, p. 403 (*The Will to Power*, § 585, p. 318).
[66] Nietzsche, *Der Wille zur Macht*, § 583, p. 398 (*The Will to Power*, § 583, p. 314).

to realize that they must think of values in a different way. Understanding that the very notion of objective truth or absolute values was an illusion to start with, they begin to reconceive values as something that can be posited by the individual. This, however, creates an entirely different dynamic from the old worldview. Now instead of the values being dictated from the outside, individuals must create them based on their own authority from the inside. This requires that individuals be strong and affirm their will to power instead of continuing to force themselves to repress it in accordance with the demands of society. But not everyone is strong; sadly, the vast majority of people are weak and have a need to conform to accepted customs and traditions. Nietzsche thus concedes that his solution is not one that will work for everyone. It will never become a mass movement. Instead, it is only possible that a small group of people will have the required creativity, strength, and desire to affirm their will to power. Only these people will be able to overcome nihilism by creating new values. Nietzsche clearly believes that the people of his own time are still wallowing in nihilism and do not yet have the strength to reverse the old values and embrace becoming and change instead of being and stability.[67]

In this regard Nietzsche can be said to go beyond Turgenev's Bazarov, who insisted that nihilism was a purely negative program and refused to give any indication of anything positive that would later replace the traditions, customs, and institutions that the nihilists were keen to destroy. The lack of any positive program was incomprehensible for Pavel and Nicholai. But as was noted, there was a tension in Bazarov's nihilism in that implicitly he clearly held certain values, such as that of science or the need to improve the lot of the peasants. So, the authenticity of the claim that his nihilism was purely negative was questionable. It seems that his position forces him into affirming some values, whether he wants to admit it or not. Nietzsche overcomes this contradiction by claiming straightforwardly that the "higher human being" or the "higher type" will be able to create new, positive values.[68] But this does not contradict the basic nihilist view in the sense that such a person is completely disabused of the illusions of the past. They know full well that whatever values they themselves posit are only their own and are thus contingent. Such people make no attempt to create new illusions by claiming some absolute or universal truth for their self-posited values.

The question of course remains about the extent to which this really solves the problem. The point of departure was that the discovery of the end of absolute values led people to a state of weakness, inertia, and helplessness. They could not imagine how to go on without these absolutes. Any value that they tried to posit on their own seemed ridiculously insignificant since it was deprived

---

[67] Nietzsche, *Der Wille zur Macht*, § 585, pp. 404f. (*The Will to Power*, § 585, p. 319).
[68] E.g., Nietzsche, *Der Wille zur Macht*, § 400, p. 273; § 544, p. 370; § 755, p. 505; § 859, p. 582 (*The Will to Power*, § 400, p. 216; § 544, pp. 292f.; § 755, p. 398; § 859, p. 458).

of any objective truth or validity. They could not even convince themselves of their own newly posited values, and without this conviction, they could not motivate themselves to do anything. Hard work, discipline, and the pursuit of goals all presuppose a motivation and a conviction that what one is doing is meaningful and worthwhile. Nietzsche seems to think that the higher men will be able to do this on the strength of their own will, but it is unclear where their motivation and conviction will come from if they remain relativists at heart.

Nietzsche believes that the death of God can in itself be inspiring and motivating since it liberates us from the chains of absolute value and external authority. We are now free to be creative and posit our own ideas of truth, justice, and beauty. The question of grounding is, for Nietzsche, still another hold-over from the old value system. For the higher man there is no need to try to justify one's newly posited values in any logical or discursive manner. This would mean submitting to the illusions of the law of contradiction and rationality that have already been rejected. But the problem remains that once these prejudices are rejected, the result seems to be relativism. Just to say that there is no need to justify one's view is not enough to provide one with a concrete motivation for a concrete task. One would end in a flippant disposition, ever moving from project to project, constantly changing goals and interests, without ever accomplishing anything. In the spirit of Møller, one could argue that it is difficult to see where the necessary degree of seriousness and discipline required to complete any more difficult task would come from.

9.7 Nietzsche and the Sciences

One aspect of Nietzsche's radicality concerns his disposition towards the sciences. We have seen throughout this study the importance of the role of the sciences in the development of the problem of nihilism. As the sciences became more precise and revealed surprising new things about the world, different aspects of the traditional Christian worldview were called into question. This explains the important role of the sciences in the works of the authors we have explored here. Some of the key figures such as Jean Paul's Karlson and Turgenev's Bazarov were scientists. Of the authors we have examined, Shelley, Schopenhauer, and Büchner all had a background in the natural sciences.

In line with this, Nietzsche seems to agree that the sciences are largely the cause of the death of God. But then in his further analysis, it becomes clear that he also believes that the sciences themselves are full of prejudices and are still grounded in many ways on the old worldview. The sciences operate with ideas such as the law of contradiction, purpose, unity, and truth, which he believes are simply fictions. Hence, when he argues against traditional Christian ideas, he does so not in the name of the sciences, as was the case with Karlson and Bazarov. Instead, it comes from a much more sweeping criticism that includes the sciences themselves. For Nietzsche, science is itself a prejudice that is based on the idea that the universe works according to certain fixed rules or constants. But this is just an illusion that results from our psychological need for metaphysical comfort. The sad truth, for Nietzsche, is that there are no such constants, but instead the universe is nothing but constant change and becoming with no *logos* behind the scenes. This picture is difficult to accept, and so people over time have developed science to satisfy their metaphysical needs.

It will be noted that some of our previous authors have anticipated Nietzsche's understanding of the universe as one governed by chaos instead of cosmos. For example, this is a part of Jean Paul's terrifying image in "The Dead Christ."[69] The same motif is found in *The Nightwatches*, where Kreuzgang rejects the idea of an orderly world but rather sees it as a "miscarried system."[70] Lord Byron also uses the motif, referring to the "chaos" in the human soul.[71] This is also found in the conclusion of Büchner's *Danton Death*, where the protagonist declares, "The world is chaos, nothingness its due messiah."[72]

Nietzsche's criticism of the very foundation of science seems to create a problem for his solution to nihilism. He claims that things like unity, substance, and cause and effect are mere prejudices, in contrast to Kant who argues that they are in fact necessary, a priori forms of our understanding. For Kant, it is impossible for us to think anything without these categories. Thus, according to his view, these are much more than simple prejudices that we can disregard as we like. They are necessary for any knowledge to be possible at all. Even if Nietzsche were right, and these were just prejudices, nonetheless, since this habit of perception or cognition is so engrained in us, it is not clear how anyone, even the higher types, would be able to come to view things differently merely by a sheer act of will. What would such a perception even look like? Here Nietzsche inadvertently seems to arrive back at Kant's long-discussed problem of the thing-in-itself.

Moreover, Nietzsche himself admits that humans would presumably have perished if they had not been capable of perceiving the world around them as

---

[69] Jean Paul, *Blumen-, Frucht- und Dornenstücke oder Ehestand, Tod und Hochzeit des Armenadvokaten F. St. Siebenkäs im Reichsmarktflecken Kuhschnappel*, vols. 1–3, Berlin: In Carl Matzdorff's Buchhandlung 1796–97, vol. 1, p. 7 (English translation: *Flower, Fruit, and Thorn Pieces; Or, The Wedded Life, Death, and Marriage of Firmian Stanislaus Siebenkæs*, trans. by Alexander Ewing, London: George Bell and Sons 1897, p. 263).

[70] *Nachtwachen. Von Bonaventura*, Penig: bey F. Dienemann und Comp. 1805, p. 94 (English translation: *The Nightwatches of Bonaventura*, trans. by Gerald Gillespie, Chicago and London: University of Chicago Press 2014, p. 41).

[71] Lord Byron, *Manfred, A Dramatic Poem*, London: John Murray 1817, p. 62, Act III, Scene I [lines 160–166].

[72] Georg Büchner, *Danton's Tod. Ein Drama*, ed. by Thomas Michael Mayer, in *Georg Büchner: Dantons Tod. Die Trauerarbeit im Schönen*, ed. by Peter von Becker, Frankfurt am Main: Schauspiel Frankfurt 1980, p. 69 (English translation in Georg Büchner, *Danton's Death* in *Complete Plays, Lenz and Other Writings*, trans. by John Reddick, London: Penguin 1993, p. 69). Quoted in Chapter 5, Sect. 5.6, p. 169.

a unity, with stable entities governed by cause-and-effect relations.[73] It thus seems that by Nietzsche's own admission, even if higher types were able to perceive without these categories, the new perception of the world, as one of change and chaos, would make it impossible for them to survive.

If Nietzsche believes that it is more truthful to reject the ideas of unity, substance, and cause and effect, how can he expect his readers to believe in his own explanation of the causes of nihilism? In other words, his account of the rise and fall of Christian theistic values depends on cause-and-effect relations, which he claims need to be rejected. This would seem to rule out any form of explanation of nihilism or anything else that requires some kind of attempt to trace the phenomenon under question back to its original source.

Along the same lines, how can Nietzsche claim that there is something called the will to power on these premises? If there is only change and nothing enduring, how can there be a unified thing called "the will" that persists over time? Nietzsche himself seems to concede that this is impossible.[74] Moreover, if everything is flux and change, how can he identify with any certainty those higher spirits or higher types and distinguish them from the rabble? In short, if the metaphysical categories are merely prejudices formed by habit, then this would seem to prevent Nietzsche from making any kind of positive statement or truth claim at all since no such claim would ever be enduring, no subject would ever be a meaningful, coherent unity, and no connection of subject and predicate would ever be anything more than a subjective impression. This view rules out any thinking or communication at all. To be sure, there is something powerful and profound in Nietzsche's criticism. However, it is so sweeping that it precludes any kind of solution to nihilism, including his own proposals.

---

[73] Nietzsche, *Der Wille zur Macht*, § 579, p. 394 (*The Will to Power*, § 579, p. 311). See also *Der Wille zur Macht*, § 583, p. 397; § 584, p. 400 (*The Will to Power*, § 583, p. 313; § 584, p. 315).
[74] Nietzsche, *Der Wille zur Macht*, § 46, pp. 34f. (*The Will to Power*, § 46, p. 28).

10

The Importance of Nihilism in the Nineteenth Century

There can be no doubt that the issue of nihilism was important in the discussions concerning philosophy, literature, and religion in the nineteenth century. Many of the leading cultural figures played a role in the discussion, which took place in different fields and spheres of culture. What has been presented in this book is only a small selection of works that treat the broad theme of nihilism in one way or another. As has been mentioned in the individual chapters, for all the authors examined here, there are many other relevant texts that could also have been treated. Moreover, there are many other authors not discussed here who might have been included. For example, mention could be made of the Italian philosopher and writer Giacomo Leopardi (1798-1837), who makes frequent use of nihilistic motifs in many of his works. Jacobi's early use of the term "nihilism" to describe the results of the failure of early German idealism to demonstrate the existence of God or the external world is also well worthy of discussion.[1] Novalis's powerful *Hymns to the Night* (1800) also explores the problem of nihilism.[2] Further, Max Stirner's work *The Ego and Its Own* (1845) has often been associated with

---

[1] See Jacobi's *David Hume über den Glauben, oder Idealismus und Realismus. Ein Gespräch*, in *Friedrich Heinrich Jacobi's Werke*, vols. 1-6, Leipzig: Gerhard Fleischer 1812-25, vol. 2 (1815), p. 108 (English translation: *David Hume on Faith or Idealism and Realism: A Dialogue*, in Jacobi, *The Main Philosophical Writings and the Novel Allwill*, trans. by George di Giovanni, Montreal: McGill-Queen's University Press 2009, p. 583): "The moment man sought to prove scientifically the veracity of our representations of an immaterial world that exists beyond them, to prove the substantiality of the human spirit, and of a free Author of this universe who is however distinct from it, of a Providence conscious of its rule, i.e. *personal* Providence, the only one that would be *truly* Providence – the moment he tried this, the object likewise disappeared before the eyes of the demonstrators. They were left with merely logical phantoms. And in this way they discovered nihilism." See also *Jacobi an Fichte*, in *Friedrich Heinrich Jacobi's Werke*, vol. 3 (1816), p. 44 (*Jacobi to Fichte*, in *The Main Philosophical Writings and the Novel Allwill*, p. 519).

[2] Novalis, *Hymnen an die Nacht*, in *Atheneum. Eine Zeitschrift*, ed. by August Wilhelm Schlegel and Friedrich Schlegel, vol. 3, part 2, Berlin: Heinrich Fröhlich 1800, pp. 188-204 (English translation: *Hymns to the Night*, trans. by Dick Higgins, Kingston, NY: McPherson & Co. 1978).

nihilism.[3] As mentioned above, Karl Gutzkow's little-known novel, *The Ring or the Nihilists* (1853), uses the term directly and presents it in part in a social-political context that seems to anticipate Turgenev.[4] This work would be useful for the story of the development of nihilism since it serves as a bridge between the concept in the German tradition and the nihilist movement in Russia. Dostoevsky treats nihilism in a number of different works. As noted, he criticizes directly the Russian movement of nihilism in *The Possessed* (1871-72).[5]

In the Anglophone tradition, Thomas Carlyle's satirical *Sartor Resartus* (1833-34) is known for the famous chapter "The Everlasting No," which is a celebrated literary expression of nihilism.[6] It represents an account of the metaphysical crisis experienced by the protagonist, Professor Teufelsdröckh, and portrays a mechanical universe indifferent to human hopes and needs. Carlyle's friend Ralph Waldo Emerson helped him to publish the work as an independent monograph in Boston.[7] Emerson himself later took up the problem of nihilism in his essay "Experience" (1844), where he addresses the sense of isolation, meaninglessness, and disorientation that is found in the face of the contingencies of the modern world.[8] This essay was written following the death of his young son, and it speaks to the sense of human vulnerability and helplessness vis-à-vis nature. The work by Scottish poet James B.V. Thomson *The City of Dreadful Night* (1874) is a profound but little-known statement of modern nihilism.[9] At the turn of the century, the American philosopher and

---

[3] Max Stirner, *Der Einzige und sein Eigenthum*, Leipzig: Otto Wigand 1845 (English translation: *The Ego and Its Own*, ed. by David Leopold, Cambridge: Cambridge University Press 1995). See R.W.K. Paterson, *The Nihilistic Egoist Max Stirner*, New York: Oxford University Press 1971.

[4] See Chapter 7, Sect. 7.1, p. 205. This work appeared in installments in Gutzkow's journal: *Der Ring oder die Nihilisten*, in *Unterhaltungen am häuslichen Herd*, 1853, no. 37, pp. 577-585; no. 38, pp. 593-601; no. 39, pp. 609-616; no. 40, pp. 628-638; no. 41, pp. 641-651; no. 42, pp. 657-662; no. 43, pp. 673-684.

[5] Chapter 8, Sect. 8.7, p. 257.

[6] The three books of Thomas Carlyle's *Sartor Resartus* were originally published serially in *Fraser's Magazine for Town and Country*, vol. 8, 1833: Book I, chapters I-IV (pp. 581-592); Book I, chapters V-XI (pp. 669-684); vol. 9, 1834: Book II, chapters I-IV (pp. 177-195); Book II, chapters V-VII (pp. 301-313); Book II, chapters VIII-X (pp. 443-455); Book III, chapters I-V (pp. 664-674); no. 50, vol. 10, 1834: Book III, chapters VI-VIII (pp. 77-87); Book III, chapters IX-XII (pp. 182-193).

[7] Thomas Carlyle, *Sartor Resartus: The Life and Opinions of Herr Teufelsdröckh*, ed. by R.W. Emerson, Boston: James Munroe 1836.

[8] Ralph Waldo Emerson, "Experience," in his *Essays: Second Series*, Boston: James Munroe 1844, pp. 49-93.

[9] James B.V. Thomson, *The City of Dreadful Night*, London: Reeves and Turner 1880. This work was originally published in the *National Reformer* in March-May 1874. See Tom Leonard, *Places of the Mind: The Life and Work of James Thomson ('B.V.')*, London: Jonathan Cape 1993.

psychologist William James addressed the question of nihilism in his essay "Is Life Worth Living?" (1896).[10] Returning to this issue in *The Varieties of Religious Experience* (1902), James explores different forms of what he refers to as "the sick soul," that is, the nihilist or pessimist.[11] The German theologian Ernst Troeltsch, in his *The Absoluteness of Christianity and the History of Religion* (1902), takes up the question of how Christianity can make an absolute claim to be in sole possession of the truth when it is merely one historical form of religion among others.[12] Using this as his point of departure, he examines the problems raised by historical relativism that have sometimes been associated with nihilism.

There are thus many other thinkers and writers who could claim a place in the history of nihilism in the nineteenth century. For the individual chapters here, I have tried to identify for analysis those works that have exercised a cultural influence on the discussion about nihilism in their own time and later in the twentieth century. I have also selected other lesser-known authors to illustrate the breadth of the issue during this period and to show how they anticipated later discussions. But I readily concede that the story about the development of nihilism in the nineteenth century could also be told with other texts and writers.

10.1 The Different Diagnoses of Nihilism

The thinkers and writers explored here all sketched a slightly different version of the problem of nihilism. The basic formula that leads to nihilism seems to consist in two main elements. First, most all the authors suffered a personal tragedy in their lives, be it the death of a loved one or a radical reversal of fortune. This plunged them into profound grief and led them to question the meaning of human existence. Second, they also had a common concern for the new secular scientific conception of nature and the universe, which seems to imply that humans are insignificant and that their lives are meaningless. These are key elements in the constellation of issues that characterize nihilism.

---

[10] William James, *Is Life Worth Living?*, Philadelphia: S. Burns Weston 1896. This essay was reprinted the following year: William James, "Is Life Worth Living?," in his *The Will to Believe and Other Essays*, New York, London, and Bombay: Longmans, Green, and Co. 1897, pp. 32–62.

[11] William James, *The Varieties of Religious Experience: A Study in Human Nature*, New York, London, and Bombay: Longmans, Green, and Company 1902.

[12] Ernst Troeltsch, *Die Absolutheit des Christentums und die Religionsgeschichte. Vortrag gehalten auf der Versammlung der Freunde der Christlichen Welt zu Mühlacker am 3. Oktober 1901*, Tübingen: J.C.B. Mohr 1902 (English translation: *The Absoluteness of Christianity and the History of Religions*, trans. by David Reid, Louisville, KY: Westminster John Knox Press 1971).

10.1 THE DIFFERENT DIAGNOSES OF NIHILISM

For Jean Paul, the clear worry is human mortality. If we are simply annihilated with death, then our existence seems meaningless. Our psychology is not designed to accept the unbearable thought that we live only for a short time and then will disappear forever. This thought is ruinous for our happiness and flourishing in the world. Despite whatever science teaches us, we must believe that there is an afterlife in one form or another. Thus, Jean Paul's point of departure is the scientific worldview that excludes any form of continued existence after death. On this view, the universe is simply a boundless void determined by chance and the forces of nature. In the end everything turns to nothingness. This idea leads to anxiety, despair, and nihilism. For the sake of our happiness and that of those we love, we must believe that our existence will continue forever. In a sense Jean Paul can be said to anticipate Nietzsche's death of God. If one were simply confronted with human finitude and mortality as the way the universe is, this might be accepted. But the problem becomes acute when one starts from the Christian context where there is a conviction that God and immortality are real, and then this conviction is disappointed by the bad news, delivered by the sciences, that these ideas are mistaken. After having once believed in God and immortality, one experiences the news that these are simply illusions or myths as crushing. This is a part of the message of "The Dead Christ," which Jean Paul seems to think captures the dilemma of his times. He clearly believes that the scientific worldview offers no help or comfort regarding these matters that are so important for us. The nihilistic view that he rejects is thus that of atheism and a denial of the notion of immortality.

In *The Nightwatches* Klingemann presents a harsh world in which all humans die and revert to nothingness. As in Jean Paul, death and mortality play an important role in Klingemann's conception of nihilism. However, while Jean Paul believes that humans are noble and elevated creatures, Klingemann's protagonist Kreuzgang regards them as scoundrels and rogues. Since, as Jean Paul pointed out, it is difficult to live with the idea that we will all one day die and turn to dust, people create elaborate forms of self-deception and distractions so that they can pretend that this is not the case. Life in society is all about this. People constantly put on masks and play roles that give them a sense of enduring truth and stability, where there is none. Only in moments of extreme crisis, such as impending death, do they put these aside. Most of our lives are spent in trivial activities and pursuits that we ridiculously invest with great importance. Hence, human society is full of irrationality and hypocrisy. Only those like Kreuzgang who stand on the fringes as outsiders are able to recognize freely the truth of the meaninglessness of existence and see human life for what it is: an absurd farce. For Jean Paul the threat of nihilism leads to a sense of the tragic. By contrast, for Klingemann the suitable response to the meaninglessness of the world also includes comedy and laughter. For Klingemann the sober natural scientific picture is in many ways the point of departure. It stands in utter contradiction to the behavior and beliefs of people. The bottom line, with which the novel ends, is that nature triumphs over human absurdity and everything ends in nothing, from which there is no escape.

Byron's *Manfred* takes as its starting point the motif of the danger of science and knowledge that can lead to despair. As has been noted with regard to Schiller's poem "The Veiled Statue at Sais," the allegory of forbidden knowledge can be interpreted as the awareness of nihilism resulting from a scientific worldview. The protagonist is haunted by the memory of his incestuous relationship with his sister. His knowledge of this makes his life miserable, and he desperately seeks some way to erase the memory. This leads him to ask for help from the supernatural powers, but he learns that the forces of nature, represented by spirits, have no interest in human affairs. With earthquakes, floods, hurricanes, tornadoes, and so on, the forces of nature are in fact destructive to human life and flourishing. Despite the poetic personification of these forces, the picture that Byron presents is otherwise in line with the modern scientific understanding of nature. The message is that humans are alone in a meaningless universe. Manfred becomes numb to the world when he realizes that there is nothing that he or anyone else can do to resolve the problem of the memory of his sin. Our lives are full of torment and pain. As a result, we are condemned to live out our days in the suffering that comes with consciousness. This anticipates the idea found in later thinkers that nihilism is a problem for those who reflect too much on such topics. Dostoevsky's underground man says that he suffers from hyperconsciousness, which he regards as a kind of disease.[13]

For Shelley, the infinite time and space of the universe mean that our lives are but a miniscule dot in the universe. In the poem "Ozymandias" he soberly points out that even the greatest achievements of the most powerful rulers will over time fall into ruin and end in dust. In agreement with Klingemann, Shelley thus criticizes human arrogance and vanity for believing in the importance of our small accomplishments. Given the limited role that we play in the grand scheme of things, any form of pride is misplaced. The appreciation of the dimensions of time and space is presumably something that came from Shelley's study of the sciences. It is this scientific view that exposes human activity for what it really is. This can be regarded as tragic (as in Jean Paul) or humorous (as in Klingemann), but in the end it is always meaningless.

Schopenhauer's philosophy can in a sense be seen as an attempt to think through a consistent atheism based on the scientific worldview. He takes his fundamental metaphysical principle of the will-to-live to be based on clear scientific evidence. As with Shelley, Schopenhauer believes that our existence is insignificant in space and time. Moreover, as natural entities, our very being is nothing but a constant cycle of drives and desires that return again and again forever. We dedicate our lives to the futile pursuit of satisfying these. But

---

[13] Fyodor Dostoevsky, *Notes from Underground and The Grand Inquisitor*, trans. by Ralph E. Matlaw, New York Penguin 1991, pp. 6–7.

happiness is only the momentary satisfaction of our desires that never endures. For this reason, human existence can be characterized as suffering. Even if we do manage to attain a degree of satisfaction, we are confronted with another problem: boredom. According to Schopenhauer's bleak picture, our lives are not only meaningless and insignificant but also full of suffering. Jean Paul and Byron acknowledge the mental anguish and despair but seem less attentive to the physical suffering that is central to Schopenhauer. For Klingemann, humans are stupid, cruel, and mendacious, but they are not suffering all the time. Most of the suffering is reserved for the lower classes and outsiders like Kreuzgang himself.

Büchner's *Danton's Death* presents a sobering view of reality. Death and anxiety are omnipresent, and suicide is commonplace. The social world that humans have created for themselves is characterized by cruelty and suffering. The protagonist Danton, formerly an engaged revolutionary who passionately fought against the *ancien régime*, is now reduced to apathy and indifference. Fully disenchanted with the direction that the revolution has taken, he is resigned to his fate and even looks forward to his death on the guillotine as a relief from suffering. Like Byron's Manfred, Danton is tormented by an inner grief caused by a sense of guilt, which leaves him no rest. From the political perspective, Danton's execution only serves a momentary purpose since his enemy Robespierre, but a short time later, follows him to the guillotine himself. None of this seems to make any sense or have any meaning despite the high-sounding political rhetoric about the great sacrifices that must be made for the revolution. Life is a terrible burden with no justice. This is a world of death and violence where little consolation or comfort is possible. The modern scientific view of nature is also important here. Büchner portrays humans as driven by their desires and passions in a manner that is wholly in line with Schopenhauer's conception of the will. Human society tries to restrain these with ethics, social mores, and laws, but this only leads to hypocrisy and makes the fulfillment of the natural side of human beings more difficult to attain. Human existence is a passionate striving that ends in nothing. Danton is by no means the only nihilist character in the work. Robespierre also regards the world as being driven by natural processes that have no meaning or significance. There is a strong tone of fatalism in his view.

Poul Martin Møller agrees with Jean Paul in the assessment that the problem of nihilism arises primarily from the denial of the idea of immortality. Møller is concerned with the rise of Hegelian philosophy, which, he claims, has no clear doctrine about the afterlife. He sees the left Hegelians as typical of the age, since they, influenced by the sciences, have called immortality into doubt. Møller fears that this can have devastating consequences, not just for individuals but also for all spheres of culture. Without a doctrine of immortality, we fall into nihilism, which undermines all sense of value concerning our own lives and those of others. We would no longer be able to take anything seriously since nothing is lasting. This prevents people from investing any time in social reforms to improve the way things are. It likewise undermines art since all artistic works would be regarded as ephemeral and meaningless. Møller thus sees his age as in a crisis that threatens to undermine everything. This diagnosis of the crisis can be seen as anticipating Nietzsche's perceptive account of the death of God and its widespread consequences for European culture.

Kierkegaard's aesthetic writer in *Either/Or*, Part I bears a certain resemblance to Klingemann's Kreuzgang. Both are outsiders who enjoy criticizing the absurdities and hypocrisies of the world, where they fail to find any deeper sense of meaning and value. The aesthete is familiar with depression, sorrow, and anguish. He is haunted by the idea of death and meaninglessness. In "At a Graveside," Kierkegaard also addresses the question of death directly. Since death is not something that we can ever experience directly in life, it remains inexplicable. This is the limit of scientific knowing. Due to this, death is a problem for people who repress the idea and try to busy themselves with trivial matters so as not to think about it. Kierkegaard's conception of nihilism is thus also related to the fact of death and meaninglessness.

Turgenev opens a new direction in the discourse on nihilism in *Fathers and Sons*. His character Bazarov understands nihilism as a negation of social norms, values, and traditions that he takes to be oppressive. Like Kreuzgang and Kierkegaard's aesthete, Bazarov enjoys provoking the older generation with his radical views. He too stands apart from the mainstream, despite his efforts to befriend the serfs. Like Schopenhauer, Bazarov takes his radical disposition to be fully grounded in science. He is himself a student of medicine and believes that science holds the key to improving the lives of the oppressed classes. Turgenev's explicit use of the term "nihilism" in the political sphere created its own tradition, where it was understood as a form of radicalism, terrorism, or anarchism. The question of death and the meaninglessness of life is only secondary, although there are points of overlap in Turgenev's characterization of nihilism and that of the other thinkers and writers examined here.

Like Turgenev, Nietzsche also uses the term "nihilism" directly. He understands it to be the situation in which Europe finds itself when it realizes that God does not exist and that the traditional values that accompany this belief come to be seen as simple fictions. This means that all the highest values lose their meaning, and people find themselves in a state of desperation and uncertainty. Their worldview has collapsed, and there seems to be no obvious way forward. If God does not exist, then there is no meaning in the world and no absolute values. Everything lapses into relativism. Nietzsche also believes that the rise of the sciences has played an important role in the collapse of the Christian worldview and has left behind a barren universe in which we find ourselves alone with no comfort or consolation. For Nietzsche, the primary focus of nihilism is not the question of human mortality but rather of values and ethics. He takes the further step of criticizing science itself, calling into question basic scientific presuppositions such as the unity and order of the universe, which he regards as metaphysical prejudices.

10.2 The Proposed Solutions to Nihilism

Given the different understandings of the problem of nihilism just outlined, it stands to reason that the thinkers and writers that we have explored propose a variety of different solutions. Each tries to develop a solution that fits with his own conception of the problem. Although a solution for death and suffering will presumably never be found, there remains a degree of *Spielraum* in what follows from this. For some people these are unfortunate facts that we have to learn to live with, while for others they are a motivation to return to religious faith. But in any case, there is clearly a need to address the issue in some way. The proposed solutions that have been explored here should be seen in this light. Most of the authors make some effort to try to help people come to terms with these facts of existence, and these can thus be regarded as perhaps *partial* solutions in the sense that no definitive solution seems possible. What are we to make of these different solutions to the problem of nihilism? Could any of these plausibly resolve this issue and the negative consequences that seem to follow from it?

For Jean Paul the threat of death is so vexing that it is impossible to live a happy life if one is constantly troubled by this idea. His proposal is simply to accept the idea of immortality and of God. He is not insistent that these must be completely in line with the traditional religious conceptions, and to this extent he grants that modern science has enjoined us to think about the issue in different ways. But nonetheless we must have a belief in immortality since the alternative is simply too terrible to contemplate. When especially we consider the death of our loved ones or small children, we realize that this is not something that we can live with. In the end Karlson agrees that, despite everything he knows about science, he too must accede to a belief in immortality. Believing is the only escape from nihilism.

Jean Paul's solution thus seems simple enough, but one cannot help but wonder if it would be truly effective. Even the most devoted religious believer periodically has crises of faith. Indeed, religious belief necessarily implies the possibility of doubt from time to time. Everyone is occasionally disturbed by thoughts of death and despair, even if they deny it or adamantly claim that they believe in immortality. In this sense, it is hard to imagine that the problem can be solved by a mere act of the will to believe. It is impossible to think that Karlson, after capitulating to belief in immortality, will from then on simply live happily without the thought ever again crossing his mind that Gione might be completely destroyed by death. He would presumably continue to be nagged by doubts and plagued with anxieties about the mortality of Gione. Jean Paul's ostensible solution can thus be seen as a form of bad faith or self-deception that really does little to eliminate the despair and anxiety that everyone feels from time to time.

Moreover, Jean Paul's idea that we must believe in immortality for the sake of our mental health and happiness seems problematic, and for this reason his portrayal of Karlson's capitulation looks implausible. According to science, something can only be taken for true if it can be proven or verified empirically. Whether someone *wants* it to be true or not is entirely irrelevant to the issue. The universe does not operate according to our wishes. If Karlson were a true scientist, as he seems to be up until the point of his conversion, then it is difficult to see how he would consent to the idea of immortality just because he would like this to be true for the sake of Gione. He even concedes that he must make an exception for this belief since it contradicts the entire scientific worldview that he subscribes to. Here the issue of self-honesty and authenticity should prevent him from going along with the urgings of his friends to believe. Science is about finding the truth and not reverting to self-deception for the sake of other reasons.

Klingemann offers a rich and wonderful portrayal of a nihilistic world. Kreuzgang's view seems consistent: at the end of *The Nightwatches* he does not seek shelter in any notions of religion or immortality. With the final scene in the graveyard, Klingemann focuses on the material side of human existence. When we die, our bodies decay and slowly disintegrate. The memories of our insignificant lives also fade and become forgotten. There is no immortality or redemption. If anything, Klingemann seems to confront readers with this sad reality and enjoins them to accept it without deflecting it with hypocrisy and lies. These deceptions then also play a role in the broader network of hypocrisy that one finds in society in general. So, in a sense one might say that, for Klingemann, nihilism is a problem without a solution. We will all die and be annihilated with death, and there is nothing that anyone can do to change this.

Although Klingemann does not try to offer a solution to the problem of nihilism, nonetheless he serves as a useful corrective to Jean Paul since Kreuzgang is constantly critical of the absurdities and hypocrisies of society. Presumably he would regard Karlson in just this light, seeing him as a person who has lied to himself since this is a convenient way for him to avoid thinking about the unpleasant prospect of death and suffering. People live in self-deceptions of this kind all their lives. These self-deceptions give us the sense that our activities have some meaning and are important. But the sad truth is that once the masks are removed, all that is left is a mortal, finite, physical being. As a scientist, Karlson should know this as well as anyone. The social criticism in *The Nightwatches* seems completely accurate, but it offers no solution to the problem. We still languish from despair and anxiety in the face of suffering, death, and our insignificance in the universe. For, whatever one might think of them, the self-deceptions about an afterlife did not arise by chance. There are good reasons why these are so widespread. So, this approach, while in many ways sympathetic and insightful, does not really resolve anything.

Byron's protagonist Manfred rejects the help of the different spirits and the pleas of the abbot, who repeatedly begs him to repent. He refuses to bow before the god of evil, Arimanes, or to make himself beholden to the witch of the Alps in exchange for her help. The message thus seems to be that humans are alone and must manage their struggles in life on their own. The only thing that has any real power is the human mind and will. These faculties alone are stronger than nature, at least in some respects. Although aware of his own imminent death, Manfred remains true to his independence. While death is a fact that cannot be changed, Manfred can determine how he will live his life, and he chooses freedom and integrity, thus rejecting servitude and unreflectiveness.

Plagued by a feeling of despair, anxiety, and guilt, Manfred, at the outset, resembles a nihilist who wishes to die. But he ultimately realizes that he must sort out this problem on his own. While Manfred is fully disabused and honest with regard to the inevitability of his own death, he nonetheless radically asserts his own freedom. He insists that for whatever wrongs he has committed, this is a matter between him and his own conscience or God. No one else can have anything to do with this. Each individual must cope with the facts of human existence on their own. There is an aspect of existentialist rebellion and heroism in Manfred's rejection of the authority of the supernatural powers and the church. Despite the power of the universe to crush him, he remains defiant to the end. In this sense the message seems to be that, despite all our limitations vis-à-vis nature, the human mind is still always something higher. It can always affirm its freedom, even in the face of death.

This approach or, if one will, *solution* is sympathetic in the sense that it calls for authenticity and self-honesty. It empowers individuals to lead their lives in the way that they wish. It allows one to look death in the eye and maintain human dignity. But, as with the case of the existentialists, this view seems to fall victim to relativism. It gives license for people to interpret their misdeeds in a way favorable to themselves. Apart from the limitations set by, for example, Sartre's theory of bad faith, there is no evaluative standard that can be imposed on anything. Ethics remains a completely open field since no definitive judgments about anyone else's actions can ever be made. One can only pass judgment on oneself, and experience shows that people tend to be unrealistically forgiving towards themselves. This was the problem of relativism that the existentialists such as Camus, Sartre, and de Beauvoir all struggled in vain to overcome.

In "Ozymandias" Shelley does not directly propose any kind of solution to nihilism, which is understood as the meaninglessness of human accomplishment. Shelley's position can be understood along the lines of Klingemann as a form of social criticism that rebukes people for taking themselves or their social roles seriously. The poem asks us to keep in mind the finitude of human existence. This is a general human problem that everyone must deal with. In a sense this can be said to anticipate Kierkegaard's reflections on the proper disposition towards one's own finitude and mortality. Given this fact of life, one should be humble and aware of one's limited meaning in the big picture. Shelley can be read as suggesting that the realization of nihilism can lead us to moral improvement

Since Shelley's assessment is in part a kind of social criticism, it can be useful to help people to see through the vanity of others who try to portray their own work and accomplishments as something of great value and significance. But this is not a positive tool that can help one to find any meaning in one's own life. On the contrary, self-honesty would seem to dictate that one regard one's own activities, achievements, and even one's own life as ultimately meaningless. But it is little consolation to criticize others for their egoism when one's own life is completely devoid of value and meaning.

For Schopenhauer, the will-to-live is the cause of human suffering since it is the source of our constant drives and desires that make life a meaningless struggle. Therefore, it stands to reason that the denial of this will is the solution. Only if one can manage to put a stop to the unending stream of drives can one be free from them. Inspired by Buddhism, Schopenhauer recommends following the model of asceticism to attain inward peace. This same sense of pleasure can be derived on a short-term basis in the form of aesthetic enjoyment by, for example, beholding a beautiful work of art or listening to a sublime musical piece.

Schopenhauer proposes the denial of the will as the best way to live since this prevents us from becoming slaves of our natural desires and drives. Yet, as has been noted, it is impossible for this to be completely successful. Even for the most extreme, iron-willed ascetic, the basic fact still holds that our drives and desires will always return. Since these are the result of the fact that we have bodies, only with death and the destruction of the body will we be free of them. But this poses the problem again instead of solving it. The fear of death and our insignificance in the universe remain. Although Schopenhauer has a much more elaborate theory, he seems to come to basically the same conclusion as Klingemann and Shelley, namely that there is no real solution to nihilism. Schopenhauer himself admits as much at the end of the first volume of *The World as Will and Representation* when he concedes that, with the complete destruction of the will with death, what is left is nothingness.[14] He thus ultimately admits that death and annihilation cannot be escaped. Likewise, the external world around us with all its stars and galaxies will revert to nothingness.

---

[14] Arthur Schopenhauer, *Die Welt als Wille und Vorstellung*, vols. 1–2, 2nd revised and enlarged ed., Leipzig: F.A. Brockhaus 1844, vol. 1, § 71, p. 464 (English translation: *The World as Will and Representation*, vols. 1–2, trans. by E.F.J. Payne, New York: Dover 1969, vol. 1, § 71, pp. 411f.).

Schopenhauer's idea of the denial of the will seems to be a recommendation for how best to live with the miserable condition of human existence, but ultimately there is no room for hope of anything more than this.

In Büchner's *Danton's Death* life is full of suffering, and the only real relief can be found in death. It might be argued that the hedonism or Epicureanism of Danton and his followers is the only logical conclusion to this picture. Since there is no real enduring happiness, it is best just to seize on whatever momentary pleasures one can find when one has the chance. But these can only provide a fleeting respite from the grim realities of death and suffering, which are the fate of everyone. They serve to numb the senses to the world and thus lead one to a nihilistic indifference. This does not really solve the problem of nihilism but instead seems to acknowledge that it is insolvable. Danton in effect commits suicide by returning to Paris, although he had a chance to escape. It will be recalled that the final casualty of the drama is Lucile, the loving wife of Camille. After her husband's execution on the guillotine, she shouts out a royalist slogan for which she is immediately arrested. Thus, she also in effect commits suicide. This ending does not bespeak any hint of a solution to the nihilist world that the work portrays.

Büchner thus seems to follow the same general line of Klingemann by offering an insightful nihilist interpretation of the human condition that leads us to be critical of the world around us but falls short of any positive recommendation or suggestion about how to deal with it. Life is full of meaningless death and suffering, and there is nothing we can do about it. Suicide is a natural result of this situation. From this perspective, there is no real point in providing a suggestion for how best to think about or cope with the issue since this will change nothing. There is a dimension of fatalism in Büchner that explains this. We are born into the world and are caught up in its struggles and miseries. Whatever we might happen to think about it is entirely irrelevant. Given this, Danton's indifference and apathy towards his own death starts to make sense. If life is nothing but a painful struggle, then death is not something to be feared but rather a relief. The natural response is resignation.

Poul Martin Møller believes that his contemporaries are beginning to realize that their age is on the brink of a crisis caused by the nihilism that has resulted from discarding the doctrine of immortality. Now it is dawning on them that science does not hold all the answers and that the results of science can be distorted when taken in isolation. Møller argues that we all have a general worldview that determines the basic points of orientation in our lives. This is a complex network of beliefs that includes all the spheres of human life and culture. He tries to demonstrate that, without the belief in immortality, one's worldview collapses since the denial of this belief has a knock-on effect for everything else. Thus, for us to make sense of our own lives, ethics, politics, art, religion, and so on, we must believe in immortality. This is not a scientific argument based on empirical evidence, but rather a conceptual one, something along the lines of Kant's postulates of practical reason. Since we cannot prove or disprove the issue of immortality empirically, we are left to examine it in this way. According to Møller, the only viable worldview is one that contains a notion of immortality. Here he can be seen as taking a hint from Jean Paul concerning the necessity of the belief in immortality due to our psychological constitution. But Møller takes the argument much further than Jean Paul by demonstrating the connections between immortality and the rest of our many views and beliefs. Thus, on pain of inconsistency, we are obliged to believe in immortality in order to maintain our interest in the different spheres of human existence.

Møller's proposal is that we can restore the doctrine of immortality to its proper place by seeing it as a necessary part of a complete life-view. The assumption is that our worldview must be consistent with all our thoughts and feelings, and therefore everything must hang together logically. It is not possible to maintain in this view the idea of our complete annihilation in death since this would imply the collapse of so many other things. This seems to be the force of Jean Paul's "The Dead Christ," which is intended to frighten the reader into religious belief. Given that the alternative to the existence of God and immortality is so terrible to contemplate, we must simply believe. However, this argument, which Møller shares with Jean Paul, is ultimately a non sequitur. It simply does not follow that the denial of immortality means that we would completely lose interest in our relations to other people and in our own lives. There are many people today who do not believe in immortality and yet are still actively engaged in their human relations and their own projects. They are still highly interested in things such as politics and art. Jean Paul and Møller seem to be still caught up in the older view that a widespread nihilism or specifically a denial of immortality will lead to the collapse of society. This might have been a great fear in earlier times, but from the perspective of our modern secular society it seems that this fear was unfounded. The elimination of key traditional religious doctrines and the lapse of religious belief in some circles have certainly not led to the destruction of civilization. Our interests and values seem to be much more firmly fixed and grounded than Møller believes. They cannot be destroyed by the refutation of a single belief, namely, the idea of immortality. So, this also proves to be an inadequate way out of the problem of nihilism.

Kierkegaard's aesthetic writer from the first volume of *Either/Or* is a merciless social critic and is flippant with regard to accepted values and customs. He seems to give advice indirectly through his way of living. He appears to recommend an indolent and self-indulgent lifestyle with points of comparison with Büchner's Danton. Kierkegaard's aesthete here seems to be a character sketch intended to evoke discussion from his readers. However, it is difficult to regard this as a serious recommendation by Kierkegaard himself for overcoming the problems of life related to nihilism. At best one might regard the aesthete as a useful model for critical thinking.

By contrast to *Either/Or*, "At a Graveside" is written in a sober tone and takes the issue of death and meaning very seriously. Contrary to both Jean Paul and Møller, Kierkegaard claims that instead of falling into despair and concluding that one's life is meaningless, the individual in fact can use the awareness of death to give his or her life great meaning. In fact, if we regard our lives as finite, then the meaning and value of every moment increases. Every day and every hour are precious since they are finite and can never be retrieved. This challenges us to rethink our lives radically since we become aware of their true value only when we think of death. This anticipates the works of the twentieth-century existentialists. It also clearly exposes the non sequitur in the thinking of both Jean Paul and Møller. The fact of the inevitability of death can be interpreted in different ways: as something that deprives one's life of all meaning or as something that bestows meaning upon it.

Although a religious writer, Kierkegaard refrains from preaching about the immortality of the soul as a certain fact. In fact, he claims that death is an enigma that transcends human knowledge. He further argues that we should be honest with ourselves about this by regarding it as something indefinable and inexplicable. This means we should resist the temptation to turn death into something concrete and certain, thus pretending that we understand it. Kierkegaard acknowledges the problem that death poses for people. Death is a certainty, and this calls into question the meaning of our lives. The very thought of death evokes anxiety and despair. Most people are unreflective and prefer not to dwell on the issue. There are plenty of other things to attend to in daily life, and so it is easy enough to avoid contemplating such unpleasant ideas. This means that most people only think about death when they are forced to, namely when someone else is gravely ill or dies. But, according to Kierkegaard, when people talk about the death of others, this is yet another distraction mechanism that allows one to avoid thinking about one's own death. Kierkegaard challenges us to think of death *earnestly*, that is, by thinking of our own death and what it means to us. While this cannot be regarded as a proposal for a solution to nihilism, it is probably good advice. Like Klingemann and Shelley, he believes that the thought of death is so uncomfortable for most people that they try to avoid it. So, there is an important point in being honest with oneself and thinking about it.

Likewise, Kierkegaard does not try to argue for the existence of God. Instead, he simply says that one should think of God while one is still alive since our relation as individuals to God is also important for giving meaning to our existence. So, in a sense Kierkegaard's solution is somewhat like that of Jean Paul. He wants us to return to certain traditional religious ideas as a solution to nihilism. He agrees that it is impossible to base one's view on any form of scientific or rational knowing, which arrogantly pretends to provide the answers for everything. But in contrast to Jean Paul, Kierkegaard fully appreciates the difficulty of doing so. Kierkegaard thus argues for a demanding form of faith that remains in *aporeia* and uncertainty. In this sense the question can be raised if this is really a solution to the problem at all and not an admission that there is no solution. The goal is not to get rid of anxiety and uncertainty but to maintain them and live with them, that is, to accept them as fundamental features of human existence.

Since Turgenev conceives of nihilism primarily in the social-political sphere, one might expect that his solution would be some kind of plan for social reform. But surprisingly this is not the case. Bazarov denies explicitly that the nihilists have any sort of positive program to reform Russian society. In fact, he criticizes such reform movements as being ideological or one-sided. To the shock of the older generation, he claims that the goal of the nihilists is purely negative. They aim simply at the destruction of the old customs, values, traditions, and institutions that have oppressed people for so long. But there is no proposal for what these would be replaced with once they are gone. Turgenev thus remains true to the etymological meaning of the word "nihilism" as a belief in nothing or simply universal negation. Suffice it to say that this is not a solution to the problem of nihilism on any definition of the term.

Although this is Bazarov's stated position, one cannot help but wonder if this is consistent. Bazarov has great sympathy for the serfs, who had only recently been liberated. He seems clearly to want to dedicate himself to ameliorating their condition by providing them with, for example, health care, if nothing else. Along the same lines, according to Kropotkin's account, the nihilists went to the countryside to educate the peasants and help them in different ways, such as showing them new agricultural methods. It is difficult to avoid interpreting this as in fact a constructive model for reform. Thus, there is a positive message lurking behind Bazarov's position of sheer negation. But this seems to contradict Bazarov's stated position. If everything is meaningless and needs to be negated, then why is the education and health of the peasants valuable and important? While these goals of the nihilists are sympathetic on their own terms, they are out of tune with their ideology, as portrayed by Turgenev.

Bazarov meets his early death with no particular reflection or deeper philosophical view. He is saddened by it and wishes that he would be able to continue with his life. It is true that he remains unwaveringly honest with himself about his approaching death, but apart from not engaging in self-deception, he meets death like most anyone else does. His nihilist credentials seem generally irrelevant for this. If anything, his request to see his beloved countess Anna Sergyevna before he dies could be interpreted as a relapse into traditional values concerning love and human relationships. Likewise, the moving image of Bazarov's old parents visiting his grave at the end of the work seems also to serve as a clear demonstration of the hopelessness and implausibility of the nihilist position. The moral to the story seems to be something along the lines of Jean Paul: love reveals that there must surely be something beyond death.

For Nietzsche, the devaluation of the highest values that comes with the death of God is a crushing psychological blow. All the things that were once believed to be certain and fixed truths are now in ruins. At first glance, it might seem completely impossible to come up with any kind of a solution to this. Either values are absolute and guaranteed by God or they are relative and thus ultimately meaningless. Since the first part of the dichotomy is now denied, the inevitable conclusion is that all values are arbitrary in the sense that they are simply made up ad hoc by individuals. But Nietzsche contests this inference. He claims that it does not follow that all values are equal and arbitrary just because God does not exist. Instead, values can still be valid and meaningful even if they are created by finite human beings. The key point is whether one, as an individual, can muster the force of will to posit such values on one's own without appealing to any higher authority.

Nietzsche sketches his theory of the will to power, according to which it is natural for humans to affirm their drives for power, which Christianity and other elements of modern culture have long warped and suppressed. While Schopenhauer argued that the will must be denied, Nietzsche disagrees: to lead a healthy and flourishing life, one must affirm and assert one's will to power. He believes that nihilism is just a temporary phase caused by the immediate shock felt by the collapse of traditional values. But once this shock has passed, certain people will be able to regenerate themselves and posit a higher set of values based on the will to power. Nietzsche thus presents a unique and challenging solution to the problem of nihilism.

He tries to imagine a world in which people in the future will be able to generate their own values to replace those that have been lost with the collapse of the Christian worldview. The coming generation of human beings will be able to escape the curse of nihilism by embracing the will to power, thus forever putting a stop to the corruption of human nature that Christianity has caused for so many centuries. But the image of this future that Nietzsche presents is in many ways a frightening one, full of cruelty, pain, and suffering. While what he regards as the negative influence on Christianity will have been removed, the root causes that produced nihilism in the first place will still be present and even increased. The weaker people will have even more reason for anxiety and despair since they will be victimized by the stronger who are exerting their will to power. So, it appears that on the most generous interpretation, Nietzsche's vision of a post-nihilistic age is one that will only be welcome for a select number of people, while the vast majority will continue to wallow in despair as before. For as much as some readers like to flatter themselves with the thought that they would be among the *Übermenschen*, most people would find this solution difficult to accept.

10.3 Nineteenth-Century Anticipations of Existentialism

In the discussions of the individual works, we have seen the many ways in which thinkers of the nineteenth century anticipated key elements of twentieth-century existentialism. The fact that so many of these discussions were already going on the nineteenth century will come as a surprise to many, who regard existentialism as a completely new movement representing the specific realities of life in the twentieth century. While existentialism, to be sure, added a new dimension, the core issue of the meaninglessness of human existence, which is so often associated with it, was already widely explored in the nineteenth century.

10.3.1 *The Realization of the Nothingness and Authenticity*

The existentialists make the plea that it is necessary to recognize nihilism and the nothingness as a basic principle of existence. This is not an easy thing to do since we all like to believe that our lives have a firm, fixed meaning. The grim prospect of death and complete annihilation is not something that people are keen to dwell on. Instead, they create numerous mechanisms for distracting themselves so they do not have to think about it. This raises the issue of authenticity or being true to oneself in the face of nihilism. Once the nothingness of existence is recognized, it is impossible to forget it completely. The difficulty is to try to avoid lying to oneself and pretending that what one does has great importance. For some, it is a struggle to acknowledge the fact that one's projects are one's own choosing and have no deeper metaphysical grounding or absolute, God-given value. Sartre begins his theory with a detailed account of nothingness as a fundamental fact of the universe. He uses this as the point of departure for his theory of individual freedom and responsibility.

This element of existentialism is anticipated by many of the authors we have explored in this work. In fact, all of them recognized the nature of nihilism in one way or another, although, as was just seen, they differ in their descriptions and diagnoses of it. Against this background, the nineteenth-century accounts provide a number of characters who are relevant for the question of authenticity. A few examples will suffice.

For most of Jean Paul's *The Valley of Campan* Karlson remains true to his scientific background, constantly refuting various arguments in favor of the idea of immortality. As was seen, these refutations all came from a materialist, scientific perspective. But when at the end he gives in to the pressure and embraces the belief in immortality, he becomes inauthentic. He deludes himself into believing that human beings are immortal and that they carry a great significance in the universe, which his scientific intuitions know cannot be the case. He finds it too difficult to live with the truth of death and annihilation, and so he abandons himself to inauthenticity.

Klingemann's anti-hero Kreuzgang represents someone aware of the meaninglessness of human existence, and this makes him an outsider in society. His failure to conform to the norms and customs of the mainstream single him out as a person in need of psychiatric care, and this in turn leads to him being institutionalized. Kreuzgang sees through the many masks that people wear in order to hide from themselves and others the contingency of their existence. This is similar to Sartre's example of the waiter acting as if he were born a waiter, as if this were his natural essence.[15] Kreuzgang suggests that behind the masks there is no substantial being at all, just as Sartre claims that humans have no fixed essence. In both cases humans create whatever essence they can be said to have by means of their own actions. Kreuzgang remains authentic and is not tempted to join the mainstream in their delusions. He does not flinch when confronted by the nothingness.

Byron's Manfred can likewise be interpreted as someone who has seen the dark side and yet remains authentic and true to himself. Although Manfred is threatened by the gods of nature, he does not bow to fear and intimidation. Likewise, when the abbot urges him to repent since death is near, Manfred refuses. He goes to his death with the idea that he takes full responsibility for the sins that weigh on his conscience. Manfred has a degree of nobility about him in his refusal to give up his dignity. He lives knowing the meaninglessness of the universe and meets his demise without any form of self-delusion. His ethical disposition in accepting, without excuse, the responsibility for his actions is very much in the spirit of Sartre's view.

Shelley's "Ozymandias" can also be understood as relevant for this theme. The ancient king described in the work allowed himself to be seduced by his own power and fame, believing that his accomplishments had a great value. But Shelley's poem draws attention to the fleetingness of these accomplishments, which becomes increasingly evident with the passage of time. The image of the broken bust in the desert of a once powerful monarch is a *memento mori* to everyone. We should remain authentic and keep in mind our own mortality and the limitations of our lives.

Nietzsche can be said to anticipate this motif of authenticity by claiming that strong people will be able to cast off the oppressive yoke of Christianity and live their lives freely in accordance with their own will to power. Such individuals will be able to accept the meaninglessness and still enjoy fulfilled lives. By contrast, he thinks that those of his time who still cling to Christianity are morally sick and wallowing in illusions made by society. According to his assessment, the modern world in his time is in such a miserable state of inauthenticity that it cannot move beyond the death of God.

10.3.2 Existential Freedom

The recognition of the nothingness and the meaninglessness of the world leads to the idea of radical freedom, which is another well-known motif in the

---

[15] See, for example, Jean-Paul Sartre, "La mauvaise foi," in his *L'Être et le Néant, essai d'ontologie phénoménologique*, Paris: Gallimard 1981 [1943], pp. 95–96 (English translation: "Bad Faith," in his *Being and Nothingness: An Essay on Phenomenological Ontology*, trans. by Hazel E. Barnes, New York: Philosophical Library 1956, pp. 59–60).

existentialist movement. Existential freedom is claimed to be the main benefit of acknowledging the metaphysical nothingness of the world. Once the nothingness is realized, then the accepted customs and traditions are no longer regarded as having any binding authority. People thus become aware of the fact that they are entirely free to do what they want. Sartre uses this insight to make the ethical claim that while one is completely at one's liberty to make one's own values, we are all obliged to take responsibility for this. We must recognize that we are the author of our own actions and not seek excuses by appealing to outside circumstances when things go wrong. Freedom from the constraints of custom, tradition, religion, and so on is thus considered a great liberation.

One might think that the figures that we have explored here do not share this positive view and that this constitutes an important difference between the nihilism of the nineteenth century and that of twentieth-century existentialism. The graphic portrayals of the world without God and immortality that are found in Jean Paul, Klingemann, Büchner, and even Møller are intended to be shocking and frightening. The authors present a picture of a world of suffering and meaninglessness that no one would want to inhabit. The horrifying images represent an unthinkable alternative to traditional beliefs that should be maintained at all costs. However, there are some nineteenth-century figures who also try to focus on what they regard as the positive side of this, namely that there is a liberating dimension to nihilism, which frees us from concern about conforming to accepted values and customs.

Kierkegaard can be said to be one forerunners of the liberating aspect of existential freedom. In "At a Graveside" he emphasizes the indefinability and inexplicability of death, urging his readers not to pretend to know anything about the mystery of death since this is something that only God can know. His suggestion is instead to think earnestly about one's own death and what it means for one's own life. He refrains from telling his readers what they should think and how they should react to this reflection. Instead, he leaves the choice entirely up to each individual reader. Everyone must take the fact of their own death and appropriate it in their own way, drawing their own conclusions from it. But this is something that only they can do, and no one else can do it for them. We are thus free to think of death as we want without the interference of other people or traditional beliefs. This freedom is liberating, but it also comes with a heightened responsibility towards oneself.

Turgenev's Bazarov is also someone who feels a sense of liberation from the value system of mainstream society. Kropotkin describes this clearly in his characterization of the Russian nihilist movement. The nihilists felt no obligation to conform to bourgeois customs and empty words of politeness and flattery. Instead, they spoke their minds directly and did not hesitate to do things that bourgeois culture might find inappropriate or even shocking. Bazarov himself is unimpressed by the pretensions of aristocrats and does not treat them with any special deference. Likewise, he mingles freely with the peasants and is apathetic about his own position in the social hierarchy. For Bazarov, this is clearly a liberating experience for him and others of his generation. Kropotkin mentions the nihilist girls and young students who reject the uninspiring futures that their families had planned for them and strike out on their own to create a life for themselves, working to help the peasants. This ability to redefine and recreate oneself in accordance with one's own values must have felt like a great personal liberation.

Along similar lines, Nietzsche believes that there will be people who, after the death of God, will be able to create their own values. The higher human beings will have a healthier value system than that found in Christianity. The previous value system of the West can be discarded and forgotten. This is intended to be a positive, liberating message, as many Nietzsche readers have found. While it is true that some of the authors examined here present nihilism in wholly negative terms and regard it as a view to be rejected, others in fact anticipate the idea of existential freedom by seeing in it a liberating element.

10.3.3 Social Criticism

If all human existence is meaningless in the grand scheme of things, then it follows that the accepted customs and traditions are also devoid of meaning. Once nihilism dawns on people, they are immediately obliged to see the world around them with different eyes. Those who were previously respected now appear to be corrupt hypocrites. Institutions and traditions look like hopeless shams. This element of social criticism was also an important aspect of the existentialist movement. Many of the existentialists were known for their outspoken rejection of bourgeois values and their criticism of contemporary society. The atheist existentialists were critical of religion and blind adherence to large political movements. This element of their program made the French existentialists, Sartre and de Beauvoir, public figures who were regularly in the spotlight for their vocal criticisms of various policies of the French government.

The connection between nihilism and social criticism has already been noted in the discussions of nineteenth-century views of nihilism, and so a few brief examples will suffice to illustrate the point. This element comes out perhaps most clearly in Klingemann's *The Nightwatches*, where Kreuzgang is merciless in his criticism of other people and every aspect of society. The scene of his announced end of the world brought out the true nature of the townspeople and demonstrated how they were all liars and phonies in normal life. Kreuzgang systematically goes through the different professions, such as lawyers, theologians, scholars, and so on, and shows the folly of all of them. He satirizes the arrogance and hypocrisy of those regarded as upstanding members of society.

Like Kreuzgang, Schopenhauer is also critical of people in general for their lack of reflection and failure to acknowledge that the world is meaningless. People do not want to regard themselves as living only to meet the constant demands of the insatiable will. He rebukes religion and bourgeois culture for pretending that there is a higher value and importance. He argues that as long as unreflective people continue in their illusions, they remain in the nefarious cycle of slavishly catering to the needs of the will. A fully disabused and self-critical approach is required for one to realize that the only way to escape this, even momentarily, is to deny the will-to-live and thus minimize one's dependence on nature.

Büchner's Danton is also disenchanted with people whom he regards as mere animals in the struggle for survival. They seek their own pleasure and try to destroy their rivals. The entire world of politics is corrupt, while the general population takes pleasure in seeing once powerful figures sent to their deaths. Given this negative view of human nature, it is no wonder that different political parties come and go, yet nothing ever changes, and the rightful grievances of the people always remain the same. Büchner is also known as a provocative writer with respect to his criticism of the sexual mores of his time. In *Danton's Death* the natural drives are continually emphasized. The story of the sexual awakening of the prostitute Marion, with her disdain for bourgeois ethics and uninhibited affirmation of sensual pleasure, was surely shocking to the sensibilities of the day.

Kierkegaard is also an important social critic. In *The Concept of Irony*, he recognizes the importance of nihilism, under the label of irony, as something important since it teaches how to think critically. This is a valuable tool, but, he claims, it should not be taken to be the truth itself. In the first part of *Either/Or* Kierkegaard's aesthete is critical of people in bourgeois society. He rejects the idea that the meaning of life can be found in making money, getting married, and reciting mindlessly the traditional phrases of politeness and social etiquette. Mention should also be made of his work *A Literary Review*, where he gives his most extended social-political criticism of his time.

Social criticism is also clearly in evidence in Turgenev's character Bazarov, who states explicitly that the goal of nihilism is to tear down everything that society has built up and then start again. He believes that traditional Russian society, even despite the liberation of the serfs, is so oppressive and reactionary that there is no other solution. In his characterization of the nihilist movement, Kropotkin lists the many aspects of contemporary Russian society that the nihilists criticized and tried to undermine. Bazarov rejects the social hierarchy and has disdain for the aristocrats. He is likewise critical of the sentimentality and superstition that stand in the way of scientific progress. He criticizes art and anything that he regards as self-indulgent or useless.

Nietzsche is also known for his harsh social criticism of Christian culture and the results of it. He criticizes all attempts of the masses, whom he regards as weak, to use their numerical advantage to defeat gifted individuals. He claims that such weak individuals know that they are weak and thus inwardly hate themselves. But they turn this hatred outward to the world, which they regard as oppressing them in some way. As was discussed, Nietzsche uses the terms *décadence* and *ressentiment* to capture this spiritual hatred of the world by the weak and disenfranchised. Christian morality was, he believes, the source of the perversion of values by teaching that the weak are actually the strong since they are loved by God and the strong are actually the weak. He sees this as a complete inversion of the more intuitive value system of the ancient Greeks. Nietzsche is also critical of mass movements in the modern world such as democracy and socialism, which he thinks are a natural result of the Christian ethic that celebrates weakness and not strength. There is thus a broad spectrum of social criticism that arises from the nineteenth-century treatments of nihilism.

10.3.4 Rebellion and the Existentialist Hero

The problem of nihilism has also been associated with rebellion. With the realization of the meaninglessness of life, there are those who refuse to accept these terms for the human condition. These rebels against God or the universe have been depicted in existentialist literature and drama in the form of the existential hero. Figures such as Sartre's Roquentin (from *Nausea*) and Orestes (from *The Flies*) and Camus's Mersault (from *The Stranger*) and Sisyphus (from his famous essay) were all important in the dissemination of existentialist ideas in the twentieth century. All these figures are readily associated with the existentialist movement, but a closer look reveals that such characters were not entirely new to literature.

Nineteenth-century literature also provides a number of examples of characters in rebellion who can be regarded as existential heroes *avant la lettre*. One of these is Klingemann's Kreuzgang. At the end of *The Nightwatches*, Kreuzgang rejects the idea of prayer as a form of self-abasement.[16] He refuses to accept submissively the rule of God and to beg for mercy. Instead, he claims that when he dies he will simply laugh as a sign of defiance.[17] Like Camus's Sisyphus, he realizes that his rebellion will ultimately have no effect on his fate. There is no life after death and no redemption. Humans are cruel hypocrites unworthy of any salvation. But it is important to rebel to show that despite the bitter truth of nihilism, one chooses to assert one's own freedom and not submit to self-delusion. Like Roquentin and Mersault, Kreuzgang is an outsider who is alienated from society. He observes the behavior of the townspeople whom he regards with bemusement. He stands alone in his rebellion, refusing to participate in the folly of the mainstream.

Kierkegaard's aesthete from *Either/Or* can surely be regarded as a kind of existentialist hero or antihero. He refuses to conform to the norms of society and seems to regard himself as standing apart from what goes on around him.

---

[16] [Klingemann], *Nachtwachen*, p. 295 (*The Nightwatches of Bonaventura*, p. 126).
[17] [Klingemann], *Nachtwachen*, p. 293 (*The Nightwatches of Bonaventura*, p. 125).

He rebels against the customary bourgeois values that the rest of society follow. Like other existentialist heroes, he suffers from anxiety, despair, and boredom. Kierkegaard's portrayal of the aesthete in the "Diapsalmata" is not really a story or narrative but rather a series of inward reflections, similar to those of Roquentin and Mersault. The aphorisms are scattered, and it is impossible for the reader to get a clear sense of space and time in order to construct any kind of meaningful storyline.

Perhaps the clearest example of existential rebellion can be found in Byron's protagonist Manfred. He suffers from inner anguish and recognizes that he will die. But he refuses to bow to the forces of the universe, represented in the poem by the spirits of nature. He insists on maintaining his human integrity and freedom by rebelling against the world. The key is that the human mind is higher than nature. This means that regardless of the external circumstances, people always have the possibility to think what they want. Manfred thus represents the existentialist focus on rebellion. Moreover, he anticipates Sartre's conception of radical freedom in the belief that, despite one's outward situation, it is always possible to act freely and rebel in order to maintain one's dignity.

Turgenev's Bazarov is also an obvious example of a rebel. He rejects everything about the old social order and wants to destroy it. His rebellion is primarily concerned with the social-political sphere and less with metaphysics. He is not in outspoken rebellion against God or mortality. When he becomes ill and knows that he will die, he passively accepts his fate. This stands in contrast to the open rebellion of Manfred, who refuses to be led to death but insists on dying on his own terms. To be sure, Bazarov is entirely clear about his impending death and does not engage in illusions about a miraculous recovery that his parents hope for. But at the end, his spirit seems to be broken. By contrast, Manfred ends in defiance, telling the spirit of death to return to hell.

10.3.5 The Absurd

Both existentialism and the theater of the absurd movements take the absurd as an important motif. Nihilism gives rise to the absurd since it contradicts our normal value system and understanding of the world, where things seem obviously meaningful. With the realization of the ultimate meaninglessness of the world, all our actions and strivings that were previously regarded as important begin to look absurd. Camus's Sisyphus is a well-known figure who captures the image of eternally laboring at a meaningless task. In Beckett's famous dramatic piece, the characters are waiting for Godot as if this were something important. Their dialogues are strange and discontinuous, and Godot never shows up, again representing the absurdity of human action and hopes in a meaningless world. While Camus's Sisyphus represents nihilism as a tragedy, Beckett's drama sees it as a comedy. Both these elements can be found in the discussions about nihilism in the nineteenth century that we have discussed.

10.3 NINETEENTH-CENTURY ANTICIPATIONS

For some of our writers and thinkers – Jean Paul, Büchner, Møller, and Turgenev – the absurdity of nihilism constitutes an important part of the argument for why it must be rejected. These thinkers regard nihilism with pathos as something tragic and sad. For Jean Paul, if God is all-knowing and all-powerful, then why would he create a universe in which people are born, struggle to achieve things, and then die and become forgotten? When the dead Christ watches the planets and suns being destroyed at the end of time, Jean Paul seems to claim that surely God could not have created all this only to have it all destroyed and come to nothing. This is an absurdity that he cannot accept.

Büchner's Danton seems to illustrate this point since his response is simply to give up on everything in his nihilistic world. In the face of the absurd, life is not worth living. At the end of the work, Danton suggests the image of human life existing just for the amusement of the gods, who sadistically watch as people labor in vain, suffer, and die. Like Jean Paul's "The Dead Christ," this is a frightening picture of a world that is intended to shock the reader. One might claim that Büchner's intent is the same as that of Jean Paul, that is, to portray a picture of the universe that is so terrifying that it cannot be accepted. With the shocking images, the reader feels the need to revert to traditional views such as the belief in the existence of God and immortality.

In his essay, Møller also argues along these lines by showing that without a belief in immortality, all spheres of life would appear absurd and would subsequently be abandoned since no one would be able to take them seriously anymore. It would be absurd to pursue the arts, philosophy, politics, or even interpersonal relationships if one did not believe in immortality. A secular worldview that denies this doctrine is simply incompatible with living a normal life. Like Jean Paul, Møller has thus presented a picture of the nihilistic world that no one could possibility accept. The resulting absurdities in the different spheres are proof enough that nihilism is not a plausible position.

At the end of *Fathers and Sons*, Bazarov's parents, full of grief, visit his grave, and an argument similar to that of Jean Paul is given by the narrator. Surely death cannot be the final word since this would be absurd. There must be something more beyond the grave that gives our lives meaning. Bazarov's parents cannot accept the idea that the death of their beloved young son is meaningless. God would never create such a universe. For these writers, embracing the nothingness and the absurdity is simply not an option.

Some of the other authors explored above – Klingemann, Shelley, and Kierkegaard – regard the absurdity of the universe as something comic and humorous. Given the utter insignificance of human beings in the universe, all our actions and investments can be made the object of satire. We struggle and toil to achieve things that appear to us to be valuable, but in the end they are fleeting and amount to nothing. In this light everyone who, with deadly seriousness, works to accomplish something looks absurd. Perhaps the clearest example of the absurd in the comic sense can be found in *The Nightwatches*.

Kreuzgang realizes the folly of society and sees the masks that people wear in their fear of the truth. Yet his sober understanding is the opposite of the principles that rule the world, and so he is consigned to a mental asylum. It is an inverted world, where those who are ostensibly insane are in fact the only ones who can see the truth. Kreuzgang finds absurd what the world regards as rational and vice versa.[18] Likewise, there is a suggestion that the universe is not a cosmos with order and structure created by God, but instead "a miscarried system."[19] Kreuzgang's amusing observations of the many absurdities of the world give the work a comic and satirical element despite the grim nature of its main theme of nihilism.

Shelley's "Ozymandias" also exposes this comic aspect of nihilism. The arrogance and condescension of the dead king appear laughable to us. His bursting pride in his military victories and building projects seems absurd from our perspective. Whatever the king managed to accomplish has long since turned to dust. This can be regarded, like *The Nightwatches*, as a form of social satire of the way in which people delude themselves by investing their actions with supreme importance, while being blind to the fact that they are ultimately meaningless. The disposition of the king makes him an absurd figure.

Kierkegaard is also quick to satirize the many forms of human folly. As noted above, his aesthete never tires of poking fun at the superficial values of bourgeois life. Moreover, Kierkegaard uses the term "absurdity" or "the absurd" explicitly to characterize his view of faith.[20] The sciences clearly speak against the belief in God or immortality. According to the scientific view, it is thus absurd to believe in such things. One might think that, as a Christian writer, Kierkegaard would reject this view and try to argue against it. Instead, he seems to agree with it. As was seen, for Kierkegaard, death is something indefinable and inexplicable. Yet he still thinks that faith is possible, but the believer must accept that this faith is absurd and runs contrary to scientific reason. Absurdity thus lies at the heart of Kierkegaard's conception of religious faith. Ultimately, he believes that it is impossible to escape the absurdity of existence as some of the authors mentioned above seem to think. It is a fact of the human condition that cannot be ignored or dismissed.

These examples demonstrate the many ways in which the nineteenth-century discussions of nihilism anticipated the key motifs of twentieth-century

---

[18] [Klingemann], *Nachtwachen*, p. 170 (*The Nightwatches of Bonaventura*, p. 73).
[19] [Klingemann], *Nachtwachen*, p. 94 (*The Nightwatches of Bonaventura*, p. 41).
[20] See Sean Turchin, "Absurd," in *Kierkegaard's Concepts*, tome I, *Absolute to Church*, ed. by Steven M. Emmanuel, William McDonald, and Jon Stewart, Aldershot: Ashgate 2013 (*Kierkegaard Research: Sources, Reception and Resources*, vol. 15), pp. 5–9; Charles I. Glicksberg, "The Kierkegaardian Paradox of the Absurd," in his *The Tragic Vision in Twentieth-Century Literature*, Carbondale, IL: Southern Illinois University Press 1963, pp. 18–28; Gregory J. Schufreider, "The Logic of the Absurd," *Philosophy and Phenomenological Research*, vol. 44, no. 1, 1983, pp. 61–83.

existentialism. This can help us to put existentialism in a new perspective and see it as part of a much longer discussion that began in the Enlightenment. It should be noted that this is not to say that the individual existentialist writers were all influenced by the figures treated here. Of course, we know that Heidegger gave a profound interpretation of Nietzsche.[21] Likewise, Kierkegaard played an important role in the thought of Buber, Jaspers, Camus, Sartre, and other leading existentialist thinkers.[22] These specific connections and others have been explored in detailed studies in source-work research. However, the question of de facto influence is secondary for our purposes. What is interesting is the fact that so many of the figures we have examined in this work are not well known and may never have been read by the existentialists, yet they made important contributions to the discussion of nihilism. This shows the richness and diversity of the tradition of nihilism in a period long before the rise of existentialism. Nihilism in the nineteenth century is not just a timeworn cliché about Nietzsche or Schopenhauer but instead includes many different figures with diverse backgrounds and approaches.

10.4 Nihilism in the Twenty-First Century

Is nihilism still a relevant issue today in the twenty-first century? While the term itself perhaps does not appear as frequently as it did in the heyday of existentialism, nihilism certainly did not disappear with that philosophical movement. However, to be sure, our historical context is considerably different from that of both the nineteenth and the twentieth century, and this needs to be noted if we are to identify accurately the expressions of nihilism in the twenty-first century.

We have focused on the important role of the rapid development of the sciences in the creation or intensification of the problem of modern nihilism. Since the Enlightenment, this development has only increased in speed, and today there can be no doubt that our lives are dominated by science and technology. This has served to ensconce the scientific worldview more firmly than was the case at the beginning of the nineteenth century, which saw the birth of the secular society that we know today. The awareness of the miniscule role of human beings in the universe is now more generally known and accepted than it was at that time when it was first starting to be understood and digested.

---

[21] See Rita Casale, *Heideggers Nietzsche. Geschichte einer Obsession*, Bielefeld: Transcript Verlag 2010.
[22] See Peter Šajda, "Martin Buber: 'No-One Can So Refute Kierkegaard as Kierkegaard Himself,'" in *Kierkegaard and Existentialism*, ed. by Jon Stewart, Aldershot: Ashgate 2011 (*Kierkegaard Research: Sources, Reception and Resources*, vol. 9), pp. 33–61; István Czakó, "Karl Jaspers: A Great Awakener's Way to Philosophy of Existence," in ibid., pp. 155–97; Leo Stan, "Albert Camus: Walled within God," in ibid., pp. 63–94; Manuela Hackel, "Jean-Paul Sartre: Kierkegaard's Influence on His Theory of Nothingness," in ibid., pp. 323–354.

Today with constantly improving telescopes, ever-more distant galaxies are still being discovered. Unlike the thinkers examined above, we know that the universe is expanding, as galaxies continue to race away from one another at colossal speeds. In step with this, the importance of humans or planet earth has continued to shrink in a way that would have been shocking to most people at the beginning of the nineteenth century. From this perspective it seems to follow that our lives are more meaningless and insignificant than ever. The only real difference is that today we have become more accustomed to this idea than people were during the Enlightenment, when the results of the new scientific developments struck most people as surprising and shocking. By contrast, we can take in stride the discovery of a new galaxy at the edge of the universe, and this does not cause us to change our worldview in any fundamental way. It does not evoke anxiety and despair about our lack of meaning in the world. The question of the meaninglessness of the universe thus might not, at first glance, seem to be so pressing as it was in the nineteenth century.

However, nihilism is still with us today. We have seen how throughout history people have struggled to give their lives a sense of meaning and importance to counter the fear of death, annihilation, and being forgotten. An important aspect of our feeling of leading a meaningful life is the recognition that we receive from others in society. In *The Nightwatches*, the people who enjoyed status and prestige in the town could live in the illusion that their lives were important in the grand scheme of things. This seemed to be confirmed by the respect and deference shown to them by other people. In this way they could keep their deep feelings of despair and hopelessness carefully hidden both to others and to themselves. Only in cases of extreme distress, such as the imminent end of the world, did these emotions emerge into the daylight.

In the ancient past people also presumably struggled with the thought of death and annihilation, and being forgotten, but for most people there was nothing that they could do about it. Widespread recognition was reserved primarily for great kings, leaders, and warriors. In addition to enjoying more recognition than others, they alone had the resources to mark their significance with great buildings and monuments. This same drive to find meaning by means of widespread recognition still exists. However, it has become democratized in the sense that now a great many people can attain some degree of fame and not just the top leaders.

The struggle for meaning and recognition today is facilitated by the expansion of technology, which makes it possible to magnify the lives of individuals in such a way that their sense of significance seems to increase. Through social media people can construct images of themselves that they can easily disseminate to large groups of people. In this way they can garner recognition from others that confirms their vision of themselves and their meaning, even if this is at great variance from the actual truth. While in antiquity powerful kings built enormous pyramids and magnificent palaces to mark their importance, today one's social media profile is the monument that one builds for oneself. The social media sites are thus one of the modern means to fulfill the basic human need for recognition and meaning, but it is not the only one.

Fulfilling this need is also facilitated by the expansion of other media such as television and film, which offer the lure of fame to those seeking recognition. The enormous growth in professional sports and athletic heroes can be seen as one example. From a certain perspective, nothing can be more trivial than throwing a ball into a basket or kicking it into a goal, but when this simple act is done in the context of professional sports with large numbers of live spectators and television viewers, suddenly it is the source of great meaning and recognition. Mention could also be made of the popularity commanded by music stars in various genres, who enjoy enormous followings. The blind struggle for fame and the adulation of those who have achieved it have led to a culture of celebrities, which presumably would have struck people from the nineteenth century as somewhat odd. Today people often work hard and make great sacrifices to attain celebrity status. No one wants to be just mediocre or average. Most people want to find some way to stand out so as to mark their importance and significance. This drive for fame is so strong that in order to get it some people are even willing to accept looking foolish or being made the object of disdain, as in, for example, reality shows. Some people enjoy being famous even though their fame always seems to be attached to some scandal. This is connected to the much-discussed phenomenon of modern narcissism. These developments would have seemed offensive to people of the nineteenth century. A great deal of human activity today can thus still be seen as a desperate attempt to establish meaning in a meaningless world or to make a lasting mark for oneself, which draws attention to one's person. This can be interpreted as motivated by the carefully hidden anxiety caused by the fact of death.

The movement from rural to urban life that came with industrialization in the nineteenth century gave rise to megacities. This phenomenon enhanced the feeling of the meaninglessness of the life of the individual. In large cities, people can easily feel lost in the crowd and develop a sense of anomie and despair that causes a crisis of meaning. The expansion of the world's population can give the impression that the value of the individual has proportionately decreased and is now at its vanishing point. As one of eight billion people on the planet, what possible meaning could my life have? In this sense it might be argued that the feeling of meaninglessness is more acute than ever.

Hence, nihilism is still clearly relevant today, even though the word itself is not bandied about so often. It is not just a passing phase of teenage rebellion but rather a fixed element in many aspects of society. The fear of death and being forgotten has not changed. The awareness of our complete insignificance in the universe has not changed. The deep need to find meaning in life today is the same as in the times of Gilgamesh. What has changed is the means available for trying to find it. Much of modern culture and much of what we do in our daily lives are desperate cries for meaning in a vast meaningless universe, where there is more nothingness than being.

SELECTED BIBLIOGRAPHY ON NIHILISM

This bibliography is confined solely to works on the concept of nihilism itself in its different usages. In the notes to the individual chapters, suggestions can be found for further reading on the specific thinkers and writers discussed here and their respective relations to nihilism.

Adams, E. M. *Philosophy and the Modern Mind: A Philosophical Critique of Modern Western Civilization*. Chapel Hill: University of North Carolina Press, 1975.

Adams, Robert Martin. *Nil: Episodes in the Literary Conquest of Void during the Nineteenth Century*. New York: Oxford University Press, 1966.

Arendt, Dieter. *Der "poetische Nihilismus" in der Romantik*, vol. 1. Tübingen: Niemeyer Max Verlag, 1972.

Arendt, Dieter. *Der "poetische Nihilismus" in der Romantik*, vol. 2. Tübingen: Niemeyer Max Verlag, 1996.

Arendt, Dieter (ed.). *Der Nihilismus als Phänomen der Geistgeschichte in der wissenschaftlichen Diskussion unseres Jahrhundert*. Darmstadt: Wissenschaftliche Buchgesellschaft, 1974.

Barrow, John D. *The Book of Nothing*. London: Vintage, 2001.

Becker, Ernst. *The Birth and Death of Meaning: An Interdisciplinary Perspective on the Problem of Man*. New York: The Free Press, 1962.

Becker, Ernst. *The Denial of Death*. New York: The Free Press, 1973.

Blocker, Gene. *The Meaning of Meaninglessness*. The Hague: Martinus Nijhoff, 1974.

Brassier, Ray. *Nihil Unbound: Enlightenment and Extinction*. New York: Palgrave Macmillan, 2007.

Cacciari, Massimo. *Architecture and Nihilism: On the Philosophy of Modern Architecture*, trans. Stephen Sartarelli. New Haven, CT: Yale University Press, 1993.

Carr, Karen L. *The Banalization of Nihilism: Twentieth-Century Responses to Meaninglessness*. Albany: State University of New York Press, 1992.

Conway, Daniel W. "Heidegger, Nietzsche, and the Origins of Nihilism." *Journal of Nietzsche Studies* 3, 1992, pp. 11–43.

Critchley, Simon. *Very Little ... Almost Nothing: Death, Philosophy, Literature*. London and New York: Routledge, 1997.

Crosby, Donald A. *The Specter of the Absurd: Sources and Criticisms of Modern Nihilism*. Albany: State University of New York Press, 1988.

Cunningham, Conor. *Genealogy of Nihilism: Philosophies of Nothing and the Difference of Theology*. London and New York: Routledge, 2002.
Diken, Bülent. *Nihilism*. London and New York: Routledge, 2009.
Dod, Elmar. *Der unheimlichste Gast. Die Philosophie des Nihilismus*. Marburg: Tectum, 2013.
Dryzhakova, Elena. "Dostoyevsky, Chernyshevsky, and the Rejection of Nihilism." *Oxford Slavonic Papers* 13, 1980, pp. 58–79.
Emden, Christian J. "Nihilism, Pessimism, and the Conditions of Modernity," in *The Cambridge History of Modern European Thought*, ed. Warren Breckman and Peter Gordon. Cambridge: Cambridge University Press, 2019, pp. 372–397.
Fries, Heinrich. *Nihilismus. Die Gefahr unserer Zeit*. Stuttgart: Schwabenverlag, 1949.
Gertz, Nolen. *Nihilism and Technology*. London and New York: Rowman & Littlefield, 2018.
Gertz, Nolen. *Nihilism*. Cambridge, MA: The MIT Press, 2019.
Gillespie, Michael Allen. *Nihilism before Nietzsche*. Chicago: University of Chicago Press, 1996.
Glicksberg, Charles I. *The Literature of Nihilism*. Lewisburg, PA: Bucknell University Press, 1975.
Goldschmidt, Hermann L. *Der Nihilismus im Licht einer kritischen Philosophie*. Zürich: Thayngen-Schaffhausen, 1941.
Goudsblom, Johan. *Nihilism and Culture*. Totowa, NJ: Rowman and Littlefield, 1980.
Harrigan, Anthony. "Post-Modern Nihilism in America." *St. Croix Review* 31, no. 5, 1998, pp. 24–32.
Heller, Peter. *Dialectics and Nihilism: Essays on Lessing, Nietzsche, Mann and Kafka*. Amherst: University of Massachusetts Press, 1966.
Jackson, Tony. "Nihilism, Relativism, and Literary Theory." *SubStance* 24, no. 3, 1995, pp. 29–48.
Kay, Wallace G. "Blake, Baudelaire, Beckett: The Romantics of Nihilism." *Southern Quarterly: A Journal of the Arts in the South* 9, 1971, pp. 253–259.
Kohlschmidt, Werner. "Nihilismus der Romantik." *Neue Schweizer Rundschau* 21, 1953–54, pp. 466–482.
Lebovic, Nitzan. "The History of Nihilism and the Limits of Political Critique." *Rethinking History* 19, no. 1, 2015, pp. 1–17.
Löwith, Karl. *Martin Heidegger and European Nihilism*, trans. Gary Steiner, ed. Richard Wolin. New York: Columbia University Press, 1995.
Marmysz, John. *Laughing at Nothing: Humor as a Response to Nihilism*. Albany: State University of New York Press, 2003.
Morgan, David R. "And Now the Void: Twentieth Century Man's Place in Modern Tragedy." *Contemporary Review* 234, 1979, pp. 315–320.
Nishitani, Keiji. *The Self Overcoming of Nihilism*, trans. Graham Parkes and Setsuko Aihara. Albany: State University of New York Press, 1990.
Novak, Michael. *The Experience of Nothingness*. New York: Harper & Row, 1970.
Pearson, Keith Ansell, and Diane Morgan (eds.). *Nihilism Now! Monsters of Energy*, Houndmills: Macmillan and New York: St. Martin's, 2000.

Pippin, Robert B. "Modernism and Nihilism," in *Idealism as Modernism: Hegelian Variations*. Cambridge: Cambridge University Press, 1997, pp. 309–371.

Pöggeler, Otto. "Hegel und die Anfänge der Nihilismus-Diskussion," in *Der Nihilismus als Phänomen der Geistesgeschichte in der wissenschaftlichen Diskussion unseres Jahrhunderts*, ed. Dieter Arendt. Darmstadt: Wissenschaftliche Buchgesellschaft, 1974, pp. 307–349.

Ponomarev, Alexey. *Der Nihilismus und seine Erfahrung in der Romantik. Das Problem des Nihilismus in der deutschen und russischen Romantik aus kulturkomparatistischer Perspektive*. Marburg: Tectum Verlag, 2010.

Pratt, Alan R. (ed.). *The Dark Side: Thoughts on the Futility of Life from the Ancient Greeks to the Present*. Secaucus, NJ: Citadel Press, 1994.

Rauschning, Hermann. *The Revolution of Nihilism: Warning to the West*, trans. E. W. Dickes. New York: Alliance Book Corporation, 1939.

Rauschning, Hermann. *Masken und Metamorphosen des Nihilismus: Der Nihilismus des XX. Jahrhunderts*. Frankfurt am Main: Humboldt-Verlag, 1954.

Ray, Matthew Alun. *Subjectivity and Irreligion: Atheism and Agnosticism in Kant, Schopenhauer and Nietzsche*. Aldershot, UK and Burlington, VT: Ashgate, 2003.

Rose, Eugene. *Nihilism: The Root of the Revolution of the Modern Age*. Platina, CA: Saint Herman Press, 1994.

Rose, Gillian. *Dialectic of Nihilism: Post-Structuralism and Law*. New York: Basil Blackwell, 1984.

Rosen, Stanley. *Nihilism: A Philosophical Essay*. New Haven, CT and London: Yale University Press, 1969.

Stevens, Brett. *Nihilism: A Philosophy Based on Nothingness and Eternity*. Melbourne: Manticore Press, 2016.

Syfret, Wendy. *The Sunny Nihilist: How a Meaningless Life Can Make You Truly Happy*. London: Profile Books, 2021.

Tartaglia, James. *Philosophy in a Meaningless Life: A System of Nihilism, Consciousness and Reality*. London: Bloomsbury, 2016.

Thielicke, Helmut. *Nihilism: Its Origin and Nature—With a Christian Answer*, trans. John W. Doberstein. New York: Schocken Books, 1969.

Vattimo, Gianni. "Optimistic Nihilism." *Common Knowledge* 1, no. 3, 1992, pp. 37–44.

Wellek, René. "The New Nihilism in Literary Studies," in *Aesthetics and the Literature of Ideas: Essays in Honor of A. Owen Aldridge*, ed. François Jost and Melvin J. Friedman. Newark, DE: University of Delaware Press, 1990, pp. 77–85.

Weller, Shane. *Literature, Philosophy, Nihilism: The Uncanniest of Guests*. Houndsmills: Palgrave Macmillan, 2008.

Weller, Shane. *Modernism and Nihilism*. Houndsmills: Palgrave Macmillan, 2011.

Young, Julian. "Nihilism and the Meaning of Life," in *The Oxford Handbook of Continental Philosophy*, ed. Michael Rosen and Brian Leiter. Oxford: Oxford University Press, 2007, pp. 463–492.

NAME INDEX

Achilles, 213
Aeschylus, 213
aesthete, the, 205–221, 237, 240, 256–257, 266, 269–270, 286, 292, 300–302, 304
Akhenaten, 7
Alexander II, Emperor of Russia, 238
Alexander the Great, 91–92
Arimanes, sc. Ahriman, 111–112, 115, 289
Aristotle, 114, 133
Artabanus, 138
Astarte, 100, 103, 105, 110, 112
Athena, 28

Bakunin, Mikhail, 245
Balzac, Honoré de, 159
Baudrillard, Jean, 16
Bauer, Bruno, 136
Bazarov, 15, 237, 241–257, 265–266, 269–270, 276, 277, 286, 294, 298–300, 302, 303
Beckett, Samuel, 17, 302–303
Beethoven, Ludwig van, 122
Belzoni, Giovanni Battista, 121
Berkeley, George, 43
Blair, Robert, 99
Borges, Jorge Luis, 200
Borup, Thomas Larsen, 228–230
Brentano, Clemens, 64
Büchner, Georg, 31, 148–173, 184, 188, 199, 209, 214, 221, 225, 235, 247, 249–250, 254, 256, 261, 269, 274, 277–278, 285, 291–292, 298, 300, 303
Büchner, Ludwig, 247
Buddha, 9
Buffon, sc. Georges-Louis Leclerc, Comte de Buffon, 23–24

Byron, Ada, 100
Byron, Annabella (neé Anne Isabella Milbanke), 100
Byron, George Gordon, 99–102, 104, 108–112, 114–115, 117–118, 121, 123–124, 147, 159, 170–171, 214, 222, 225, 230, 256, 278, 284–285, 289, 297, 302

Cabet, Étienne, 25
Caesar, Julius, 91, 116
Callicles, 11
Camus, Albert, 17, 78, 93, 124, 171, 199–200, 289, 301–302, 305
 The Myth of Sisyphus, 17, 199–200
 The Rebel, An Essay on Man in Revolt, 98
Carlyle, Thomas, 281
Châtelet, Émilie du, 24
Chaumette, Pierre-Gaspard, 162
Chernyshevsky, Nicholas, 237
Chronos, 125
Cicero, Marcus Tullius, 12
Clairmont, Claire, 100
Colli, Giorgio, 260
Conan Doyle, Arthur, 257
Condorcet, Nicolas de, 25
Copernicus, Nicolaus, 262

d'Alembert, Jean Le Rond, 24
Dante Alighieri, 45, 138
Danton, Georges, 150–173, 184, 189, 209, 214, 221, 235, 247, 249–250, 254, 256, 261, 269, 274, 278, 285, 291–292, 300, 303
Danton, Julie, 152, 164, 166–167, 254
Darwin, Charles, 22, 242
Darwin, Erasmus, 22, 72

De Beauvoir, Simone, 124, 289, 299
Delacroix, Jean François, 153
Derrida, Jacques, 16
Descartes, René, 12, 243
Desmoulins, Camille, 153, 155–156, 163–165
Desmoulins, Lucile, 164–167, 170, 221, 254, 291
Devil, the, 66, 73, 79, 81, 85, 87, 90, 92, 208
d'Holbach, Paul Henri Thiry, 124–125
Diderot, Denis, 14, 15, 24
Diodorus of Sicily, 119–121
Dostoevsky, Fyodor, 14, 31–32, 64, 78, 195, 257, 281, 284
　The Brothers Karamazov, 14, 195
　Notes from Underground, 64, 284
　The Possessed, 257, 281

Emerson, Ralph Waldo, 281
Enkidu, 2
Epicurus, 153
Eremita, Victor, 205–206, 240

Faust, 27, 65, 101, 104, 115, 116
Feuerbach, Ludwig, 13, 51, 90, 136
Fichte, Johann Gottlieb, 18, 36, 43, 65, 69, 78, 91, 97, 126, 128, 280
Förster-Nietzsche, Elisabeth, 259–260
Foucault, Michel, 79
Fourier, Charles, 25

Garrick, David, 45–46, 96
Gast, Peter, sc. Heinrich Köselitz, 259
Genet, Jean, 17
Gilgamesh, 2, 4, 307
Gione, 44, 46–48, 57–62, 77, 87, 95, 96, 134, 139, 146, 162, 169, 182, 186, 225, 235, 264, 265, 274, 287, 288
Glaucus, 3
Godot, 302
Goethe, Johann Wolfgang von, 27, 28, 65, 101, 122, 126, 244
Gorgias, 11
Gray, Thomas, 99
Gutzkow, Karl, 151, 205, 281

Halley, Edmund, 20–21
Hamlet, 73, 79, 82–85, 91, 101, 106–108, 133, 208–209, 214
Hecataeus of Abdera, 119–121
Hegel, G.W.F., 224, 262
　Lectures on the History of Philosophy, 18, 19
　Lectures on the Philosophy of History, 194
　Phenomenology of Spirit, 18, 19
　Philosophy of Right, 18, 19
　Science of Logic, 179
Hegesias of Cyrene, 185
Heiberg, Johan Ludvig, 174, 176, 187, 193–195, 204
Heidegger, Martin, 17, 97, 305
Heine, Heinrich, 188
Heraclitus, 11
Hérault de Séchelles, Marie Jean, 168
Hérbet, Jacques-René, 151
Hermann, Johann Bernhard, 35
Herodotus, 11, 138
Herschel, William, 21
Hipparchus, 20
Hobbes, Thomas, 30
Hogarth, William, 44, 87–88, 96, 98
Hölderlin, Friedrich, 122
Horneffer, August, 259
Horneffer, Ernst, 259
Hubble, Edwin, 262
Hume, David, 280

Ionesco, Eugène, 17
Isis, 27–28
Ivanovna Zasulich, Vera, 258

Jacobi, Friedrich Heinrich, 280
James, William, 282
Jean Paul, sc. Johann Paul Friedrich Richter, 31, 61, 35–63, 65, 70, 72, 73, 76, 77, 80, 82–83, 86–87, 89–90, 92, 94–97, 98, 102, 117–118, 123, 125, 134, 136, 139, 145–146, 148, 159, 162, 164–165, 168–169, 175, 181–184, 186, 188, 197, 199, 201, 210, 211–213, 220–221, 225–227, 234–236, 241, 253, 255–256, 261, 264–267, 274, 277–278,

283–285, 287–288, 292–294, 296, 298, 303
Clavis Fichtiana, 43
"The Dead Christ," 36–39, 43–48, 58, 62, 65, 90, 93, 95, 182, 212, 220, 278, 283, 292, 303
"Die Neujahrnacht eines Unglücklichen," 226
Flower, Fruit, and Thorn Pieces, 36–42, 90, 212, 220, 278
Preschool of Aesthetics, 36
Selina or on Immortality, 61
The Valley of Campan, 36, 43–62, 65, 72, 77, 80, 86, 95–96, 117, 134, 139, 146, 182, 188, 225, 296
Jesus of Nazareth, 39, 40, 140, 155, 156, 163, 212, 264
Juvenal, 98

Kant, Immanuel, 13, 25, 43–44, 48–50, 58–60, 69–71, 84–85, 91–92, 97, 127–129, 137, 140, 143, 145, 264–265, 271, 273, 278, 292
Critique of Practical Reason, 49–50
Critique of Pure Reason, 70
Lectures on the Philosophical Doctrine of Religion, 13
Religion within the Boundaries of Mere Reason, 49
Karamazov, Ivan, 14, 195
Karlson, 44–60, 62, 70, 77, 83, 87, 95, 96, 117, 134, 139, 145–147, 162, 164–165, 169, 182, 184, 186, 197, 199, 225, 235, 241, 256, 264, 265, 274, 275, 277, 287–288, 296
Keats, John, 7, 99
Kierkegaard, Søren, 18–19, 33, 37, 78, 139, 163, 173–176, 187–189, 200–238, 240, 249, 254–257, 261, 266, 269, 286, 290, 292–294, 298, 300, 301, 303–305
The Concept of Anxiety, 187
The Concept of Irony, 19, 189, 249, 269, 300
Either/Or, 202, 240, 286, 300, 301
A Literary Review, 202, 300
Philosophical Fragments, 215, 219
Repetition, 202, 205
The Sickness unto Death, 189, 202
Three Discourses on Imagined Occasions, 222–234
Kirsanov, Arkady, 238, 241–243, 245–249
Klingemann, August, 31, 64–98, 104, 108, 110, 114, 117–118, 123, 136–138, 145–148, 152, 157, 159, 164, 169, 172, 184, 199, 210, 211, 213, 216, 219, 221, 225–226, 232, 235, 236, 250, 255, 261, 265–266, 269, 283–286, 288–291, 293, 296, 298, 299, 301, 303, 304
Klopstock, Friedrich Gottlieb, 122
Kreuzgang, 65–72, 75–86, 88–99, 108, 110, 118, 123, 136, 139, 143, 146, 158, 164–167, 169–170, 184, 203, 207–208, 212, 213, 215–219, 221, 230, 237, 240, 244, 246, 250, 254, 256–257, 265–266, 269–270, 278, 283, 285, 286, 288, 296, 299, 301, 304
Kropotkin, Peter, 238–241, 244–246, 257, 294, 298, 300

Lamarck, Jean-Baptiste, 23
Legendre, Louis, 153
Leibniz, Gottfried Wilhelm, 43, 83, 138, 177
Leigh, Augusta, 100
Leopardi, Giacomo, 280
Lessing, Gotthold Ephraim, 12, 25, 207
Lichtenberg, Georg Christoph, 44, 87
Linnaeus, Carl, 22–23
Locke, John, 30
Lyotard, Jean-François, 16

Macbeth, 72, 73, 132, 156, 168
Manfred, 99–118, 121, 123–124, 147, 159, 170–171, 209, 214, 222, 230, 256, 278, 284, 285, 289, 297, 302
Marx, Karl, 209
Melpomene, 45
Mephistopheles, 27, 104
Merleau-Ponty, Maurice, 37
Michelangelo, 26, 68, 69
Milton, John, 45

Møller, Poul Martin, 31, 201, 173–201, 235–237, 255, 261, 265, 277, 285, 291–293, 298, 303
Montinari, Mazzino, 260
Moritz, Karl Philipp, 35

Nadine, 44, 49, 55, 57–58, 61, 169
Napoleon Bonaparte, 121–122, 126
Newton, Isaac, 24
Nietzsche, Friedrich Wilhelm, 10, 15–16, 18, 20, 32, 33, 36, 91, 98, 100, 146, 199, 202, 237, 259–280, 283, 286–287, 294, 295, 297, 299, 300, 305
  Twilight of the Idols, 259, 261
  Untimely Meditations, 270
  The Will to Power, 279
Novalis, sc. Georg Philipp Friedrich Freiherr von Hardenberg, 280

Oedipus, 81, 105
Oerthel, Adam Lorenz von, 35
Oerthel, Christian von, 35
Olsen, Regine, 206
Ophelia, 82–86, 91, 95, 96, 110, 165, 167
Ormuzd, 111
Otto, Christian Georg, 62
Ovid, 6
Owen, Robert, 25

Paine, Thomas, 162–163
Parnell, Thomas, 99
Pellisson, Paul, 207
Philippeaux, Pierre Nicolas, 157, 168
Pindar, 3, 11, 155
Pisarev, Dmitry, 237
Plato, 11, 233, 234, 273
Pliny the Younger, 6
Plutarch, 28
Polidori, John, 100
Polybius, 5
Prahl, Niels, 228–230
Prometheus, 98
Prospero, 94
Ptolemy II Philadelphus, 186
Pushkin, Alexander, 247

Rameses II, 119, 121
Raphael, 26, 244

Ray, John, 21
Reynolds, Joshua, 45–46, 96
Richter, Friedrich, 176–177, 184
Richter, Heinrich, 35
Richter, Max, 61
Robespierre, Maximilien, 50, 151–157, 159–160, 164, 172, 285
Rousseau, Jean-Jacques, 25, 30

Saint-Just, Louis Antoine Léon de, 151, 160, 161
Saint-Simon, Henri de, 25
Sallust, 6
Sartre, Jean-Paul, 17, 74, 98, 117, 124, 170, 289, 296–299, 301, 302, 305
  Being and Nothingness, 74, 117, 297
  Nausea, 98, 301
Schelling, Friedrich Wilhelm Joseph, 65, 89, 91, 122, 128, 189, 203, 269
Schiller, Friedrich von, 26–28, 51, 101–102, 105–106, 131, 196, 244, 284
Schlechta, Karl, 260
Schlegel, Friedrich von, 15, 19, 64, 78, 203, 269, 280
Schleiermacher, Friedrich, 126
Schopenhauer, Arthur, 9, 33, 126–148, 153–154, 156–160, 169, 171–173, 175, 184, 188, 192–194, 199, 201, 207, 209–211, 214–215, 218–219, 221, 225, 227, 238, 244, 254–256, 261–262, 265–266, 270–272, 277, 284–286, 290–291, 295, 299, 305
Schuyler, Eugene, 257
Segner, Johann Andreas, 28
Shakespeare, William, 68, 72, 73, 75, 79, 82–83, 85, 91, 94, 101, 107, 132–133, 156, 157, 168, 208, 214
  As You Like It, 68, 75
  Hamlet, 73, 79, 82–83, 85, 91, 101, 107, 133, 208, 214
  Macbeth, 72, 73, 132, 168
  The Tempest, 94
Shelley, Mary (née Godwin), 100, 119
Shelley, Percy Bysshe, 99, 118–126, 147, 171, 236, 250, 277, 284, 289–290, 293, 297, 303–304
  The Necessity of Atheism, 124

NAME INDEX

"Ozymandias," 99, 118–120, 123–125, 236, 250, 284, 289, 297, 304
Queen Mab, 124, 125
Rosalind and Helen, A Modern Eclogue, 119, 120
Sibbern, Frederik Christian, 174, 193–195
Sisyphus, 17, 301–302
Socrates, 11, 50, 54, 56, 72, 78, 159, 175, 203, 233–234, 236, 269
Solger, Karl, 203, 269
Sophocles, 81, 105
Spinoza, Baruch (de), 177
Steensen, Niels, 23
Steffens, Henrik, 89
Stepniak, Sergius, sc. Sergey Mikhaylovich Stepnyak-Kravchinsky, 237, 257
Stirner, Max, 280, 281
Swedenborg, Emanuel, 197

Thalia, 45
Thomson, James B.V., 281
Thrasymachus, 11
Tieck, Ludwig, 203, 269
Troeltsch, Ernst, 282

Turgenev, Ivan, 15, 18, 20, 237–238, 241, 244, 246–247, 249–259, 263, 266, 269, 276, 277, 281, 286, 294, 298, 300, 302–303

Ugolino, 138
Ussher, James, 21

Vinci, Leonardo da, 26
Virgil, 3, 265
   Aeneid, 3
   The Eclogues, 265
Voltaire, 12, 24, 25

Weiding, Friedrich Ludwig, 150
Wilde, Oscar, 257, 258
Wilhelm, Judge, 43, 72, 127, 174, 192, 194, 206, 221, 262, 280
Wilhelmi, 44, 47, 48, 50, 54–57
Willughby, Francis, 21
Woolf, Virginia, 96

Xenophanes, 11
Xerxes, 138

Yorick, 91
Young, Edward, 99

SUBJECT INDEX

abandonment, 9, 14, 24, 30, 59, 98, 115, 117, 123, 134, 182, 186, 188, 195–196, 215, 263–267, 296, 303
absolute spirit, 187
abstract reasoning, 48
absurd, the, 14, 17, 25, 42, 51, 59, 67, 69, 78, 80, 83–85, 89–90, 93, 95, 97–98, 136, 169, 182, 190, 195, 199–200, 202, 206, 212, 216, 218, 232, 235, 243, 246, 250, 253, 283, 286, 288, 302–304
active nihilism, 270
actuality, 132, 180, 203, 204, 214, 215
aesthetics, 105, 239
afterlife, 3, 40, 57, 61, 66, 80, 88, 104, 107, 167, 182, 188, 197, 198, 209, 212, 214, 234–235, 253, 264, 265, 267, 274, 283, 288
agnosticism, 54
alienation, 14, 16–17, 56, 96, 109
American Revolution, 30
anarchism, 12, 15, 241, 257, 286
anatomy, 149
ancestors, 5
anguish, 41, 96, 102, 108, 110, 185, 210, 256, 285, 286, 302. *See also* anxiety
annihilation, 3, 15, 41, 47, 54, 60, 62, 66, 74, 80, 93–94, 163, 182, 185, 225, 234, 235, 253, 255, 261, 290, 292, 296, 306
anxiety, 2, 4–5, 8, 17, 26–27, 31, 41, 69, 93, 96, 102, 106, 108, 110, 115, 139, 182–185, 202, 210, 214, 226, 256, 283, 285, 286, 288, 289, 293–295, 302, 306, 307
appropriation, 224, 233, 298

art, 6–7, 24, 36, 39, 57, 87, 105, 116, 121, 133–135, 150, 186–189, 195, 239, 240, 244, 262, 263, 286, 290–292, 300, 303
asceticism, 141–142, 147, 171, 290
Asian Studies, 127
atheism, 10, 12–14, 31, 162, 177, 192, 220, 271, 283, 284
authenticity, 146, 212, 239, 276, 288, 289, 296, 297
autonomy, 25, 92, 123, 176

bad faith, 74, 266, 288, 289
beauty, 44–45, 53, 56–57, 59–61, 80, 94, 96, 105, 165, 168, 187, 210, 233, 239, 247, 263, 277
being, 17, 39, 41, 52, 56, 66, 74, 85, 88, 90–91, 104, 129, 131, 135, 139, 143–145, 183, 210, 214, 223–225, 240, 272, 274, 276, 284, 297, 307
being-towards-death, 17
Bible, 21, 207, 220
   Ecclesiastes, 1, 2, 4, 10, 14, 26, 42, 101, 131, 132, 156, 207, 209, 220
   Genesis, 5, 26, 76, 102, 112, 220
   Job, 9, 111
   John, 40, 205, 264
   Matthew, 39, 142
   Psalms, 207
Bildungsroman, 65
biology, 21, 89, 267
boredom, 96, 132–134, 137, 156–158, 172, 207, 219–221, 256, 285, 302
botany, 21, 22

SUBJECT INDEX

bourgeois ethics, 83, 99, 162, 206, 215, 246, 269–270, 298–300, 302, 304
bourgeois philistine, 207
Buddhism, 9, 126–127, 147, 176, 192–195, 271, 290

capitalism, 18, 265
censorship, 150, 216
chance, 10, 38, 41, 141, 155, 283, 288
chaos, 14, 18, 39, 67, 70, 87, 113, 114, 126, 169, 267, 274, 278–279
chemistry, 44, 47, 54
children, 3, 8, 15, 38, 40, 46, 48, 66, 79–81, 83, 86, 91, 160, 161, 168, 170, 179, 181, 201, 212–214, 216, 226, 230, 240, 243, 246, 287
chivalry, 7
Christianity, 7, 40, 43, 51, 59, 63, 66, 72, 111, 139–142, 145, 174, 180–181, 186, 189, 192–193, 199–201, 207, 217, 223, 230, 232, 234, 242, 261, 263–267, 269, 271, 272, 275, 277, 279, 282–283, 286, 295, 297, 299, 300, 304
Church, 26, 30, 269, 289
colonialism, 18
comedy, 45–46, 73, 84, 85, 95, 96, 136, 159, 217, 219, 283, 302
Committee of Public Safety, 151
conceptual analysis, 97, 137
conceptual knowledge, 191
conformism, 14, 18, 49, 75, 76, 96, 158, 184, 211–212, 221, 276, 296, 298, 301
Congress of Vienna, 122
conscience, 14, 30, 107, 113, 114, 117, 147, 154, 155, 159, 170, 225, 269, 289, 297
contradiction, 59, 140, 186, 188, 195–197, 201, 209, 219, 227, 245, 271, 276, 283
cosmos, 63, 67, 92, 125, 266, 278, 304
Creation, the, 21, 163
cult of Aten, 7

Dadaism, 18
damnatio memoriae, 7
dance, 41, 80, 82, 92, 160, 169, 230
David Garrick Between Tragedy and Comedy, 45–46, 96

death, 2–5, 6–10, 15–17, 27, 35, 38–42, 45–46, 48–49, 51, 53–55, 57–63, 66–67, 69, 74, 78–83, 85–94, 98–100, 102–108, 110–114, 116, 117, 122, 124–125, 130–133, 136–138, 141, 145, 147, 152–172, 174–175, 178, 180–181, 183, 185, 191–193, 196–198, 200–202, 208–209, 211–215, 220–236, 252–256, 261, 264, 272–275, 281–283, 285–294, 296–304, 306–307
death of God, 10, 261, 272, 274–275, 277, 283, 286, 294, 297, 299
décadence, 274, 301
decisiveness of death, 228
defiance, 93, 116–118, 163, 230, 232, 289, 301–302
deism, 10, 26, 30
democracy, 30, 301
denial of the will-to-live, 141, 143, 271
despair, 10, 16–18, 26, 31, 36, 47, 51, 65, 69, 71, 80, 86, 93, 97, 99, 102, 112, 115, 120, 122, 131, 132, 139, 159–160, 182, 185, 189, 198, 200, 202, 208–210, 235, 254, 256, 261, 263, 283–285, 287–289, 293, 295, 302, 306–307
dignity, 26, 72, 75, 77, 93–94, 98, 117, 118, 136, 170–171, 183, 242, 268, 289, 297, 302
disorientation, 3, 30, 281
divine right of kings, 30, 262
doctrine of annihilation, 60, 182
doubt, 30, 43, 107, 139, 146, 154, 187, 202, 210, 219, 220, 243, 256, 258, 275, 285, 287
drama, 12, 16, 17, 28, 31, 32, 65, 82, 96, 100, 116–118, 150–152, 157, 169–170, 172, 193, 257, 291, 301, 302
dreams, 3, 37, 38, 41–43, 66, 76, 80–82, 84, 85, 89, 90, 93–95, 107, 137, 154, 155, 160, 189, 211, 218, 225–226, 235, 255
dust, 2, 3, 11, 38, 40, 42, 74, 81, 85, 88, 90, 91, 93–94, 98, 113–114, 121, 164–165, 183, 208, 211, 213, 265, 283–284

earnestness, 86, 187, 224–227, 230–235, 254, 293, 298
echo, 1, 3, 42, 65, 72, 80, 85, 89, 90, 93–95, 97, 106, 154–155, 158, 163, 168, 177, 205, 209, 211
ecstasy, 61, 144, 155
education, 181, 251
Elysium, 3, 47, 61, 212
emancipation, 25, 193, 238, 252, 268
emotion, 48, 57–60, 71, 82, 83, 91, 96, 100, 117, 162, 169, 181, 182, 184, 228, 235, 256, 265, 306
encyclopedists, the, 27
Enlightenment, the, 12, 20, 24–26, 28–30, 32, 47, 63, 67, 69, 76–77, 98, 124, 150, 154, 238, 305–306
epic poetry, 135
Epicureanism, 153, 171, 291
epistemology, 16, 18, 84
equality, 25, 67, 166, 232, 248, 251
eternity, 6, 38, 40, 43, 49–50, 74, 86, 104, 198, 200, 213
ethics, 12–15, 18, 48, 50, 53, 108, 123, 140–141, 147, 153, 162, 171, 185, 195, 199, 206, 226, 243, 256, 261, 271, 275, 285, 286, 291, 297–298, 301
evolution, 9, 22, 72, 242, 262, 274
existentialism, 14, 16–18, 20, 33, 37, 48, 67, 93, 97–99, 101, 104, 117, 124, 170, 199, 266, 289, 293, 295–299, 301–302, 305
   existential freedom, 298–299
   existential nihilism, 17
   existentialist hero, 301

facticity, 117
faith, 1, 2, 7, 9–10, 13–15, 24–26, 30–31, 38–39, 42–44, 57–59, 62, 71, 78, 82, 84, 85, 93–95, 98, 112, 115, 117–118, 124–125, 139, 146–147, 159, 169, 172, 176–178, 181–183, 186–188, 195, 197–201, 203, 207, 218–220, 223, 225, 227, 234–235, 239, 243–245, 250–253, 262, 264, 265, 267–270, 274, 283–284, 286–288, 291–294, 296, 298, 302–304
Fall, the, 103
fascism, 17, 265
Fates, the, 110–111, 214

feeling, 9, 14, 48, 53, 58, 61, 62, 66, 83, 92, 96, 108, 110, 133, 147, 154, 159–160, 162, 164, 181–184, 186–188, 195, 215–216, 224, 225, 239, 246, 265, 270, 273, 275, 289, 292, 306–307
feminism, 240
finitude, 3, 4, 8, 10, 17, 45, 74, 96, 103–104, 113, 122, 136, 175, 183–186, 208, 211, 215, 231, 235–236, 283, 289
The Flight of Human Life, or the Death-Dance, 228–230, 232
Flood, the, 21
forbidden knowledge, 26, 28, 102, 103, 284
freedom, 17, 25, 30, 104, 117–118, 122, 124, 153, 170–172, 203, 206, 216, 239, 241, 245, 248, 263, 266, 270, 289, 297–298, 301, 302
   existential freedom, 298–299. *See also* individual freedom
   freedom of speech, 216
   individual freedom, 30, 115–117, 124, 222, 238, 241, 245, 296
French Revolution (1789), 25, 30–32, 121, 151, 172, 269

Garden of Eden, 102
geometry, 60, 178
German idealism, 32, 69, 89, 97, 128, 280
graveyard poets, 99
grief, 3, 46, 48, 53, 57, 61, 83, 86, 93, 101–103, 109, 282, 285, 303

harmony, 42, 45, 47–48, 52, 55, 59, 61, 65, 67, 82, 94, 114, 125, 135, 180, 187, 198
heaven, 5, 7, 40, 47, 56, 66, 78, 86, 88–90, 92–93, 101, 115, 139, 159, 168–169, 227
hedonism, 14, 141, 145, 231, 291
Hegelianism, 161, 174, 176–181, 186–187, 194–195, 198, 205, 285
heliocentric universe, 20
herd instinct, 266
Hinduism, 126, 192
history, 5–7, 9, 14–20, 24, 30, 31, 34, 69–70, 72, 75, 91, 95, 111, 119, 125–126, 129, 137, 151–152, 161, 175–176, 185, 189–190, 196, 208, 260, 262–263, 265, 269, 273, 282, 305–306

SUBJECT INDEX

history of ideas, 31
Holocaust, the, 28
hope, 5, 7, 32, 34, 40, 48, 51, 57–58, 62, 72–73, 81, 95, 105, 111–112, 121, 124, 127, 136, 160, 165, 169, 177, 182, 184, 185, 211, 216, 226, 235, 252, 254, 267, 269, 275, 281, 291, 302
hopelessness, 11, 18, 29, 97, 98, 122, 210, 244, 247, 261, 294, 299, 306
humor, 44, 46, 65, 71, 73, 95, 148, 169, 216, 219, 284, 303
hypocrisy, 15, 68–71, 74, 81, 94, 139, 146, 152, 153, 203, 204, 218, 238–241, 251, 283, 285–286, 288, 299, 301

idealism, 91
ideology, 78, 124, 244, 251, 262, 294
immanent thinking, 189–190
immortality, 3, 6–7, 22, 26, 31, 35, 43–63, 66, 70, 74–77, 83, 85–91, 93–97, 104, 112, 116–118, 124, 131, 134, 139, 146, 162, 165, 168–169, 173–193, 195–201, 218–219, 221, 223–227, 234–236, 257, 264, 267, 275, 283, 285, 287–288, 291–293, 296, 298, 303, 304
incest, 100, 103, 105, 117, 159, 284
indefinability, 231–233, 235–236, 293, 298, 304
inexplicability, 201, 211, 232–233, 235–236, 286, 293, 298, 304
irony, 71, 73, 78–79, 176, 202–206, 249, 270
    controlled irony, 204–205
    Romantic irony, 203, 205, 206, 269
irrationality, 14, 18, 25, 76, 89, 117, 157, 216, 219, 235, 242, 252, 283

Jacobinism, 151, 152
July Revolution of 1830, 216
justice, 11–14, 49, 67, 133, 140–141, 159, 202, 232–233, 250, 272, 277, 285

knowledge, 6, 9, 24, 26–28, 36, 51, 54, 57, 62, 78, 94, 101–106, 108, 109, 112, 114, 116, 125, 130–131, 133, 142–145, 160, 181, 183, 185, 189–191, 196, 233–234, 242, 247, 263, 264, 278, 284, 293

Last Judgment, the, 40, 67–71, 75, 89, 96, 143
laughter, 46, 72, 85, 93, 95–96, 158–159, 168–170, 206, 215–219, 242, 246, 248, 283, 301, 304
law of contradiction, 267, 277
law of excluded middle, 214
left Hegelianism, 174, 178, 180, 205, 285
loneliness, 9, 96, 210, 212, 226
love, 2, 3, 6, 8–10, 41, 46–48, 54, 57–60, 65, 73, 80–87, 90–94, 96, 100, 105, 110–112, 133, 135, 140–143, 146, 148, 152–153, 157, 162, 164–168, 171, 173, 183, 186, 198, 211, 215, 218, 224, 226, 239–240, 246, 252–255, 264, 265, 282, 283, 287, 291, 294, 301, 303

marriage, 36, 100, 240, 246, 255
masks, 38, 68–69, 73–74, 77–78, 81–82, 166, 239–240, 283, 288, 296, 304
materialism, 32, 49, 50, 52–54, 169, 237, 239, 242, 247, 253, 255, 296
mathematics, 60, 178, 179, 181, 246
meaninglessness, 1–2, 4, 8–9, 15, 17, 27, 31, 36, 58, 62–63, 65, 70–71, 79, 80, 82, 95–98, 104, 106, 109, 111, 118, 122–123, 125, 136–137, 141, 145–148, 157–158, 161, 166, 167, 171, 172, 175, 183, 185, 186, 199, 203, 208–211, 215–217, 219–220, 223, 226–227, 230, 233, 235, 243, 244, 249, 256, 257, 261, 264, 267–268, 270, 275, 281–286, 289–291, 293–299, 301–304, 306, 307
medicine, 4, 7, 9, 78, 126, 131, 145, 149–150, 241, 247, 252, 286
melancholy, 7, 59, 86, 110, 188, 212, 215, 219, 252, 256
memory, 4–8, 15, 37, 52, 90, 93, 103–104, 112, 114, 116, 122, 125, 133, 135, 147, 155, 159, 168, 180, 185, 213, 218, 224, 227, 239, 242, 254, 265, 284, 288, 296, 299, 303, 306, 307
metaphysical need, 272, 274, 278
metaphysics, 16, 18, 84, 97, 140–141, 143, 177, 179, 200, 261, 267, 271–274, 278–279, 281, 284, 287, 296, 298, 302
misanthropy, 71, 82, 218, 237, 256

monads, 177
monuments, 5, 7, 57, 80, 116, 119–121, 306
mood, 47–48, 57, 65, 90, 203, 208, 225–226, 244

nationalism, 18, 32, 250, 265
naturalism, 23, 30, 44, 54, 62, 87, 149, 177, 186
nature, 2–4, 10, 11, 22–26, 28, 36, 38–45, 56, 61, 72, 76–77, 79–80, 83, 88–89, 92–94, 103–104, 107–110, 112–114, 116–118, 123–125, 129–132, 137–138, 144, 145, 153–155, 160–162, 165, 166, 169, 179–180, 192, 213, 214, 217–218, 228, 241, 242, 246–247, 253, 267, 281–285, 289, 297, 300, 302
negation, 13, 135, 144, 177, 204, 239, 241, 249, 257, 269, 286, 294
Nemesis, 111
Niban, 192, 196
nihilist women, 240
Nirvana, 192
nominalism, 84
nonsense, 18, 30, 240
nothingness, 2, 12, 17, 38, 40, 41, 52, 60, 66, 69–75, 82, 84–86, 91–95, 111, 118, 120–123, 127, 134, 136, 143–146, 148, 152, 155, 156, 159–160, 163, 168–169, 185, 192, 194, 199, 207–210, 213, 215, 218, 220, 231, 243–245, 251–254, 267, 272–274, 278, 283–286, 290, 294, 296–298, 303, 307

Owl of Minerva, 51, 189

pain, 8–9, 37, 47, 48, 57, 109–111, 115, 117, 130–135, 137, 139–141, 143, 146, 155, 156, 158, 162, 165, 210–212, 218, 220, 226, 284, 291, 292, 295
pantheism, 10, 177, 181, 186, 189, 191, 193, 195
paradise, 45, 47
paradox, 52, 190, 201, 235
passive nihilism, 270, 272
pessimism, 65, 95, 129, 131, 133, 139, 145, 169, 256, 261, 270, 282
philosophical anthropology, 77, 113

philosophy of nature, 89, 101
philosophy of subjectivity, 18
physiology, 54, 246
political nihilism, 15
politics, 15, 18, 25, 29–32, 69, 87, 121, 124, 150–153, 156, 167, 170, 172, 184, 205, 216, 241, 250, 256–258, 262–264, 266, 281, 285, 286, 291–292, 294, 299–300, 302–303
postmodernism, 16
postulate of practical reason, 50
practical nihilism, 185
prayer, 68, 93, 115, 136, 139, 223, 230, 255, 301
principle of individuation, 140, 148
proofs for immortality, 178
Protestantism, 30
Providence, 48, 280

rationalism, 30, 124, 243, 261
realism, 91
reason, 13, 25, 28–30, 49, 59, 60, 67, 69–70, 76, 78, 89, 95, 97, 113–114, 119, 123, 130, 154, 155, 161–162, 168, 179, 181, 186, 191, 200, 216, 219, 239, 242–247, 249, 266–267, 269, 274, 277, 287, 290, 292, 293, 304
rebellion, 17, 93, 98, 116, 118, 123, 132, 147, 162, 167, 170–171, 204, 230, 289, 301–302, 307
recognition, 4–6, 74, 75, 147, 213, 218, 297, 306–307
recollection, 56, 198, 213, 223, 226, 227
reconciliation, 40, 57, 95, 151, 167, 187, 252
Reign of Terror, 30, 149, 151, 167, 170, 172
relativism, 4, 10–12, 14, 18, 30, 51, 117, 144, 193, 194, 203–204, 263, 267, 268, 277, 282, 286, 289, 295
religion, 3, 10–14, 18, 20, 25, 28, 30–32, 35, 38, 40, 43, 47, 49, 62, 66, 70, 77, 91, 93, 95, 97, 106, 113–117, 121, 123–124, 126, 136, 139, 141, 153, 179, 181, 186, 188, 191, 194–195, 198, 199, 201, 207, 217, 219, 221–223, 227, 235, 239, 271, 280, 282, 287–288, 291–293, 298–300, 304
Renaissance Humanism, 26

repetition, 102, 118, 132, 156–157, 159, 172, 202
reputation, 6–7
resignation, 67, 118, 141, 156, 160, 163, 167, 169–172, 191, 222, 235, 249, 252, 261, 269, 272, 274–275, 285, 291
ressentiment, 274, 301
Resurrection of the Dead, the, 40
Revolutions of 1848, 205
right Hegelianism, 174, 176, 179
Romanticism, 246
  English Romanticism, 99
  German Romanticism, 18, 36, 203, 206

salvation, 112, 141, 143, 147, 156, 219, 254, 255, 301
satire, 44, 65, 71, 77, 83, 87, 91, 95, 98, 123, 148, 169, 214, 281, 299, 303–304
science, 3, 4, 6, 10, 15, 20–21, 24–32, 34, 36–38, 40, 42–43, 46, 51–55, 57–63, 67, 69, 72, 76, 87, 94, 96–98, 101–102, 106, 107, 112, 115–117, 123–125, 131, 134, 139, 145–146, 149, 162, 168–169, 176–177, 181, 184, 186, 189–191, 195–198, 208–209, 212–213, 217, 220–221, 235, 237, 239, 241–245, 247, 250, 253, 256, 262, 264–265, 267, 274, 276–278, 280, 282–288, 291, 293, 296, 300, 304, 305
Second Coming, the, 40, 68
secular worldview, 20, 180, 193, 303
secularism, 11, 20, 25, 42, 112, 180, 189, 191–193, 196, 227, 282, 292, 303, 305
self-deception, 69, 74, 95, 112, 117, 134, 188, 197, 224, 283, 287–288, 294
self-positing ego, 36
sentimentalism, 239, 244
serfdom, 238, 252, 286, 294, 300
sickness, 16, 78–79, 189, 200, 202, 282
sincerity, 239
single individual, the, 224
skeletons, 85, 89, 94, 228
skepticism, 12, 16, 51–52, 198, 204, 224
social criticism, 14, 66, 98, 139, 153, 169, 203, 204, 215, 238, 243, 244, 249, 251, 257, 288–290, 299–301

Sophists, the, 11
suffering, 5, 8–9, 15, 58–59, 66, 79, 83, 85–86, 102–104, 106–112, 114–118, 122, 125, 130–132, 134, 136–147, 152–156, 158–159, 162, 164, 165, 167–169, 171–172, 184, 186, 188, 195, 207, 209–215, 226, 230, 232, 256, 263, 271, 272, 275, 284–285, 287, 288, 290–291, 295, 298, 303
suicide, 1, 17, 35, 71–72, 85, 96, 106–107, 133, 150, 152, 167, 170–171, 185, 209, 214, 230, 232, 254, 285, 291
supersensuous, the, 180
superstition, 136, 239, 250

The Tailpiece, or the Bathos, 88
theater, 17, 45, 65, 68, 71, 73–75, 83–85, 125, 138, 302
theater of the absurd, 17, 302
thing-in-itself, 84–85, 140, 267, 271, 273, 278
time, 1, 3–5, 7, 10, 14, 21–23, 38, 40–42, 49, 50, 56, 69–70, 75, 81, 84, 86, 87, 90, 103, 109–112, 121, 122, 125, 130–132, 136–140, 144–145, 147, 155, 167–168, 176, 180, 185–186, 188, 196, 198, 200, 205, 208–210, 227–232, 244, 250, 254, 265, 267, 273, 279, 283–286, 297, 302, 303, 305, 307
Tower of Babel, 5
tragedy, 45–46, 71–72, 75, 77, 96, 99, 101, 136, 159, 184, 213, 219, 282, 302
transcendental idealism, 128
transcendental unity of apperception, 273
Tree of Knowledge, 26, 102, 106
truth, 10, 11–12, 15–16, 19, 25, 27, 30, 36, 42, 50, 53, 56–57, 59–61, 66, 68, 70, 71, 74–76, 79, 80, 82–84, 92–94, 98, 101, 105, 120, 137, 140, 142, 143, 156, 158, 161, 166, 168–169, 172, 178–179, 181–185, 190–192, 195–196, 198–200, 203–206, 208, 212, 215, 217, 219–220, 233, 249–250, 253, 256, 262, 264, 266–267, 272–274, 276–279, 282, 283, 288, 294, 296, 300, 301, 304, 306

utilitarianism, 91, 244

values, 1, 2, 5, 7–8, 10–15, 18, 19, 31, 33, 36, 37, 60, 67, 72, 77, 83, 99, 101, 104, 106, 108, 109, 117, 166, 175, 183, 188, 190, 193, 198–200, 203–204, 206, 211, 216, 218–219, 231, 237–239, 242–244, 246, 248, 252, 256–257, 261, 263–271, 274–277, 279, 285–286, 290, 292–302, 304, 307
vanity, 1, 2, 14, 77–78, 87, 94, 105, 116, 118, 123, 142, 147, 166, 218, 227, 242, 245, 258, 284, 290
veil of Maya, 140, 192, 218
violence, 11, 18, 80, 140, 152, 154, 168, 172, 285
virtue, 12–13, 49, 53, 56–57, 59–60, 93–94, 157, 158, 162, 179, 202, 226, 249, 262, 264
void, the, 10, 38, 41, 43, 86, 155, 163, 244, 283

Wandering Jew, 163
warrior ethic, 5, 6
will to power, 199, 271–272, 275–276, 279, 295, 297
will-to-live, 137, 140–143, 145, 160, 214, 261, 271, 284, 290, 300
world history, 70, 77, 95
World War I, 18
World War II, 17, 171
worldview, 19, 24–27, 29, 30, 32, 36, 42–43, 46, 51–53, 57–59, 62, 69, 90, 98, 102, 106, 112, 124–125, 128, 134, 139, 145–149, 158, 177–182, 184, 186, 188–189, 192, 194, 196–199, 201, 217, 220, 235, 243, 256, 263–267, 275–277, 283, 284, 286, 288, 291–292, 295, 305

Young Germany, 149, 188

zoology, 21, 22, 119
Zoroastrianism, 111